092858

KU-490-123

B23.5 DEF S
STOLER
856108

DISCARD
B.C.H.E. — LIBRARY

00133291

DANIEL DEFOE

GARLAND REFERENCE LIBRARY
OF THE HUMANITIES
(VOL. 430)

DANIEL DEFOE
An Annotated Bibliography of Modern Criticism, 1900–1980

John A. Stoler

GARLAND PUBLISHING, INC. • NEW YORK & LONDON
1984

© 1984 John A. Stoler
All rights reserved

Library of Congress Cataloging in Publication Data

Stoler, John A., 1935–
    Daniel Defoe, an annotated bibliography of modern
criticism, 1900–1980.

    (Garland reference library of the humanities ; vol.
430)
    Includes index.
    1. Defoe, Daniel, 1661?–1731—Bibliography.
I. Title. II. Series: Garland reference library of the
humanities ; v. 430.
Z8221.S87 1984 [PR3406] 016.823′5   83-48262
ISBN 0-8240-9086-1 (alk. paper)

BATH COLLEGE
OF
HIGHER EDUCATION
NEWTON PARK
LIBRARY

CLASS
No.   823·5 DEF S

ACC
No.   856108

Printed on acid-free, 250-year-life paper
Manufactured in the United States of America

For:

Oliver F. Sigworth
and
Edwin Nierenberg

Scholars, Teachers, Friends

ACKNOWLEDGMENTS

The first person I wish to thank for the successful completion of this project is my wife, Mandy, who has skillfully directed our marriage through two extensive bibliographical projects over the past five years and who has been a diligent and patient proofreader for both. To Professor Gene Koppel of the University of Arizona go my thanks for stimulating my interest in Defoe through a rigorous independent study of that author that I made under him a decade and a half ago. I also wish to thank Alan Craven, Director of the Division of English, Classics, and Philosophy, University of Texas, San Antonio, for providing financial support for xeroxing and interlibrary loan fees in the preparation of this bibliography; Sue McCrory, Interlibrary Loan Librarian, John Peace Library, University of Texas, San Antonio, for her diligence in obtaining hard-to-locate items for this work; and the thoroughly competent staff of the Perry-Castaneda Library, University of Texas, Austin—where I did the bulk of the work for this project—for its efficiency and cooperation.

CONTENTS

INTRODUCTION

This bibliography is the result of a perceived deficiency in Defoe scholarship. The only previous attempts to draw together a comprehensive listing of modern criticism on Defoe are the useful but now-outdated checklists by Maximillian E. Novak (item 7) and William L. Payne (item 21). The former contains only about four hundred critical items and the latter, although it lists over twice as many works, is plagued with numerous serious inaccuracies. I have attempted to correct those errors—although undoubtedly committing some of my own—and have greatly expanded the listing of works about Defoe written since 1900 to the almost-1600 items that make up this book.

This bibliography attempts a comprehensive, although not exhaustive, listing of critical materials on Daniel Defoe published from 1900 through 1980. A few items from 1981, 1982, and 1983 that came to my attention also are included, but no thorough search of journals published after 1980 was attempted. Works published prior to 1900 are included only if they constitute part of an exchange that carries over into the twentieth century or if they have been republished since 1900. In listing reprinted works, I have given first the publication information of the edition I used for my annotation; in some cases this is the original edition, in others it is the reprint. I have chosen this method in order to be entirely accurate because some reprints add supplementary information to the original.

Unless otherwise noted, all works listed in the first six sections have been seen by the compiler. Foreign-language materials generally are not annotated because I saw but few of them myself, picking up most of them from bibliographical guides and references in critical works. Many of these items are not readily available in the United States, and the cost of collecting and translating them was prohibitive. Likewise, it was too expensive to attempt to purchase and read dissertations, and it seemed futile to annotate from abstracts since most of the latter are available in complete form in *Dissertation Abstracts* or *Dissertation Abstracts International* (abbreviated in the bibliography as *DA* and *DAI*). Even though the foreign-language materials and dissertations are but lightly annotated, they are cross-referenced in the appropriate sections of the bibliography whenever I could determine their subjects from the titles.

The annotations tend to be objective summaries of a work's content. I chose this method of annotation because I believe it best suits the needs of both novice researcher and scholar and because I wished to avoid the impression, especially with inexperienced Defoe students, of passing off my biases as fact. Where serious controversy has arisen over a specific work, I have directed the reader to appropriate commentary. As further aid to the reader's assessment of a given work, reviews have been listed after the work reviewed. Additionally, to help the researcher group closely-related items and follow controversy, I have cross-referenced within the annotations. Finally, I have cross-listed in appropriate sections those items which treat more than one of Defoe's works, but to avoid padding the bibliography, such items are numbered and annotated only once, and the reader is referred to the section in which the annotation is printed. A researcher pursuing a particular subject should not rely solely on the above devices, however, but also should use the subject index and should browse in Section III for promising titles. In fact, the entire book has been organized to facilitate browsing through general subject areas.

The groupings of items into subject sections may at first seem somewhat arbitrary—and perhaps they are—but the Defoe canon poses more problems than most for the bibliographer. First, there is the sheer bulk of Defoe's production; he now is credited with at least 550 separate works. Second, there is the problem created by Defoe's practice of blending fact and fiction; some works are pure fact, some works are pure fiction, and most works are a combination of the two. The bibliographer, then, is faced with extreme difficulties in classifying certain items. For example, does *Captain Carleton* (if it is a Defoe production at all) belong with real memoirs, falsified memoirs, or pure fiction?

(One must remember that as late as 1919, Watson Nicholson was arguing that *A Journal of the Plague Year* was an authentic history rather than a novel.) In any case, each section of the bibliography has its own logic and principles of organization.

Section I, "Selected Bibliographies," contains bibliographies of both primary and secondary materials. Excluded are bibliographical listings printed in critical books of Defoe. The researcher should consult—in addition to the bibliographies listed here—the standard reference guides, particularly the *MLA International Bibliography*, *The Annual Bibliography for English Language and Literature*, and *The Eighteenth-Century: A Current Bibliography*. *The Scriblerian* also should be consulted; that journal now annotates works on Defoe from all over the world.

Section II, "Selected Collections and Editions," does not attempt to be comprehensive. The items here were selected on the following principles: (1) they represent authoritative texts; (2) they contain important critical materials such as introductions, essays, or explanatory notes; (3) they are editions easily accessible to the general reader; or (4) they are the only editions in print. In the first subdivision, "Novels," the works are arranged according to the date of publication. However, the works listed in the "Other Writings" and "Specialized Collections" subsections are alphabetically ordered to facilitate finding lesser-known works and works with uncertain dates of publication.

No matter what subject the researcher is pursuing, he should carefully check the materials listed in Section III, "General Works on Defoe's Life and Art." Many of these items are cross-referenced, but some that are not may still contain valuable commentary on the topic under investigation. Items here are listed alphabetically according to the author's last name.

The next section, "The Major Novels," is divided into eight parts; the first contains general criticism of the fiction and each of the following seven is devoted to one of the major novels. The latter are ordered according to their dates of publication, beginning with the earliest (*Robinson Crusoe*, 1719). The items within each subdivision are alphabetized by the author's last name. Section V, "Miscellaneous Writings," has six subsections which roughly group Defoe's works according to type. After a section of general criticism, Defoe's writings are fitted into five separate categories. The criticism within each division is alphabetically arranged according to the last name of the author.

Section VI, "Discussions of the Canon," was included because Defoe's incredible rate of production and his habit of writing anonymously or pseudoanonymously combine to create a number of canonical questions. There is enough specialized material on the Defoe canon to merit separating it from general criticism and placing it in its own section. The listings of foreign-language materials and dissertations (Sections VII and VIII) conclude the bibliography proper. Because few of these items were seen by the compiler, they are not subdivided but are simply listed alphabetically by author.

Author, title, and subject indices are appended to the text. The first two of these are designed to aid the researcher who may know, for example, that G. S. Starr wrote on Defoe but who may not have the titles of his studies, as well as the person who knows a title but cannot place its author. The author index also enables the researcher to check all the studies made by a particular scholar. The subject index is designed to supplement the cross-reference in the text. In general, it is limited to the subjects mentioned in the titles and annotations and does not necessarily cover all the material in every work listed herein. The guiding principle of the indices, as well as that of the rest of the bibliography, is that of usefulness to both the scholar and the novice researcher. I hope that I have succeeded in combining these somewhat diverse interests.

Daniel Defoe

I

SELECTED BIBLIOGRAPHIES

1. Abernethy, Peter L., Christian J.W. Kloesel, and Jeffrey
    R. Smitten. *English Novel Explication: Supplement I.*
    Hamden, Conn.: Shoe String Press, 1976.

    Supplements Palmer and Dyson (item 20) and Bell and
    Baird (item 4) by listing about 75 items on Defoe pub-
    lished up to 1975.

2. Baine, Rodney M. "Chalmers' First Bibliography of Daniel
    Defoe." *Texas Studies in Literature and Language*, 10
    (1969), 547-68.

    Condenses and reprints Chalmers' bibliography and argues
    that Chalmers' inclusion of a work does not provide suf-
    ficient evidence that the work is actually Defoe's.

3. Beasley, Jerry C. *English Fiction, 1660-1800.* Detroit:
    Gale Research Co., 1978.

    Annotates 100 Defoe items including editions, letters,
    bibliographies, biographies, and critical studies.

4. Bell, Inglis F., and Donald Baird. "Daniel Defoe."
    *The English Novel, 1578-1956: A Checklist of Twentieth-
    Century Criticism.* Denver and Chicago: Swallow, 1958.
    Pp. 30-32.

    Lists 26 basic works on *Captain Singleton*, *Moll
    Flanders*, *Robinson Crusoe*, and *Roxana*.

*   Boucé, Paul-Gabriel. "D. Defoe: Bibliographie selective
    et critique." (See item 1229.)

5. Brigham, Clarence E. "Bibliography of American Editions
    of *Robinson Crusoe* to 1830." *Proceedings of the
    American Antiquarian Society*, 67 (1958), 137-83.

    Describes 125 editions of *Robinson Crusoe* published
    in America between 1774 and 1830. The bibliography

gives the full title, an abstract of the imprint, the
number of plates, the pagination of the separate
divisions of the text, the first and last lines of the
Crusoe narrative, and the location of copies in libraries.

6. *A Catalogue of the Defoe Collection in the Boston
    Public Library*. With a Preface by John Alden.
    Boston: G.K. Hall, 1966.

    Catalogs approximately 1350 Defoe items held by the
    Boston Public Library, many of them from the collection
    assembled by Professor W.P. Trent.

7. *Daniel Defoe: An Excerpt from the General Catalogue of
    Printed Books in the British Museum*. London: British
    Museum, 1953.

    Includes all the museum's Defoe holdings: works *by*
    Defoe, works *usually* attributed to Defoe, works *sometimes*
    assigned to Defoe; an appendix lists bibliographies,
    biographies, and criticism on Defoe.

8. "Daniel Defoe Desiderata." *Yale University Library
    Gazette*, 45 (1970), 25-31.

    Prints a list of 116 Defoe items included in John
    Robert Moore's *Checklist* (item 14) but missing from
    the Yale collection of Defoe material.

9. *Daniel Defoe the Journalist: A Collection of Scarce
    Tracts*. Metuchen, N.J.: Charles F. Heartman, 1934.

    Lists and describes 88 Defoe items to be auctioned
    off by Charles F. Heartman.

10. Downie, J.A., and Pat Rogers. "Defoe in the Pamphlets:
    Some Additions and Corrections." *Philological Quar-
    terly*, 59 (1980), 38-43.

    Emends 51 of the 165 titles listed in William L.
    Payne's "Defoe in the Pamphlets" (item 22) and adds
    57 new titles to the bibliography.

*   Harris, John. "Manuscript Dates on Pamphlets Collected
     by Thomas Bowdler II With Examples from Defoe."
     (See item 195.)

11. Hutchins, Henry C. "Daniel Defoe (1660-1731)." *The
    Cambridge Bibliography of English Literature*. Ed.
    F.W. Bateson. Vol. 2. Cambridge: Cambridge University

Press, 1969. Pp. 495-514. Originally published
1940.

Lists approximately 400 works thought to be by Defoe
and about 175 works about Defoe.

12. ————. *Daniel Defoe, 1660-1731: A Bibliography Com-*
piled for the Forthcoming Edition of the Cambridge
Bibliography of English Literature. New Haven,
1936.

An early typescript version of item 11 which was
donated to the University of Texas at Austin.

13. Lloyd, William S. *Catalogue of Various Editions of*
Robinson Crusoe and Other Books by and Referring to
Daniel Defoe. Philadelphia: Library of William S.
Lloyd, 1915.

The compiler did not personally review this catalogue,
listed in Payne (item 71). Also see Nicholls, "Some
Early Editions," item 625.

14. Moore, John Robert. *A Checklist of the Writings of*
Daniel Defoe. Indiana University Humanities Series,
No. 47. Bloomington: Indiana University Press, 1960.
Reprinted and augmented, Hamden, Conn.: Archon, 1971.

Stands as the major bibliography of Defoe's writings.
Moore identifies 548 Defoe works and provides information
on when each item was published, why it was written,
who printed and sold it, and where copies of first
editions can be found. Items are arranged according
to their dates of publication; sections on "Undated Works
Published Posthumously" and "Periodicals" are appended
to the body of the bibliography; the work concludes with
two indices: "Index of Printers and Booksellers" and
"Index of Titles."

Reviews: J. Béranger, *Etudes Anglaises*, 15 (1962), 77-
78; Bernhard Fabian, *Archiv für das Studium der neueren*
Sprachen, 201 (1964), 460-61; George Harris Healey,
Philological Quarterly, 40 (1960), 383-84; C.J. Rawson,
Notes and Queries, 207 (1962), 468-71; J.G. Riewald,
English Studies, 47 (1966), 150-52; James Sutherland,
Library, 5th series, 17 (1963), 323-25; William B.
Todd, *Book Collector*, 10 (1961), 493-94, 497-98;
Daniel Whitten, *Papers of the Bibliographical Society*
of America, 55 (1961), 164-67.

15. ————. *John Robert Moore: A Bibliography.* Bloomington: Indiana University Foundation, 1961.

Includes a complete list of Moore's writings on Defoe.

16. Nash, N. Frederick. "Additions and Refinements to Moore's *A Checklist of the Writings of Daniel Defoe.*" *Papers of the Bibliographical Society of America*, 72 (1978), 226-28.

Turns up in the John Robert Moore collection of Defoe material, now owned by the University of Illinois Library, several previously unrecorded editions and variants.

*   Nicholls, Norah. "Some Early Editions of Defoe." (See item 625.)

17. Novak, Maximillian E. "Daniel Defoe." *The New Cambridge Bibliography of English Literature.* Ed. George Watson. Vol. 2. Cambridge: Cambridge University Press, 1971. Pp. 882-918.

Attributes about 500 works to Defoe and lists over 400 items about him.

18. ————. "Defoe." *The English Novel: Select Bibliographical Guides.* Ed. A.E. Dyson. London: Oxford University Press, 1974. Pp. 16-35.

Evaluates the criticism of Defoe in an essay that is followed by a listing of about 150 works by and about Defoe.

19. ————. "Recent Studies in the Restoration and Eighteenth Century." *Studies in English Literature*, 22 (1982), 531-54.

Reviews the more important recent works on Defoe.

20. Palmer, Helen H., and Anne Jane Dyson. *English Novel Explication: Criticisms to 1972.* Hamden, Conn.: The Shoe String Press, 1973.

Updates Bell and Baird (item 4) by adding to their bibliography 55 items on Defoe published between 1958 and 1972.

21. Payne, William L. "An Annotated Bibliography of Works about Daniel Defoe, 1719-1974: Parts I-III." *Bulletin*

       of Bibliography, 32 (1975), 3-14, 27, 32, 63-75, 87, 89-100, 132.

       Forms the most complete (approximately 900 items) listing of Defoe scholarship prior to this volume. Most articles are briefly annotated, and reviews are listed for some book-length studies.

22. ————. "Defoe in the Pamphlets." *Philological Quarterly*, 52 (1973), 85-96.

       Lists 165 pamphlets which mention Defoe. For emendations and additions, see Downie and Rogers, item 10.

23. Rogers, Pat. "Addenda and Corrigenda: Moore's *Checklist of Defoe*." *Papers of the Bibliographical Society of America*, 75 (1981), 60-64.

       The compiler did not check this item personally.

24. Schutt, J.H. "Hermann Ullrich: A Bibliography." *English Studies*, 13 (1931), 87-89.

       Names 38 of Ullrich's works which treat Defoe, *Robinson Crusoe*, or Robinsonaden.

25. Sherbo, Arthur. "Eighteenth-Century British Fiction in Print: An Uncritical Census." *College English*, 21 (1959), 105-11.

       Lists fourteen inexpensive editions of Defoe's novels on a chart which shows whether or not the edition includes an introduction, notes, and a bibliography.

*   Sherburn, George, and Donald F. Bond. "Defoe and Journalism." (See item 331.)

26. Staves, Susan. "Studies in Eighteenth-Century Fiction, 1979." *Philological Quarterly*, 59 (1980), 465-514.

       Presents an analytic review of the year's major Defoe studies.

*   Trent, William P. "Bibliographical Notes on Defoe. I." (See item 1202.)

*   ————. "Bibliographical Notes on Defoe. II." (See item 1203.)

*   ————. "Bibliographical Notes on Defoe. III." (See item 1204.)

27. ————. "A Collection of Newspaper Clippings, Manu-
     script Notes, Etc., Including Some on Defoe." 3 port-
     folios. Boston Public Library.

     Listed by Payne, item 21, but not confirmed by the
     compiler.

II

SELECTED COLLECTIONS AND EDITIONS

A. Novels

28. *Robinson Crusoe: An Authoritative Text, Backgrounds and Sources, Criticism.* Ed. Michael Shinagel. New York: Norton, 1975.

Bases the text on Defoe's first edition, but also collates all six of the authorized editions published by William Taylor in 1719. The book contains background and critical materials from Defoe's lifetime to the present day. Modern materials, all annotated under their original titles, include: J. Paul Hunter, three selections from *The Reluctant Pilgrim*, item 565; Gustav L. Lannert, from *An Investigation of the Language of Robinson Crusoe*, item 585; Virginia Woolf, "Robinson Crusoe," item 692; Ian Watt, "Robinson Crusoe as Myth," item 689; Eric Berne, "The Psychological Structure of Space with Some Remarks on Robinson Crusoe," item 483; John Robert Moore, from *Daniel Defoe: Citizen of the Modern World*, item 255; Maximillian E. Novak, from *Defoe and the Nature of Man*, item 431; James Joyce, "Daniel Defoe," item 213; George A. Starr, from *Defoe and Spiritual Autobiography*, item 453; and James Sutherland, from *Daniel Defoe: A Critical Study*, item 349.

Review: Max Byrd, *The Eighteenth Century: A Current Bibliography*, n.s. 1 (1978), 270.

29. *The Life and Strange Surprising Adventures of Robinson Crusoe.* Ed. J. Donald Crowley. London and New York: Oxford University Press, 1972.

Includes an Introduction (see item 505), Note on the Text, Bibliography, Chronology, Textual Notes, and Explanatory Notes. The text is based on the first edition (prepared from the Bodleian Library copy).

*   *Robinson Crusoe and Other Writings*. (See item 92.)

30.   *The Life and Adventures of Robinson Crusoe, of York,
      Mariner*. Ed. Angus Ross. Baltimore: Penguin, 1965.

      Not reviewed by the compiler but listed in the *Annual
      MLA Bibliography* for 1965, item 5493.

31.   *Robinson Crusoe*. New York: New American Library, 1961.

      Contains no information on the copy-text. For the
      Afterword by Harvey Swados, see item 672.

32.   *The Life and Strange Surprising Adventures of Robinson
      Crusoe*. Ed. J. Cuthbert Hadden. New York: The
      Heritage Press, 1930.

      "Corrects" the text of 1719 "for ease of reading:
      possibly by children as well as adults." For Hadden's
      introduction, see item 543.

33.   *The Life, Adventures, and Pyracies of the Famous Captain
      Singleton*. Ed. Shiv K. Kumar. London: Oxford Uni-
      versity Press, 1969.

      Consists of an Introduction (see item 701), Note on
      the Text, Bibliography, Chronology, and Explanatory
      Notes. The text is based on "an almost literal reprint
      ... of the first edition."

      Reviews: Robert James Merrett, *Yearbook of English
      Studies*, 2 (1972), 276-77; James H. Simms, *Seventeenth-
      Century News*, 29 (1971), 79-80.

34.   *The Life, Adventures and Piracies of the Famous Captain
      Singleton*. Introduction by James Sutherland. London:
      Dent; New York: Dutton, 1963.

      Reprints the first (1720) edition with corrections of
      obvious printer's errors. See Sutherland's "Introduction"
      under item 707.

35.   *The Life, Adventures, and Piracies of the Famous Captain
      Singleton*. London: Dent; New York: Dutton, 1906.

      Begins with a Preface by Edward Garnett (see item 700)
      and a list of Defoe's works. No reference is made to
      the copy-text.

36.   *Memoirs of a Cavalier*. Ed. James T. Boulton. London:
      Oxford University Press, 1972.

Uses as copy-text the 1720 edition (the only edition
published in Defoe's lifetime) and contains a basic
bibliography, a chronology, explanatory notes, a glossary
of military terms, a biographical index of persons mentioned in the text, and Boulton's introduction (for the
latter, see item 709).

37. *The Fortunes and Misfortunes of the Famous Moll Flanders.*
Ed. Juliet Mitchell. Harmondsworth and New York:
Penguin, 1978.

Not reviewed by the compiler.

38. *Moll Flanders: An Authoritative Text, Backgrounds and
Sources, Criticism.* Ed. Edward Kelly. Norton Critical
Editions New York: Norton, 1973.

Reprints the first edition of the novel and contains
three sections of background and critical materials from
Defoe's own lifetime to the present day. Modern criticism,
annotated under original titles, includes: John Robert
Moore, from *Daniel Defoe: Citizen of the Modern World*,
item 255; Gerald Howson, "Who Was Moll Flanders?" item
755; Virginia Woolf, "Defoe," item 827; E.M. Forster,
from *Aspects of the Novel*, item 742; Alan Dugald McKillop,
from *The Early Masters of English Fiction*, item 424;
Ian Watt, from *The Rise of the Novel*, item 688; Terence
Martin, "The Unity of *Moll Flanders*," item 775; Wayne C.
Booth, from *The Rhetoric of Fiction*, item 722; Martin
Price, from *To the Palace of Wisdom*, item 796; Arnold
Kettle, "In Defense of *Moll Flanders*," item 762; Robert
Alan Donovan, "The Two Heroines of *Moll Flanders*," item
734; Michael Shinagel, "The Maternal Paradox in *Moll
Flanders*," item 811; Maximillian E. Novak, "Defoe's
'Indifferent Monitor,'" item 787; G.A. Starr, from *Defoe
and Casuistry*, item 452.

39. *The Fortunes and Misfortunes of the Famous Moll Flanders.*
Ed. G.A. Starr. London and New York: Oxford University
Press, 1971.

Contains an Introduction (see item 816), Bibliography,
Chronology, and both textual and explanatory notes.
The text is based on the first edition (published January
27, 1722, by Chetwood and Edling) and records approximately 1,000 second-edition substantive variants.

Review: (London) *Times Literary Supplement*, 11 February
1972, p. 148.

40. *The Fortunes and Misfortunes of the Famous Moll Flanders*
     (1722). Menston: Scolar Press, 1970.

     A facsimile reprint of the third edition.

41. *Moll Flanders*. Ed. J. Paul Hunter. New York: Crowell,
     1970.

     Follows the text of the first edition rather than the
     third edition, corrected, which usually is the basis of
     modern reprints. The person who edited the third edition
     seems frequently to have misunderstood the original and
     to have altered the text in ways contrary to Defoe's
     intentions and usual practice. An Appendix lists those
     places in which the editor has regularized spellings.
     Twelve critical essays from the nineteenth and twentieth
     centuries are reprinted. The nineteenth century items
     include two anonymous pieces and essays by John Ballantyne,
     Charles Lamb, Bayard Tuckerman, and Wilbur Cross. The
     modern works, annotated in Section IV of this collection,
     are Virginia Woolf, "Defoe" (item 827); Dorothy Van Ghent,
     "On Moll Flanders" (item 819); Ian Watt, "Defoe as
     Novelist: *Moll Flanders*" (item 464); Arnold Kettle, "In
     Defence of *Moll Flanders*" (item 762); Maximillian E.
     Novak, "Conscious Irony in *Moll Flanders*: Facts and Prob-
     lems" (item 786); G.A. Starr, "*Moll Flanders*" (item 453).

42. *Moll Flanders*. Ed. Nancy L. Arnez. New York: Barnes
     and Noble, 1969.

     Listed in the *Annual MLA Bibliography* for 1969 (item
     3663) but not seen by the compiler.

43. *Moll Flanders*. Introduction by Elizabeth Tate. New
     York: Airmont, 1969.

     Not reviewed by the compiler, but listed in the
     Annual MLA Bibliography for 1969 (item 3482).

44. *The Fortunes and Misfortunes of the Famous Moll Flanders*.
     Afterword by Kenneth Rexroth. New York: Signet, 1964.

     Bases the text on the third edition of December 1722
     which contains Defoe's corrections of the first edition.
     See Rexroth's Afterword under item 800.

45. *Moll Flanders*. Ed. Mark Schorer. New York: Random House,
     1950.

     Fails to mention the copy-text. See Schorer's intro-
     duction under item 806.

46. *The Fortunes and Misfortunes of the Famous Moll Flanders.*
    Ed. Godfrey Davies. New York: Rinehart, 1949.
    Not reviewed by the compiler.

47. *The Fortunes and Misfortunes of the Famous Moll Flanders.*
    Ed. John T. Winterich. New York: The Heritage Press,
    1942.

    Illustrated by Reginald Marsh and introduced by John T.
    Winterich (for the latter, see item 382). The copy-text
    is not mentioned.

48. *The Fortunes and the Misfortunes of the Famous Moll
    Flanders.* New York: Knopf, 1923.

    The compiler did not see this item.

    Reviews: Robert Littel, *New Republic*, 2 January 1924,
    p. 152; Andrew Carey, *Spectator*, 27 December 1924,
    pp. 1027-29.

49. *The History and Remarkable Life of the Truly Honourable
    Col. Jacque, Commonly Call'd Col. Jack.* Ed. Samuel
    Holt Monk. London and New York: Oxford University
    Press, 1965.

    Contains an Introduction (item 833), Bibliography,
    Chronology, and several pages of notes. The text "is
    based on an almost literal reproduction of the first
    edition."

50. *The History and Remarkable Life of the Truly Honourable
    Colonel Jack.* London: Hamish Hamilton, 1947.

    Begins with an introductory Note by A.H. (see item
    830). Provides no information on the copy-text.

51. *A Journal of the Plague Year.* Ed. Louis Landa. London:
    Oxford University Press, 1969.

    Contains a long introduction (see item 854), copious
    notes, and a brief section on the plague. The copy-text
    is the first edition of 1722 with minor changes.

    Review: Robert James Merrett, *Yearbook of English
    Studies*, 2 (1972), 276-77.

52. *A Journal of the Plague Year.* Eds. Anthony Burgess and
    Christopher Bristow. Harmondsworth and Baltimore:
    Penguin, 1966.

Bases the text on the original edition of 1722 with some modernization of spelling and punctuation; contains an Introduction by Anthony Burgess (item 847) and a note on the nature of the plague.

53. *Journal of the Plague Year*. London: Falcon Press, 1950.

Not seen by the compiler.

Review: (London) *Times Literary Supplement*, 15 September 1950, p. 580.

54. *"A Journal of the Plague Year" and Other Pieces*. Ed. Arthur W. Secord. New York: Doubleday Doran, 1935.

See Introduction under Secord, item 862.

* *Ein Bericht vom Pestjahr*. Translated by Ernst Betz with a Postscript by Ernst Gerhard Jacob. (See item 1318.)

55. *A Journal of the Plague Year*. Introduction by Kenneth Hopkins. London: The Folio Society, 1960.

Contains a dozen woodcuts by Peter Pendrey. See Hopkins' Introduction at item 849.

56. *A Journal of the Plague Year*. Ed. G.A. Aitken. London: Dent and New York: Dutton, n.d.

Has an appendix of contemporary accounts of the plague and an Introduction by Aitken (see item 842).

57. *Roxana*. Ed. Jane Jack. London and New York: Oxford University Press, 1981.

Issued originally in the Oxford English Novel series, this edition is a less expensive reprint in a new series, The World's Classics. For information on the text and Introduction, see item 873.

58. *Roxana, The Fortunate Mistress*. New York and London: Signet, 1979.

Fails to note the copy-text. For Katherine Rogers' Afterword, see item 887.

59. *Roxana, The Fortunate Mistress*. Ed. Jane Jack. London and New York: Oxford University Press, 1964.

Combines an Introduction, Bibliography, Chronology, and textual notes with the text, which is based on the first edition of 1724 (with obvious misprints corrected).

The Introduction is annotated under Jack, item 873.

Review: John Fuller, *New Statesman*, 69 (1965), 283-84.

60. *The Fortunate Mistress.* Introduction by Willa Cather.
New York: Knopf, 1924.

Begins with an Introduction by Willa Cather (see item
869). No information is given on the source of the text.

B. Other Writings

61. *An Account of the Conduct and Proceedings of the Pirate
Gow.* New York: Burt Franklin, 1970.

Contains no information on the source of this text,
but it apparently is taken from the copy in the British
Museum and was first published in this form in 1896.
There is a Preface by John R. Russell (see item 1063)
and a few notes appended to the text.

62. *Atalantis Major.* Ed. John J. Perry. Augustan Reprint
Society, No. 198. Los Angeles: Clark Memorial Library
and University of California Press, 1979.

Reprints this 1711 pamphlet directed against the
second Duke of Argyll's participation in the 1710 election of Scottish peers. See Perry's Introduction at
item 1007.

63. *A Brief History of the Poor Palatine Refugees* (1709).
Introduction by John Robert Moore. Augustan Reprint
Society, No. 106. Los Angeles: Clark Memorial Library
and University of California Press, 1964.

Reproduces the original tract (London: J. Baker, 1709)
from the only known copy, which is held by the British
Museum.

64. *The Complete English Tradesman.* New York: Burt Franklin,
1970.

Prints an 1889 edition.

65. *Conjugal Lewdness; or, Matrimonial Whoredom* (1727).
Scolar Students' Facsimiles, PR 4. Menston: Scolar
Press, 1970.

A facsimile reprint of the first edition.

66. *Conjugal Lewdness; or, Matrimonial Whoredom. A Treatise
    concerning the Use and Abuse of the Marriage Bed* (1727).
    Introduction by Maximillian E. Novak. Gainesville,
    Fla.: Scholars' Facsimiles and Reprints, 1967.

    Reproduces this facsimile edition from a copy in the
    British Museum.

67. *The Consolidator, or Memoirs of Sundry Transactions from
    the World in the Moon.* Ed. Malcolm J. Bosse. New York
    and London: Garland, 1972.

    A facsimile edition (part of Garland's "Foundations of
    the Novel" series) made from a copy in the Beinecke
    Library of Yale University. See the Introduction under
    Bosse, item 896.

68. *Daniel Defoe and Others: Accounts of the Apparition of
    Mrs. Veal.* Ed. Manuel Schonhorn. Augustan Reprint
    Society, No. 115. Los Angeles: Clark Memorial Library
    and University of California Press, 1965.

    Reprints eight accounts of the appearance of Mrs. Veal's
    apparition to Mrs. Bargrave: a letter from E.B. to an
    unknown lady, L. Lukyn's letter to her aunt, Stephen
    Gray's letter to John Flamsteed, an account printed in
    the *Loyal Post* of London, Defoe's famous account (both
    the first and fourth editions), a translation of Latin
    manuscript notes in the Defoe fourth edition, a "re-
    arrangement" of Defoe's account which was prefixed to
    John Spavin's abridgement of Drelincourt's *The Christian
    Defense against the Fears of Death*, and the Rev. Thomas
    Payne's version. See Schonhorn's commentary under item
    1015.

69. *Defoe's Review.* 9 Vols. Ed. A. Wellesley. New York:
    A.M.S. and London: Cassell, 1967.

    Listed in the *Annual Bibliography of English Litera-
    ture and Language* for 1967 (item 4746) but unseen by the
    compiler.

70. *Defoe's Review Reproduced from the Original Editions.*
    22 Vols. Ed. Arthur W. Secord. New York: Columbia
    University Press, 1938.

    Reviews: A.D. McKillop, *Modern Language Notes*, 55
    (1940), 218-20; (London) *Times Literary Supplement*,
    11 June 1938, p. 408; (London) *Times Literary Supple-
    ment*, 18 June 1938, p. 424; (London) *Times Literary*

Supplement, 30 July 1938, p. 508; (London) *Times Literary Supplement*, 8 July 1939, p. 412; *Philological Quarterly*, 18 (1939), 172; James R. Sutherland, *Modern Language Review*, 35 (1940), 540-42.

71. "Defoe's *True born Englishman*." Ed. Adolph C.L. Guthkelch. *Essays and Studies by Members of the English Association*, 4 (1913), 100-50.

    Reprints the first edition with added notes.

72. *An Essay on the Regulation of the Press*. Ed. John R. Moore. Luttrell Reprints, No. 7. Oxford: Blackwell, 1948.

    Set from a photostat of the tract owned by Indiana University. Six misprints have been corrected, the pagination of the original has been ignored, and some changes in spacing have been made; otherwise, the reproduction conforms to the 1703-04 original. See Moore's Introduction at item 988.

73. Item deleted.

74. *A General History of the Pyrates*. Ed. Manuel Schonhorn. Columbia, S.C.: University of South Carolina Press, 1972.

    Review: Michael Shinagel, *Modern Philology*, 72 (1975), 314-16.

75. *The Meditations of Daniel Defoe*. Ed. George Harris Healey. Cummington, Mass.: The Cummington Press, 1946.

    Prints for the first time seven verse meditations taken from a notebook, now owned by the Huntington Library, written in Defoe's hand.

    Reviews: H.C. Hutchins, *Philological Quarterly*, 26 (1947), 116-17; John R. Moore, *Journal of English and Germanic Philology*, 45 (1946), 466-68; A.W. Secord, *Modern Language Notes*, 62 (1947), 350-52; (London) *Times Literary Supplement*, 24 August 1947, p. 404.

76. "*Memoirs of an English Officer (The Military Memoirs of Capt. George Carleton)*" with "*The History of the Remarkable Life of John Sheppard*" and "*The Memoirs of Major Alexander Ramkins, A Highland Officer*." Preface by James T. Boulton. London: Gollancz, 1970.

Uses the third edition of May 27, 1728, for the text
of *Memoirs of an English Officer* because Carleton himself
made some changes and additions in that edition. The
text of *Ramkins* is the original of December 9, 1718, and
the text of *Sheppard* is from the first issue of 1724.

77. *Memoirs of Captain Carleton*. Ed. Cyril H. Hartmann.
London: Routledge, 1929.

Bases this edition on the 1808 Sir Walter Scott edition
with modernized spelling and punctuation and selected
emendations. The latter are noted in Hartmann's Introduction (item 1181).

Review: (London) *Times Literary Supplement*, 18 April
1929, p. 306.

78. *Of Captain Mission* (1728). Introduction by Maximillian
E. Novak. Augustan Reprint Society, No. 87. Los
Angeles: Clark Memorial Library and University of
California Press, 1961.

Reproduces a section of Defoe's *The History of the
Pyrates* from the first edition copy of the second volume
held by the Huntington Library. Novak's Introduction is
listed under item 1058.

79. *A Plan of English Commerce*. Oxford: Blackwell, 1927.

Listed in the *Annual Bibliography of English Literature
and Language* for 1927, item 2136, but not seen by the
compiler.

*   *Defoe's Review*. (See items 69 and 70.)

80. *A Short Narrative of the Life and Actions of His Grace
John, D. of Marlborough* (1711). Introduction by Paula
R. Backscheider. Augustan Reprint Society, No. 168.
Los Angeles: Clark Memorial Library and University of
California Press, 1974.

Reproduces this facsimile from a copy in the William
Andrews Clark Memorial Library. An Appendix draws upon
internal evidence and cites Moore to establish Defoe's
authorship of the pamphlet. See Backscheider's Introduction at item 1035.

81. *Street-Robberies Consider'd: The Reason of Their Being
So Frequent*. Ed. Geoffrey M. Sill. Stockton, N.J.:
Carolingian Press, 1973.

Prints the text from a microfilm of the 1728 original with some editorial restoration. See Sill's Introduction at item 1023.

Reviews: *The Eighteenth Century: A Current Bibliography*, n.s. 1 (1978), 270-71; *Eighteenth-Century Studies*, 8 (1974), 124.

82. *A System of Magick*. Introduction by Richard Landon. East Ardsley, Wakefield: EP Publishing; distributed through Totowa, N.J.: Rowman and Littlefield, 1973.

Reproduces the 1728 edition held by the University of London Library. See Landon's Introduction at item 967.

Review: Maximillian E. Novak, *Philological Quarterly*, 53 (1974), 686-87.

83. *A Tour Through England and Wales*. 2 Vols. Introduction by G.D.H. Cole. London: Dent and New York: Dutton, 1968.

Set up from the 1927 Peter Davies edition, which was a verbatim reprint of the first edition. See Cole's Introduction at item 1083.

84. *A Tour thro' London about the year 1725 being Letter V and parts of Letter VI of "A Tour thro' the whole island of Great Britain,"* containing a description of the City of London, as taking in the City of Westminster, Borough of Southwark, and parts of Middlesex. Edited and Annotated by Sir Mayson M. Beeton and E. Beresford Chancellor. London: Batsford, 1929.

Reprints the letters from the original edition.

Review: (London) *Times Literary Supplement*, 12 December 1929, p. 1045.

85. *A Tour Thro' the Whole Island of Great Britain*. Ed. Pat Rogers. Harmondsworth and Baltimore: Penguin, 1965.

Not reviewed by the compiler.

86. *A Tour thro' the Whole Island of Great Britain*. Introduction by G.D.H. Cole. 2 Vols. London: Peter Davies, 1927. Reprinted London: Frank Cass and New York: Augustus M. Kelley, 1968.

Reprints the first edition. For Introduction, see Cole, item 1084.

Reviews: *Philological Quarterly*, 10 (1928), 151; A.W.
Secord, (London) *Times Literary Supplement*, 26 January
1928, p. 62; (London) *Times Literary Supplement*, 12
January 1928, p. 25.

*   *A True Account of the Apparition of Mrs. Veal*. (See
item 68.)

*   *The True-Born Englishman*. (See item 71.)

87. *A Vindication of the Press* (1718). Introduction by Otho
Clinton Williams. Augustan Reprint Society, No. 29.
Los Angeles: Clark Memorial Library and University of
California Press, 1951.

Reprints the New York Public Library copy of this 1718
tract. (The only other copy known to exist is in the
Indiana University Library.) See Williams' Introduction
under item 1032.

C. Collections

88. *The Best of Defoe's "Review": An Anthology*. Ed. William
L. Payne. New York: Columbia University Press, 1951.

Groups 69 essays from Defoe's *Review* into five sec-
tions: "Portrait of the True-Born Englishman," "The
Press," "Economics and Trade," "Politics," and "Curiosa."
See Marjorie Hope Nicolson's Introduction under item 998.

Reviews: *Deutsche Literaturzeitung*, Jahrg. 73, Heft 10
(1952), 592-94; *Listener*, 49 (1953), 983; John Robert
John Robert Moore, *South Atlantic Quarterly*, 51 (1952),
466-67; (London) *Times Literary Supplement*, 25 July
1952, p. 482.

89. *Daniel Defoe*. Ed. James T. Boulton. London: B.T. Batsford and New York: Schocken Books, 1965.

Collects several letters and the following works, some
complete and some abridged: "An Essay Upon Projects,"
"An Argument Shewing That a Standing Army ...," "The
True-Born Englishman," "Legion's Memorial," "The Shortest
Way with the Dissenters," "A Hymn to the Pillory," "A
Review," "A True Apparition of One Mrs. Veal," "And What
If the Pretender Should Come?", "An Appeal to Honour and
Justice," "The Family Instructor," "Memoirs of a Cavalier,"

"The Complete English Tradesman," "The History of the Pyrates: Of Captain Bellamy," and "The Compleat English Gentleman." Boulton's Introduction is listed as item 119.

Reviews: Ben W. Fuson, *The Library Journal*, 90 (1965), 4980; *Johnsonian Newsletter*, 25 (1965), 6; (London) *Times Literary Supplement*, 18 November 1965, p. 1024.

90. *The Letters of Daniel Defoe*. Ed. George Harris Healey. Oxford: Oxford University Press, 1955. Reprinted from corrected sheets of the first edition, 1969.

Brings together sixteen letters written *to* Defoe and 235 written *by* him; two of the former and four of the latter are printed here for the first time. Healey has traced the holographs of 218 of Defoe's known letters; for the others, he has in general used the earliest published version. The letters are thoroughly annotated and a detailed index is appended to the collection.

Reviews: Richmond P. Bond, *Philological Quarterly*, 35 (1956), 288; Robert W. Chapman, *Time and Tide*, 36 (1955), 141–42; Paul Dottin, *Etudes Anglaises*, 8 (1955), 330–34; J. Hamard, *Les Langues Modernes* (1955), 273; Gerhard Jacob, *Archiv für das Studium der neueren Sprachen*, 194 (1957), 70–71; *Listener*, 53 (1955), 119; Harold Nicolson, *Observer*, 9 January 1955, p. 9; Cecil Price, *Neuphilologische Mitteilungen*, 56 (1955), 153–55; A.W. Secord, *Modern Philology*, 54 (1956), 45–52; Roger Sharrock, *Modern Language Review*, 52 (1957), 103–05; (London) *Times Literary Supplement*, 29 April 1955, p. 208; Mark A. Thomson, *English Historical Review*, 71 (1956), 296–98; Harold Williams, *Review of English Studies*, n.s. 8 (1957), 95–96.

91. *Poems on Affairs of State: Augustan Satirical Verse, 1660–1714*. Vol. 6. Ed. Frank H. Ellis. New Haven: Yale University Press, 1970.

Contains eleven poems by Defoe: *An Encomium upon a Parliament* (1699); *The Pacificator* (1700); *The True-Born Englishman* (1700); *A New Satyr on the Parliament* (1701); *England's Late Jury* (1701); *The Mock Mourners* (1702); *Reformation of Manners* (1702); *The Spanish Descent* (1702); *More Reformation. A Satyr upon Himself* (1703); *A Hymn to the Pillory* (1703); and *The Address* (1704). All available witnesses to the texts have been collated and substantive variants recorded in the notes. See Ellis' remarks on Defoe under item 1138.

92. *Robinson Crusoe and Other Writings*. Ed. James Suther-
    land. Riverside Editions. Boston: Houghton Mifflin,
    1968. Reprinted as part of the Gotham Library series
    by New York University Press, 1977.

    Contains complete texts of *Robinson Crusoe*, "The Poor
    Man's Plea," "The Shortest Way with the Dissenters," "The
    Apparition of Mrs. Veal," and "Every-Body's Business Is
    No-Body's Business." Includes selections from *The True-
    Born Englishman, The Review, A Journal of the Plague
    Year*, and *The Complete English Tradesman*. For the Intro-
    duction, see item 353.

93. *Selected Poetry and Prose of Daniel Defoe*. Ed. Michael
    F. Shugrue. New York: Holt, Rinehart and Winston,
    1968.

    Includes *The True-Born Englishman, The Mock-Mourners,
    The Shortest Way with the Dissenters, An Appeal to Honour
    and Justice, The History* ... *of John Sheppard*, and *The
    Time and Genuine Account of* ... *Jonathan Wild*; also in-
    cludes selections from *An Essay Upon Projects, The Con-
    solidator, The Review, Applebee's Journal*, and *Augusta
    Triumphans*. The texts for the most part are reprinted
    from first editions in the University of Illinois Library.
    See Shugrue's Introduction at item 335.

    Review: Johnsonian Newsletter, 28 (1968), 12.

94. *Selected Writings of Daniel Defoe*. Ed. James T. Boulton.
    Cambridge: Cambridge University Press, 1975.

    Review: Paul Gabriel Boucé, *Etudes Anglaises*, 29 (1976),
    95-97.

95. *Selections from the Prose of Daniel Defoe*. Ed. Roger
    Manvell. London: Falcon Press, 1953.

    Cites portions of the following works: *Robinson
    Crusoe, Duncan Campbell, Memoirs of a Cavalier, Captain
    Singleton, Moll Flanders, A Journal of the Plague Year,
    Colonel Jack, Roxana, A Tour Through the Whole Island of
    Britain*, and *The Political History of the Devil*.

96. *The Shakespeare Head Edition of the Novels and Selected
    Writings of Daniel Defoe*. 14 Vols. Oxford: Black-
    well, 1927-28.

    Review: (London) *Times Literary Supplement*, 16 August
    1927, pp. 585-86.

97. *The Versatile Defoe: An Anthology of Uncollected Writings
     of Daniel Defoe.*   Ed. Laura Ann Curtis.   Totowa, N.J.:
     Rowman and Littlefield, 1979.

     Collects and critically comments on eighteen works by
     Defoe: "King William's Affection to the Church of
     England Examined," item 934; "A Declaration of Truth to
     Benjamin Hoadley," item 930; "An Answer to a Question
     that Nobody Thinks of, viz. But What if the Queen Should
     Die?," item 927; "Reasons Why This Nation Ought to Put a
     Speedy End to This Expensive War," item 936; "A Letter
     from a Gentleman at the Court of St. Germains," item 935;
     "Some Thoughts upon the Subject of Commerce with France,"
     item 1088; "A Brief Deduction of the Original Progress,
     and Immense Greatness of the British Woollen Manufac-
     ture," item 928; "A Brief State of the Inland or Home
     Trade, of England," item 1086; "An Essay upon Loans,"
     item 931; "The Freeholder's Plea against Stock-Jobbing
     Elections of Parliament Men; The Villainy of Stock-
     Jobbers Detected; The Anatomy of Exchange Alley," item
     933; "The Storm; or a Collection of the Most Remarkable
     Casualties and Disasters which Happened in the Late
     Dreadful Tempest, Both by Sea and Land," item 1045; "The
     Military Memoirs of Captain George Carleton," item 1043;
     "A True Account of the Proceedings at Perth," item 938;
     "Minutes of the Negotiation of Monsr. Mesnages at the
     Court of England during the Four Last Years of the Reign
     of Her Late Majesty, Queen Anne," item 1044; "The Com-
     plete English Tradesman," item 1087; "Two Andrew Moreton
     Pamphlets: 1. The Protestant Monastery; 2. Augusta
     Triumphans," item 939; "The Family Instructor," item
     932; and "Religious Courtship," item 937. Each selection
     is preceded by a brief critical evaluation. The Intro-
     duction is annotated at item 897.

     Review: John Wilkinson, *The Scriblerian*, 13 (1980), 45-
     46.

*   *Works*. (See item 96.)

98. *Works*. Ed. G.H. Maynadier. (In addition to the 1903-04
     Sproul edition, entered separately in this section, the
     National Union Catalog records the editions listed be-
     low as edited by Maynadier. The compiler has not com-
     pared them but suspects that they are various reprints
     of the same edition.)

     16 Vols., New York: F. DeFau, 1903; 8 Vols., Philadel-
     phia: John D. Morris, 1903; 16 Vols., Boston and New York:

C.T. Brainard, 1903-04; 16 Vols., New York: Crowell,
1903-04; 16 Vols., New York: Jenson Society, 1907.

99. *The Works of Daniel Defoe.* 16 Vols.   Ed. G.H. Maynadier.
    New York: Sproul, 1903-04.

    Provides no textual information. See Maynadier's
    introductions under individual titles in the appropriate
    sections of this bibliography.

III

GENERAL WORKS ON DEFOE'S LIFE AND ART

100. A., T.P. "German Translations of Defoe." *Notes and Queries*, 172 (1937), 11.

   Responds to F.A.M., item 229, that a wave of German imitations of *Robinson Crusoe*, called "Robinsonaden," followed in the wake of the novel's publication and continued to 1880. There also appeared German translations of *An Essay on Projects* (1890), *Moll Flanders* (1903), *Captain Singleton* (1919), and *Memoirs of a Cavalier* (1919).

101. Adolph, Robert. *The Rise of Modern Prose Style.* Cambridge, Mass.: Harvard University Press, 1968.

   Calls Defoe's style "modern" in that it is both "plain" and "impersonal." It is a businessman's prose, one which accounts for everything, carefully spelling out exact times and spatial relationships. There is no stylistic heightening in Defoe's works even when, for example, Crusoe tells us of his despair and panic; passions are described in the same style as the most mundane events.

102. Aitken, G.A. "Daniel Defoe's Wife." *Notes and Queries*, Tenth Series, 11 (1909), 516.

   Points out to "Diego" (item 155) that the author's articles in *The Contemporary Review* for February 1890 and *The Athenaeum* for August 23, 1890, give in detail the facts about Defoe's date of birth and his marriage.

103. Amakawa, Junjiro. *Defoe.* Tokyo: Miraisha, 1966.

   The compiler was unable to locate this work, listed in the *Annual Bibliography of English Language and Literature for 1966*, item 4689.

104.   ———. "Defoe as an Economist." *Kwansei Gakuin University Annual Studies*, 15 (1966), 101-26.

Sees Defoe as a knowledgeable economist who anticipates Adam Smith's views, the growth of capitalism, and the Industrial Revolution.

105.   Andersen, Hans H. "The Paradox of Trade and Morality in Defoe." *Modern Philology*, 39 (1941), 23-46.

Demonstrates that some of Defoe's professed moral views are at odds with his attitudes toward slavery and luxury. Although Defoe expresses the conventional morality against slavery in his *Reformation of Manners* (1702), he advocates slavery whenever he believes it is advantageous to trade. Likewise, he rails against drunkenness and other varieties of sinful luxuries, but he says in his *Review* that what "may be a Vice in Morals may at the same time be a Vertue [sic] in Trade." Defoe's paradoxical views are founded in the conflicts of his age between Puritanism and economic aspiration.

106.   Askew, H. "Daniel Defoe's Descendants." *Notes and Queries*, 167 (1934), 160.

Identifies the lineage of the Rev. Defoe Baker mentioned in V., item 370, and remarks that three "maiden ladies" bearing Defoe's name were given government pensions in 1877.

107.   B., R.S. "Ancestry of Daniel Defoe: Registration of Baptisms." *Notes and Queries*, 175 (1938), 86.

Corrects a remark by Mundy, item 277, that it was unusual for parish registers to record births without baptisms; in 1653 a Parliamentary Ordinance was passed requiring the entry of births not baptisms. Also see Ellison, item 177.

108.   Backscheider, Paula R. "Defoe and the Edinburgh Town Council." *Scriblerian*, 14 (1981), 44-46.

Remarks on two of Defoe's transactions with the Edinburgh council—he received permission to print *Caledonia* and to print the Edinburgh *Courant*—in order to demonstrate the esteem with which Defoe was held in Scotland for his work on the Union.

108A.   ———. "Defoe's Lady Credit." *Huntington Library Quarterly*, 44 (1981), 89-100.

This item was not seen by the compiler.

109. Baine, Rodney. *Daniel Defoe and the Supernatural.*
Athens, Georgia: University of Georgia Press, 1968.

Explores Defoe's "belief in an unseen world and his
employment of occult materials in his writings." Baine
believes that in order to fully comprehend Defoe's religious thought, one must understand that Defoe believed in
"the ministry of the blessed angels, the power and temp-
tation of the Devil, and the medium of the apparition,
as it was used not only by these angelic powers but by
inferior spirits." In his occult works, Defoe attempts
to show God's care for man and the Devil's persistent
attacks on him. Previous criticism on Defoe's super-
naturalism has focused on "Mrs. Veal" and all but ignored Defoe's other occult publications, but Baine
attempts to rectify this critical deficiency by discussing such works as "A Vision of the Angelick World,"
The Political History of the Devil, A System of Magick,
and *An Essay on the History and Reality of Apparitions.*
He also produces evidence to show that Defoe did *not*
write *The Life and Adventures of Duncan Campbell* or *The
Dumb Philosopher,* both of which are attributed to him
by all Defoe bibliographers.

Reviews: *Johnsonian Newsletter,* 29 (1969), 6-7; Samuel
Holt Monk, *South Atlantic Bulletin,* 34 (1969), 27-29;
Manuel Schonhorn, *Philological Quarterly,* 48 (1969),
345-47.

110. ————. "Defoe and the Angels." *Texas Studies in
Literature and Language,* 9 (1967), 345-69.

Contends that an understanding of Defoe's "angelology"
in both "A Vision of the Angelick World," appended to
the *Serious Reflections* (1720), and *Essay on the History
and Reality of Apparitions* (1727) will help clarify his
religious interests and purposes. Such an understanding
shows Defoe to be a sincere Puritan trying to demonstrate
through credible evidence the existence of "God's per-
sisting care, through angelic ministry, to reclaim and
guide lost man."

111. Baird, Theodore. "The World Turned Upside Down."
American Scholar, 27 (1958), 215-23.

Argues somewhat impressionistically that Defoe has
shaped the way readers read because he "relocated the
place of the imagination" by denying its existence.
Defoe's literal treatment of every subject and his in-
difference to literary tradition makes him literature's
great realist.

*   Baker, Ernest A. *The Later Romances and the Establish-*
           ment of Realism. (See item 390.)

112.   Bastian, F. "Daniel Defoe and the Dorking District."
           Surrey Archeological Collection, 55 (1958), 41-64.

           Examines Defoe's comments in his *Tour* on the Dorking
           area and checks their accuracy against maps and other
           contemporary documents, concluding that he shows a de-
           tailed, though not always accurate, knowledge of the
           district. This knowledge, coupled with a remark in *An
           Essay on the History and Reality of Apparitions*, leads
           Bastian to believe that Defoe attended a boarding school
           at Dorking and could not have been enrolled in Morton's
           Academy prior to autumn of 1676.

113.   ————. *Defoe's Early Life.* Totowa, N.J.: Barnes and
           Noble, 1981.

           This book came to the compiler's attention too late
           to be annotated for the bibliography, but see Novak's
           remarks, item 19.

114.   ————. "James Foe, Merchant, Father of Daniel Defoe."
           Notes and Queries, n.s. 11 (1964), 82-86.

           Draws upon records in the Guildhall Library and the
           London Records Office to develop a brief biography of
           Defoe's father which should shed light upon Defoe's
           background and upbringing.

115.   Bateson, Thomas. "The Relations of Defoe and Harley."
           English Historical Review, 15 (1900), 238-50.

           Condemns Defoe for his "degradation" in working for
           Harley. Defoe was a turncoat, a hypocrite, a "hanger-
           on," and a "wretch" who served Harley against all
           principle and solely for his own financial gain, although
           he was actually paid little for his efforts. (For a
           different view of Defoe's economic relationship with
           Harley, see Downie, "Secret Service Payments," item
           171.)

116.   Bensly, Edward. "Daniel Defoe in the Pillory." *Notes
           and Queries*, Twelfth Series, 8 (1921), 118.

           Quotes Courthope and the author of the *Encyclopaedia
           Britannica* article on Defoe as stating that Pope knew
           that Defoe did not lose his ears in the pillory but
           that he wanted to compare Defoe with Prynne. See G.B.M.,
           item 230, and Druett, item 173.

117. Bentley, A.L.C. "The Mother of Daniel Defoe." *Notes and Queries*, 193 (1948), 151.

      Refers to the oft-repeated notion that Defoe's mother was socially superior to her husband and that her father kept a pack of hounds and asks for further information on her.

118. Blunden, Edmund. "Daniel Defoe." *Votive Tablets*. Freeport, N.Y.: Books for Libraries Press, 1967. Pp. 87-100. Originally published London, 1932.

      Ranges over the body of Defoe's work, emphasizing the triumphs of *Robinson Crusoe*, *The True-born Englishman*, and *The Shortest Way with the Dissenters*. Defoe's talent lies in his "laconic and shrewd reporting," his ability to present the most minute and realistic events of everyday life. His deficiencies include his prolexity and his inability to objectively assess his own works.

119. Boulton, James T. "Introduction. Daniel Defoe: His Language and Rhetoric." *Daniel Defoe*. London: B.T. Batsford and New York: Schocken Books, 1965. Pp. 1-22.

      Presents a detailed analysis of Defoe's style, emphasizing its "plainness" which is consciously designed to be appropriate to the subject at hand and to suggest that the narrator is telling the truth. When Defoe does use imagery, it is usually of the "homely" variety found in proverbs and close to the everyday experience of the average reader. Although Defoe never multiplies words or indulges in copious figures to make his work more artistic or "poetic," he does show "the popular orator's tendency to repeat himself," heaping illustration on illustration and adding details which are superfluous to the event being described but which are important in psychologically describing the narrator.

120. Boyce, Benjamin, and Dorothy G. Boyce. "Dr. Johnson's Definitions of 'Tory' and 'Whig.'" *Notes and Queries*, 198 (1953), 161-62.

      Observes that Dr. Johnson's slanted definitions of "Whig" and "Tory" were traditional, and as one bit of evidence cites Defoe in the *Review* (1710, VI, no. 75) where "Tory" is defined, in part, as "one who will give up his Nation to *Popery* and *Arbitrary Power....*"

A "Whig," Defoe says, is one who "*Blesses God from the bottom of his Heart for the Legal Provisions made against Popery*, in a Parliamentary Succession."

121. Bredvold, Louis. "Daniel Defoe." *The Literature of the Restoration and the Eighteenth Century, 1660-1798.* Vol. 3 of *A History of English Literature.* Ed. Hardin Craig. New York: Collier Books, 1962. Pp. 56-61.

Surveys superficially Defoe's life and literary career, finding him to be a "slovenly" writer with no "capacity for self-criticism" but the Augustan age's greatest representative of middle-class culture.

122. Brown, Lloyd W. "Defoe and the Feminine Mystique." *Transactions of the Samuel Johnson Society of the Northwest.* Vol. 4. Ed. Robert H. Carnie. Calgary: Samuel Johnson Society of the Northwest, 1972. Pp. 4-18.

Draws together the views of Defoe as "revolutionary pro-feminist" (see Fitzgerald, item 179) and as a male conservative (see Novak, *Defoe and the Nature of Man*, item 431), concluding that Defoe is neither the one nor the other but rather combines both extremes in an ambiguous position. Defoe's insistence on individualism is offset by the influence of established custom: "the emancipation of woman is desirable, but her equality is unholy, for that way lie the destruction of male pre-rogative and the institution of female government."

123. Brown, T.J. "English Literary Autographs XXIV: Daniel Defoe, 1661?-1731." *Book Collector*, 6 (1957), 387.

Prints two examples of Defoe's handwriting and re-marks on its "wild elegance."

124. Bulloch, J.M. "Defoe's Relations." *Notes and Queries*, Twelfth Series, 8 (1921), 432.

Requests information on William Gordon, a supposed relative of Daniel Defoe.

125. Burch, Charles Eaton. "Attacks on Defoe in Union Pamphlets." *Review of English Studies*, 6 (1930), 318-19.

Cites passages from three pamphlets which vigorously attack Defoe for his support of the Union between England and Scotland.

126.   ————. "Benjamin Defoe at Edinburgh University, 1710-
       1711." *Philological Quarterly*, 19 (1940), 343-48.

       Believes that Defoe helped advertise Scottish uni-
       versities as appropriate for educating the sons of
       Dissenters.

127.   ————. "Daniel Defoe's Views on Education." *London
       Quarterly Review* (October 1930), 220-29.

       Demonstrates Defoe's progressive attitudes about
       education by showing that he advocated the education of
       women, more adequate teaching of the language, improving
       the quality of English used in the pulpit and the press,
       a more practical method of training for business,
       university reform, and support of serious research.
       See Leinster-Mackay, items 220-25.

128.   ————. "Defoe and His Northern Printers." *Publications
       of the Modern Language Association of America*, 60
       (1945), 121-28.

       Traces Defoe's professional relationship with the
       three northern printers with whom he worked from 1706
       to about 1713: Mrs. Agnes Campbell Anderson, John
       Moncur, and Joseph Button. Burch also notes that Defoe
       probably was part owner of the *Newcastle Gazette* in
       1710.

129.   ————. "Defoe and the Edinburgh Society for the Reforma-
       tion of Manners." *Review of English Studies*, 16
       (1940), 306-12.

       Outlines Defoe's participation in the affairs of The
       Edinburgh Society for the Reformation of Manners between
       March and December of 1707. Defoe withdrew from the
       Society because he objected to its emphasis on the
       wickedness of the common people while it overlooked the
       vices of the upper classes.

130.   ————. "Defoe's British Reputation, 1869-1894."
       Englische Studien, 68 (1934), 410-23.

       Follows the fluctuating tide of Defoe's literary and
       personal reputation from the publication of Lee's
       Daniel Defoe, His Life and Recently Discovered Writings
       (1869) to near the end of the nineteenth century, con-
       cluding that the criticism of the twenty-five years
       following the publication of Lee's book was more thorough
       and thoughtful than it was previous to Lee's study.

131. ————. "An Equivalent for Daniel Defoe." *Modern Language Notes*, 44 (1929), 378.

Shows that the *Equivalent* (1706) is not, as Wilson stated in his 1830 life of Defoe, a Tory attack upon Defoe in the pillory, but is instead a Scotch satire attacking Defoe for his part in the negotiations over the Union.

132. Byrd, Max, ed. *Daniel Defoe: A Collection of Critical Essays*. Twentieth Century Views. London and Englewood Cliffs, N.J.: Prentice-Hall, 1976.

Introduces twelve pieces on Defoe with a brief essay which surveys Defoe's fiction, notes his depiction of "economic man" and his conception of gentility, mentions his view of salvation, and concludes with a brief summation of modern critical trends. The twelve articles, each annotated separately under the author's name, include: Virginia Woolf, "Defoe" (item 827); Martin Price, "Defoe's Novels" (item 796); Benjamin Boyce, "The Question of Emotion in Defoe" (item 396); Ian Watt, "*Robinson Crusoe*" (item 688); Maximillian E. Novak, "Robinson Crusoe's Original Sin" (item 631); George A. Starr, "Robinson Crusoe's Conversion" (item 453); J. Paul Hunter, "The Conclusion of *Robinson Crusoe*" (item 565); Ian Watt, "*Moll Flanders*" (item 688); Mark Schorer, "*Moll Flanders*" (item 806); Dorothy Van Ghent, "On *Moll Flanders*" (item 819); James R. Sutherland, "The Conclusion of *Roxana*" (item 349); W. Austin Flanders, "Defoe's *Journal of the Plague Year* and the Modern Urban Experience" (item 848).

133. Cadbury, Henry J. "Defoe, Bugg, and the Quakers." *Journal of the Friends' Historical Society*, 42 (1950), 70-72.

Reviews Defoe's literary quarrel with the ex-Quaker Francis Bugg and points out that Defoe often defended Quakers from attacks by their enemies.

*   Carnochan, W.B. *Confinement and Flight*. (See item 496.)

134. Chalmers, George. *The Life of Daniel De Foe*. London, 1790. Reprinted New York: Folcroft Library Editions, 1972 (reprints the 1841 Oxford Press edition).

Now almost totally outdated, this biography is included here only because of this modern reprint. Con-

tains a "List of Defoe's Works, Arranged Chronological-
ly" of use to those interested in the historical development of Defoe bibliographic studies.

135. Champion, Larry S. *Quick Springs of Sense: Studies in
the Eighteenth Century.* Athens, Georgia: University
of Georgia Press, 1974.

Includes two essays which treat Defoe: Benjamin Boyce,
"The Shortest Way: Characteristic Defoe Fiction" (item
914), and A.S. Knowles, Jr., "Defoe, Swift, and Fielding:
Notes on the Retirement Theme" (item 580).

136. Ch'en, Shou-Yi. "Daniel Defoe, China's Severest
Critic." *Nankei Social and Economic Quarterly*, 8
(1935), 511-50.

Unseen by the compiler, this piece is listed by Payne
(item 21) who says it treats Defoe's contempt for the
Chinese.

137. Churchill, R.C. *English Literature of the Eighteenth
Century.* London: University Tutorial Press, 1953.

Covers Defoe's entire literary career but emphasizes
the *Review*, *Robinson Crusoe*, and *Moll Flanders*. Unlike
many critics, Churchill believes that Defoe was an entirely honest journalist, often expressing views contrary to the official position of the government that
was paying him. The novels are seen as realistic
narratives of "self-help" that remain appealing because
they deal with "the everyday affairs of common humanity."

138. Clayton, Herbert D. ["Family of James William Defoe."]
Notes and Queries, 7 (1901), 395.

Prints additional information on the family of James
William De Foe, thought by Hibgame (item 201) to be the
last of Defoe's male descendants. Also see King,
items 214 and 215; Oxon, item 290; and A.H., item 190.

139. Clinton, K.B. "Femme et Philosophe: Enlightenment
Origins of Feminism." *Eighteenth-Century Studies*,
8 (1975), 283-99.

Notes briefly (in three paragraphs) Defoe's view that
women are the intellectual equals of men.

140. Cockburn, J.D. "Daniel Defoe in Scotland." *Scottish
Review*, 36 (1900), 250-69.

Uses recently discovered Defoe letters to support the view that Defoe is an "unsavory" person.

141. Coetzee, J.M. "The Agentless Sentence as Rhetorical Device." *Language and Style: An International Journal*, 13 (1980), 26-34.

Points out that passive constructions dominate the passage in which Robinson Crusoe's father counsels his son against going to sea; these passives enable Defoe to present Crusoe's father without mentioning God or Providence. Defoe's intention is to present the bourgeois success story as in the nature of things, a kind of destiny without divine author, in order to reinforce the bourgeoisie's good opinion of itself as all-deserving.

142. Cole, G.D.H. "Daniel Defoe." *From Anne to Victoria*. Ed. Bonamy Dobrée. New York: Scribner's, 1937. Pp. 56-74.

Generalizes about Defoe's life and career. Defoe's moralizing strain is sincere; its apparent hypocrisy is due to the manners of the times and Defoe's own vulgarity and coarseness. He created both English journalism and the modern novel. His finest qualities are his directness, force, and simplicity.

*   Constantine, J. Robert. "The Negro in Defoe's *Religious Courtship*." (See item 920.)

143. Cross, A.G. "Don't Shoot Your Russianists; Or, Defoe and Adam Brand." *British Journal for Eighteenth-Century Studies*, 3 (1980), 230-33.

The compiler was unable to locate this item.

144. Curtis, Laura. *The Elusive Daniel Defoe*. Totowa, N.J.: Barnes and Noble, 1981.

The compiler received notice of the above too late to annotate it for this collection.

145. Daiches, David. *A Critical History of English Literature*. Vol. II. New York: Ronald Press, 1960.

Calls Defoe "shrewd and humane" and sees *Robinson Crusoe* as epitomizing middle-class economic values; even religion to Defoe is "businesslike." Defoe reduces "all literature to journalism," writing everything as

if it were a factual account of a real event. Defoe is
an innovator in literature because his heroes and
heroines seek comfort and safety rather than honor.

146. Dallett, F.J. "Charles Lodwick." *Notes and Queries*,
      n.s. 5 (1958), 452.

      Identifies Charles Lodwick to whom Defoe was appren-
      ticed and who was bondsman for Defoe's marriage.

147. D'Angelo, Michael J. "A Descendant of Daniel Defoe."
      Notes and Queries, 175 (1938), 117.

      Uncovers information that a Daniel Defoe VI, a cook
      aboard the British bark, *Priorhill*, landed in New York
      on October 3, 1893, and asks for information on his
      whereabouts or fate.

148. "Daniel Defoe." *The Library of Literary Criticism of
      English and American Authors*. Vol. IV. Ed. Charles
      Wells Moulton. New York: Moulton, 1902. Reprinted
      New York: Peter Smith, 1933. Pp. 23-51.

      Consists of a biographical sketch and brief extracts
      of critical commentary from the early eighteenth century
      to the late nineteenth century.

149. "Daniel Defoe." (London) *Times Literary Supplement*,
      23 April 1931, pp. 313-14.

      Surveys Defoe's work and discovers his genius to be in
      his "laconic and shrewd reporting." The prose master-
      pieces are *Robinson Crusoe* and *The Shortest Way with
      the Dissenters* (the latter, somewhat surprisingly, is
      referred to here as one of "the perfections of litera-
      ture"). The author also praises "The True-born
      Englishman" and says that Defoe deserves a higher
      reputation than he has as a poet.

150. *Daniel Defoe, 1660-1731: Commemoration in Stoke Newington
      of the Tercentenary of His Birth: An Exhibition of
      Books, Pamphlets, Views, Portraits and Other Items,
      1960, in the Library Hall at the Central Library,
      Stoke Newington*. London: Stoke Newington Central
      Library, 1960.

      Unseen by the compiler but listed in the *Philological
      Quarterly* annual bibliography for 1960.

151. Davis, Andrew McFarland. *Colonial Currency Reprints,*
     1682-1751. 2 Vols. Boston: Prince Society, 1910-11.

     Reprints (in Vol. II, 266-70) *News from the Moon,*
     first thought to be an original pamphlet in the colonial
     currency question but discovered by the author to be a
     reprint of an issue of No. 15, Vol. VII, of Defoe's
     Review (see Davis, item 941). Vol. II, 109-37, also
     reprints two works which mention Robinson Crusoe in their
     titles but which are not connected with Defoe.

152. Dearing, Vinton A. "A Walk Through London with John Gay
     and a Run with Daniel Defoe." *Some Aspects of*
     Eighteenth-Century England. Los Angeles: Clark
     Memorial Library and University of California Press,
     1971. Pp. 27-59.

     Reconstructs sections of eighteenth-century London
     from Gay's *Trivia* and Defoe's *Colonel Jack.* The source
     for the four pages devoted to Defoe is the scene in
     which Jack escapes after stealing the gentleman's pocket-
     book.

153. "Defoe as a Soldier." *Academy,* 69 (1905), 1077.

     Lauds Defoe's knowledge of military tactics as re-
     flected in *Memoirs of a Cavalier* and contends that
     Defoe was for a time "captain-lieutenant" in Colonel
     Desborde's dragoons.

154. "Defoe Tercentenary Exhibition." *Notes and Queries,*
     n.s. 7 (1960), 162.

     Announces the exhibition at Stoke Newington from
     May 7 to May 28, 1960, in celebration of Daniel Defoe's
     birth. Also see item 150.

155. Diego. "Daniel Defoe's Wife." *Notes and Queries,*
     Tenth Series, 11 (1909), 466.

     Uncovers an application for a wedding license by a
     Daniel Foe and a Mary Tuffley on December 28, 1683.
     Also see Aitken, item 102.

156. Dixon, Ronald. "Defoe." *Notes and Queries,* Ninth
     Series, 10 (1902), 32.

     Reprints a death notice from the Hull *Eastern Morning*
     News which announces the death of Mary Ann Defoe, Daniel's
     great-great-granddaughter and the last of his lineal
     descendants.

157. ————. "Defoe at Tooting." *Notes and Queries*, Ninth Series, 9 (1902), 318.

    Denies that there is evidence that Defoe ever lived at Tooting-Graveny and presents a brief outline of the places he did live with accompanying dates. See S.K.R., item 303; Hibgame, item 200; and Taylor, item 360.

158. Dobrée, Bonamy. "Daniel Defoe." *Milton to Ouida*. London: Frank Cass, 1970. Pp. 41-63.

    Reprints the text of a 1946 Amsterdam lecture which surveys Defoe's life and work. Defoe was "astonishingly seminal," creating the novel, pioneering in essay-writing, and inventing the newspaper lead-article. His most distinctive characteristic is his ability to enter so completely into the person he is portraying that he seems almost to become that person; this ability adds an "artless" authenticity to Defoe's best work. But his very success raises a major question: How much of the apparently artless is really art? Defoe is either a consummate artist or almost unbelievably innocent.

159. ————. "Daniel Defoe." *Neophilologus*, 30 (1946), 97-106. Reprinted as *Daniel Defoe* (Allard Pierson Stichtung Afdeling voor Modern Literatuur wetenschap Universteit van Amsterdam, No. 20). Gronningen und Batavia: J.B. Wolters, 1946.

    Surveys Defoe's life and career, finding him a man of "immense energies" and "astonishingly seminal." He is one of England's most versatile writers and is a genius in creating vivid pictures and showing "so many sides of human emotion."

160. ————. *English Literature in the Early Eighteenth Century, 1700-1740*. Oxford: Clarendon Press, 1959. Pp. 34-53, 84-102, 395-431.

    Devotes almost eighty pages of this volume of the *Oxford History of English Literature* to Defoe. The first section on him, "Defoe to 1710," discusses the early pamphlets but emphasizes the verse--called "lively swinging prose"--which often is doggerel but which sometimes contains felicitous passages. Defoe, whose prose ranks second only to Swift's in this period, is England's first middle-class literary genius. In "Swift, Defoe, Arbuthnot," the next section to treat Defoe, he is seen as "the only popular moderating voice" in politics during Harley's rise to power: he is

"extraordinarily fair, temperate, and explanatory" in
his many lucid *Review* essays. Defoe's versatility--"he
is 'simple' only when speaking through the mouths of
simple people"--is emphasized in "Defoe, 1715-1731," the
final section on his work. Because Defoe's fictions lack
form, they are only embryonic novels. Yet, he was a
genius in narrative technique, he established the
realistic novel, and he showed the way to the psychological novel.

*   ————. "The Matter-of-Fact Novelist." (See item 408.)

161.   ————. "Some Aspects of Defoe's Prose." *Pope and His
        Contemporaries: Essays Presented to George Sherburn.*
        Eds. James L. Clifford and Louis A. Landa. Oxford:
        Clarendon Press, 1949. Pp. 171-84.

        Disputes the generalization that early eighteenth-
        century prose emulated the conversation of gentlemen and
        attempted to reflect "the voice of society" rather than
        the author's individual speech. Actually, there were
        many styles, ranging from that of Addison to that of
        Ned Ward. Defoe's style is eclectic: he has no style
        "because he has a hundred." His prose is undisciplined,
        spontaneously vigorous, prolix; it employs irony, parody,
        burlesque, and a wide variety of set rhetorical figures.
        His style and his material meshed superbly in his later
        years when he turned to his long prose fictions, par-
        ticularly *Moll Flanders.*

162.   ————. "The Writing of Daniel Defoe." *Journal of the
        Royal Society of Arts*, 108 (1960), 729-42.

        Challenges the critical cliché that Defoe's style is
        simple and plain. Actually it varies enormously,
        depending on his subject and audience; it is by turns
        hortatory, admonitory, ironic, humorous, exalting, and
        direct. Defoe is particularly adept at irony and at
        imagining himself "into the being of his creations."

163.   Dos Passos, John. "Two Eighteenth-Century Careers: II.
        Daniel Defoe." *New Republic*, 18 November 1940, pp.
        689-91.

        Begins with a comparison of Defoe and Benjamin Frank-
        lin and then traces Defoe's biography in order to claim
        that while London life stunted the Englishman, the
        great outdoors and the prosperity boom in America enabled
        Americans to grow and develop free of caste or station.

164. Dottin, Paul. *The Life and Strange and Surprising Adventures of Daniel De Foe.* Translated by Louise Ragan. New York: Macaulay, 1929. Reprinted New York: Octagon Books, 1971. Originally published as Vol. I of *Daniel Defoe et ses romans* (see item 1251).

    Traces Defoe's life and attempts to mitigate some of its less savory aspects. Although most of the biographical and bibliographical material is now outdated, the work still contains useful information on Defoe, his environment, and the various influences on his writings. The chronological "List of Daniel De Foe's Works," lightly annotated, forms an interesting historical link in the developing study of the Defoe canon.

    Reviews: American Mercury, January 1930, p. xii; Arthur Colton, *Saturday Review of Literature,* 1 March 1930, pp. 769-71; F.P. Mayer, *Virginia Quarterly Review,* 6 (1930), 274-83; C.P. Rollins, *Saturday Review of Literature,* 1 November 1930, p. 296; (London) *Times Literary Supplement,* 8 May 1930, p. 389; C. Wilkinson, *London Mercury,* 22 (1930), 277-79.

*   ————. *Robinson Crusoe Examin'd.* (See item 513.)

*   ————. *La Vie et aventures de Daniel De Foe.* (See item 1258.)

165. Downie, J.A. "Daniel Defoe and the General Election of 1708 in Scotland." *Eighteenth-Century Studies,* 8 (1975), 315-28.

    Reviews Defoe's role in helping effect the union of Scotland and England and in analyzing the results of the election of 1708. Although Defoe viewed himself as a major figure in the Union, he actually was an insignificant pawn of important politicians. As an analyst of the election, Defoe did not understand the various political maneuverings that transpired.

166. ————. "Defoe and *A Dialogue Between Louis le Petite, and Harlequin le Grand.*" *American Notes and Queries,* 12 (1973), 54-55.

    Points out that Sutherland (item 350) and Moore (item 255) err in assuming that several lines of poetry cited as *A Dialogue Between Louis le Petite and Harlequin le Grand* refer to Defoe's relationship with Harley: the *Dialogue* has nothing to do with Defoe and is in prose; the lines of verse are from a prefatory poem.

167.   ————. "Defoe in the Fleet Prison." *Notes and Queries*,
       n.s. 22 (1975), 343–45.

       Investigates Defoe's financial affairs and concludes
       that there is good reason to doubt his veracity about
       them and consequently about other matters as well.
       Although Defoe wanted people to think his first bank-
       ruptcy in 1692 was due to his insuring ships in the war
       with France, in fact he failed because of mismanagement.
       He attributed his second business failure, in 1702, to
       his prosecution for writing *The Shortest Way*, but,
       actually, evidence suggests that he was in difficulties
       prior to his writing the pamphlet.

168.   ————. "Defoe the Spy." *British Society for Eighteenth-
       Century Studies Newsletter*, 9 (1976), 17–18.

       The compiler was unable to locate this journal,
       listed in the *Annual Bibliography of English Language
       and Literature* for 1976, item 6337.

169.   ————. "Defoe's Review, the Theatre, and Anti-High-
       Church Propaganda." *Restoration and 18th Century
       Theatre Research*, 15, no. 1 (May 1976), 24–32.

       Shows that Defoe's negative remarks on the theater
       in the *Review* served both as sincere expressions of
       his belief that the playhouses encouraged vice and as
       anti-High-Church propaganda. Although the complexion
       of early eighteenth-century drama was decidedly
       Whiggish, Defoe persisted in presenting it as Tory and
       High-Church in order to serve his political purposes;
       for example, he suggested that High-Churchmen were
       behind the building of the Queen's Theater in Haymarket,
       whereas his Whig allies had actually been responsible.

170.   ————. "Eighteenth-Century Scotland as Seen by Daniel
       Defoe." *Eighteenth-Century Life*, 4 (1977), 8–12.

       Outlines Defoe's views of Scotland, emphasizing his
       economic ideas. In 1707, Defoe was highly optimistic
       about the Union's favorable effect on Scotland's economy,
       but by 1726, when he published the third volume of *A
       Tour Thro' the Whole Island of Great Britain*, he was
       much more pessimistic. However, eventually all the
       economic benefits that he predicted for the Scots came
       their way.

171.   ————. "Secret Service Payments to Daniel Defoe, 1710–
       1714." *Review of English Studies*, 30 (1979), 437–41.

Uncovers evidence that Defoe, in spite of his protests
to the contrary, was not slighted financially for his
services as a secret agent for Harley. In fact, in the
first seven months of 1714 alone, Defoe received from
Harley five hundred pounds, quite a large amount for
the time.

172. Drew, Bernard. "The London Assurance--a corporation
established by Royal charter in 1720." *Notes and
Queries*, 193 (1948), 342.

Presents details concerning Defoe's son, Daniel Junior,
who was a founding investor in The London Assurance.
Both the elder and the younger Defoes held policies with
the corporation.

173. Druett, W.W. "Daniel Defoe in the Pillory." *Notes and
Queries*, Twelfth Series, 8 (1921), 78.

Extracts from the *London Gazette* of August 2, 1703,
details of Defoe's punishment, which include standing
in the pillory for three days, a fine of two hundred
marks, and sureties for his good behavior for seven
years. See G.B.M., item 230, and Bensly, item 116.

174. Earle, Peter. "The Economics of Stability: The Views
of Daniel Defoe." *Trade, Government and Economy in
Pre-Industrial England: Essays Presented to F.J.
Fisher.* London: Weidenfeld and Nicolson, 1976. Pp.
274-92.

Puts Defoe's economic beliefs in terms of an economic
structure supported by three pillars: (1) the best wool
in the world; (2) the high wages--well above subsis-
tence--of the workers; and (3) the high employment rate.
He felt that the cloth industry should be expanded and
that wool should not be exported; the center of production should be far from the final market so that
more workers being paid high wages could handle the
merchandise along the way. Sometimes Defoe's expansion-
ist views bordered on the fantastic as they did in his
belief that if millions of native Africans could be
made ashamed of their nakedness, they would demand
English suits and stockings. His project for colonizing
South America, however, was more practical. Even though
he advocated expansion, Defoe opposed changes within the
woolen industry because he did not wish to alter, perhaps for the worse, a system that had served England so
well.

175. ————. *The World of Defoe*. London: Weidenfeld and
        Nicolson, 1976; New York: Atheneum, 1977.

        Bases a study of British society from 1660 to 1731 on
        the writings of Daniel Defoe, attempting to summarize
        Defoe's view of that society. The book is divided into
        four parts: "The Observer," a biography of Defoe; "The
        World of Defoe," a survey of Defoe's ideas; "England,"
        a study of the nation's economy and social structure;
        and "The Individual in Society," a discussion of
        various English life-styles.

        Reviews: Maximillian E. Novak, *The Eighteenth Century:
        A Current Bibliography*, n.s. 3 (1977), New York: AMS
        Press, 1981, pp. 188-90; Pat Rogers, (London) *Times
        Literary Supplement*, 21 January 1977, p. 56.

176. Edd. "Rumour Is a Lying Jade." *Notes and Queries*, n.s.
        14 (1967), 424.

        Responds to a query about the source of "rumour is a
        lying jade" by noting Defoe's "Fame, a lying jade, would
        take me up for I know not what of courage."

177. Ellison, A.V. "The Ancestry of Daniel Defoe." *Notes
        and Queries*, 174 (1938), 266.

        Like Mundy, item 275, checks parish registers for
        evidence of Defoe's ancestors and discovers that the
        family name occurs infrequently in London records; lists
        those names that do appear. Also see R.S.B., item 107.

178. Firestone, Clark B. *The Coasts of Illusion: A Study of
        Travel Tales*. New York and London: Harper, 1924.

        A lengthy search through interlibrary loan facilities
        failed to turn up a copy of this work.

179. Fitzgerald, Brian. *Daniel Defoe: A Study in Conflict*.
        London: Secker and Wartburg, 1954; Chicago: Regnery,
        1955.

        Speculates a good deal about Defoe's life and opinions,
        frequently prefacing statements with such phrases as "we
        might picture Defoe" or "one can guess that Defoe might"
        and so on. The author has the curious habit of ending
        many of his statements with four periods, thus sig-
        nalling an ellipsis, as though he has more to say but
        wishes to keep it to himself. His purported thesis is
        that Defoe's life was a ceaseless conflict which mir-
        rored the conflicts of his age, the clashes between

Puritanism and emerging capitalism. The novel, which
Defoe invented, is "the epic of that conflict." The
controversy that this book aroused is reflected in the
reviews listed below.

Reviews: Listener, 52 (1954), 493; Winifred Lynskey,
Philological Quarterly, 34 (1955), 400-01; Helen Mc-
Carthy, *Arizona Quarterly*, 12 (1955), 358-60; (London)
Times Literary Supplement, 9 July 1955, p. 438.

180.   Fletcher, Edward G. "Defoe and the Theatre." *Philological Quarterly*, 13 (1934), 382-89.

Covers Defoe's views of the stage as he expressed
them in the *Review*. Although he attacks the theater's
immorality, Defoe believes that the stage has potential
as a tool for the reformation of manners. Finally,
because that potential is not realized, Defoe calls for
the closing of the theaters.

181.   ————. "Defoe on Milton." *Modern Language Notes*, 50
(1935), 31-32.

Quotes a passage from the August 18, 1711, *Review* in
which Defoe refers to the public consensus on the relative merits of *Paradise Lost* and *Paradise Regained*.

182.   Foot, Michael. *The Pen and the Sword*. London: Mac-
Gibbon and Kee, 1957.

Paints a brief portrait of Defoe as a turncoat with a
"twisted mind."

183.   Freeman, William. *The Incredible De Foe*. London:
Jenkins, 1950. Reprinted Port Washington and London:
Kennikat Press, 1972.

Finds Defoe's genius a result of four qualities:
(1) an ability to select key details; (2) "an adequate
vocabulary expertly used"; (3) objectivity in viewing
his own work; and (4) a power to visualize both remembered facts and imaginary events. The first three
of these are the tools of every good journalist; the
last is a unique quality which lies at the heart of
Defoe's genius. The consequence of Defoe's talent is
that the reader is uncertain about where facts end and
fancy begins, and it is this quality which is the
strength of his fiction. Defoe's life, on the other
hand, is a "disappointment for those who look to find
the greatness which his art reflects." This study

emphasizes Defoe's biography, glossing over the works
except for *Robinson Crusoe*, to which two rather
general chapters are devoted.

Reviews: *Listener*, 45 (1952), 231; Arthur W. Secord,
Journal of English and Germanic Philology, 51 (1952),
432-34.

184.   Friday [Henry C. Hutchins]. "Defoe at Yale." *Yale
       University Library Gazette*, 22 (1948), 99-115.

       Presents a resumé of the collection of materials by
       and about Defoe held by the Yale University Library
       and speculates about Defoe's personal library.

185.   G., E.L. ["A Defoe Portrait."] *Notes and Queries*, 6
       (1900), 156.

       Notes briefly that a recent Guildhall exhibit con-
       tained a portrait by Eyre Crowne of Defoe in the pillory.
       Also see Hope, item 204, and Gnomon, item 187.

186.   Girdler, Lew. "Defoe's Education at Newington Green
       Academy." *Studies in Philology*, 50 (1953), 573-91.

       Records some discoveries about "the books, courses,
       and pedagogical methods" of Defoe's education under
       Charles Morton at Newington Green Academy. Morton and
       the Academy had a profound influence on Defoe, who
       wrote about his education frequently and who used in
       his writing what he had learned in his courses. Even
       his plain prose style is a product of his early training.

187.   Gnomon. "Daniel Defoe." *Notes and Queries*, 6 (1900),
       270-72.

       Treats the custom of displaying the heads of executed
       traitors in public places and also refers to Eyre
       Crowne's portrait of Defoe. See E.L.G., item 185, and
       Hope, item 204.

188.   Gray, Christopher W. "Defoe's Literalizing Imagina-
       tion." *Philological Quarterly*, 57 (1978), 66-81.

       Discusses Defoe's use of figurative speech: Defoe's
       Puritan background makes him almost ashamed of using
       metaphoric language (which he limits to "an absolute
       minimum"). His use of metaphor is at odds with his
       belief that direct and literal communication is the
       goal of the writer.

189. Guimaraens, A.J.C. "Daniel Defoe and the Family of
     Foe." *Notes and Queries*, Eleventh Series, 5 (1912),
     241-43.

     Traces Defoe's family tree back to his grandfather;
     speculates that the H.F. of *A Journal of the Plague
     Year* is Daniel's uncle, Henry Foe; outlines three
     suits in which Defoe was plaintiff; and discusses
     letters of administration granted to one Mary Brooke.

190. H., A. "The Last Male Descendant of Daniel Defoe."
     Notes and Queries, 7 (1901), 177.

     Refers to the Defoe family tree (see Hibgame, item
     201) and points out that the original family name was
     Foe or Fooe. Also see King, items 214 and 215; Oxon,
     item 290; and Clayton, item 138.

191. Hall, Basil. "Daniel Defoe and Scotland." *Reformation,
     Conformity, and Dissent: Essays in Honour of Geoffrey
     Nuttall*. Ed. R. Buick Knox. London: Epworth, 1977.
     Pp. 221-38.

     Reviews the circumstances surrounding Harley's choice
     of Defoe as an agent to advance the cause of Scotland's
     union with England and outlines Defoe's activities during
     this period. A month after he arrived in Scotland,
     Defoe was in print with two pamphlets urging the Union,
     and he simultaneously hammered away on the topic in his
     Review. Defoe's work for Harley on the Union was not
     entirely mercenary; he was sincerely concerned about
     Scotland's economic strength and was interested in the
     sound establishment of the Church of Scotland.

192. Haraszti, Zoltán. "A Great Defoe Library." *More Books*,
     6 (1931), 1-14.

     Describes W.P. Trent's Defoe collection, acquired by
     the Boston Public Library and consisting of 1600 Defoe
     items and approximately 3000 other works by Defoe's
     contemporaries. Also see "A Catalog of the Defoe Collec-
     tion," item 6.

192A. Hargevik, Stieg. "Daniel Defoe and King Charles XIII
      of Sweden." *Studies in English Philology, Linguistics
      and Literature Presented to Alarik Rynell, 7 March
      1978*. Eds. Mats Rydén and Lennart A. Björk. Stock-
      holm: Almqvist & Wiksell, 1978. Pp. 50-63.

      The compiler was unable to locate a copy of this work
      prior to the publication of the bibliography.

193. Harlan, Virginia. "Defoe's Narrative Style." *Journal of English and Germanic Philology*, 30 (1931), 55-73.

    Seeks to explain Defoe's success in making fiction appear to be truth. One of his methods is to provide a detailed source for the story he is about to tell and then to frequently say such things as, "This the young lady told me herself." Another device is for Defoe to establish the honesty of the narrator by having the latter tell the reader that the story is so incredible he can't believe it himself. The use of a first-person narrator who speaks exactly as a garrulous person would speak also adds to the verisimilitude of Defoe's stories. And, finally, his plain style seems to be that of a non-professional, an amateur inartistically telling his or her own story.

194. Harris, Frances. "Paper-Round: The Distribution of Whig Propaganda in 1710." *Factotum*, 9 (1980), 12-13.

    Mentions a Defoe tract, *Counter Queries*, and a ballad sometimes attributed to him, *The age of wonders: to the tune of Chevy Chase*, as part of the free mass distribution of Whig propaganda supervised by the Earl of Sunderland in 1710.

195. Harris, John. "Manuscript Dates on Pamphlets Collected by Thomas Bowdler II with Examples from Defoe." *The Book Collector*, 30 (1981), 225-31.

    Uses notes on the Bowdler pamphlets as a guide to the publication dates of 52 Defoe works; many of these dates correct Moore's *Checklist* (item 14).

196. Hassan, M.A. "Lockhart's 'Life' of Defoe." *Notes and Queries*, n.s. 20 (1973), 294-96.

    Identifies the first excursion into biography by J.G. Lockhart, the eminent biographer, as the "Biographical and Critical Preface, Written expressly for this edition" of *Robinson Crusoe*, published in 1820 by Cadell and Davies.

197. Hayward, John. "Commentary [Defoe Exhibition at Stoke Newington and the Sale of Defoe's Library]." *Book Collector*, 9 (1960), 268-69.

    Notes the exhibition, held to celebrate the tercentenary of Defoe's birth, of 400 items at Stoke Newington and laments the lack of a copy of Olive Payne's catalog of Defoe's library. On the latter, see O'Donovan, item 289, and Heidenreich, item 199.

198. Heal, Ambrose. "Daniel Defoe's Descendants: Sophia (Defoe) Standerwick." *Notes and Queries*, 167 (1934), 192.

Desires information on a Defoe descendant whose obituary appeared in the *Gentleman's Magazine* in 1784.

199. Heidenreich, Helmut, ed. *The Libraries of Daniel Defoe and Phillips Farewell: Olive Payne's Sales Catalogue (1731).* Berlin: W. Hildebrand, 1970.

Precedes the reprint of the catalog with 49 pages of prefatory material on its importance, its characteristics, and its revelations about Defoe's sources. There also are sections identifying Farewell and Payne and three indices: Collector's Items, Subjects, and Names. Unfortunately, the usefulness of the catalog is marred because Payne failed to list the two libraries separately.

200. Hibgame, Frederick T. "Defoe Methodist Chapel, Tooting." *Notes and Queries*, Eleventh Series, 2 (1910), 505.

Reprints an article from the *Daily Chronicle* of December 9, 1910, which refers to the sale of a chapel said to have been founded by Defoe. See S.K.R., item 303; Dixon, item 157; and Taylor, item 360.

201. ————. "The Last Male Descendant of Daniel Defoe." *Notes and Queries*, 7 (1901), 86.

Notes the death on January 12, 1901, of Defoe's great-great-great grandson, James William De Foe, at the age of 82. Also see A.H., item 190; Oxon, item 290; King, items 214 and 215; and Clayton, item 138.

202. Hope, Henry Gerald. "Daniel Defoe." *Notes and Queries*, 5 (1900), 483–84.

Paraphrases information from John Forster's "Works of Daniel Defoe" (1843) concerning Defoe's flight to Bristol to avoid imprisonment for debt and his writing of *The Essay on Projects* while he was in hiding there.

203. ————. "Daniel Defoe." *Notes and Queries*, 6 (1900), 156.

Remarks on the popularity of Defoe's *Robinson Crusoe* and cites Dr. Johnson's praise of that book.

204.   ————. "Daniel Defoe." *Notes and Queries*, 6 (1900),
       219.

       Refers to E.L.G.'s remarks on a portrait of Defoe in
       the pillory (item 185), but the note is mainly about the
       "custom of placing the heads and quarters of traitors
       on Temple Bar." Also see Gnomon, item 187.

205.   Horsley, L.S. "Rogues or Honest Gentlemen: The Public
       Characters of Queen Anne Journalists." *Texas Studies
       in Literature and Language*, 18 (1976), 198-228.

       Contends that in order to influence his readers, the
       eighteenth-century journalist--whose private life was
       expected to conform to his public image--had to appear
       honest, straightforward, and qualified to speak out;
       naturally, his enemies attempted to discredit him by
       noting discrepancies between his public and private
       characters. Defoe spent a great deal of time defending
       himself from a variety of such charges. His detractors
       attacked him for standing in the pillory, for lacking a
       proper education, for running up debts, for being
       socially inferior, and for possessing the negative
       characteristics of avarice and immorality.

206.   Howard, William J. "Truth Preserves Her Shape: An
       Unexplored Influence on Defoe's Prose Style."
       Philological Quarterly, 47 (1968), 193-205.

       Attributes Defoe's use of "veiled" or ironic writing
       to the development of rhetorical methods designed to
       circumvent the new libel laws. At first Defoe was only
       a crude practitioner of this new rhetorical technique,
       but he learned rapidly and his fully developed abilities
       are seen in his *Minutes of the Negotiations of Monsr.
       Mesnager at the Court of England*.

207.   Huddleston, J. "Defoe and Charles Morton." *Notes
       and Queries*, n.s. 25 (1978), 37-38.

       Shows the possibility of Charles Morton's direct
       influence on Defoe's prose style by reconstructing a
       Morton lecture and indicating its parallels with Defoe's
       stylistic development.

208.   Humphreys, A.L. "Daniel Defoe and Martock, Somerset."
       Notes and Queries, 183 (1942), 25.

       Responds to P.D.M., item 231, with information on
       the Martock school and refers him to Wilson's *Defoe*,
       Vol. III, for a list of Defoe's descendants to 1830.

209. Jackson, Holbrook. "Daniel Defoe." *Great English Novelists*. Philadelphia: George W. Jacobs, 1908. Pp. 17-38.

    Surveys Defoe's life and career, seeing him as "a bridge between two literary eras." Defoe was a mixture of artist and controversialist, but "his art was almost unconscious."

210. Jacobson, Daniel. "Commonwealth Literature: Out of Empire." *New Statesman*, 8 (January 1965), 153-54.

    Notes that Defoe was the first English writer to treat the colonies.

211. James, E. Anthony. *Daniel Defoe's Many Voices: A Rhetorical Study of Prose Style and Literary Method.* Amsterdam: Rodopi N.V., 1972.

    Covers three categories of Defoe's work: the non-fiction which he acknowledged he wrote; the ironic works which he pretended someone else wrote; and the fictional narratives written in the first person. The aim of this study is to demonstrate through close reading that Defoe is a conscious artist, "capable of a wide range of pointed stylistic effects and a variety of studied techniques," and not a haphazard bungler as some critics portray him as being. Defoe always modifies his method to fit his audience, always maintains a consistent voice for his speakers, and always attempts to manipulate the responses of his audience. When writing in his own voice, Defoe is extremely careful to be as clear as possible so he eschews irony and extended figures of speech in favor of extreme concreteness. In the ironic works which he pretended someone else wrote, Defoe assumes a variety of masks--a poor man, a merchant, a Turk, a Jacobite, etc.--and he is almost perfectly able to mimic the tone and attitude of his pretended speakers. The latter works provide a training ground for Defoe's fictional first-person narratives, which also are con-sistent in point of view and characterization. James demonstrates Defoe's technical consistency in *Robinson Crusoe*, *Moll Flanders*, and *Roxana*. He admits that Defoe is hasty and careless, but he argues that Defoe's use of detail and his skill in characterization enable him to transcend these technical limitations so that his narrators "emerge as full-fleshed personages."

212. Johnson, Clifford R. *Plots and Characters in the Fic-*
      tion of Eighteenth-Century English Authors. Vol. I.
      Folkestone, Kent: William Dawson, 1977.

      Summarizes the following works by Defoe: *Mrs. Veal,*
      Captain Singleton, Colonel Jacque, Due Preparations for
      the Plague, The Dumb Philosopher, Duncan Campbell,
      Farther Adventures of Robinson Crusoe, A General History
      of the Pirates, John Gow, Jonathan Wild, A Journal of
      the Plague Year, The King of Pirates (Captain Avery),
      The Life of John Sheppard, Memoirs of a Cavalier, Moll
      Flanders, Narrative of John Sheppard, A New Voyage
      Round the World, Robert Drury's Journal, Robinson Crusoe,
      Roxana, and *The Six Notorious Street-Robbers.* Some of
      the summations contain interpretive remarks. An alpha-
      betical list of characters concludes the book.

213. Joyce, James. *Daniel Defoe.* Edited and Translated
      from the Italian manuscripts by Joseph Prescott.
      Buffalo Studies I, i. Buffalo, N.Y.: State Univer-
      sity of New York, 1964.

      Presented originally as a 1912 lecture in Trieste.
      Joyce admires Defoe's realistic techniques and his
      refusal to turn his fiction into polemic. The essay
      is accompanied by extensive notes. Some of this
      material is reprinted in Kelly, item 38.

214. King, Charles. "The Last Male Descendant of Daniel
      Defoe." *Notes and Queries,* 7 (1901), 297.

      Says that James William De Foe was not Daniel Defoe's
      last descendant as stated by Hibgame (item 201) and
      takes issue with several of A.H.'s details on Defoe's
      family tree (see item 190). Also see King, item 215;
      Oxon, item 290; and Clayton, item 138.

215. ————. "The Last Male Descendant of Daniel Defoe."
      Notes and Queries, 7 (1901), 395.

      Uncovers an article in the *Sketch* for September 27,
      1893, on the Defoe family which is illustrated by a
      portrait of Daniel De Foe the elder, James William De
      Foe, and Daniel De Foe the younger. See King, item 214;
      Oxon, item 290; A.H., item 190; Hibgame, item 201; and
      Clayton, item 138.

216. Kramnick, Isaac. *Bolingbroke and His Circle: The*
      Politics of Nostalgia in the Age of Walpole. London:

Oxford University Press and Cambridge, Mass.: Harvard University Press, 1968.

Refers to Defoe throughout and contains a chapter on "Defoe and the Literature of the New Age" (pp. 188-204). Defoe's entire (and "huge") literary output consistently accepts "the new world of bourgeois liberalism" and propounds ideas dreaded by Bolingbroke and his circle: for instance, Defoe believed that the new men of business should become the nation's political leaders, replacing those born of gentle and ancient families. "Defoe, not Colley Cibber, was the true laureate of the age."

217. Kronenberger, Louis. "Defoe." *Kings and Desperate Men*. New York: A.A. Knopf, 1959. Originally published 1942. Pp. 153-58.

Summarizes briefly Defoe's literary career. Although Defoe was a pioneer in prose fiction, he was less of an artist than almost any other great writer in English letters.

218. ————. "Defoe the Great Materialist." *Saturday Review of Literature*, 20 (30 September 1939), pp. 3-4, 17.

Believes that Defoe was less of an artist than any other great English writer. He had a "concrete and empirical mind" that focused on facts; this quality enabled him to excel as a journalist. His journalistic genius is the source of his success in fiction, in which his realistic story-telling is his strength and his lack of psychological depth is his weakness.

219. Kropf, C.R. "The Sale of Defoe's Library." *Papers of the Bibliographical Society of America*, 65 (1971), 123-33.

Discusses Olive Payne's sales catalog for the libraries of Defoe and Phillips Farewell, speculating that probably all but a hundred or so of the titles listed belonged to Defoe. Also see Heidenreich, item 199.

220. Leinster-Mackay, D.P. "Daniel Defoe: An Eighteenth Century Educationist?" *Education Research and Perspectives*, 5 (1978), n.p.

The annotator was unable to peruse this article, referred to in the author's *The Educational World of Daniel Defoe*, item 222.

221.   ————. "Daniel Defoe––the Great Projector: A Con-
        sideration of the Ideas of Defoe for the Improvement
        of English Education." *History of Education Society
        Bulletin*, No. 25 (Spring 1980), n.p.

        The author refers to this essay in his *The Educational
        World of Daniel Defoe*, item 222, but the compiler was
        unable to locate a copy.

222.   ————. *The Educational World of Daniel Defoe*. English
        Literary Studies. Victoria, B.C.: University of
        Victoria Press, 1981.

        Systemizes and analyzes Defoe's ideas on education,
        ideas drawn from forty-five of his works (which are
        listed in an appendix). Defoe was highly critical of
        education in his day, particularly upper class education
        which inculcated a love of pleasure rather than a love
        of learning. He was one of the first advocates for
        adult education, encouraging ignorant adult members of
        the gentry to educate themselves, but he also supported
        education for tradesmen, thus separating himself from
        the Lockean tradition of education for gentlemen only.
        In addition, he advocated education for women and for
        the deaf and dumb. He believed in a Christian education
        that began at home and saw the value of an early educa-
        tion when a child was still malleable and subject to
        parental influences. See Burch, item 127, and note the
        extremely hostile review listed below.

        Review: *The Scriblerian*, 15 (1982), 4.

223.   ————. "Regina v. Hopley. Some Historical Reflections
        on Corporal Punishment." *Journal of Educational
        Administration and History*, 9 (1977), n.p.

        Referred to in Leinster-Mackay's *The Educational World
        of Daniel Defoe*, item 222, but not seen by the compiler.

224.   ————. "A Review of the Affairs of France: A Continuity
        Factor in Defoe's Interest in English Education."
        Paedagogica Historica, 16 (1976), n.p.

        Leinster-Mackay notes this article in his *The Educa-
        tional World of Daniel Defoe*, item 222, but the compiler
        was unable to verify it personally.

225.   ————. "Rousseau and Defoe: A Case of Misguided Ad-
        vocacy or Paradox *Par Excellence* in Eighteenth Century

Eduaction?" *Journal of Educational Thought* (University of Calgary), 13 (1979), 121-28.

Argues that *Robinson Crusoe* is not typical of Defoe's educational ideas and therefore Rousseau was misguided in citing it in *Emile* as a work advocating natural education. See the negative review of this article in *The Scriblerian*, 15 (1982), 4.

226. Levett, Ada E. "Daniel Defoe." *The Social and Political Ideas of Some Thinkers of the Augustan Age*. Ed. F.J.C. Hearnshaw. London: Harrap, 1928. Pp. 157-88.

Distills from Defoe's various writings his views on politics, trade, and social reform. His main contribution to political thought was to clarify and popularize Locke's ideas. On trade, Defoe was a "not unworthy forerunner of Adam Smith," but his ideas are eclectic and must be distilled from a wide number and variety of his works. His most important reform measures dealt with the poor; he was interested in this area because he believed that his country's strength was based on the wealth and education of the population, not on its size.

227. Lovett, Robert Morss. "Franklin and Defoe." *New Republic*, 3 November 1926, pp. 303-04.

Reviews Phillips Russell's *Benjamin Franklin* and points out similarities between Franklin and Defoe: both were journalists and shared the same sense of humor; both recognized the equality of women; both were exponents of the art of "getting ahead"; and, most importantly, both were the prophets of their generations.

228. M., A.R.L. "Daniel Defoe's Descendants." *Notes and Queries*, 166 (1934), 350-51.

Reprints a letter by W.J. Tucker from the *Daily Express* of May 3, 1934, which traces Defoe's descendants.

229. M., F.A. "German Translations of Defoe." *Notes and Queries*, 171 (1936), 421.

Asks for information in German translations of Defoe's works.

230. M., G.B. "Daniel Defoe in the Pillory." *Notes and Queries*, Twelfth Series, 8 (1921), 12.

Requests verification of Pope's remark that Defoe had
his ears cut off when he stood in the pillory in 1703.
Also see Druett, item 173, and Bensly, item 116.

231. M., P.D. "Daniel De Foe and Mertock, Somerset."
      Notes and Queries, 182 (1942), 302.

      Seeks Martock school records in order to track down a
      schoolmaster relative of Defoe's referred to in the
      Tour.

232. M., R.B. "Raleigh and Defoe." *Devon and Cornwall Notes
      and Queries*, 20 (1938), 137.

      Inquires if there is any truth in Defoe's claim to be
      related to Sir Walter Raleigh.

233. Macaree, David. "Daniel Defoe and *The Memoirs of John,
      Duke of Melfort*." *Transactions of the Samuel Johnson
      Society of the Northwest*, 11 (1980), 82-98.

      Shows how Defoe could write ironically from the per-
      spective of the position he was attacking; here he writes
      an apparent Jacobite tract to expose the Jacobite menace
      to England. "Memoirs" such as this tract anticipate
      Defoe's techniques in his novels.

233A. ————. *Daniel Defoe and the Jacobite Movement*.
      Salzburg: University of Salzburg, 1980.

      This book has not been reviewed by the compiler.

234. ————. "Daniel Defoe, the Church of Scotland, and the
      Union of 1707." *Eighteenth-Century Studies*, 7 (1973),
      62-77.

      Demonstrates how Defoe's breadth of sympathy and
      openmindedness enabled him to overcome his initial
      difficulties in handling Scots clerical opposition
      to the Union. At first Defoe was unaware of deeper
      issues, but he learned quickly and soon was able to
      classify opponents of the Union in various groups and
      to work out appropriate strategies for dealing with
      each. Defoe made important contributions to the Union,
      providing Harley with valuable information, helping
      smooth over a dangerous uprising in Glasgow, and making
      the Union as palatable as possible to both Englishman
      and Scot.

235. McCarthy, B. Eugene. "Defoe, Milton, and Heresy."
     Milton Newsletter, 3 (1969), 71-73.

     Shows Defoe's concern with Milton's historical vera-
     city in *Paradise Lost*; whenever Milton departed from
     Scripture, as he did in portraying hell as a local
     place and in denying that Christ was Son of God from
     all eternity, Defoe attacked him for heresy.

236. MacDonald, W.L. "Daniel Defoe (1660-1731)." *Queen's
     Quarterly*, 38 (1931), 89-103.

     Views Defoe as an economic, social, and political
     commentator whose greatest contributions to modern
     thought are his plans for increasing trade and helping
     the poor.

237. McEwen, Gilbert D. "'A Turn of Thinking': Benjamin
     Franklin, Cotton Mather, and Daniel Defoe on 'Doing
     Good.'" *The Dress of Words: Essays on Restoration
     and Eighteenth Century Literature in Honor of
     Richmond P. Bond*. University of Kansas Publications,
     Library Series 42. Ed. Robert B. White, Jr. Lawrence:
     University of Kansas Libraries, 1978. Pp. 53-65.

     Suggests that Mather and Defoe influenced Benjamin
     Franklin's Silence Dogood letters. Franklin seems to
     have especially admired Defoe's *Robinson Crusoe, Moll
     Flanders, Religious Courtship, Family Instructor*, and
     An Essay on Projects. Several of Defoe's projects from
     the latter were paralleled by Franklin.

238. McVeagh, John. "'The Blasted Race of Old Cham': Daniel
     Defoe and the African." *Ibadan Studies in English*,
     1 (1969), 85-109.

     Distills Defoe's views of Africa and Africans from
     his tracts and novels, concluding that J.R. Moore
     (see his *Daniel Defoe, Citizen of the Modern World*,
     item 255) and others are wrong in seeing Defoe ahead
     of his time in condemning the slave trade. He may
     have objected to slavery in the abstract, but as a
     practical commercial matter, he often noted its economic
     advantages. His main interest in Africa centers on
     its potential for trade favorable to England; his
     opinion of Africans is that they are culturally in-
     ferior to Europeans.

*   ————. "Rochester and Defoe: A Study in Influence."
         (See item 1150.)

239.   Manvell, Roger. "Introduction" to *Selections from the*
        Prose of Daniel Defoe. London: Falcon Press, 1953.
        Pp. 7-17.

        Skims over Defoe's life and then concentrates on his
        prose style. His writing is almost always clear and
        straightforward, and he is the first important pro-
        fessional journalist in England.

240.   Marriott, J.A.R. "Daniel Defoe (Born 1661; died April
        26, 1731)." *Cornhill Magazine*, 70 (1931), 531-43.

        Celebrates Defoe's life and career on the occasion
        of the two hundredth anniversary of his death. Although
        an "attractive reprobate," Defoe was infused with "the
        fire of indisputable genius" in both politics and
        literature.

241.   Martin, Burns. "Defoe's Conception of Poetry." *Modern*
        Language Notes, 44 (1929), 377-78.

        Cites an item from Robert Wodrow's *Analecta* which
        quotes Defoe's praise for the preaching of Robert M'Cala,
        who Defoe called a true poet because of his "poeticall
        flight and imagination."

242.   Masefield, John E. "Daniel Defoe." *Fortnightly Review*,
        91 (1909), 65-73.

        Presents a generalized biography of Defoe, who is
        seen as a fine political writer but who is not an artist.
        Defoe's vision is "common," and all he beheld in life
        was "a broken-down mariner alone on an island, a penitent
        whore in Newgate, and a dirty little pickpocket asleep
        on an ash-heap."

243.   ————. "Defoe." *Masters of Literature*. London: G.
        Bell, 1909.

        Payne (item 21) lists the above--unseen by this com-
        piler--and says that Masefield views Defoe as a sincere
        writer who lacks the "finer emotions." It appears to
        this compiler that this item is an introduction to a
        Defoe collection assembled and perhaps edited by Mase-
        field for Bell's "Masters of Literature" series.

244. Mason, Shirlene. *Daniel Defoe and the Status of Women.*
Monographs in Women's Studies. St. Albans, Vt. and
Montreal: Eden Press, 1978.

Examines "Defoe's attitudes toward women in light of
their legal and social status, with a comparison of
eighteenth-century law and social conditions to the
ideas Defoe sets forth in his didactic works, in his
journalism, and in his fiction." The discussion is
divided into sections on The Young Maiden, The Wife,
The Widow, The Divorced Woman, The Old Maid, and The
Fallen Woman. The author concludes that Defoe sincerely
desires better conditions for women and that he views
them as intellectual equals to men and as often superior
to men in spiritual and cultural matters. He also "continually proposes new laws that will help them." However, Defoe is unwilling or unable to face the logical
consequences of the equality of the sexes because he
tends to see the female's natural role as occurring
within marriage and not in the independent economic
marketplace.

Review: Paula R. Backscheider, *The Eighteenth Century:
A Current Bibliography*, n.s. 4 (for 1978), New York:
AMS Press, 1981, 303.

245. Maxfield, Ezra Kempton. "Daniel Defoe and the Quakers."
*Publications of the Modern Language Association of
America*, 47 (1932), 179-90.

Adduces evidence to refute Thomas Wright's statement
in his *Life of Daniel Defoe* (item 383) that Defoe
always went out of his way to portray Quakers in a
positive light. In fact, although Defoe did them no
harm, he often wrote facetiously about them; in the
so-called "Quaker Letters," Defoe's series of pamphlets
purportedly written by Quakers, Defoe ridicules and
distorts their beliefs.

246. Maynadier, G.H. "Introduction" to *Robinson Crusoe* by
Daniel Defoe. New York: Sproul, 1903. Pp. ix-xxviii.

Covers Defoe's life and literary career briefly before
focusing on *Robinson Crusoe*. Maynadier sees Defoe as
intrinsically "vulgar" and devious, but finds his "low-
ness" an aid to his fiction, in which he was able to
depict even the lowest ranks of society accurately.
Crusoe is important for its realism and for bringing
the picaresque into the mainstream of English fiction.

247. Mead, D.S. "D. Foe--Defoe." *College English*, 5 (1943),
      163.

      Speculates that Defoe's name changed from "D. Foe" to
      "Defoe" through a process similar to that which leads
      people to mistakenly write "O'Henry" for author "O.
      Henry."

248. "Memorabilia." *Notes and Queries*, n.s. 5 (1958), 461,
      488.

      Reports that Defoe's missing tombstone has been dis-
      covered and returned to the Stoke Newington Library.

249. Meyerstein, E.H.W. "Daniel, the Pope, and the Devil:
      A Caricaturist's Portrait of the True Defoe." (London)
      Times Literary Supplement, 15 February 1936, p. 134.

      Notes that no contemporary painting or drawing of
      Defoe is known to exist, but suggests that "The Three
      False Brethren" (1711), a so-called "medley" by George
      Bickham, may well contain both a caricature and a
      representation of Defoe.

250. Minto, William. *Daniel Defoe*. London: Macmillan, 1909.
      Originally published 1879.

      Chronicles Defoe's life in a now-outdated biography,
      but one which provides a valuable insight into Victorian
      attitudes toward Defoe's character and works. Minto--
      who refers to Defoe as a truly great liar--believes that
      Defoe "was a wonderful mixture of knave and patriot."
      Although he often was immoral in his actions, his aims
      were high. He consistently sought the best for his
      country. Defoe essentially was a journalist, and the
      success of his fiction, particularly *Robinson Crusoe*,
      rests on his journalistic talents: plain style and
      realistic detail.

251. "Miscellaneous News Items." *Johnsonian Newsletter*, 18
      (December 1958), 7.

      Reports that Defoe's original gravestone has been
      presented to the Stoke Newington Library.

252. Mitchell, Velma E.M. "Charles Eaton Burch: A Scholar
      and His Library." *College Language Association
      Journal*, 16 (1974), 369-76.

      Comments on Burch, a noted Defoe scholar whose book
      collection was acquired by Howard University, and pre-

sents a bibliography of his writings. Mitchell lists
Burch's major contributions to Defoe scholarship.

253. Moore, John Robert. "The Character of Daniel Defoe."
      Review of English Studies, 14 (1938), 68-71.

      Objects to Newton's claim (see item 282) that Defoe
      was guilty of chicanery in the matter of the civet cats
      which cost his mother-in-law £600. Defoe was a victim
      in the incident and remained on good terms with his
      mother-in-law and her family.

254. ────. "Daniel Defoe and Modern Economic Theory."
      Indiana University Studies, 104 (1934), 1-28.

      Believes Defoe to be quite modern in his economic
      thought. He was against long term credit for merchants
      and the use of workhouse labor in established indus-
      tries; the former led to overextension and bankruptcy
      and the latter led to reduced wages, a lower standard
      of living, and the undermining of the country's pros-
      perity. He favored government regulation of business
      only when it was absolutely necessary. Although he
      regarded home trade as the principal source of English
      wealth, he outlined several schemes for foreign trade
      and proposed a system of Empire Trade two centuries
      before the Empire Traders.

255. ────. *Daniel Defoe: Citizen of the Modern World*.
      Chicago: University of Chicago Press, 1958. Pp. 222-
      28 are reprinted in Ellis, item 521.

      Portrays Defoe as deeply religious but not bigoted,
      slow to anger but courageous when angered, highly in-
      formed and intelligent but more concerned with using
      these qualities to advance civil and religious liberty
      than to advance himself. He was an abstemious and
      hardy person, retaining his verve and writing skills
      until the very end of his life. "His influence lies
      under much that is best in modern literature, and under
      much that is best in modern life." Defoe's influence
      on specific works and authors--*The Rime of the Ancient
      Mariner*, Rousseau, Scott, etc.--is enormous. Even today
      Defoe's influence is everywhere; he is still important
      for his theories on treating the insane, economics,
      city planning, trade, and so on. A detailed chronology
      of Defoe's life is appended to the text; and the notes,
      which contain a bibliography, are detailed and useful.

      Reviews: Jean Béranger, *Etudes Anglaises*, 13 (1960),

62-63; Benjamin Boyce, *South Atlantic Quarterly*, 58
(1959), 495-96; Matthew J. Bruccoli, *William and Mary
Quarterly*, 3rd series, 17 (1960), 122-23; George Falle,
University of Toronto Quarterly, 30 (1960), 95-100;
Adolph O. Goldsmith, *Journalism Quarterly*, 36 (1959),
77; R.W. Ketton-Cramer, *Listener*, 62 (1959), 451;
W.L. Payne, *Modern Language Notes*, 75 (1960), 267-69;
Spiro Peterson, *Philological Quarterly*, 38 (1958),
316-19; Simon Raven, *Spectator*, 31 July 1959, p. 142;
George Sherburn, *Journal of English and Germanic
Philology*, 58 (1959), 705-07; Robert Walcott, *Journal
of Modern History*, 31 (1959), 361-62; F. Wölcken,
Review of English, n.s. 12 (1961), 86-88.

256.   ————. "Daniel Defoe: Precursor of Samuel Richardson."
        *Restoration and Eighteenth-Century Literature: Essays
        in Honor of Alan Dugald McKillop*. Ed. Carroll Camden.
        Chicago: University of Chicago Press, 1963. Pp. 351-
        69.

        Studies Defoe's use of letters in his tracts and
        novels to explain "offstage" action and to express
        strong emotion or to provide a climax for a situation.
        Defoe's epistolary method anticipates Richardson's
        narrative technique. Particularly influential on
        Richardson are Defoe's *The Family Instructor* and *Religious
        Courtship*.

257.   ————. "Daniel Defoe: Star Reporter." *Boston Public
        Library Quarterly*, 6 (1954), 195-205.

        Fills a gap in Defoe's journalistic history by
        tracing his career as star reporter for Fonvive's
        London triweekly, *The Post-Man*, during 1706-1708 while
        he was serving as Queen Anne's agent in promoting the
        Union with Scotland.

258.   ————. "Defoe Acquisitions at the Huntington Library."
        Huntington Library Quarterly, 28 (1964), 45-57.

        Identifies and describes ten Defoe tracts recently
        acquired by the Huntington Library.

259.   ————. "Defoe and Shakespeare." *Shakespeare Quarterly*,
        19 (1968), 71-80.

        Cites approximately two dozen allusions to and quota-
        tions from Shakespeare in Defoe's works, and notes
        briefly the structural parallels between *The Tempest*
        and *Robinson Crusoe*. Also see Moore, item 621.

260.   ———. "Defoe and the Rev. James Hart: A Chapter in
        High Finance." *Philological Quarterly*, 19 (1940),
        404-09.

        Speculates about the implications of a hitherto
        unnoted Defoe financial transaction on December 21,
        1714, in Scotland and suggests that Defoe bribed the
        Rev. James Hart, an influential Scots minister.

261.   ———. *Defoe in the Pillory and Other Studies*.
        Indiana University Publications, Humanities Series
        No. 1. Bloomington: Indiana University Press, 1939.

        Consists of eight separate studies. Chapter I, "Defoe
        in the Pillory: A New Interpretation," attributes the
        severity of Defoe's punishment for the *Shortest Way with
        the Dissenters* to the personal resentment of his judges
        over Defoe's having satirized them in print. Chapter
        II, "Whitney's Horses," explains the reference to
        "Whitney's Horses" in Defoe's *A Hymn to the Pillory*;
        it refers to an absurd speech by Sir Salathiel Lovell,
        one of Defoe's judges, made when he sentenced a highway-
        man. In Chapter III, "Two Sources for Defoe's Roxana,"
        Moore discovers in Abel Boyer's translation of Hamilton's
        Mémoires du Comte de Gramont a source for Roxana's
        dance and he reveals details about Sir Robert Clayton,
        the only historical figure in *Roxana*. "Defoe's First
        Collected Works," Chapter IV, argues that of the two
        collections of Defoe's works issued in 1703, the first,
        the so-called "spurious" collection, is just as
        authentic as the "true" collection; all thirteen tracts
        in the first collection are genuine. In Chapter V, Moore
        analyzes the methods which previous scholars have used to
        assign works to the Defoe canon. Chapter VI, "The
        Authorship of *The Voyage of Don Manuel Gonzales*," sug-
        gests that Defoe wrote parts of the *Voyage*; the Defoe-
        like sections are remarkably similar to parts of Defoe's
        Tour. In "The Authorship of *Madagascar; Or, Robert
        Drury's Journal*," Chapter VII, Moore attributes the
        Journal to Defoe after tracing its critical history
        from its acceptance as an authentic record to the certain
        knowledge that it is a fictitious account. (Also see
        Moore's *Defoe's Sources*, item 1053.) Chapter VIII,
        "The Authorship of *A General History of the Pirates*,"
        contends that the *History*, substantially Defoe's
        throughout, is an original work of history interspersed
        with some passages of fiction and romance; the work has
        created the modern conception of pirates. The Epilogue,
        "Defoe as Poetic Dreamer," disagrees with Sean O'Faoláin's
        view that Defoe lacked a sense of "the poetry of life."

The volume concludes by reprinting a rare 1705 tract,
A Letter from Scotland to a Friend in London, which
Moore assigns to Defoe.

Reviews: Hans H. Anderson, *Modern Philology*, 39 (1941),
215-17; F.E. Budd, *Review of English Studies*, 16
(1940), 226-28; F. Haster, *Anglia Beiblatt*, 52 (1941),
251-60; *Notes and Queries*, 177 (1939), 90; Rudolph
Stamm, *English Studies*, 24 (1942), 25-27; James
Sutherland, *Modern Language Review*, 35 (1940), 540-
42; Mark A. Thompson, *English Historical Review*, 60
(1945), 258-60.

262.   ————. "Defoe, Steele, and the Demolition of Dunkirk."
        Huntington Library Quarterly, 13 (1950), 279-302.

Records Defoe's views of the lengthy controversy over
the disposal of Dunkirk. In 1693, he lamented Charles
II's sale of Dunkirk to the French; in 1713, after
England had regained the port, he urged that the government should not hurry to return it to France or demolish
it as some plans called for; and in 1730, he expressed
regrets that England no longer held Dunkirk. Defoe was
consistent in his opposition to destroying the port;
he believed that in the interest of trade, Dunkirk
should be preserved.

Review: John Loftis, *Philological Quarterly*, 30 (1951),
265-66.

263.   ————. "Defoe, Stevenson, and the Pirates." *ELH:
        A Journal of English Literary History*, 10 (1943),
        35-60.

Explores the influence of Defoe's work on Robert
Louis Stevenson. *Robinson Crusoe* certainly influenced
Treasure Island and perhaps *Kidnapped*, but it is Defoe's
writings on pirates that most strongly kindled Stevenson's imagination. In spite of being directly influenced by Defoe, however, Stevenson handled pirates and
piracy differently than did his predecessor. For
Stevenson, the "piratic" is make-believe, a literary
tradition, but to Defoe piracy is a bitter experience
of real life; not only did pirates cost Defoe money for
marine insurance, but he knew several of them personally,
and he actually saw the pirate Gow hanged.

264.   ————. "Defoe, Thoresby, and 'The Storm.'" *Notes and
        Queries*, 175 (1938), 223.

Points out that Defoe's religious appeal was not confined to Dissenters but that his religious writings were valued by pious Anglicans as well.

* ———. "Defoe's 'New Discovery' and 'Pacificator.'" (See item 1151.)

265. ———. "Defoe's Project for Lie-Detection." *American Journal of Psychology*, 68 (1955), 672.

Reprints a passage from *An Effectual Scheme for the Immediate Preventing of Street Robberies* in which Defoe suggests taking the pulse of a suspected criminal as a means of lie detection.

266. ———. "Defoe's Religious Sect." *Review of English Studies*, 17 (1941), 461-67.

Determines that if Defoe had a religious denomination, it was Presbyterian.

267. ———. "Defoe's Workshop." *More Books*, 23 (1948), 323-30.

Expostulates on Defoe's wide-ranging interests, his habit of storing up information in his notes and memory, and his continuity of ideas. For example, he was fascinated by the plague and wrote about it from a variety of perspectives: in 1711 he urged the danger of the plague as a reason for peace; in 1719 he wrote on the spread of the plague toward Hungary; in 1720 he used the plague in *Memoirs of a Cavalier* and wrote of it in three newspaper articles; in 1721 he devoted five articles to it; in 1722 he produced both *Due Preparations for the Plague* and *A Journal of the Plague Year*. This continuity of ideas in Defoe's writings provides one way for the bibliographer to identify his anonymous or pseudonymous work.

268. ———. "A Footnote to a Charge of Scandal against Defoe." *Huntington Library Quarterly*, 36 (1973), 159-62.

Refutes charges made in "The Review Review'd"—an anti-Defoe letter—that Defoe had betrayed his benefactor, Nathaniel Sammen, by having an affair with Sammen's wife.

269. ———. "Gildon's Attack on Steele and Defoe in *The Battle of the Authors*." *Publications of the Modern*

Language Association, 66 (1951), 534-38.

Identifies Charles Gildon, an inveterate enemy of
Defoe, as the author of *The Battle of the Authors* (1720),
a tract which contains an attack on Defoe's personal
and professional life.

270. ———. "Mandeville and Defoe." *Mandeville Studies:
New Explorations in the Art and Thought of Dr.
Bernard Mandeville, 1670-1733.* International Archives
of the History of Ideas 81. The Hague: Nijhoff, 1975.
Pp. 117-25.

Shows that Defoe was more nearly in agreement with
Mandeville than any other major writer of the period.
They agreed on the famous paradox concerning private
vice and public benefits, the desirability of paying
ministers more and restraining the clergy from political
activity, the intellectual equality of women to men,
and basic economic principles, among other things.

271. ———. "'Robin Hog' Stephens: Messenger of the Press."
Papers of the Bibliographical Society of America,
50 (1956), 381-87.

Elaborates on an earlier article on the career of
Robert Stephens, a notorious Messenger of the Press
under William III and Queen Anne, by tracing Defoe's
remarks on the man in letters to Harley and in the
Review. Defoe hated Stephens because the latter was
one of the agents who arrested him for his *Shortest
Way* and because he felt Stephens abused his authority
and harmed Harley's cause.

272. Morgan, William T. "The Versatility of Daniel Defoe."
More Books, 21 (1946), 327-46.

Covers Defoe's literary career, emphasizing the
non-fiction. Defoe's work is characterized by its
versatility and the unparalleled curiosity and industry
behind it. His political writings, especially his
Review, are invaluable for the historian. Morgan believes that Defoe's greatest achievements are his
journalistic work on the *Review*, his authorship of
Robinson Crusoe, and his influence on the Union with
Scotland.

273. Morley, Henry. *The Earlier Life and the Chief Earlier
Works of Daniel Defoe.* London: George Routledge and

Sons, 1889. Reprinted New York: Burt Franklin, 1970.

Intersperses selections from Defoe's works with Morley's biography. The latter is now completely out-dated but is carried here because of the modern reprint; in addition, the work is useful for reflecting nine-teenth-century attitudes towards Defoe.

274. Morris, Frank D. "Pilloried Pamphleteer." *Mentor*, 17 (September 1929), 42-44, 80.

Retells the story of Defoe's sentence in the pillory and surveys his life and literary career in a non-scholarly manner (the author refers to Defoe as "Dan").

275. Mundy, P.D. "The Ancestry of Daniel Defoe." *Notes and Queries*, 174 (1938), 112-14.

Checks various parish registers in order to trace Defoe's ancestry more accurately than have previous biographers. Questions some of the biographical "facts" concerning Defoe's noble lineage. See Mundy's other notes under this same title, items 276-79; also see R.S.B., item 107, and Ellison, item 177.

276. ————. "The Ancestry of Daniel Defoe." *Notes and Queries*, 175 (1938), 44.

Adds to his previous note on Defoe's ancestry (item 275) information from the parish registers of the church at St. Giles, Cripplegate. Mundy discovers that Defoe's mother was named Alice and suggests that her family might be the source of the relationship to Sir Walter Raleigh that Defoe was so proud of. See Mundy's other notes under this same title, items 275 and 277-79; also see R.S.B., item 107, and Ellison, item 177.

277. ————. "The Ancestry of Daniel Defoe." *Notes and Queries*, 197 (1952), 382-83.

Locates several families by the name of Foe or Foo and tries to link them with the family of Daniel Defoe. The connections cannot be made certain, however, until the parentage of Defoe's grandfather, Daniel Foe of Etton, is proved. See Mundy's other notes under this title, items 275-76 and 278-79; also see R.S.B., item 107, and Ellison, item 177.

278. ————. "The Ancestry of Daniel Defoe." *Notes and Queries*, 197 (1952), 459.

     Tracks down a John Foe, one of Daniel Defoe's ancestors. See Mundy's other notes under this title, items 275-77 and 279; also see R.S.B., item 107, and Ellison, item 177.

279. ————. "The Ancestry of Daniel Defoe." *Notes and Queries*, 202 (1957), 242.

     Clears up a problem concerning the remarriage of Daniel Defoe's grandmother, Rose, who married a Solomon Fall in 1631 after her first husband and Daniel Defoe's grandfather died. See Mundy's other notes under this same title, items 275-78; also see R.S.B., item 107, and Ellison, item 177.

280. ————. "The Wife of Daniel Defoe." *Notes and Queries*, 203 (1958), 296-98.

     Identifies Defoe's wife, née Mary Tuffley, and presents a family tree of the Tuffley family.

281. Newman, S.A. Grundy. "Defoe Arms." *Notes and Queries*, 159 (1930), 152.

     Desires information on Defoe's 1706 grant of arms.

282. Newton, Theodore F.M. "The Civet-Cats of Newington Green: New Light on Defoe." *Review of English Studies*, 13 (1937), 10-19.

     Tracks down a 1706 reference to Defoe as a civet-cat merchant. In 1693, Defoe purchased, partially on credit, seventy civet-cats which were seized when he could not come up with the rest of the money he owed. Defoe's mother-in-law was involved in financing Defoe's scheme to market civet, and she eventually sued him for defrauding her of sixty pounds in this affair. See Moore, item 253.

283. Novak, Jane. "Verisimilitude and Vision: Defoe and Blake as Influences on Joyce's Molly Bloom." *Carrell*, 8 (1967), 7-20.

     Demonstrates that Joyce was influenced by Defoe's realism and Blake's myth-making in his development of Molly Bloom's character in *Ulysses*. Like Defoe, Joyce observes and records "the prosiness of physical experience and the indefatigable activity of the human ego." He also employs two narrative devices that he admired in Defoe: the meticulous enumeration of trivial details and the undifferentiated juxtaposition of incidents greatly differing in importance.

284. Novak, Maximillian E. "Defoe and the Machine Smashers." *Notes and Queries*, n.s. 7 (1960), 288-90.

Revaluates Defoe's economic views, sometimes praised for being very modern, and discovers them to be quite conservative. For example, Defoe opposed the use of many new inventions on the grounds that they would create unemployment.

285. ————. "Defoe's Use of Irony." *The Uses of Irony.* *Papers on Defoe and Swift Read at a Clark Library Seminar, April 2, 1966.* Los Angeles: Clark Memorial Library and University of California Press, 1966. Pp. 5-38. Also published in *Stuart and Georgian Moments*. Ed. Earl Miner. Berkeley: University of California Press, 1972. Pp. 189-220.

Takes issue with those critics who assert that Defoe was no ironist. Certainly Defoe's contemporaries regarded him as a writer who "revelled" in paradox and deceit, and in fact scarcely a year went by without Defoe writing at least one long work of extended irony. Novak surveys several of Defoe's tracts to demonstrate that irony lies at the very heart of his literary method.

Review: C.J. Rawson, *Notes and Queries*, n.s. 14 (1967), 432-34.

286. ————. "'Simon Forecastle's Weekly Journal': Some Notes on Defoe's Conscious Artistry." *Texas Studies in Literature and Language*, 6 (1965), 433-40.

Answers those critics who—like Ian Watt (see item 688)—contend that Defoe was inartistic. Novak uses "Simon Forecastle's Weekly Journal," a parody of a seaman's journal that Defoe wrote for Mist's *Weekly*, to show that Defoe used his punctuation and the juxtaposition of trivial details with important ones to achieve ironic effects. He employs this method in other works as well, most notably in *Robinson Crusoe* when Crusoe addresses the gold he finds on the wrecked ship.

287. ————. "A Whiff of Scandal in the Life of Daniel Defoe." *Huntington Library Quarterly*, 34 (1970), 35-42.

Reprints "The Review Review'd," a 1707 attack on Defoe, and comments that its allegations about Defoe's sexual misconduct can never be proved.

288. O'Donoghue, Freeman. *Catalog of Engraved British Portraits Preserved in the Department of Prints and Drawings in the British Museum.* II, 27. London: British Museum, 1908-25.

Catalogs seven unauthenticated portraits of Defoe.

289. O'Donovan, Anne. "Sale Catalogue of Defoe's Library." *Book Collector*, 9 (1960), 454-55.

Responds to Hayward, item 197, by locating in the British Museum a copy of the Olive Payne catalog of Defoe's personal library.

290. Oxon, M.A. ["A Defoe Descendant."] *Notes and Queries*, 7 (1901), 297-98.

Writes reply to Hibgame (item 201) that he met another descendant of Defoe, now--if living--about eighteen years old, and obtained for the family money from the Crown. Also see King, items 214 and 215; A.H., item 190; and Clayton, item 138.

291. Page, John T. "Defoe." *Notes and Queries*, Ninth Series, 10 (1902), 137-38.

Reprints two letters to the *Daily Mail* which note that, contrary to Dixon (item 156), there are still living descendants of Daniel Defoe.

292. Page, Norman. *Speech in the English Novel.* London: Longman, 1973.

Sees Defoe's narrative style as consciously different from his "normal competent journalistic prose" in that it reflects a "calculated absence of polish and economy" and is based on actual speech patterns.

293. Partington, Wilfred. "End-Papers and Marginalia: the Strange and Surprising Adventures of Daniel Defoe and Paul Dottin." *The Bookman's Journal*, Third Series, 18 (1931), 123-26.

Takes issue with Arnold Bennett's view that there is little French interest in English literature and refutes it with a positive commentary on Paul Dottin's *La Vie et les aventures étranges et surprenantes de Daniel de Foe.*

*   Payne, William L. "Defoe in the Pamphlets." (See item 22.)

294.   Peterson, Spiro. "Daniel Defoe." *Notes and Queries*, n.s. 6 (1959), 118.

        Asks F.J. Dallett, item 146, for further information on the Lodwick family.

295.   ————. "Daniel Defoe and 'City Customes.'" *Notes and Queries*, n.s. 5 (1958), 400-01.

        Shows that Defoe had a good understanding of "proprietary law" by defining the term "City Customes," used by Defoe in a letter to his future son-in-law, Henry Baker, on the dowry promised for Defoe's daughter, Sophia.

296.   ————. "Defoe and Westminster, 1696-1706." *Eighteenth-Century Studies*, 12 (1979), 306-38.

        Bases this study of Defoe "as a Londoner" on twenty-eight documents and records recently discovered at the London Guildhall Library and listed here in a valuable Appendix. These documents enable Peterson to fill in a major gap in Defoe biography--the years around 1696; they include, among other items, a memorandum in Defoe's hand which proposes a land-development scheme for Westminster Market. A photograph of the Defoe holograph is reprinted and quoted in full.

297.   ————. "Defoe in Edinburgh, 1707." *Huntington Library Quarterly*, 38 (1974), 21-33.

        Believes that more was known about Defoe's activities on behalf of the Union than Defoe ever suspected and discusses the attack on him in *The Review Review'd*.

298.   Pickford, John. "Defoe: The Devil's Chapel." *Notes and Queries*, Tenth Series, 9 (1908), 331.

        Although the title alludes to several items on Defoe (see items 1133, 1134, 1135, and 1149), it really has only to do with a poem, not by Defoe, inscribed on a building at Ness Cliff.

*   Poston, Lawrence, III. "Defoe and the Peace Campaign, 1710-1713: A Reconsideration." (See item 1009.)

299.   Potter, George Reuben. "Henry Baker, F.R.S. (1698-1774)." *Modern Philology*, 29 (1932), 301-21.

Presents many biographical facts about Defoe's son-
in-law, including Baker's own account of his courtship
of Sophia Defoe.

300. Powell, Frederick York. "Daniel Defoe." *Frederick York
      Powell: A Life and a Selection from His Letters and
      Occasional Writings.* Vol. II. Ed. Oliver Elton.
      Oxford: The Clarendon Press, 1906. Pp. 281-97.

      Sees Defoe as a "bourgeois genius" who was extremely
      successful as a politician, prose stylist, biographer,
      and novelist. Although Defoe's works are too "preachy,"
      they still delight because of the practical knowledge
      artistically expressed in the non-fiction and the accurate
      reproduction of "the tone of the past life he is describ-
      ing" in the fiction.

301. Praz, Mario. "De Foe and Cellini." *English Studies,*
      13 (1931), 75-87.

      Compares Cellini and Defoe in an attempt to define
      "the characteristics of that kind of unpremeditated
      narrative which marks the beginning of modern novel-
      writing." The two authors are similar in their use of
      a colloquial, unadorned prose style, precise detail,
      repetition, characters who act but are not introspective,
      and pervasive Christian attitudes, particularly when
      they or their characters are isolated.

302. Purves, William L. "Literary Output of Daniel Defoe."
      Library, 3 (1912), 333-35.

      Lists the number of pages produced by Defoe at various
      stages of his literary career; because Defoe was so pro-
      lific, Purves suggests that perhaps he managed a literary
      partnership with others writing under his name.

303. R., S.K. "Defoe at Tooting." *Notes and Queries,* Ninth
      Series, 9 (1902), 207.

      Asserts that Defoe's biographers are incorrect in
      their belief that Defoe lived at Tooting, Graveney, in
      1688 and helped form the first Nonconformist congregation
      there. This belief is founded on tradition not fact,
      and no local records refer to Defoe. See Dixon, item
      157, and Hibgame, item 200.

304. Rawson, C.J. "The Phrase 'Legal Prostitution' in Field-
      ing, Defoe, and Others." *Notes and Queries,* n.s. 11
      (1964), 298.

Notes that the phrase "legal prostitution" appears
first in Defoe and becomes a stock saying in eighteenth-
century literature.

305. Riffe, Nancy Lee. "Milton on *Paradise Regained*." *Notes
and Queries*, n.s. 13 (1966), 25.

Cites Defoe as the first person to record (in the *Review*, no. 63, August 18, 1711) the anecdote about Milton's
preference for his *Paradise Regained* over his *Paradise
Lost*.

306. Robbins, Alfred F. "Daniel Defoe." *Notes and Queries*,
5 (1900), 285.

Discover's Defoe's name in the *House of Lords' MSS*
for 1693/94 on a list of debtors to be relieved by the
eventually defeated Merchants' Insurers' Bill.

307. ————. "Defoe and the St. Vincent Eruption of 1718."
Notes and Queries, Ninth Series, 9 (1902), 461-62.

Corrects Defoe's biographers who all regard Defoe's
article on the volcanic eruption on St. Vincent's Island
as a fabrication. The article, which appeared in *Mist's
Journal* for July 5, 1718, is corroborated by an article
in *Applebee's Journal* for the same date; the latter is
reprinted here in full.

308. Rogers, Katherine. "The Feminism of Daniel Defoe."
Woman in the 18th Century and Other Essays. Eds. Paul
Fritz and Richard Morton. Toronto: Hakkert, 1976. Pp.
3-24.

Sees Defoe as committed to feminism. He recognized
the "full humanity" of women and wished to free them
from both economic and sexual dependence on men. He believed that the rights and obligations of marriage were
mutual and that a wife should participate in her husband's business so that she could run it successfully
if necessary. Defoe also believed that an unchaste woman
could be an excellent wife, and in *Moll Flanders* and
Roxana he seems to imply that "unchastity" is "necessary
for freedom." Defoe had complete confidence that women
were the equals of men and could fend for themselves.

309. Rogers, Pat. "Defoe in the Fleet Prison." *Review of
English Studies*, 22 (1971), 451-55.

Cites documents from the Public Records Office to
place Defoe's first bankruptcy in October 1692.

310.   ———, ed. *Defoe; The Critical Heritage.* Boston:
       Routledge and Kegan Paul, 1972.

       Traces Defoe's critical reputation over the years and
       sums up the current (1972) state of Defoe scholarship in
       a detailed introduction. The anthologized criticism in-
       cludes selections ranging from 1703 to 1879, including
       commentary by Swift, Gay, Pope, Rousseau, Dr. Johnson,
       Scott, Coleridge, Lamb, Carlyle, Hazlett, Taine, Marx,
       and Stephens.

311.   ———. "Defoe's First Official Post." *Notes and
       Queries*, 18 (1971), 303.

       Confirms Defoe's service as Accomptant to the Commis-
       sioners of the Glass Duty in 1695 and notes that the
       form "de Foe" was used for his name.

312.   ———. "The Dunce Answers Back: John Oldmixon on
       Swift and Defoe." *Texas Studies in Literature and
       Language*, 14 (1972), 33-43.

       Extracts from a variety of John Oldmixon's works his
       views of Swift and Defoe in order to assess the con-
       temporary grounds on which these two authors were
       criticized. Oldmixon reviles both men as Harley's
       mercenary henchmen, but he distinguishes between them
       in seeing Defoe as an upstart double-dealer and Swift
       as an established, straightforward time-server. Rogers
       does not attempt to validate these charges but simply
       to record them in order to show the flexibility of
       personal invective in the Augustan period.

313.   ———, ed. *The Eighteenth Century.* New York: Holmes
       and Meier, 1978.

       Draws together essays on the writer and society,
       politics, religion, science, and art in order to provide
       a cultural context for eighteenth-century literature.
       The sections on the mechanics of publication and on
       politics contain many scattered references to Defoe's
       work.

314.   ———. *Grub Street: Studies in a Sub-Culture.* London:
       Methuen and New York: Barnes and Noble, 1972.

       Makes frequent references to Defoe throughout with a
       section on his inclusion among Pope's dunces. He was
       classified as a dunce because of his social status, his
       legal problems, his literary popularity with the masses,

his subject matter (especially the crime literature),
and his noisy encounters with opposing journalists like
John Tutchin and Ned Ward.

315. Roscoe, Edward S. "Harley and De Foe, 1703-1714."
*Robert Harley, Earl of Oxford, Prime Minister, 1710-
1714*. London: Methuen, 1902. Pp. 47-74.

Presents a positive picture of Defoe's connection
with Harley: the relationship was "creditable to both
men." Defoe did not "sell out" by working for Harley;
in fact, Defoe's advocation of political and social progress, religious freedom, and personal moderation represent both his and Harley's real views. Moreover, both
men believed in the common sense of their countrymen,
and Defoe's journalistic appeal to this characteristic
marked a legitimate new way to influence public opinion.
Defoe is both a diplomat and a journalist.

316. Ross, John F. *Swift and Defoe: A Study in Relationship*.
University of California Publications in English,
Vol. 11. Berkeley and Los Angeles: University of
California Press, 1941.

Identifies Swift, "looking back pessimistically," as
"the last of the aristocrats," and Defoe, "looking for-
ward optimistically," as "the herald of the middle
class." Their hostile attitudes toward each other are
not so much personal as they are the products of class
conflicts. Swift, the "gentleman," held in utter contempt dissenting middle-class tradesmen like Defoe,
while Defoe, the bourgeois, regarded with jealousy and
resentful admiration the upper-level person represented
by Swift. As literary craftsmen, they have virtually
nothing in common except that they both created masterpieces with "Everyman" protagonists in *Robinson Crusoe*
and *Gulliver's Travels*.

Reviews: Louis Landa, *Philological Quarterly*, 21 (1942),
221-23; A.W. Secord, *Modern Language Notes*, 58 (1943),
642; W.D. Taylor, *Review of English Studies*, 19 (1943),
89-90.

317. Rothman, Irving N. "Defoe." *The Milton Encyclopedia*.
Vol. 2. Ed. William B. Hunter, *et al.* Lewisburg:
Bucknell University Press, 1978. Pp. 135-40.

Comments in detail on Defoe's opinions on Milton and
his art. Defoe has high praise for Milton's artistry,
but he often attacks Milton's theology for departing

from conventional interpretations of biblical history.
In his attacks on Jacobitism, Defoe often imitates the
rhetoric of Milton's satanic council in *Paradise Lost*.

318. Rowe, Arthur F. "Daniel Defoe." *Notes and Queries*, 6
      (1900), 337.

      Not really on Defoe but on the custom of displaying
      the heads of executed traitors in public places. See
      the notes by Hope, items 202-04, and the article by
      Gnomon, item 187.

319. Sampson, George. "Daniel Defoe." *Bookman* (London), 34
      (1908), 93-99.

      Calls Defoe's literary life "the political history of
      England from the Revolution to the accession of George
      II." Defoe's political ideas are traced from *The True-
      born Englishman* through *The Shortest Way with the Dis-
      senters* to *The Review*. He was pre-eminently a journalist
      whose fictions are simply extensions of his journalistic
      methods.

320. Schonhorn, Manuel. "Defoe: The Literature of Politics
      and the Politics of Some Fictions." *English Literature
      in the Age of Disguise*. Ed. Maximillian E. Novak.
      Berkeley and Los Angeles: University of California
      Press, 1977. Pp. 15-56.

      Traces in detail Defoe's discussions of "societal evo-
      lution and civil leadership" in his pamphlets, poetry,
      and fiction. Defoe's first political pamphlet, *Reflec-
      tions Upon the Late Great Revolution* (1689), is "a dis-
      orderly assemblage of commonplaces," but *Jure Divino*
      (1706) is a more mature work showing evidence of wide
      and intelligent reading. The latter poem presents a
      defense of a patriarchally divine kingship. Even
      Robinson Crusoe and the *Farther Adventures* can be given
      political readings; in both works, Crusoe plays the role
      of king as Defoe explores the development of society and
      defines good government. Central to his expression of
      his political ideas are metaphors of crown, sword, and
      scepter, as well as allusions to and images from Scrip-
      ture.

321. ———, and Maximillian E. Novak. "Defoe Edition." (Lon-
      don) *Times Literary Supplement*, 19 June 1969, p. 663.

      Announces the Southern Illinois University Press forty-
      volume edition of *The Collected Writings of Daniel Defoe*.

322. Schücking, Levin L. *The Puritan Family*. Translated by
     Brian Battershaw. London: Routledge and Kegan Paul,
     1969; New York: Schocken, 1970. Originally published
     as die Familie im Puritanismus. Leipzig: Teubner,
     1929. Republished as *Die puritanische Familie in
     Literarsoziologischer*. Bern und München: A. Francke
     Verlag, 1964.

     Calls Defoe "an enthusiast for marriage" (also see
     Vaid, item 371) and remarks that Defoe demonstrates how
     Puritanism helped emancipate women; he shows them be-
     coming more responsible for themselves, a by-product
     of Puritan teaching. Dozens of references to Defoe's
     views on Puritanism and the family are made throughout
     this work.

     Review: (London) *Times Literary Supplement*, 5 March
     1970, p. 253.

323. Schwoerer, Lois G. "The Literature of the Standing
     Army Controversy, 1697-1699." *Huntington Library
     Quarterly*, 28 (1965), 187-212.

     Notes briefly Defoe's support of King William's
     position favoring a standing army in peacetime.

324. Scott, Sir Walter. "Daniel Defoe." *Sir Walter Scott
     on Novelists and Fiction*. Ed. Ioan Williams. New
     York: Barnes and Noble, 1968. Pp. 164-83.

     Includes Scott's piece on Defoe among fifteen Scott
     essays on eighteenth-century novelists. Scott praises
     Defoe's versatility--"he wrote on all occasions and on
     all subjects"--and his realistic techniques. Defoe's
     works, with the exception of his political writings,
     are for "the amusement of children and the lower classes."

325. Secord, Arthur. "Defoe in Stoke Newington." *Publica-
     tions of the Modern Language Association*, 66 (1951),
     211-25.

     Consists of sixteen biographical notes which correct
     previously accepted "facts" about Defoe's life. For ex-
     ample, Secord shows that Defoe never owned the famous
     "Defoe house" on Church Street; he also discovers the
     precise date for Defoe's move to Stoke Newington and
     demonstrates that previous biographers have erred in
     placing Defoe in Scotland before April 1707/08. The
     article contains information on the Drury family and
     its relationship with Defoe.

Review: George Harris Healey, *Philological Quarterly*,
31 (1952), 265.

326.   ⸺. "Defoe's Release from Newgate." (London) *Times
Literary Supplement*, 26 January 1928, p. 62.

Provides evidence to show that Defoe was released
from Newgate before November 10, 1703, and did not remain in prison until March or April 1704 as stated in
recent editions of Defoe's works.

327.   ⸺. *Studies in the Narrative Method of Defoe*.
Urbana: University of Illinois Press, 1924.

Selects three works for study: *Robinson Crusoe*, *Captain
Singleton*, and *The Memoirs of Captain Carleton*. The
section called "The Composition of *Robinson Crusoe*" is
not really about the act or method of composing the
novel but about its sources, primarily the published
accounts of Selkirk's adventures, Knox's *Ceylon*, and
Dampier's *Voyages*. Defoe develops the basic incidents
he takes from such sources by adding details drawn from
his imagination and his widespread reading in economics,
geography, history, and sea-lore. The discussion of
Captain Singleton also focuses on the way in which Defoe
bases the action on a variety of adventure stories,
including those of Dampier and Knox. The section on
The Memoirs of Captain Carleton, however, emphasizes
the problem of authorship. Secord rejects the idea
that Carleton wrote any considerable portion of the book
and attributes it solely to Defoe, who used Carleton's
career only as a central thread around which he wove
details and events taken from Boyer, Freind, and newspaper accounts. Defoe's principal sources for his novels
were drawn from the literature of voyages, travels, and
actual adventure and fleshed out with details taken
from histories and newspaper reports. His novels do not
have "plots" in the traditional sense, for by imitating
true records, he imitates the shapelessness of life itself.

Reviews: Howard Buck, *Modern Language Notes*, 42 (1927),
121-24; Paul Dottin, *Revue Anglo-Américain*, 2 (1925),
444-45; Bernhard Fehr, *Deutsche Literaturzeitung*
(1924), 2204-08; H.V.R., *Modern Language Review*, 20
(1925), 109; Henry Clinton Hutchins, *Journal of English
and Germanic Philology*, 28 (1929), 443-52; S.B. Liljegren, *Anglia Beiblatt*, 36 (1925), 340-43; *Notes and
Queries*, 147 (1924), 291-92; F.A. Pompen, *Neophilologus*,

12 (1926), 31-34; H. Ullrich, *Englische Studien*, 59 (1925), 457-67.

328. Sen, Sri C. *Daniel Defoe: His Mind and Art.* Calcutta: University of Calcutta Press, 1948. Reprinted New York: Folcroft Press, 1969.

Presents an almost totally positive view of Defoe and his art. Defoe is practical, moderate, sane, versatile, accurate, and imaginative; he is a "born realist" with an eye for detail. Sen's method is to analyze a particular work in order to illuminate a specific aspect of Defoe's thought. *A Journal of the Plague Year* is examined in Chapter I in order to show the workings of Defoe's memory and imagination. In Chapter II, a discussion of the *Compleat English Gentleman* demonstrates Defoe's ideas on education. Chapter III focuses on the *Complete English Tradesman*, which reflects Defoe's views on trade. The *Essay Upon Projects* (Chapter IV) illustrates his social criticism, and the *Appeal to Honour and Justice* (Chapter V) presents his political opinions. Chapter VI is devoted to his "narrative and dramatic qualities and other cognate matters." An examination of *Robinson Crusoe* in Chapter VII reveals the didacticism basic to Defoe's novels. Chapter VIII examines Defoe's methods of characterization, and Chapter IX treats the symbolism of *Robinson Crusoe*. This work was originally produced as a dissertation and reflects the limitations of that scholarly form.

329. Sena, John F. "Daniel Defoe and 'The English Malady.'" *Notes and Queries*, n.s. 16 (1969), 183-84.

Examines a brief passage in *Robinson Crusoe* to show medical knowledge of "the English malady" or melancholia.

330. Sharp, R.F. *Architects of English Literature: Biographical Sketches of Great Writers from Shakespeare to Tennyson.* London: Swan Sonnenchein, 1900.

The compiler has not seen this item but apparently pages 43-53 cover Defoe.

331. Sherburn, George, and Donald F. Bond. "Defoe and Journalism." *The Restoration and Eighteenth Century (1660-1789)*. Vol. III of *A Literary History of England*. Ed. Albert C. Baugh. 2nd Ed. New York: Appleton-Century-Crofts, 1967. Originally published 1948. Pp. 847-56.

Surveys briefly Defoe's life and career and contains
a short but useful bibliography. Defoe had "a natural
gift for ingenious episode and specific detail" and his
abilities in characterization generally are underrated.
His "spontaneous, unsophisticated methods of narration"
are more fundamental to the novel form than the techniques which dominated fiction later in the eighteenth
century.

332. Shinagel, Michael. *Daniel Defoe and Middle-Class Gen-
     tility.* Cambridge, Mass.: Harvard University Press,
     1968.

Examines "the significance of the theme of middle-
class gentility in Defoe's life, works, and age," a theme
which Defoe treats throughout his entire career. This
examination is divided into three broad sections: "The
Making of a Middle-Class Gentleman," consisting of four
chapters which include remarks on *The True-born Englishman* and *The Review*; "Middle-Class Gentility in Defoe's
Fiction," consisting of five chapters with discussions
of *Moll Flanders*, *Colonel Jacque*, and *The Fortunate
Mistress*; and "The Tradesman as Gentleman," consisting
of three chapters which contain remarks on *The Compleat
English Gentleman*. Defoe spent his entire life seeking
middle-class gentility, and his aspirations and ideals
are reflected in his writings. He was the embodiment
of developing middle-class attitudes, and he became a
spokesman for middle-class interests. His life and
works give us insights into a period of flux in which
the middle class was becoming assertive.

Reviews: J. Paul Hunter, *Journal of English and Germanic
     Philology*, 70 (1971), 315-18; *Johnsonian Newsletter*,
     28 (1968), 9-10; Maximillian E. Novak, *Philological
     Quarterly*, 48 (1969), 348-49; James Sutherland, *Studia
     Neophilologica*, 41 (1969), 192-94; (London) *Times
     Literary Supplement*, 16 October 1968, p. 1179.

333. Shirren, Adam J. *Daniel Defoe in Stoke Newington.*
     London: Central Library, 1960.

Listed by Payne, item 21, as a typescript, but unseen
by the compiler.

334. Shroff, Homai J. *The Eighteenth Century Novel: The Idea
     of the Gentleman.* New Delhi: Arnold Heinemann, 1978.

Points out that Defoe's conception of a "gentleman"
is based on money; thus, the merchant's son, who spends

his time in trade, is more worthy of the title of "gentleman" than the aristocrat's son, who might well spend his time in riding, hunting, and drinking.

335. Shugrue, Michael F. "Introduction" to *Selected Poetry and Prose of Daniel Defoe*. New York: Holt, Rinehart and Winston, 1968. Pp. v-xxiii.

Discusses the growth of the Defoe canon and justifies the inclusion of essays from *Applebee's Journal* in that body of work. Shugrue also provides contexts for the Defoe works collected here. Emphasized is Defoe's political activity, which is seen as consistently moderate and not at all that of a political opportunist. The sources for Defoe's detailed knowledge of criminal life also are explored briefly.

336. Sill, Geoffrey M. "A Brief Digression on Daniel 'De' Foe." *Notes and Queries*, n.s. 25 (1978), 39-40.

Discusses Defoe's change of his name from "Foe" to "De Foe" not as a pretension to an aristocratic lineage but rather as a possible attempt to reclaim the original form of the family name.

337. ————. "A Report to Hanover on the 'Insolent Defoe.'" *Notes and Queries*, 28 (1981), 224-25.

Suggests that the Hanoverian hostility toward Oxford and Defoe was due to Defoe's ironic *Reasons against the Succession of the House of Hanover*.

338. Simmons, James C. "A Victorian Plagiarism of Defoe." *American Notes and Queries*, 10 (1971), 36-37.

Says that Anne Manning plagiarized her plague scenes in *Cheery and Violet: a Tale of the Great Plague* (1853) from Defoe's *Journal of the Plague Year*.

339. Skydsgaard, Niels Jørgen. "Defoe on the Art of Fiction." *Essays Presented to Knud Schibsbye on His 75th Birthday, 29 Nov. 1979*. Eds. Michael Chesnutt, Claus Fairch, Torben Thrane, and Graham D. Caie. Copenhagen: Akademisk, 1979. Pp. 164-71.

Believes that Defoe's frequent "claims to authenticity and a moral purpose" often obscure his "active commitment to the artistic aspects of his craft...." Defoe was an artist first and a moralist second.

340. Snow, Malinda. "The Origins of Defoe's First-Person
      Narrative Technique: An Overlooked Aspect of the Rise
      of the Novel." *Journal of Narrative Technique*, 6
      (1976), 175-87.

      Contends that one source for Defoe's first-person
      narrative method, not fully considered by critics like
      Ian Watt, is the scientific writing of the late seven-
      teenth century. Certainly Defoe's education at Newington
      Green and the sale catalog of his library suggest a
      more-than-passing interest in science. In addition,
      science writers like Robert Hooke and Robert Boyle
      employed a simple, direct style similar to Defoe's and,
      like the latter's narrators, they not only describe
      things but also describe *themselves* perceiving and
      interacting with the objects of their perceptions.

340A. Sokolyansky, Mark G. "The Diary and Its Role in the
      Genesis of the English Novel." *Zeitschrift für
      Anglistik und Amerikanistik*, 28 (1980), 341-49.

      The compiler did not personally review this item.

*   Snyder, Henry L. "Daniel Defoe, the Duchess of Marl-
      borough, and the *Advice to the Electors of Great
      Britain*." (See item 1200.)

341. Southam, Herbert. "Defoe: The Devil's Chapel." *Notes
      and Queries*, Tenth Series, 10 (1908), 134.

      Refers not to Defoe, but to Pickford, item 298.

342. Spearman, Diana. *The Novel and Society*. London:
      Routledge and Kegan Paul, 1966.

      Sees Defoe as an isolated writer; he is not repre-
      sentative of any "class, sect, or opinion," and he did
      not directly influence other authors. He successfully
      portrayed his age because he knew it so well, but he
      is an "eccentric" writer whose ideas are not always
      those of his time. Defoe's religious and economic
      views, for instance, are often highly individualistic,
      and *Robinson Crusoe* is not nearly such a moral or
      "capitalistic" novel as is usually argued.

343. Stamm, Rudolf G. "Daniel Defoe: An Artist in the Puri-
      tan Tradition." *Philological Quarterly*, 15 (1936),
      225-46.

      Describes "a desperate battle" between Defoe's artistic
      drives and his Puritan views on art. Defoe was suspicious

of all imaginative literature, aggressively hostile to
erotic works, and antagonistic to the theater. Because
of his Puritan conditioning, the bulk of Defoe's works
was practical, journalistic efforts within the limits of
the Puritan view of art. In an attempt to remain within
such limits in his novels, he added Calvinistic interpretations to his faked autobiographies in order to conceal their essentially amoral and fictional natures.

344. Starr, G.A. "Defoe's Prose Style: 1. The Language of
      Interpretation." *Modern Philology*, 71 (1974), 277-94.

      Warns against generalizing about Defoe's prose, basing
      arguments on the "shaky evidence" of accidentals, and
      neglecting the relevance of literary history to dis-
      cussions of style. In the rendering of character,
      Defoe's style is highly adverbial because the emphasis
      is on how a character perceives things rather than on
      how those things really are in themselves; Defoe is
      interested in the subjective perception of experience
      rather than in an objective depiction of that experience.
      Defoe's realism derives from his ability to precisely
      render that subjectivity.

345. ————. "From Casuistry to Fiction: The Importance of
      the *Athenian Mercury*." *Journal of the History of
      Ideas*, 28 (1967), 17-32.

      Discovers in Dunton's *Athenian Mercury* the source
      for Defoe's casuistry, which influences his subject
      matter and narrative method. Defoe also was exposed
      to casuistical divinity at Morton's academy.

346. ————. "'Sauces to whet our gorg'd Appetites': Defoe
      at Seventy in the Anchovy Trade." *Philological Quar-
      terly*, 54 (1975), 531-33.

      Discovers evidence to show that Defoe remained active
      in trade at least until a year before his death; ap-
      parently, he was an importer of anchovies at the same
      time he was condemning the food as one of the corrupting
      luxuries of English life.

347. Stauffer, Donald. *The Art of Biography in Eighteenth-
      Century England*. Princeton: Princeton University
      Press, 1941.

      Contends that Defoe's work demonstrates the interdepen-
      dency of biography and the novel. Although Defoe's ap-
      plication of the art of biography to fiction enhanced
      the novel form, his gift for "telling a lie" was a

negative influence on biographers. Defoe's "art that
conceals art also conceals the artist," and this makes
it difficult to establish a canon of Defoe's works.

348. Steensma, Robert C. "A Legal Proverb in Defoe, Swift,
and Shenstone." *Proverbium*, 10 (1968), 248.

Records the use in English literature of a legal proverb taken from Anacharsis; Defoe uses it in his *Poor
Man's Plea*: "These are all Cob-web Laws, in which the
small Flies are catch'd, and the great Ones break thro'."

349. Sutherland, James R. *Daniel Defoe: A Critical Study*.
Cambridge, Mass.: Harvard University Press, 1971.
Sections reprinted in Byrd, item 132, and Shinagel,
item 28.

Opens and concludes with biographical chapters, in
between which are a chapter on Defoe's journalism, one
on his poetry, and two on his fiction. The seventy-
page chapter on journalism concentrates on Defoe's
pamphlets, finding them much superior in irony, style,
and clarity to those of his contemporaries; he retained
his pamphleteering skills until the end of his life.
His "conscious artistry" is likewise evident in his
periodical writing. As a poet, Defoe was less successful, although "once or twice ... he succeeded in writing
effective satire." Ultimately, of course, Defoe will
be remembered for his fiction, which is characterized
by the author's "constant endeavor to create in his
reader's mind a belief in the absolute veracity of
the narrator." Defoe's stories also focus on "the
isolated human being contending with circumstances."
The bulk of Sutherland's discussion deals with *Moll
Flanders*, an innovation for Defoe in that it depicts
life through the eyes of a woman. In this story, as in
most of his other work, Defoe shows a remarkable
"psychological understanding" that many critics have
been unwilling to grant him. In all of his fiction,
Defoe was a sincere moralist, but interpretive problems
arise because that morality often is in conflict with
the autobiographical form which forces him to convincing-
ly narrate events of which he ethically disapproves.

Reviews: Leo Braudy, *Johnsonian Newsletter*, 32 (1972),
3; *Philological Quarterly*, 51 (1973), 665-66; Manuel
Schonhorn, *Review of English Studies*, n.s. 24 (1973),
87-89; Arthur Sherbo, *Journal of English and Germanic
Philology*, 71 (1973), 251-52; Keith Stewart, *English*

Language Notes, 9 (1973), 306-10; (London) *Times Literary Supplement*, 28 April 1972, pp. 461-63.

350. ————. *Defoe*. London: Methuen, 1937 and New York: J.B. Lippincott, 1938. Second Edition, 1950. Pp. 227-46 are reprinted in Ellis, item 520.

Combines biography with literary criticism, but emphasizes the former. Literary works discussed are selected on the basis of the extent to which they illuminate Defoe's "mind and motives." A short survey of Defoe's early life culminates in a chapter on his relationship with Robert Harley and his establishment of *The Review*, which Sutherland calls Defoe's "most astonishing performance." Following this is a chapter on Defoe's satiric and controversial writings which focuses on *The Shortest Way with the Dissenters*, a work that Sutherland finds puzzling. After several more biographical chapters, Sutherland devotes Chapter XI to a specific study of *Robinson Crusoe* and generalized remarks on the rest of his fiction. The concluding two chapters on Defoe's last years are followed by an Appendix which prints a never-before published memorandum in Defoe's handwriting to Robert Harley.

Reviews: S.C. Chew, *New York Herald Tribune Books*, 20 February 1938, p. 5; H. Davis, *Modern Philology*, 36 (1938), 79-80; Paul Dottin, *Etudes Anglaises* (April 1938), 160-61; P. Geyl, *Tijdschrift voor geschiedens*, 52 (1937), 419-20; T. Good, *Life and Letters Today*, 17 (1937), 181; E. Johnson, *New Republic*, 23 March 1938, pp. 199-200; H.M. Jones, *Saturday Review of Literature*, 26 February 1938, p. 10; Louis Kronenberger, *New York Times Book Reviews*, 13 February 1938, p. 5; R. Lewin, *Mercury*, 35 (1937), 491-92; J.R. Moore, *Review of English Studies*, 16 (1940), 224-26; *More Books*, 13 (1938), 117; W.T. Morgan, *American Historical Review*, 44 (1939), 360-61; S. Potter, *Fortnightly*, 148 (1937), 247-48; V.S. Pritchett, *Spectator*, 16 July 1937, p. 113; *Quarterly Review*, 269 (1937), 367; D.A. Roberts, *Nation*, 26 February 1938, p. 250; Rudolph Stamm, *Englische Studien*, 72 (1938), 413-16; Geoffrey Tillotson, *Modern Language Review*, 33 (1938), 587-88; (London) *Times Literary Supplement*, 26 June 1937, p. 476; (London) *Times Literary Supplement*, 16 July 1954, p. 462.

351. ————. *Defoe*. Writers and Their Work, No. 51. London: Longmans, Green and Co., 1954. Revised edition, 1970.

Surveys Defoe's life and works after a brief introduction which claims that "whereas in his prose fiction Defoe is not much more than a fascinating primitive, in his controversial and journalistic writings he is one of the great English masters." Despite this statement, about one-half of the book is devoted to the fiction because it is the most popular of Defoe's writings with modern readers. The fiction is characterized by Defoe's verisimilitude, his use of his personal experiences, and his consistent moral overview. Defoe is usually so convincing that it is hard to believe that his narratives are not authentic first-hand accounts; he accomplishes this by overwhelming the reader with details so trivial that no one would believe that the author would go to the trouble of making them up and by admitting uncertainty as to the accuracy of some of his "facts." The result is that we admire the honesty of the narrator and therefore accept what he says as true. Defoe further authenticates his stories by incorporating into them factual material drawn from his reading and personal experience. The Puritan in Defoe is very strong, and his moralizing in such works as *Moll Flanders* and *Roxana* is sincere and consistent with his non-fictional moral writings.

Review: (London) *Times Literary Supplement*, 16 July 1954, p. 462.

352. ————. "Down Chancery Lane." *Evidence in Literary Scholarship: Essays in Memory of James Marshall Osborn.* Eds. René Wellek and Alvaro Ribeiro. Oxford: Clarendon, 1979. Pp. 165-78.

Reminisces about (among other things) the author's fortuitous discoveries of important biographical information on Defoe; these discoveries resulted in the publication of items 350 and 357.

353. ————. "Introduction" to *Robinson Crusoe and Other Writings* by Daniel Defoe. The Gotham Library. New York: New York University Press, 1977. Pp. vii-xvi. Originally published as a Riverside Edition by Houghton Mifflin, 1968.

Surveys the works included in this collection (for a listing of them, see item 92), emphasizing Defoe's direct, journalistic approach. Sutherland regards *Crusoe* as a reflection of Defoe's own sharing in the solitude and sufferings of his title character.

354. ————. "A Note on the Last Years of Defoe." *Modern
      Language Review*, 29 (1934), 137-41.

      Tries to explain the mystery of Defoe's August 12,
      1730, letter to his son-in-law in which he refers to
      his unhappiness and to "a wicked, perjur'd, and con-
      temptible Enemy." This latter has never been identified
      but probably is Mary Brooke, a widow who had claims
      against Defoe's estate and who filed suit against him.

355. ————. *On English Prose*. Toronto: University of
      Toronto Press, 1957.

      Remarks briefly on Defoe's prose style, which was
      influenced by Roger L'Estrange and was part of the re-
      action against the elaborate structure and learned
      vocabulary of John Milton, Thomas Browne, and Jeremy
      Taylor.

356. ————. "The Relation of Defoe's Fiction to His Non-
      Fictional Writings." *Imagined Worlds: Essays on
      Some English Novels and Novelists in Honour of John
      Butt*. Eds. Maynard Mack and Ian Gregor. London:
      Methuen, 1968. Pp. 37-50.

      Looks at Defoe's non-fictional writings which employ
      a persona in order to explain how Defoe was able to
      become such a successful novelist so late in his life.
      The main characters of his novels are merely more sus-
      tained versions of the speakers he had employed
      earlier. The problem that concerned him above all
      was "necessity," the will to survive that conflicts
      with economic facts and accepted morality, and this
      central interest explains why he chose criminal types
      and the autobiographical form for so much of his fiction.

      Review: Frank Kermode, *Modern Language Quarterly*, 24
          (1968), 476-78.

357. ————. "Some Early Troubles of Daniel Defoe." *Review
      of English Studies*, 9 (1933), 275-90.

      Locates nine lawsuits involving Defoe in Chancery
      records.

358. Sweeting, W.D. ["Defoe's Family Residence."] *Notes
      and Queries*, 7 (1901), 298.

      Corrects a widely held belief that Daniel Defoe's
      grandfather lived in Elton; his actual residence was
      in Etton.

359.   Sypher, Wylie. *Guinea's Captive Kings: British Anti-*
        Slavery Literature of the XVIIIth *Century.* Chapel
        Hill: University of North Carolina Press, 1942.

        Claims that Defoe is both the first poet and the
        first novelist to deal with slavery in any comprehensive
        way. Although he attacked the slave trade in his poem,
        "Reformation of Manners" (1702), he advocates purchasing
        slaves in the *Essay on Projects* (1698) and *Plan of the*
        English Commerce (1728). In *Robinson Crusoe* (1719),
        Captain Singleton (1720), and *Colonel Jack* (1722), Defoe
        treats slavery from several points of view, all of them
        characterized by a matter-of-fact attitude. His
        handling of slavery is the most accurate of any
        eighteenth-century novelist.

360.   Taylor, Henry. "Defoe Methodist Chapel, Tooting."
        Notes and Queries, Eleventh Series, 3 (1911), 54.

        Corrects Hibgame, item 200, by noting Defoe's burial
        monument in Bunhill Fields.

361.   Temple, R.C. "Daniel Defoe and Thomas Bowrey." *Notes*
        and Queries, 160 (1931), 39-40.

        Prints two letters Defoe wrote to Bowrey concerning
        the possibility of trade with the island of Juan Fer-
        nandez.

*   Titlebaum, Richard. "Some Notes Towards a Definition
        of Defoe's Demonology." (See item 1027.)

362.   Trent, William P. *Daniel Defoe. How to Know Him.*
        Indianapolis: Bobbs Merrill Co., 1916.

        Mixes biographical and critical commentary with selec-
        tions from Defoe's various writings. Trent believes
        that Defoe's morals have been too harshly judged and
        that, in any case, he is a literary genius who portrays
        his age with greater clarity and fulness than any of
        his contemporaries. In addition to his writing talents,
        Defoe was a shrewd and influential politician and a
        sound economist. Ultimately, however, his fame will
        rest on *Robinson Crusoe.*

363.   ————. "Defoe: The Newspaper and the Novel." *The*
        Cambridge History of English Literature. Vol. 9.
        Eds. A.W. Ward and A.R. Waller. Cambridge: University
        Press, 1968. Pp. 1-25. Originally published 1912.

Intersperses biographical information with a survey
of Defoe's literary career. Trent contends that "as a
writer and an important figure of his age," Defoe is
second to no one except perhaps Swift. Defoe's contribution to journalism is his abandonment of the inflammatory
style of his age in favor of moderation and accuracy
aimed at gaining acquiescence. The novelist in Defoe
evolved out of the journalist, and that is why his fictions are realistically detailed stories aimed at the
moral edification of his readers. His "power to make
alive" is best manifested in *Robinson Crusoe*--"the most
indisputable English classic"--but all his later novels
are testimonies to his talent for realism.

364. ————. "A New Edition of Defoe." *Forum*, 36 (1904),
     624-34.

     Reviews the Crowell edition of Defoe's *Works* (edited
     by G.H. Maynadier) and comments on Defoe's life, correct-
     ing such "fantasies" as Wright's declaration that Defoe
     did not speak to his family for 29 years and the
     generally accepted view that Defoe was an impious rascal.

365. ————. "New Light on De Foe's Life." *Nation*, 87 (1908),
     259-61.

     Unearths in the sixty-six-volume Nichols Collection
     of Newspapers in the Bodleian Library a number of facts
     about Defoe's life. Among them are the following: Defoe
     spent but five months in jail for his *Shortest Way*; he
     probably began infiltrating opposition newspapers as
     early as 1711; and Defoe went to jail for two weeks in
     1713 for some pamphlets that his enemies claimed were
     written in support of the Pretender.

366. ————. "A Talk About Defoe ... 28th of December,
     1911." *Papers of the Hobby Club of New York City,
     1911-1912*. Boston, 1912.

     Not seen by the compiler, this item is listed by
     Payne, item 21.

367. Trevelyan, G.M. *England Under Queen Anne: Blenheim*.
     London and New York: Longmans, Green, 1930. The
     first four chapters are reprinted as *The England of
     Queen Anne*. London and New York: Longmans, Green,
     1932. Chapter I appears as "Defoe's England" in
     English Social History. London and New York: Longmans,
     Green, 1942.

Uses Defoe, "the first who saw the old world through
... modern eyes," to characterize England under Queen
Anne. Defoe's *Tour*, although written in the reign of
George I, was based on observations made during the
early and middle years of Anne and depicts a prosperous,
contented populace. Defoe, the middle-class businessman,
was a truer spokesman for his age than was Swift. This
is the first volume of a trilogy (also see items 368
and 369).

368.   ————. *England Under Queen Anne: The Peace and the
       Protestant Succession.* London and New York: Longmans,
       Green, 1934.

       Contains several scattered remarks on Defoe's political
       activities. This is part three of a trilogy: also see
       items 367 and 369.

369.   ————. *England Under Queen Anne: Ramellies and the
       Union with Scotland.* London and New York: Longmans,
       Green, 1933.

       Contains several scattered remarks on Defoe's political
       activities. This is part two of a trilogy: also see
       items 367 and 368.

370.   V. "Daniel Defoe's Descendants." *Notes and Queries*,
       167 (1934), 122.

       Notes that in the 1890's, the Vicar of Claxby was a
       descendant of Daniel Defoe. See Askew, item 106.

371.   Vaid, Sudesh. *The Divided Mind: Studies in Defoe and
       Richardson.* New Delhi: Associated Publishing House,
       1979.

       Views *Moll Flanders* and *Roxana* from a feminist per-
       spective. Although Defoe's attitudes toward women are
       progressive for his day, they are not radical. He
       advocates a better education and greater matrimonial
       rights for women, but he still believes in paternal
       authority, especially in religious matters. He sym-
       pathizes with the plights of his heroines, but he re-
       mains sympathetic only with Moll because she ultimately
       accepts marriage and therefore patriarchy. Defoe's
       commitment to patriarchy forces him to punish Roxana
       because she rejects marriage and motherhood and seeks
       to become a "man-woman." In both of his "feminist"
       novels, Defoe shows a deep awareness of the complex

economic and moral problems that confront women in a patriarchal society.

372. Walker, Emery. "Portraits Wanted." *Notes and Queries*, Eleventh Series, 2 (1910), 307-08.

Asks for information on a portrait of Defoe by Kneller.

373. Watson, Francis. "The Civet-Cats of Stoke Newington." *Listener*, 63 (1960), 1142-43.

Repeats, for no apparent reason, Newton's information on the civet-cat episode in Defoe's life (see item 282) and then rambles on about how many works he wrote, where he lived, and why he failed in trade.

374. ————. *Daniel Defoe*. Port Washington: Kennikat Press, 1969. Originally published London: Longmans, 1952.

Opens with a chapter--"Who Wrote *Robinson Crusoe?*"-- which summarizes Defoe's life and work and which views him as an accidental genius who "found an unexpected immortality" as he tried to earn a living for his family and in the process created *Robinson Crusoe*. The emphasis throughout the study is on Defoe's uniqueness: "There is nobody quite like Defoe in the literatures of other lands. Even in the abundant variety of English he is unique...." The book is primarily biographical and Defoe's writings, except for *Crusoe* which is praised again and again, receive only perfunctory commentary. There are few annotations and the works cited were outdated even in 1952 when this study was published.

Reviews: Pierre Danchin, *Etudes Anglaises*, 6 (1954), 158; Gerhard Jacob, *Archiv für das Studium der neueren Sprachen*, 191 (1955), 233; *Listener*, 48 (1952), 351; Harold Nicolson, *Observer*, 17 August 1952, p. 7; (London) *Times Literary Supplement*, 8 August 1952, p. 518.

375. Weitzman, Arthur J. "Defoe's Opinion of *The Beggar's Opera* Considered." *American Notes and Queries*, 13 (1975), 148-49.

Finds in *Augusta Triumphans* and *Street Robberies Consider'd* two jibes by Defoe at the immorality of Gay's *Beggar's Opera*.

376. Westley, W. Arthur. "Gehoe." *Notes and Queries*, 188 (1945), 197.

Says that Defoe is the first to use the word "gehoe" (in the second edition of the *Tour*).

377. Wherry, Albinia L. *Daniel Defoe*. London: George Bell & Sons, 1905. Reprinted Folcroft Library Editions, 1973.

Begins with four biographical chapters and follows with a chapter on non-fiction writings, one on the fiction excluding *Crusoe*, one each on *Crusoe* and the *Serious Reflections*, and a final one on Defoe's style. Both biographical and critical commentary are now out-dated.

378. White, A.S. "Defoe's Military Career." (London) *Times Literary Supplement*, 28 January 1926, p. 63.

Corrects Charles Dalton who, in his *English Army Lists and Commission Registers, 1661-1714*, identifies a half-pay officer as Daniel Defoe; actually the officer's name was Daniel Dufaur.

379. Whitten, Wilfred. *Daniel Defoe*. Westminster Biographies. London: Kegan Paul, 1900.

Emphasizes in this now-outdated biography Defoe's use of his education and experience in both his journalistic and literary works. The value of Defoe's writing is not in its moral lesson which is "too crude for instructed minds," but rather in its "photographic vividness." Even in his journalism, Defoe makes "fiction look like sworn evidence."

380. "Who Founded London University? Daniel Defoe's Claim." (London) *Times Educational Supplement*, 11 July 1936, n.p.

Not seen by the compiler but referred to by Leinster-Mackay, *The Educational World of Daniel Defoe*, item 222.

381. Wingrave, Wyatt. "Defoe at Lyme Regis." *Notes and Queries*, 154 (1928), 390.

Asks for information on Defoe's relationship with Monmouth at Lyme Regis and on what happened to Defoe after Monmouth's defeat.

382. Winterich, John T. "How This Book Came to Be." *The Fortunes and Misfortunes of the Famous Moll Flanders*

by Daniel Defoe. New York: The Heritage Press, 1942.
Pp. vii-x.

Praises Defoe's fecundity in writing eleven books
between his sixtieth and sixty-fifth years, and then
briefly traces Defoe's life and career in a lively and
non-scholarly fashion.

383. Wright, Thomas. *The Life of Daniel Defoe.* 2nd Ed.
London: C.J. Farncombe, 1931. Originally published
1894.

Pays Defoe homage as a genuinely heroic man throughout
this almost completely rewritten critical biography.
Wright superficially surveys Defoe's literary productions, regarding as his masterpieces *Robinson Crusoe*,
Colonel Jacque, *Moll Flanders*, and *Roxana*. The other
fictions also are rated highly along with *Due Preparations for the Plague* and *Mrs. Veal*. The rest of Defoe's
work contains "a large quantity of chaff." At several
places in this study, Wright attempts to parallel
Crusoe's fictional life with certain events in Defoe's
life.

IV

THE MAJOR NOVELS

A. General

384. Alkon, Paul K. *Defoe and Fictional Time*. Athens: University of Georgia Press, 1979.

Divides the discussion into six chapters: Fictional Time and Real Time, Setting and Chronology, Time-Consciousness, The Reader's Memory, Tempo, and Implications. The focus is on three aspects of fictional time: "the question of how temporal settings within narratives may be related to the outside world of clock- and calendar-time, the question of how time-concepts shared within a culture may influence expectations about the writing and reading of fiction, and above all the question of how narratives shape the phenomenal time experienced by their readers." In Chapter 2, Alkon shows that in *Colonel Jack* Defoe uses biographical time to reinforce his portrayal of moral growth, but in *Moll Flanders*, biological time is used to create doubts about Moll's moral state. Chapter 3 emphasizes Defoe's preference for "retrospective narrations shaped like autobiographies" which demonstrate his interest in "the structure of experiential time." Alkon focuses on "the effects of spatial form that are a significant part of Defoe's emblematic method" in Chapter 4. In the fifth and longest chapter, Alkon explores in detail the "pace" of *A Journal of the Plague Year*, arguing that the narrative is slow-moving in order to seem to parallel the duration of the action portrayed. The final chapter discusses the implications of Defoe's experiments with time and his influence on such later writers as Fielding.

Review: Maximillian E. Novak, *Eighteenth-Century Studies*, 13 (1980), 449-51.

385. Allen, Walter. "Daniel Defoe." *Six Great Novelists*.
      London: Hamish Hamilton, 1955. Pp. 9-37.

      Rates Defoe with Shakespeare and Dickens as one of
      the three most famous English writers throughout the
      world. Defoe's pretence of presenting literal reality
      and his calling his fictions "histories" marks the
      difference between the old kind of prose fiction and
      the new, and this makes possible the modern novel.
      Defoe's illusion of reality is obtained through his
      method of presenting a plethora of details which seem
      too trivial for anyone to have bothered to invent them.
      The bulk of this essay is a fairly general critical
      biography.

386. ————. *The English Novel*. New York: E.P. Dutton,
      1954.

      Calls Defoe the "father of the novel." In *Robinson
      Crusoe* he creates "the first great individualist" and in
      Moll Flanders he creates the first sociological novel.
      Unlike many critics, like E.M. Forster (item 742), who
      see Moll as a flat character, Allen sees her as existing
      "completely in the round"; Defoe's obsession with im-
      parting a fully realized character makes him "the
      archetypal novelist."

387. Backscheider, Paula. "Defoe's Women: Snares and Prey."
      Studies in Eighteenth-Century Culture, 5 (1976),
      103-20.

      Offers a feminist reading of Defoe's treatment of
      women in his novels. Because characters like Moll and
      Roxana are trapped by social codes favorable only to
      married women, they become predators. They grow in-
      creasingly independent, learning to act more like men
      in order to survive. Although Defoe can objectively
      condemn his women's predatory and immoral actions, he
      still has created "models of courage, ingenuity, and
      aspiration."

388. Baine, Rodney M. "The Evidence from Defoe's Title
      Pages." *Studies in Bibliography*, 25 (1972), 185-91.

      Shows that many misinterpretations of Defoe's work
      stem from the erroneous belief of some scholars that a
      novel's title page reproduces the author's own title
      and provides evidence of his original plan. In fact,
      in Defoe's age, the title page was primarily the
      publisher's advertisement and was set in type last, so

it is unlikely that an author would even see it prior
to publication.

389. Baker, Ernest A. "Defoe as Sociological Novelist."
Academy, 70, 26 May 1906, pp. 502-03.

Attributes Defoe's special talents as a novelist to
his journalistic experience; from the latter, he gained
his talent for observation and recording details as
well as his interest in the political, religious, and
social issues of his time. His exploration of the conditions that shape the human character makes him a
sociological novelist.

390. ————. *The Later Romances and the Establishment of
Realism.* Vol. 3 of *The History of the English Novel.*
London: H.F. and G. Witherby, 1929. Reprinted New
York: Barnes and Noble, 1969.

Contains two lengthy chapters on Defoe. The first
of these, Chapter VI, "The Establishment of Realism--
Defoe and Robinson Crusoe," surveys Defoe's life and
literary production to 1719 and the writing of *Crusoe.*
The material on Crusoe emphasizes the novel's sources:
current travel literature, Selkirk's adventures, Robert
Knox's *An Historical Relation of Ceylon*, William Dam-
per's *New Voyage*, Henry Neville's *Isle of Pines*, Grimmelshausen's *Simplicissimus*, Hendrik Smeeks' *Krinke
Kesmes*, and many others. Chapter VII, "The Later
Fiction of Defoe," also emphasizes sources. Baker concludes that although Defoe lacked the necessary knowledge
of psychology to create life-like characters, he still
contributed to the modern novel with a circumstantial
method that grounded fiction on solid earth and wedded
it to the common man.

391. Baker, Sheridan. "The Idea of Romance in the Eighteenth-
Century Novel." *Papers of the Michigan Academy of
Science, Arts, and Letters*, 49 (1963), 507-22.

Contends that eighteenth-century novelists did not use
the term "romance" as a synonym for "novel," as many
critics believe, but instead employed it in its more
traditional chivalric sense. The conventions of chivalric romance are easily adapted to the more realistic
demands of the new novel. Defoe uses these conventions
when his "nobodies rise to riches"; the romance's at-
tainment of "glory" is replaced in the novel by "a new
suit and a nest egg." Furthermore, *Robinson Crusoe*

treats romance as one of the realities of life. Crusoe romanticizes his adventures, sometimes consciously and sometimes unconsciously, but he always remains a realistic figure. This novel is an example of how novelists use the "stuff of romance" to dramatize the conflict of illusion and reality which is the central "business" of the modern novel.

*   Bellessort, André. "Les romans picaresques de Defoe." (See item 1218.)

392. Bishop, Jonathan. "Knowledge, Action and Interpretation in Defoe's Novels." *Journal of the History of Ideas*, 13 (1952), 3-16.

Discovers a common pattern in Defoe's major fiction: "the soul progresses from primeval innocence through the depths of immoral experience to the point where it becomes aware of its sins, turns against its former life, and is reconciled to God." As part of this pattern, Defoe presents a picture of the mind's reacting to its environment which illustrates Locke's epistemology.

393. Black, Sidney J. "Eighteenth Century 'Histories' as a Fictional Mode." *Boston University Studies in English*, 1 (1955), 38-44.

Contends that Defoe pretended his novels were biographies, histories, memoirs, and journals because to the middle-class mind of his era the term "novel" represented a type of moral dishonesty. By disguising his fiction in order to appeal to the Puritan mind, Defoe helped create what amounts to a new fictional mode. Defoe developed three "types" within the new "mode": (1) stories with imaginary characters involved in imaginary events but with overriding moral elements which he could claim are "real" (*Robinson Crusoe*); (2) stories with imaginary characters involved in real events (*A Journal of the Plague Year*); and (3) stories with real characters involved in imaginary events (*Memoirs of Captain George Carleton*).

394. Blackburn, Alexander. *The Myth of the Picaro: Continuity and Transformation of the Picaresque Novel, 1554-1954*. Chapel Hill: University of North Carolina Press, 1979.

Says that although Defoe shares the spirit of the picaresque novelists with his "behaviorism," he essentially stands in antithesis to the myth of the picaro.

Unlike picaresque novels, Defoe's works never question the validity of experience. They also have a pattern of Christian redemption that "is diametrically opposed to the disintegration pattern of the picaresque novels."

395. Blewett, David. *Defoe's Art of Fiction: "Robinson Crusoe," "Moll Flanders," "Colonel Jack," and "Roxana."* Toronto: University of Toronto Press, 1979.

Traces Defoe's "developing artistic self-consciousness" through his four "best" novels. The repeated pattern of the novels is "disaster and slow recovery" which comes about through "the struggle of erring individuals against an indifferent, and often hostile, society." Defoe's sense--perhaps derived from his own economic and political experience--that human affairs in general are permeated with deception infuoes the four works treated here. The discussion of *Robinson Crusoe* focuses on "the rhythm of danger and deliverance" and on the novel's language, particularly the imagery of prisons and animals, which conveys this "rhythm." *Moll Flanders* is a darker vision, reflected in the extended use of false appearance and disguise "to suggest a world of equivocation and hypocrisy." *Colonel Jack* is the male version of *Moll Flanders* with the main difference being that Jack is less engaging than Moll because his disguises and deceptions "do not spring from any pressing need." Defoe's darkest novel is *Roxana* because in it "there is no period of spiritual awakening," and the novel closes with a dispirited heroine. Although Defoe is unable to deal with emotional subtleties, in his best work he is able to focus intensely within a limited range on the universal passions of love, hate, envy, and fear.

Review: Ian A. Bell, *The Scriblerian*, 13 (1980), 37-38.

395A. Boardman, Michael M. *Defoe and the Uses of Narrative.* New Brunswick, N.J.: Rutgers University Press, 1983.

This book came to the compiler's attention too late to read for this work.

396. Boyce, Benjamin. "The Question of Emotion in Defoe." *Studies in Philology*, 50 (1953), 45-58. Reprinted in Byrd, item 132.

Rejects the popular critical view that although Defoe is skilled in presenting facts, he is unable to depict emotional states realistically. In fact, Defoe's

fiction is rendered so powerful precisely because he is
able to show the submerged but never forgotten anxiety
that haunts his characters. He depicts emotional stress
so well because he was prey to it himself, his anxiety
stemming from his occasional adoption of the "prudent"
course rather than the honest one.

*   ————. "The Shortest Way: Characteristic Defoe Fiction."
         (See item 914.)

397.   Braga, Thomas. "Daniel Defoe and the Portuguese."
         Enlightenment Essays, 4 (1973), 47-51.

         Shows that Defoe's opinion of the Portuguese moves
         from a positive one in *Robinson Crusoe* to a negative one
         in *Captain Singleton* and attributes this shift to
         anti-Catholicism and the developing English ideal of
         self-reliance.

398.   Braudy, Leo. "Daniel Defoe and the Anxieties of Auto-
         biography." *Genre*, 6 (1973), 76-97.

         Considers Defoe's first-person novels "as the record
         of his exploration of what constitutes human individual-
         ity and how to write about it." Defoe's characters
         attempt to package and merchandise themselves in a
         publicly acceptable way while still preserving a "private
         self," and disguise is the means by which they accom-
         plish this dual end. These characters feel their iden-
         tities to be threatened by everything that exists before
         them—family, society, culture, etc. The latter can
         only be accepted when the characters gain a sense of
         self, and one of the means to do so is to create a book.
         The pseudo-autobiography enables Defoe's characters to
         achieve their personal identities.

399.   Brooks, Douglas. *Number and Pattern in the Eighteenth-
         Century Novel: Defoe, Fielding, Smollett, and Sterne.*
         London and Boston: Routledge and Kegan Paul, 1973.

         Treats five of Defoe's novels—*Robinson Crusoe*, *Captain
         Singleton*, *Colonel Jack*, *Moll Flanders*, and *Roxana*—in
         terms of their contrasts, correspondences, parallels,
         and repetitions in order to discover significant struc-
         tural patterns. The patterns that emerge express the
         human desire to impose order on the chaos of everyday
         life and to resolve the religious-secular conflicts
         that are treated in the novels. Brooks' thesis is con-
         troversial and should be considered in conjunction with

the two important reviews that are listed below.
Reviews: Eric Rothstein, *Philological Quarterly*, 53 (1974), 587-88; Robert W. Uphaus, *Eighteenth-Century Studies*, 8 (1974), 116-19.

400. Brown, Homer O. "The Displaced Self in the Novels of Daniel Defoe." *Studies in Eighteenth-Century Culture, IV.* Ed. Harold E. Pagliaro. Madison: University of Wisconsin Press, 1975. Pp. 69-94. Originally published in *ELH: A Journal of English Literary History*, 38 (1971), 562-90.

Points to the *Confessions* of Saint Augustine as the "ultimate source" of Defoe's confessional fiction and emphasizes the paradox of characters who expose their lives to the reader while attempting to conceal their true identities and motives.

401. Burch, Charles E. "British Criticism of Defoe as a Novelist, 1719-1860." *Englische Studien*, 67 (1932), 178-98.

Points out that Defoe's work, except for *Robinson Crusoe*, was largely ignored during the eighteenth century. Scott's 1810 edition of Defoe's novels, however, produced positive criticism by Coleridge, Lamb, and Hazlitt which revitalized Defoe's reputation as a novelist.

402. ———. "The Moral Elements in Defoe's Fiction." *London Quarterly and Holborn Review*, 162 (1937), 207-13.

Challenges that view of Defoe which questions the sincerity of his moralizing in his novels and which sees it as a hypocrite's way of covering up essentially immoral stories. In fact, Defoe was consistent and sincere in upholding "a practical, if not lofty standard of morality," one which was never questioned by his contemporaries.

403. Bushnell, Nelson S. "Walter Scott's Advent as a Novelist of Manners." *Studies in Scottish Literature*, 1 (1963), 15-34.

Generalizes--*very* briefly--about Defoe's influence on Scott's novelistic techniques. Also see J.P. Moore's "Defoe and Scott," item 427.

*   Cather, Willa. "Introduction" to *Roxana, or the Fortunate Mistress* by Daniel Defoe. (See item 869.)

404. Church, Richard. *The Growth of the English Novel*. London: Methuen, 1951.

Payne (item 21) lists this item, but the compiler did not review it.

*   Colaiacoma, Paola. *"Captain Singleton* fra *Robinson Crusoe* e *Moll Flanders."* (See item 1238.)

405. Davis, Lennard J. "A Social History of Fact and Fiction: Authorial Disavowal in the Early English Novel." *Literature and Society*. Ed. Edward W. Said. Baltimore: Johns Hopkins University Press, 1980. Pp. 120-48.

Investigates the question of why seventeenth- and early eighteenth-century novelists consistently claimed to be recording facts instead of writing fictions. Such authorial disavowals, of course, skirted the Puritan sanction against fiction and made the novels appear more realistic. More significant, however, is that by denying the fictitious quality of their works, the early novelists were claiming kinship with history and journalism. They felt that, in fact, they were writing news, but "news stripped of its reference to immediate public events"; they were writing "news of the ideology" of their nation. Thus, authorial disavowal in early English fiction is more than a literary convention; it demonstrates that these novelists saw themselves "as part of a news-synthesizing and disseminating system."

406. Dawson, William J. "The Fathers of English Fiction." *The Makers of English Fiction*. London and New York: Fleming H. Revell, 1905. Pp. 7-18.

Says that Defoe "stumbled upon" the art of successful prose fiction in *The Shortest Way with the Dissenters*. This work failed because Defoe's perfect imitation of the speaker precludes irony and hence destroys the satire, but this skill in imitation lies at the heart of such successful first-person narrative fictions as *Robinson Crusoe* and *A Journal of the Plague Year*. Defoe's attention to detail and apparent sincerity make his works highly realistic.

407. Dennis, John. *The Age of Pope (1700-1744)*. London: G. Bell and Sons, 1928. Originally published 1894.

Praises *Robinson Crusoe* as a fine book "for boys," but finds most of the rest of Defoe's fiction disgusting.

Defoe, a "base" individual, inspects "filth with a
microscope."

* Dobrée, Bonamy. *English Literature in the Early
Eighteenth Century, 1700-1740.* (See item 160.)

408. ———. "The Matter-of-Fact Novelist." *Listener*,
22 March 1951, pp. 468-69.

Defines Defoe's "creative imagination" as his ability
to "live" his scenes, to "become" his characters. This
ability, combined with his amazing capacity for accurate
observation and his use of factual material even in his
fiction makes him the master of verisimilitude.

409. Ernle, R.E.P. *The Light Reading of Our Ancestors:
Chapters in the Growth of the English Novel.* New
York: Brentano's, n.d.

Attributes Defoe's emergence as a novelist to his
awareness that a new literate class, demanding facts
and suspicious of the imagination, was forming. His
journalistic training and his Puritan background ad-
mirably suited him to supply the wants of this new
public.

410. Faller, Lincoln B. "In Contrast to Defoe: the Rev.
Paul Lorrain, Historian of Crime." *Huntington Library
Quarterly*, 40 (1976), 59-78.

Contrasts Defoe's portrayal of his fictional criminals
with Paul Lorrain's treatment of the real criminals
whose public hangings he described in more than forty
papers published the morning after the executions.
Lorrain took a severe and unsympathetic view of the
criminals whose deaths he witnessed whereas Defoe
pleaded necessity and never allowed his fictional
criminals to be executed,

411. Freedman, Richard. *The Novel.* New York: Newsweek
Books, 1975.

Withholds from Defoe the title of "father of the
modern novel" for several reasons: (1) novels strive
for a *sense* of reality, but Defoe pretends to the
literal truth; (2) Defoe's novels lack the unity associated with modern fiction; and (3) unlike modern
novelists, Defoe concentrates on vividly presenting
life's externals rather than attempting to portray his
characters' inner psychological and spiritual lives.

*   Giles, Edward L. "Shipwrecks and Desert Islands."
            (See item 533.)

412.   Goldknopf, David. *The Life of the Novel.* Chicago:
            University of Chicago Press, 1972.

            Develops three main themes: (1) "the contribution of
            a first-person narrator to the total sense of a novel";
            (2) the "socializing" of plot in the Victorian novel;
            (3) "the relationship between the novel and the objec-
            tive situation which it absorbs into art." Chapter
            Three, which helps develop the first of the above
            themes, is devoted to Defoe's narrative techniques.
            Because Defoe always uses the first-person narrative
            format, which directs our attention to the inner life
            of the speaker, and yet conveys his meaning through
            external action, he appears to be working at cross-
            purposes. Actually, however, this apparent conflict
            is less of a conflict than a subtle "counterpoint" in
            which the external nature of his narrative approach is
            balanced by the subjectivity of the pseudo-memoir
            format. Furthermore, this "subjectivity" is projected
            through the objective situation: the physical or social
            isolation of the main character.

            Review: (London) *Times Literary Supplement*, 9 March
            1973, p. 272.

*   Gondebeaud, Louis. *Le Roman "picaresque" anglais,*
            1650-1730. (See item 1285.)

413.   Hahn, H. George. "An Approach to Character Development
            in Defoe's Narrative Prose." *Philological Quarterly*,
            51 (1972), 845-58.

            Rejects the approach to Defoe's characters that sees
            them as subordinated to the genre--conduct books,
            spiritual autobiography, memoirs, etc.--which is assumed
            to have produced them. Defoe's characters are "organic"
            figures who gradually develop and mature and who are
            presented with complete credibility. In their presenta-
            tion there is a "three-phase pattern of character
            development": first, a pattern in which character
            dominates event; then, a pattern in which event dominates
            character; and finally in the major novels, a pattern
            of interplay between character and event. After ex-
            ploring these patterns, Hahn outlines "a paradigm ...
            for the typical hero's progress in a Defoe novel" as
            that hero moves from moral transgression to repentance.

414. Holliday, Carl. *English Fiction*. New York: Century, 1912.

Not read by the compiler, but listed by Payne, item 21.

* Johnson, Clifford R. *Plots and Characters in the Fiction of Eighteenth-Century English Authors*. (See item 212.)

415. Karl, Frederick R. "Daniel Defoe: The Politics of Necessity." *The Adversary Literature: The English Novel in the Eighteenth Century, A Study in Genre*. New York: Farrar, Straus and Giroux, 1975. Pp. 68-98.

Regards Defoe--like the other major eighteenth-century novelists--as a "subversive," undermining with his fiction the bourgeois values of his age. Robinson Crusoe, for example, seems to accept his father's values, but ultimately he rejects them by setting out on his own to "see the world." Moll Flanders also rejects the standards of behavior for her era when she refuses to accept her lower-class status and insists on asserting her "basic democratic rights." Defoe's prose style is suitable for his realistic effects but it is ineffective in differentiating among various states of feeling; an arrangement for room and board is treated stylistically no differently than a confrontation with death. Defoe's importance in the development of the novel cannot be overestimated; he gave form to his picaresque model; character to the picaro; embodiment to female aspirations; a realistic frame of reference to his stories; and a flexible, denotative prose style to fiction writers.

* ————. "Moll's Many-Colored Coat: Veil and Disguise in the Fiction of Defoe." (See item 761.)

416. Kettle, Arnold. "The 18th Century Novel in England." *Estudios sobre los géneros literarios, I: Grecia clásica e Inglaterra*. Eds. Javier Coy and Javier de Hoz. Salamanca: University de Salamanca, 1975. Pp. 149-60.

Assigns the rise of the novel to the 1688 English settlement from which a new England and a new Englishman emerged. Defoe's fiction "embodies both the perils and the power of the new bourgeois individualism." Based on the earlier picaresque tales, Defoe's novels differ from them in that his protagonists win over adversity through effecting "an endurable compromise." Defoe's

realism comes from the tension that exists in his fiction between what his protagonists want to be and what
the world forces them to become.

417.   ———. *An Introduction to the English Novel*. Vol. I.
        New York: Harper and Row, 1960. Originally published
        London: Hutchinson and Company, 1951.

        Places Defoe in the picaresque tradition because of
        "his anti-romantic, anti-feudal realism, his concern
        with the feel and texture of the life he conveys and
        his lack of pattern." He also achieves "utter verisimi-
        litude" by his insistence on minute detail.

418.   ———. "The Precursors of Defoe: Puritanism and the
        Rise of the Novel." *On the Novel: A Present for
        Walter Allen on His 60th Birthday from His Friends
        and Colleagues*. Ed. B.S. Benedikz. London: Dent,
        1971. Pp. 206-17.

        Contends that Puritanism at first prevented the growth
        of the realistic novel (fiction was bad because it was
        untrue) but eventually aided in its development through
        the influence of allegory and spiritual autobiography,
        both of which the Puritans approved. Defoe's fiction
        links the realistic picaresque tradition with the "moral
        tensions" of Puritan writing. Defoe's novels reflect
        the practical turn that Puritanism took as the Puritan
        middle class became more affluent and powerful.

419.   Kinkead-Weekes, Mark. "Defoe and Richardson--Novelists
        of the City." *Dryden to Johnson*. Ed. Roger Lonsdale.
        London: Barrie and Jenkins, 1970. Pp. 226-56.

        Surveys Defoe's life, emphasizing his Puritanism and
        social status; discusses his style ("highly selective")
        and his imagination; and then analyzes *Robinson Crusoe*
        and *Moll Flanders*. The former work gives us a "synoptic
        economic history of man" combined with an "archetypal
        vision of sinful man brought to regeneration by divine
        grace." In *Moll Flanders*, Defoe creates another
        archetype, that of Everywoman coping with a male-
        dominated economic society. Defoe's strength as a
        novelist lies in his ability to project himself into
        the imagined situations of his protagonists.

420.   Knight, Grant C. *The Novel in English*. New York:
        Richard R. Smith, 1931.

        Regards *The Apparition of Mrs. Veal* as the work in
        which Defoe polished the circumstantial method which he

used so successfully in his fiction. *Robinson Crusoe* is an allegory of Defoe's own struggles against ill-luck. *Moll Flanders* and *Roxana* almost establish the modern novel; all that they lack is a believable cause and effect pattern for their characters.

421. Leavis, Q.D. *Fiction and the Reading Public*. London: Chatto and Windus, 1965.

Judges Defoe to be no artist. All his ingenuity was directed toward passing off fiction as fact in order to cater to the tastes of a Puritan audience; his methods are "childishly cunning, transparent, and spasmodic."

422. Lovett, Robert M., and Helen S. Hughes. *The History of the Novel in England*. London: George G. Harrap, 1932.

Covers Defoe's fiction in a fairly standard survey, but concludes that his realistic method combined with his sensational material results in "bourgeois realism."

423. McBurney, William. "Mrs. Penelope Aubin and the Early Eighteenth-Century Novel." *Huntington Library Quarterly*, 20 (1957), 245-67.

Points out that novelist Penelope Aubin owed much of her literary success to her ability to fuse the methods and subjects of the popular Eliza Haywood with those of Defoe. She emphasizes slavery, shipwreck, piracy, catastrophe caused by disobeying one's parents, and necessity as a cause for sin just as did Defoe. She even imitates Defoe's title pages and prefaces and often borrows specific details from him.

*   McCullough, Bruce. "The Conquest of Realistic Incident." (See item 770.)

423A. Macey, Samuel L. *Money and the Novel: Mercenary Motivation in Defoe and His Immediate Successors*. Victoria, B.C.: Sono Nis Press, 1983.

Unseen by the compiler.

424. McKillop, Alan D. "Daniel Defoe." *The Early Masters of English Fiction*. Lawrence: University of Kansas Press, 1956. Pp. 1-46. Some of this material is reprinted in Kelly, item 38.

Regards Defoe's fiction as a development of his jour-nalism: his novels are ostensibly designed to improve morals or at least convey useful information; they do not purport to be entertainments; they are packed with supportive, realistic detail; and they are written in a plain, reportorial style. Defoe's protagonists show that the profit motive is natural but that it conflicts with accepted moral and religious standards; this reduction of life to acquisition and calculation results in the protagonists' spiritual impoverishment and constitutes the moral lesson in almost all the novels. The apparently unstudied simplicity of character presentation and the monotonous evenness of emphasis in reporting events from incest to the contents of a stolen bundle demonstrate a genuine artistic intent on Defoe's part.

425.   Manlove, C.N. *Literature and Reality, 1600-1800*. London: The Macmillan Press, 1978.

Regards Defoe's novels as stories about survival and "validates" this assessment by comparing them to John Wyndham's science fiction novels in which the same concern is paramount. Both the latter and Defoe's novels focus on whether or not the protagonist will survive, and they are episodic, linear narratives with "emasculated" moral values. In Defoe's work the moral point usually is lost because of his overwhelming desire to render life as it really is. Because of his emphasis on the actual, his novels have no art, structure, theme, or sense of language.

*   Merrett, Robert James. *Daniel Defoe's Moral and Rhetorical Ideas*. (See item 899.)

426.   ————. "Defoe's Presentation of Crime and Criminals: An Examination of His Social Philosophy." *Transactions of the Samuel Johnson Society of the Northwest*. Vol. 4. Ed. Robert H. Carnie. Calgary: Samuel Johnson Society of the Northwest, 1972. Pp. 68-85.

Defines Defoe's social philosophy in terms of his belief that in the sight of God all men are criminals because they cannot meet His absolute standards. Each individual's physical and mental weaknesses form a barrier to a proper moral perspective. Because of these weaknesses, the individual must work at rigidly controlling his passions so that the devil cannot tempt him. Defoe's fictions dramatize this philosophy: for example, in *Moll Flanders* Defoe relates the protagonist's excesses, vanity, and acquisitiveness to the power of the devil and to Moll's ignorance of human nature, and in *Robinson Crusoe* the hero's lack of moral insight and "unjustifiable wanderings exacerbate his original sin."

*   Moore, John Robert. *Daniel Defoe: Citizen of the Modern World.* (See item 255.)

427. ————. "Defoe and Scott." *Publications of the Modern Language Association*, 56 (1941), 710-35.

Discusses both Sir Walter Scott's influence on Defoe's reputation and Defoe's influence on Scott's fiction. Scott did more than any other person to elevate Defoe's literary reputation. And Scott himself was deeply influenced by Defoe; allusions and parallels to him abound throughout Scott's fiction and letters, and Defoe provided much source material--especially in his writings on pirates--for Scott. These two authors also resemble each other in the ways in which they have been undervalued by readers who generally are ignorant of their real skills as writers of fiction.

428. Morgan, Charlotte E. *Rise of the Novel of Manners: A Study of English Prose Fiction between 1600 and 1740.* New York: Columbia University Press, 1911.

Contends that Defoe's apprenticeship in journalism is reflected in his "opportune" subjects, catchy title-pages, sensational methods, colloquial style, abundant detail, and apparently disinterested narration. His novels do not derive from the picaresque tale but rather from actual criminal biographies. His criminal characters gain sympathy because they are the victims of circumstance, not happy in their evil ways but instead longing for a life of respectability.

429. Mylne, Vivienne. "Changing Attitudes Towards Truth in Fiction." *Renaissance and Modern Studies*, 7 (1963), 53-77.

Contends that many readers show a "preference for truth" which has affected the development of narrative fiction. In order to cater to this preference, many authors, like Defoe, blend fact and fiction and pass off pseudo-memoirs and pseudo-histories as authentic.

430. Neill, S. Diana. *A Short History of the English Novel.* Rev. ed. New York: Collier Books, 1964. Originally published 1951.

Presents a general survey of Defoe's fiction, empha-

sizing his appeal to the middle class and his journalistic style.

431.   Novak, Maximillian E. *Defoe and the Nature of Man.*
        London: Oxford University Press, 1963. A section is
        reprinted in Shinagel, item 28.

        Asks whether there is any standard of morality in
        Defoe's fiction, and if so, what relationship exists
        between it and his theology. The answer to these ques-
        tions is found in Defoe's allegiance to the laws of
        nature--"it is by this standard that almost all of
        Defoe's characters must be judged." The opening chapter
        surveys Defoe's didactic works in order to determine his
        views of natural law and human nature, and the following
        five chapters demonstrate how these ideas are manifested
        in *Robinson Crusoe*, *Moll Flanders*, *Colonel Jack*, and
        Roxana. These novels are not entirely successful in
        characterization because Defoe's "characters operate in
        a universe of unchanging natural law and natural
        morality" which makes them somewhat uniform in their
        psychology. Defoe is willing to sacrifice the realistic
        creation of character in order to draw a moral from
        natural law. Most critics fail to understand the moral
        nature of Defoe's fiction and its relationship to his
        methods of characterization because they are unaware of
        the importance of natural law in his work.

        Reviews: Jean Béranger, *Etudes Anglaises*, 18 (1965), 44-
        52; Arnold Kettle, *Modern Language Review*, 60 (1965),
        256-57; James W. Nichols, *Personalist*, 45 (1964),
        578-79; John Robert Moore, *Journal of English and
        Germanic Philology*, 63 (1964), 795-97; C.J.H. O'Brien,
        *Journal of the Australasian Universities Language and
        Literature Association*, No. 22 (1964), 305-07; Martin
        Price, *Philological Quarterly*, 43 (1964), 353-55;
        J.E.P. Thomson, *Southern Review* (Australia), 1 (1965),
        82-83; (London) *Times Literary Supplement*, 2 April
        1964, p. 274; and F. Wölcken, *Review of English
        Studies*, n.s. 16 (1965), 205-06.

432.   ————. "Defoe's Theory of Fiction." *Studies in Phil-
        ology*, 61 (1964), 650-58.

        Examines three aspects of Defoe's view of fiction:
        (1) his attitude toward the fiction of his era and his
        opinion of the audience of the time; (2) his theory of
        reality; and (3) his defense of fiction on moral grounds.
        Although Defoe never developed an adequate critical
        theory, he was aware of certain formal divisions between

history and fiction, and theoretically, at least, he objected to the blending of the two. He believed that in
order to find readers, the author must place his "moral"
in the context of entertaining but realistic adventures.
In his attitude toward reality, he was a disciple of
Locke. Defoe enlisted realism in the service of morality;
his realistic method was designed to more effectively
convey his moral intention to his readers--and all of
his fictions were written with a moral aim.

433.   ————. *Economics and the Fiction of Daniel Defoe.*
University of California English Studies, 24. Los
Angeles: University of California Press, 1962. Pp.
32-48 are reprinted in Byrd, item 132, and pp. 49-50,
53-60, and 62-66 are reprinted in Ellis, item 521.

Explicates Defoe's fiction in the light of his awareness of economics as a science. Defoe held to the older
mercantile theories and not the newer, evolving beliefs
in capitalist expansion and invention; these conservative views are embodied in *Robinson Crusoe*, which attacks
laissez faire and economic individualism. Novak contends
that the portrait of Crusoe as "economic man" is an un-
satisfactory abstraction and that he should be seen as
"a shrewd merchant, a skilled craftsman, a tough-minded
colonizer," but also as a wanderer, a typical figure
from an age of exploration. However, Defoe's wanderers
are not the rogues of the picaresque tradition; Defoe
transforms the antiheroic picaro into the realistic hero
and focuses on his social problems, thus originating the
social novel. His awareness of his own society also is
seen by the analogies he develops between trade and
piracy in his piratical works and *Captain Singleton*.
Defoe's constant concern with business, economics, and
trade is reflected in *Roxana* in which the protagonist
serves as a focus for the author's attack on greed and
the luxuries of the rich; Roxana herself is condemned
because she is an economic parasite. Moll Flanders, on
the other hand, is not punished, because as a colonist
she works hard and contributes to the wealth of England.

Reviews: Jean Béranger, *Etudes Anglaises*, 15 (1962), 391-
92; Arnold Kettle, *Modern Language Review*, 58 (1963),
244-45; Alan D. McKillop, *Philological Quarterly*, 42
(1963), 340-42; Michael F. Shugrue, *College English*,
23 (1962), 71; Michael F. Shugrue, *Journal of English
and Germanic Philology*, 62 (1963), 403-05; (London)
Times Literary Supplement, 8 February 1963, p. 94;
F. Wölcken, *Review of English Studies*, n.s. 15 (1964),
89-91.

434. ———. "The Extended Moment: Time, Dream, History, and
      Perspective in Eighteenth-Century Fiction." *Probability,*
      Time, and Space in Eighteenth-Century Literature. Ed.
      Paula Backscheider. New York: AMS, 1979. Pp. 141-66.

      Suggests that Defoe prefigures certain narrative tech-
      niques generally associated with the Gothic novel. For
      example, Defoe is able to focus on an object and expand
      "the time experience of a work of fiction," which is one
      of his contributions to realism. He also uses, in both
      his novels and his travel pieces, sublime scenes. And
      finally, Defoe employs dreams and visions to convey
      important messages in highly dramatic moments that exist
      outside of time.

435. ———. "Fiction and Society in the Early Eighteenth
      Century." *England in the Restoration and Early*
      Eighteenth Century: Essays on Culture and Society.
      Ed. H.T. Swedenberg, Jr. Berkeley: University of
      California Press, 1972. Pp. 51-70.

      Makes frequent references to Defoe in this essay,
      which is designed as a correction to Watt and others
      who offer narrow or simplistic reasons for the emergence
      of the so-called "modern novel." Novak briefly explores
      the influence of social events on writers of fiction and
      notes that Defoe rendered "in fictional form the same
      ideas that he thought worthy of a treatise." Unlike
      most commentators on Defoe's "uniqueness" as a writer
      of fiction, Novak finds Defoe's originality in his
      "psychological realism."

436. ———. "Freedom, Libertinism, and the Picaresque."
      Racism in the Eighteenth Century. Ed. Harold E. Pag-
      liaro. Cleveland: Case Western Reserve Press, 1973.
      Pp. 35-48.

      Disagress with those "prescriptive theories of
      picaresque fiction" which regard Lesage, Defoe, and
      Smollett as unpicaresque. Sexual liberation and freedom
      of movement in space are the defining characteristics of
      the picaresque, and *Moll Flanders* and *Roxana* possess
      these features.

437. ———. "The Problem of Necessity in Defoe's Fiction."
      Philological Quarterly, 40 (1961), 513-24.

      Defines "necessity" as "a state of desperation,
      usually associated with starvation and destitution, in
      which the victim is forced to choose between certain

death and a life prolonged only by violating the laws of society, religion, or personal honor." Several of Defoe's main characters--especially Moll Flanders, Colonel Jack, and Roxana--plead their "necessity" in order to excuse their crimes. Defoe is sympathetic to such a plea, and in his *Review* he argued against rigid principles of honesty as being incompatible with the realities of human nature. Because his characters do not fall into necessity through vice, he does not see them as guilty of their original crimes which are "committed in accordance with the laws of nature." See Starr, item 452.

*   Oda, Minoru. "Allegory and History: A Study of Daniel Defoe's *Roxana*." (See item 879.)

438. Paulson, Ronald. *Satire and the Novel in Eighteenth-Century England*. New Haven: Yale University Press, 1967.

Sees Defoe as an important figure in the evolution of that kind of novel which presents psychological reality and complexity without trying to analyze it. Defoe also is important in the secularization of spiritual autobiography. This secularization, however, produces difficulties because the pious commentary which is a holdover from spiritual autobiography usually does not fit the new criminal or economic situation. The same kind of tensions are produced by the survival of satiric conventions in non-satiric works; thus in the introduction to *Roxana*, Defoe says he describes vice only to expose it, and in *Moll Flanders*, he treats marriage satirically.

439. Phelps, William Lyon. *The Advance of the English Novel*. New York: Dodd, Mead, 1916.

Regards Defoe as the first true novelist and focuses almost exclusively on his realistic techniques. Phelps praises *Crusoe* as a great book for boys and believes that *Journal of the Plague Year* is history not fiction.

440. Pollin, Burton R. "Poe and Daniel Defoe: A Significant Relationship." *Topic*, 16 (1976), 3-22.

Discovers more than a dozen references to Defoe in Poe's letters and published works. Defoe's narrative methods helped Poe "codify some of his ideas about the necessary identification of an author with the creatures of his imagination." Poe believed that Defoe's contribu-

tion to fiction was his realism directed toward the
simulation of true reports.

441. Pritchett, V.S. "Defoe." *The English Novelists: A
      Survey of the Novel by Twenty Contemporary Novelists.*
      Ed. Derek Verschoyle. London: Chatto and Windus,
      1936. Pp. 51-65.

      Generalizes about Defoe as novelist. Defoe, devious
      in his personal life, was "the greatest liar in English
      letters"; his "gusto" for lying adds to the realism of
      his fiction, as does his genius in the use of detail.
      His characters, like him, are pragmatic moralists who
      do not sin out of viciousness but because they are
      victims of circumstance.

442. Proper, Coenraad Bart Anne. *Social Elements in English
      Prose Fiction Between 1700 and 1832.* Amsterdam: H.J.
      Paris, 1929.

      Contends that the novel with a moral purpose, like
      Defoe's works, paved the way for the novel with a social
      purpose. Defoe's concern over social issues is seen
      particularly clearly in the *Essay on Projects* and in
      such novels as *Moll Flanders*. There is a superficial
      survey of the fiction which emphasizes the social cir-
      cumstances of Defoe's protagonists.

443. Pugh, Charles W. "Defoe's Repentance Theme." *Southern
      University Bulletin*, 46 (1959), 57-64.

      The compiler was unable to locate this article, listed
      in Payne's checklist, item 21.

444. Raleigh, Walter. *The English Novel, Being a Short
      Sketch of Its History from the Earliest Times to the
      Appearance of "Waverley."* New York: Charles Scribner's
      Sons, 1909. Originally published London, 1894.

      Believes that Defoe learned his method of realistic
      narrative from his experience writing *The Shortest Way*
      and *Mrs. Veal*, both of which skillfully give the im-
      pression of artlessness. The only novel discussed in
      detail is *Robinson Crusoe* which "typifies the spirit of
      the Anglo-Saxon race."

445. Richetti, John J. *Defoe's Narratives: Situations and
      Structures.* Oxford: Clarendon Press, 1975.

      Rejects as incomplete the two major views of Defoe as
      novelist; he is neither "a proto-realistic author" treat-

ing individualism nor a profoundly religious writer dealing with the "anguish of surviving in a secular world with a religious ideology." Defoe's fiction actually explores "the tangled relationships between the free self and the social and ideological realities which that self seems to require." His books possess "an imaginative unity" and they contain "energies" which are lacking in more sophisticated fiction. This study attempts "to locate these energies and to find the sources of that imaginative unity" through a close reading of the major narratives: *Robinson Crusoe*, *Captain Singleton*, *Moll Flanders*, *Colonel Jack*, *Roxana*, and *A Journal of the Plague Year*.

Reviews: Paul Gabriel Boucé, *Etudes Anglaises*, 29 (1976), 95-97; Leopold Damrosch, Jr., *The Eighteenth Century: A Current Bibliography*, n.s. 1 (1978), 271-73; Robert Alan Donovan, *Journal of English and Germanic Philology*, 75 (1976), 596-98; Frederick R. Karl, *Studies in the Novel*, 8 (1976), 470-73; Clive Probyn, (London) *Times Literary Supplement*, 23 January 1976, p. 88; Pat Rogers, *British Society for Eighteenth-Century Studies Newsletter*, 8 (1976), 6-7.

446. ————. *Popular Fiction Before Richardson*. Oxford: Clarendon Press, 1969.

Makes frequent and detailed comments on Defoe's work in an attempt to define "the idealogical matrix" out of which Richardson and Fielding emerge. At the heart of this "matrix" lies the conflict between the religious and the secular which fascinated the reader of early eighteenth-century fiction. Rogue stories, pirate tales, and travel narratives all provide appropriate contexts for the presentation of such a conflict. Defoe's *Captain Singleton*, for instance, presents "a compromise between the compelling egoism of the pirate-adventurer and the self-effacement and submission of the repentant sinner." Likewise, Crusoe on his island is a paradigm of economic man and at the same time "a pious *exemplum*." *Robinson Crusoe* exploits to the fullest "the interplay of religious-passive and secular-active values," and Crusoe's integration of these two sets of values makes him "a secular saint."

447. Robert, Marthe. *Origins of the Novel*. Translated by Sacha Rabinovitch. Bloomington: Indiana University, 1980.

Reviewed by Novak, item 19, but not seen by the compiler.

448. Rogers, Pat. *The Augustan Vision*. New York: Barnes
      and Noble and London: Weidenfeld and Nicolson, 1974.

      Presents a general survey of Defoe's life and novels.
      Robinson Crusoe is his greatest work because its hero
      is "absolutely convincing psychologically" and the
      routine of his life on the island melds ideally with
      Defoe's factual and unvaried method; *A Journal of the
      Plague Year* is a private vision of disaster, admirably
      told, rather than a piece of faked reporting; *Moll
      Flanders* is popular because of its vibrant heroine; the
      other novels are weaker pieces.

449. Saintsbury, George. *The English Novel*. London: Dent
      and New York: Dutton, 1913.

      Ranks Defoe among the greatest novelists but says that
      the secret of his greatness is a mystery because in
      plot, character, description, and dialogue he is not
      outstanding. Perhaps his secret is his ability to
      serve up the fictitious as absolutely real.

450. [Schorer, Mark.] "Surprising Adventures." (London)
      Times Literary Supplement, 15 September 1950, p. 580.

      Presents a brief biography of Defoe followed by re-
      marks on his novelistic skills and influences, particu-
      larly emphasizing the *Journal of the Plague Year* and *Moll
      Flanders*. The former's realism caused it to be regarded
      for years as a factual account, and it surpasses Poe in
      the creation of atmosphere; the latter is remarkable for
      the reality of its title character. Defoe is the first
      exponent of the novel of action.

*   Scrimgeour, Gary J. "The Problem of Realism in Defoe's
      Captain Singleton." (See item 706.)

*   Shinagel, Michael. *Daniel Defoe and Middle-Class
      Gentility*. (See item 332.)

450A. Sill, Geoffrey M. *Defoe and the Idea of Fiction*. Newark,
      Del.: University of Delaware Press, 1983.

      Not seen by the compiler but the book is advertised
      as linking Defoe's fiction to European political events
      from 1713 to 1717.

*   Singleton, Robert R. "English Criminal Biography, 1651-
      1722." (See item 838.)

451. Skilton, David. "Defoe and the Augustan Age." *The*
      English Novel: Defoe to the Victorians. London: David
      and Charles and New York: Harper and Row, 1977. Pp.
      7-18.

      Contrasts Defoe's life and attitudes with those of the
      Augustans as typified by Swift and Pope. Augustanism
      was an aristocratic myth, but Defoe represented the
      common man and celebrated the "middle station" of life.
      Unlike the Augustans who depicted the city--and by
      extension the world--symbolically, Defoe used circum-
      stantial detail to provide fictions which also were
      realistic social documents. Finally, whereas the Augus-
      tans believed character was determined by the laws of an
      immutable "human nature," Defoe saw character as the
      product of environment.

*   Spearman, Diana. *The Novel and Society.* (See item 342.)

452. Starr, George A. *Defoe and Casuistry.* Princeton:
      Princeton University Press, 1971. Sections of this
      work appear in Elliott (item 737) as "Moll Flanders"
      and in Kelly (item 38) as "Defoe and Casuistry: Moll
      Flanders."

      Examines "the influence of traditional casuistry on
      the subject matter, narrative technique, and ethical
      outlook of Defoe's writings." Much of Defoe's literary
      material in his periodicals, pamphlets, and novels is
      derived from traditional cases of conscience used in
      casuistical divinity. The use of such material tends
      to fragment the novels into a series of discrete epi-
      sodes. Many episodes are organized around traditional
      casuistical ways of posing and resolving moral dilemmas,
      constantly outlining motives and sanctions, choices and
      circumstances, precedents and hypothetical analogues.
      Such a procedure interferes with a book's overall de-
      sign, but it offers parallels among episodes and
      gives them a fullness and complexity lacking in earlier
      fiction. This complexity accounts for some of the
      critical confusion over Defoe's ethical viewpoint and
      its irony or lack thereof. He has recourse to natural
      law, divine law, positive law, and expediency depending
      on the occasion. The effect of refusing consistent
      allegiance to any one of these sanctions is an apparent
      moral confusion compounded by a rhetoric designed to
      make the reader sympathize with characters whose actions
      at times can be viewed as morally reprehensible. This
      study explores these elements in *A Journal of the Plague*

Year, *Colonel Jack*, *Moll Flanders*, and *Roxana*. Also see
Novak, item 437.

Reviews: F. Bastian, *Review of English Studies*, 23 (1972),
500-02; Martin C. Battestin, *Journal of English and
Germanic Philology*, 71 (1972), 140-42; J.
Donald Crow-
ley, *Studies in the Novel*, 4 (1972), 124-28; Hans-
Göran Ekman, *Samlaren*, 93 (1973), 261-62; Maximillian
E. Novak, *Modern Language Quarterly*, 33 (1972), 456-59;
Manuel Schonhorn, *Philological Quarterly*, 51 (1972),
664-65; Keith Stewart, *English Language Notes*, 9 (1972),
306-10; David W. Tarbet, *Eighteenth-Century Studies*, 6
(1972), 274-77.

453.   ————. *Defoe and Spiritual Autobiography*. Princeton:
Princeton University Press, 1965. Reprinted New York:
Gordian Press, 1971. Sections reprinted in Byrd, item
132; Ellis, item 521; Hunter, item 41; and Shinagel,
item 28.

Sketches the tradition of spiritual autobiography in
order to show its influence on *Robinson Crusoe*, *Moll
Flanders*, and *Roxana*. In such biography, the individual
must "note every symptom of [spiritual] progress or re-
lapse" through constant self-evaluation in order to
learn the error of his ways and improve himself. Defoe
blends this spiritual instruction with his narrative
skills to create unique fictions. *Robinson Crusoe* follows the plan of the spiritual autobiography: Crusoe
"sins" by flouting family, social, and divine order when
he refuses "to follow the calling chosen for him by his
father" and runs away, but he undergoes a spiritual
transformation which is clearly and precisely delineated.
Moll's fall is due first to her vanity, analogous to
Crusoe's rebelliousness, and she undergoes the same
kind of spiritual development as does Crusoe, characterized by hardening, repentance, hardening, repentance--
relapses interspersed with a gradually expanding spiritual awakening until true repentance is achieved. *Roxana*
departs from the conventional spiritual autobiography,
but the *norms* of the latter help to illuminate the
book's meaning. Although "Roxana's spiritual predicament is very similar to Moll's," she remains impenitent
"with the distinct prospect of damnation." This de-
parture "from the conventional form of spiritual autobiography" makes the book a tragedy.

Reviews: W.B. Carnochan, *Modern Language Quarterly*, 17
(1966), 224-26; William Cobau, *Seventeenth-Century
News*, 24 (1966), 14; William H. Halewood, *Modern*

Philology, 66 (1969), 274-78; Florence Higham, Church
Quarterly Review (October 1966), 531-32; Johnsonian
Newsletter, 25 (1965), 6; Maximillian E.
Novak, Journal
of English and Germanic Philology, 66 (1967), 153-55;
Rachel Trickett, Essays in Criticism, 16 (1966), 336-
40; (London) Times Literary Supplement, 18 August 1966,
p. 738; John Preston, Review of English Studies, n.s.
18 (1967), 337-39; Aubrey Williams, Yale Review, 55
(1966), 312-15.

454.   Steeves, Harrison. "Man on an Island." Before Jane
Austen: The Shaping of the English Novel in the
Eighteenth-Century. New York: Holt, Rinehart, and
Winston, 1965. Pp. 22-42.

Calls Defoe "the father of modern realism." His
realism hinges on his method of concealing conscious
techniques and giving his works a sense of artlessness.
Defoe's most serious limitations are his shallow presentation of the emotional life and his adherence to the
picaresque, which does not permit a sufficiently re-
flective view of society.

455.   Štěpaník, Karel. "Fact and Fiction in the Novels of
Daniel Defoe." Philologica Pragensia, 3 (1960),
227-40.

Contends that the autobiographical nature of Defoe's
fiction--he used all of his experience and his learning
in his novels--gives it a realistic aura. Because Defoe
mixed historical truth with fiction, the factual reliability of the specific details of the novels is ques-
tionable; however, his fiction does depict "the general
social character of the time" and so is an invaluable
aid to the historian.

456.   Stevenson, Lionel. The English Novel: A Panorama. Boston: Houghton Mifflin, 1960.

Believes Defoe's particular genius to be his "practical imagination," his "ability to develop existing
facts in original directions without sacrificing
plausibility." His realism is a result of his use of
unselected details: "an inventory of furniture or the
menu of a meal is recorded as fully as a life-and-death
crisis." Defoe is not a major novelist because he only
chronicles life and does not analyze it.

457.   Swallow, Alan. "Defoe and the Art of Fiction." Western Humanities Review, 4 (1950), 129-36. Reprinted

in *The University of Denver Quarterly*, 2 (1967), 82-
92.

Finds four elements of Defoe's fiction significant in
launching the novel form: (1) he made narrative thematic;
(2) he presented a middle-class view of man as an isolated, individual conscience whose most important problem
is economic; (3) he used moral choice as the dramatic
tension in fiction; and (4) he was committed to fiction
as an imaginative act.

458.   Uphaus, Robert W.   "Defoe, Deliverance, and Dissimula-
       tion." *The Impossible Observer: Reason and the Reader
       in 18th-Century Prose.* Lexington: University of
       Kentucky Press, 1979. Pp. 46-70.

       Defines Defoe's methods of characterization as "dis-
       simulation." Defoe does not mimetically represent his
       characters; rather, he imaginatively becomes them.
       This technique of "dissimulation" breaks down the dis-
       tance between reader and character in two ways: (1) by
       projecting the author totally into a character in order
       to authenticate the way that figure thinks and acts,
       and (2) by luring the reader into participating in the
       way a particular character's mind works.

       Review: Serge Soupel, *Etudes Anglaises*, 35 (1982), 88-89.

459.   Utter, Robert P.   "On the Alleged Tediousness of Defoe
       and Richardson." *University of California Chronicle*,
       25 (1923), 175-93.

       Disagrees with those critics who say Defoe's accumula-
       tion of details is boring. The use of detail is the
       essence of Defoe's realistic technique and the reason
       that such novels as *Robinson Crusoe* and *Captain Singleton*
       have a romantic appeal to young people.

460.   Wagenknecht, Edward.   *Cavalcade of the English Novel.*
       New York: Henry Holt, 1943.

       Finds in *A True Relation of the Apparition of One Mrs.
       Veal* all of "Defoe's salient qualities" in miniature;
       these qualities include verisimilitude, corroborative
       and irrelevant detail, and minute particularity. Defoe's
       positive qualities are undermined by his inaccuracies
       and his failure to create individual characters; his
       incessant moralizing also is a negative characteristic
       attributed to the "Puritanism-gone-to-seed that he knew
       as a religion." Defoe pointed the way to the modern
       novel.

461. Walton, James. "The Romance of Gentility: Defoe's
     Heroes and Heroines." *Literary Monographs*. Vol. 4.
     Ed. Eric Rothstein. Madison: University of Wisconsin
     Press, 1971. Pp. 91-135.

     Begins with an investigation of the link of myth,
     romance, and the novel, particularly the old "child
     exile" theme which is adapted to the new novel form.
     In Defoe this theme is modified by the rogue biography--
     a "debased" form of romance which greatly influenced
     him--so that his novels use the concept of gentility as
     a middle-class analogue to noble birth. Defoe's heroes
     and heroines define themselves subjectively as royalty
     in rogue's disguise, but they cannot escape objective
     definition as real rogues who must disguise themselves
     as royalty in order to pass themselves off as noble.
     Captain Singleton, Colonel Jack, and Moll Flanders all
     fit this pattern, and Roxana represents a modification
     of it.

     Review: C.J. Rawson, *Notes and Queries*, n.s. 20 (1973),
     237.

462. Watson, George. *The Story of the Novel*. London: Mac-
     millan, 1979.

     Comments briefly throughout on Defoe's first-person
     narrative, emphasizing its source in the autobiography
     and diary forms.

463. Watt, Ian. "Defoe and Richardson on Homer: A Study of
     the Relation of Novel and Epic in the Early Eighteenth
     Century." *Review of English Studies*, n.s. 3 (1952),
     325-40.

     Uses commentary by Defoe and Richardson to demonstrate
     the antipathy between novel and epic in the early
     eighteenth century. The general contempt of Defoe for
     most things classical is illustrated by his *Applebee's
     Journal* article of 31 July 1725 in which he depicts Homer
     as a commercial ballad-monger and plagiarist. In a later
     work, the *Essay upon Literature* (1726), Defoe says that
     historical truth is corrupted by the ancients because
     they "adorn" truth instead of recording it accurately.
     Elsewhere, Defoe objected to the ancients on the grounds
     that they were foolishly superstitious.

464. ———. "Defoe as Novelist." *From Dryden to Johnson*.
     The Pelican Guide to English Literature, Vol. 4.
     Ed. Boris Ford. Baltimore: Penguin, 1957. Pp. 203-
     16.

Concentrates on *Robinson Crusoe* and *Moll Flanders*.
The former, employing an unprecedented realism, is a
travel story used for the purpose of religion and
morality; it also, inadvertently, creates in its hero
a symbol of economic man. The latter is his best novel
but is marred by its ethical disunity--its purported
moral does not tally with the plot--and by the lack of
any psychological development in its heroine. Defoe's
forte as a novelist is the brilliant episode.

465.   ------. "The Naming of Characters in Defoe, Richardson,
        and Fielding." *Review of English Studies*, 25 (1949),
        322-38.

        Explains Defoe's practice of naming characters. Minor
        figures are referred to by a description of their roles--
        "the Quaker," "the honest Dutch merchant," etc.--because
        of the severely functional view the protagonists take
        of others. The protagonists themselves go by nicknames
        (Colonel Jack), pseudonyms (Moll Flanders), and aliases
        (Roxana) because they move in societies in which it is
        dangerous to reveal one's identity completely and be-
        cause they avoid ceremonies of religion and law from
        which personal names derive their sanctions.

466.   ------. "Serious Reflections on *The Rise of the Novel*."
        Novel, 1 (1968), 205-18.

        Traces the genesis of the *Rise of the Novel*, responds
        to the book's critics, and explores the ways the author's
        "execution fell short of [his] intentions." Scattered
        references are made to Defoe. See Watt's *Rise of the
        Novel* at item 688.

467.   Wehrung, Maurice. "The Literature of Privateering and
        Piracy as a Source of the Defoean Hero's Personality."
        *Tradition et innovation: Littérature et paralittéra-
        ture*. Paris: Didier, 1975. Pp. 159-92.

        Unreviewed by the compiler.

468.   West, Alick. *The Mountain in the Sunlight: Studies in
        Conflict and Unity*. London: Lawrence and Wishart,
        1958.

        Takes a Marxist approach to Defoe's fiction. His
        novels are given unity and their realism is given depth
        by the conflict between "money relations and human
        relations" in them. This conflict is embodied in
        Robinson Crusoe who at first rejects "the middle station

of life" but who eventually becomes a bourgeois ex-
ploiter himself. Moll Flanders is like Crusoe: she
typifies the insatiable appetite of the bourgeoisie
for money but she also exemplifies the wretchedness
that money causes. This theme is intensified in *Roxana*.
Defoe reveals throughout his fiction how the bourgeois
exploit the poor and control the state through terror.
Review: (London) *Times Literary Supplement*, 21 November
1958, p. 674.

469. Williams, Harold. *Two Centuries of the English Novel*.
London: John Murray, 1911.

Lauds the versatility and energy of Defoe's fiction.
Although Defoe "scarcely knew what art was," he still
created it through his innate ability to "fix con-
vincingly lifelike pictures in our mind." The one
great defect in his novels is the absence of pathos.

470. Williams, Ioan. "Between Truth and Lie: the Problematic
Case of Defoe." *The Idea of Novel in Europe, 1600-
1800*. London: Macmillan, 1978. Pp. 146-54.

Finds the irony in Defoe's fiction a result of "a
deep-rooted confusion in his mind" which was the result
of the clash between his religious principles and his
artistic impulses. His fictions demolish his own moral
and religious convictions because his attitudes are ir-
reconcilable with the actual conditions of life in his
day.

471. Wyatt, Edith. "The Author of *Robinson Crusoe*." *North
American Review*, 198 (1913), 87-99.

Presents a brief biography and a short, descriptive
survey of the major fiction, concluding that the
"clear-thinking ingenuity throughout Defoe's work is
indescribably beautiful."

472. Zimmerman, Everett. *Defoe and the Novel*. Berkeley and
Los Angeles: University of California Press, 1975.

Treats Defoe's major fiction: *Robinson Crusoe, Captain
Singleton, Moll Flanders, A Journal of the Plague Year,
Colonel Jack*, and *Roxana*. In the course of writing
these works, Defoe consistently improved his technical
skills, eventually overcoming the problems he had in
presenting "a seemingly autonomous central character
while at the same time marking his judgments of the

character." *Robinson Crusoe* is a circular novel, ending
where it began as far as Crusoe's character is concerned; Crusoe's "attempts to get out of himself," to
discover the spiritual, end in rage, despair, and dis-
order. Because Defoe is unable to order the many dis-
parities of *Captain Singleton* without fragmenting his
narrator, he is unable to convince the reader of that
narrator's "psychological validity," and thus the novel
fails. Both *Crusoe* and *Singleton* have double perspectives—those of the narrator as he is and of the person
he once was—but *Moll Flanders* has a third perspective,
the editor's; thus, "Defoe prepares the reader to understand more than Moll does." However, there are unresolved contradictions in these perspectives which
identify Defoe himself with his narrator. *A Journal
of the Plague Year* differs from the earlier fiction in
that it describes an historical event and does not
create a social world. The success of the novel lies
in the psychologically complex and interesting central
character whose attempts to morally instruct the reader
demonstrate his own psychological turmoil. With increasing clarity, Defoe displayed his characters' self-
deceptions, and the title character of *Colonel Jack* is
the most self-possessed of Defoe's narrators in his
confidence in the linguistic subterfuge he uses to
"conceal appalling truths." *Roxana* is the logical conclusion to Defoe's fictional exploration of "a de-
spiritualized world" because, unlike the earlier narrators who engage in "obsessive behavior that is rational-
ized but not explained," Roxana understands the moral
implications of her actions but persists in them even
when she knows they are evil and repulsive to her.
Zimmerman notes that each of Defoe's narrators has a
dominant metaphor that becomes the motif of the work:
Crusoe's is travel; Singleton's, trade; Moll's, gold;
Colonel Jack's, gentility; H.F.'s, the plague; and
Roxana's, the loss of sensation. "Each character's
emotional stability is dependent upon his preventing
his metaphor from collapsing." Also see Richetti,
item 445.

Reviews: Leopold Damrosch, Jr., *The Eighteenth-Century:
A Current Bibliography*, n.s. 1 (for 1975), New York:
AMS Press, 1978, 271-73; Frederick R. Karl, *Studies
in the Novel*, 8 (1976), 468-73; Robert James Merrett,
Eighteenth-Century Studies, 10 (1976-77), 264-66;
Maximillian E. Novak, *Modern Language Quarterly*, 38
(1977), 194-96; Sam Pickering, *Sewanee Review*, 85

(1977), 651-60; Clive Probyn, (London) *Times Literary Supplement*, 23 January 1976, p. 88.

B. *Robinson Crusoe* (1719)

*   A., T.P.   "German Translations of Defoe."   (See item 100.)

*   Adolph, Robert.   *The Rise of Modern Prose Style*.   (See item 101.)

473.   Alkon, Paul K.   "The Odds Against Friday: Defoe, Bayes, and Inverse Probability."   *Probability, Time, and Space in Eighteenth-Century Literature*.   Ed. Paula R. Backscheider.   New York: AMS, 1979.   Pp. 29-61.

Discusses probability theory, particularly de Moivre's *The Doctrine Chances*, in order to "explore Defoe's resort to the language of probability" in *Robinson Crusoe*. Crusoe gives the odds of certain events transpiring, but the numbers used are "mathematically incoherent" and are chosen by Defoe for rhetorical effect only. Defoe also "uses non-mathematical statements about probability to show how seldom probability is the best guide to future conduct." Instead, Defoe suggests, man should rely on his Christian faith in God's mercy.

474,   Anderson, J.L.   "Robinson Crusoe."   *Notes and Queries*, Ninth Series, 10 (1902), 286.

Inserts an obituary notice from the *Scotsman* of September 20, 1902, which records the death of James Gillies, the last descendant of Alexander Selkirk.

475.   Andreae, G.   *The Dawn of Juvenile Literature in England*.   Amsterdam: H.J. Paris, 1925.

Mentions that because of its detailed adventures, *Robinson Crusoe* started a new line of children's literature, inspiring such works as *The Swiss Family Robinson*.

*   Angelino, Paolo.   *Il problema etico-religioso nel "Robinson Crusoe."*   (See item 1212.)

*   Arnold, Heinz Ludwig.   "Robinson Crusoe: Notizen zu einer Illusion."   (See item 1213.)

476. Armstrong, T. Percy. "Robinson Crusoe's Island." *Notes and Queries*, Twelfth Series, 8 (1921), 415.

     Responds to "Constant Reader," item 502, to indicate that Defoe invented Crusoe's island but that it is confused with Juan Fernandez because the latter is where Selkirk, Defoe's source for Crusoe, was marooned. See Freeman, item 529; Hubbard, item 561; Lynn, item 594; and Wainwright, item 683.

477. Askham, F.W. "Daniel Defoe, 'Robinson Crusoe,' and Brixham." *Devon and Cornwall Notes and Queries*, 15 (1928), 76-77.

     Discovers a Richard Cruso in Brixham in 1724 and suggests that he is the source of Robinson Crusoe's name.

478. Ayers, Robert W. "*Robinson Crusoe*: 'Allusive Allegorick History.'" *Publications of the Modern Language Association*, 82 (1967), 399-407.

     Proposes a reading of *Robinson Crusoe* which takes it to be exactly what Crusoe says it is, an "allusive, allegorick History," that is, a work which operates both on a literal and a symbolic level. A perception of the biblical allusions employed by Defoe and a knowledge of traditional Puritan interpretations of the passages from which the allusions are drawn leads to a fuller understanding of the novel's treatment of a spiritual experience and reveals a conscious artistry usually denied to Defoe.

479. B., C.W. "The Genesis of Robinson Crusoe." (London) *Times Literary Supplement*, 13 May 1939, p. 282.

     Suggests that perhaps the desert island episodes in *Robinson Crusoe* were not part of Defoe's original plan and that he "invented as he went on."

*   Baer, Joel H. "'The Complicated Plot of Piracy': Aspects of English Criminal Law and the Image of the Pirate in Defoe." (See item 1036.)

480. Baine, Rodney M. "Blake and Defoe." *Blake Newsletter*, 6 (1972), 51-53.

     Identifies three Blake illustrations for *Robinson Crusoe*, including one never before properly identified. These drawings show that Blake understood Defoe's central thesis--"God's providential care of Crusoe."

*   ————. "Defoe and the Angels." (See item 110.)

*   Baker, J.N.L. "The Geography of Daniel Defoe." (See
          item 1075.)

*   Bantas, Andrei. [Introduction to] Robinson Crusoe by
          Daniel Defoe. (See item 1215.)

481.   Beattie, James. "On Fable and Romance." Eighteenth-
          Century Critical Essays. Vol. II. Ed. Scott Elledge.
          Ithaca, N.Y.: Cornell University Press, 1961. Pp.
          924-26.

          Uses Robinson Crusoe to define "serious romances" of
          the type which present a chronological account of a
          person's life from birth to the end of his adventures.
          Beattie praises Crusoe for its piety and for its por-
          trayal of the blessings of labor.

*   Beck, Richard. "Höfunder Robinson Crusoes." (See
          item 1217.)

482.   Benjamin, Edwin B. "Symbolic Elements in Robinson
          Crusoe." Philological Quarterly, 30 (1951), 206-11.
          Reprinted in Ellis, item 521.

          Rejects Robinson Crusoe as an allegory of Defoe's life
          in favor of the view that the book is a symbolic account
          of a spiritual experience. The story really tells of
          Crusoe's conversion, and his deliverance from the island
          symbolizes "his deliverance from sin through the mercy
          of God." Even the geography of the island is conceived
          of in moral terms, and many of Crusoe's experiences have
          biblical analogues.

483.   Berne, Eric. "The Psychological Structure of Space with
          Some Remarks on Robinson Crusoe." Psychoanalytic
          Quarterly, 25 (1956), 549-67. Reprinted in Ellis,
          item 561, and Shinagel, item 28.

          Argues that "interest in space" has three varieties
          (the exploration of space, the measurement of space, and
          the utilization of space) which correspond to three sub-
          limations (oral, anal, and phallic). Robinson Crusoe
          is based on an oral fixation of the author: "He who
          eats shall be eaten." The entire story of the novel is
          an elaboration of this theme.

484.   Bhattacharya, Debipada. "Don Quixote, Robinson Crusoe,

and Rabindranath Tagore." *Revista de Istoria si
Teorie Literară*, 29 (1980), 441-46.

Records a number of references to *Robinson Crusoe* by
Indian author Rabindranath Tagore and asserts that the
novel exerted a great influence on the development of
Tagore's attitudes toward adventure and nature.

485.   "Bibliographical Terms." (London) *Times Literary Supple-
       ment*, 22 October 1925, p. 695.

       Reviews H.C. Hutchins' *Robinson Crusoe and Its Printing*
       (item 567) and praises its minuteness of detail. The
       reviewer, however, disagrees with Hutchins' use of the
       term "issue." Also see McKerrow, item 599.

486.   Biles, Jack I., and Carl R. Kropf. "The Cleft Rock of
       Conversion: *Robinson Crusoe* and *Pincher Martin*."
       Studies in the Literary Imagination, 2 (1969), 17-43.

       Discovers numerous parallels to and inversions of
       Robinson Crusoe in William Golding's *Pincher Martin*.
       Not only do similar details abound, but the two books
       share a three-part thematic design which deals with
       spiritual experience.

*   Blewett, David. *Defoe's Art of Fiction*. (See item 395.)

487.   Boas, F.S. "Sheridan's Robinson Crusoe at Oxford."
       (London) *Times Literary Supplement*, 29 January 1944,
       p. 60.

       Draws attention to a performance of Sheridan's Drury
       Lane pantomime of *Robinson Crusoe* in 1799 as proof of
       the pantomime's continuing popularity. Also see Nettle-
       ton, item 623, and Rosenfeld, item 653.

488.   Bonner, Willard H. *Captain William Dampier, Buccaneer-
       Author*. Palo Alto: Stanford University Press, 1934.

       Assesses in great detail Dampier's influence on Defoe
       who used Dampier's *Voyages* almost as a standard reference
       book for over twenty years. The most convincing details
       in *Robinson Crusoe*, such as the inept building of the
       canoe, come from the *Voyages*. Dampier also furnished
       some details for the second part of *Captain Singleton* and
       for the five-day storm in *Colonel Jack*.

489.   ————. "The Man Who Was Friday: Tracing Defoe's Second
       Most Famous Character to His Source." *Bookman* (New
       York), 75 (1932), 556-59.

Discovers a source for Friday in Dampier's character, Will.

490.   ——————, and Mary Alice Budge. "Thoreau and Robinson Crusoe: An Overview." *Thoreau Journal Quarterly*, 5 (April 1973), 16-18.

Links Thoreau with Robinson Crusoe because of the "similarity of problems of subsistence in solitude." Allusions, both direct and oblique, to Defoe's character appear throughout *Walden*, and for Thoreau, Crusoe was "the archetype of man traveling to a potentially richer life."

491.   Boreham, Frank William. *The Gospel of Robinson Crusoe*. London: Epworth Press, 1955.

Takes a non-scholarly, evangelical view of *Robinson Crusoe*, which "is the throbbing record of a notable spiritual pilgrimage." In effect, Boreham uses the novel as the inspiration for an extended sermon which preaches the glories of Christianity.

*   Braga, Thomas. "Daniel Defoe and the Portuguese." (See item 397.)

*   Brandl, Leopold. "Krinke Kesmes und Defoes *Robinson*." (See item 1230.)

492.   Briden, Earl F. "Huck's Island Adventure and the Sel-kirk Legend." *Mark Twain Journal*, 18 (1976), 12-14.

Mentions Twain's admiration for Defoe and says that Twain "used the Crusoe story as an explicit normative and structural model in *A Connecticut Yankee*."

493.   Bridges, Richard M. "A Positive Source for Daniel Defoe's *The Farther Adventures of Robinson Crusoe*." *British Journal for Eighteenth-Century Studies*, 2 (1979), 231-36.

Traces Crusoe's Archangel journey to Adam Brand's *A Journey of the Embassay from their Majesties John and Peter Alexievitz, Emperors of Muscovy, etc. Over Land into China* (1698). The embassy in the latter follows the same path as Crusoe did, albeit in the opposite direction. Many of the details of the two works are similar enough to strongly suggest Brand's influence on Defoe.

*   Brigham, Clarence S. "Bibliography of American Editions
      of *Robinson Crusoe* to 1830." (See item 5.)

494. Brink, Andrew W. "*Robinson Crusoe* and *The Life of the
      Reverend Mr. George Trosse*." *Philological Quarterly*,
      48 (1969), 433-51.

      Believes that traditional spiritual autobiography,
      because it lacks concreteness, narrative substance, and
      continuity, does not lead directly to a work like
      Robinson Crusoe (see Starr, item 453). However, *The
      Life of the Reverend George Trosse* (1714) fills the
      gap between "Puritan accounts of the quest for grace and
      the extended fictional narrative of a life which includes
      that quest." The main features, both in the method of
      presentation and the spiritual content, of Trosse's book
      are remarkably similar to those of *Robinson Crusoe*.
      The two works treat "conversion under circumstances of
      adversity" in a concrete and detailed way, conveying the
      narrative in a "confiding conversational manner" which
      gives "a disarming naturalness to all that is said."

*   Broich, Ulrich. "Robinsonade und Science Fiction." (See
      item 1232.)

*   Brunner, Horst. "Kinderbuch und Idylle: Rousseau und
      die Rezeption des *Robinson Crusoe* im 18. Jahrhundert."
      (See item 1234.)

*   Buisine, Alain. "Repères, marques, gisements: A propos
      de la robinsonade vernienne." (See item 1235.)

495. Bullen, Frank T. "*Robinson Crusoe*." *The Bibliophile*,
      1 (1908), 243-48.

      Muses about the influence of *Robinson Crusoe* on Bul-
      len's own life and questions Defoe's morality in
      asserting his fictions to be true tales.

*   Calvet, J. *Les types universels dans les littératures
      étrangères*. (See item 1236.)

496. Carnochan, W.B. *Confinement and Flight: An Essay on
      English Literature of the Eighteenth Century*. Berkeley
      and Los Angeles: University of California Press, 1977.

      Subordinates the standard readings of *Robinson Crusoe*
      as spiritual biography or as an economic tract to a
      reading of the novel as bourgeois psychology. Crusoe
      is the ultimate collector, depending on his store of

things to give order to his world. The discovery of
the footprint, however, turns Crusoe away from his world
of things and into himself. Symbolically, the footprint
may be "the evidence of an authorial presence" for the
progress of the novel from *Crusoe* to *Tristram Shandy*
is toward an increasing authorial self-consciousness.
As the artist-figure emerges, he takes on different
forms as disparate as "master of revels" (*Tom Jones*)
and "psychic invalid" (*Journal of the Plague Year*).

497. Cassell and Co. "Cassell's Illustrated *Robinson Crusoe*."
     Notes and Queries, Twelfth Series, 3 (1917), 194.

     Replies to Williams, item 691, by listing the artists
     responsible for illustrating Cassell's (c. 1860) edition
     of *Crusoe*. See Makeham, item 602.

498. Charlton, Aydon. "The Appeal of *Robinson Crusoe*."
     Sphinx, 2 (1974), 21-37.

     Reads *Robinson Crusoe* psychoanalytically to reveal
     patterns--oral, anal, phallic, and Oedipal--that are
     deeper than those uncovered by other intrepretations.
     It is valid to read the novel as a story of adventure
     or economics or repentance, but these readings are not
     as integrated and complete as a psychological reading.

499. Clarke, William A. "*Robinson Crusoe*." *Notes and Queries*,
     9 (1902), 48.

     Asks for information concerning the first and fifth
     editions of *Robinson Crusoe*.

500. Codman, John S. "Robinson Crusoe Up-to-Date." *The
     Freeman*, 9 August 1922, pp. 514-16.

     Presents a modern version of Robinson Crusoe on his
     island to demonstrate the evil consequences of the
     private ownership of land and natural resources.

*   Colaiacoma, Paola. "*Captain Singleton* fra *Robinson
     Crusoe* e *Moll Flanders*." (See item 1238.)

501. Collier, Barnard L. "The 744 on Crusoe's Island Are
     Dimly Aware of Legend." *New York Times*, 8 November
     1967, p. 49.

     Describes modern life on Más a Tierra Island, identified
     as the place of Alexander Selkirk's sojourn and the
     source of Robinson Crusoe's island. Also see Elliott,
     item 519.

*   Comarnescu, Petru. [Introduction to] *Robinson Crusoe*.
        (See item 1240.)

502.   Constant Reader. "Robinson Crusoe's Island." *Notes
        and Queries*, Twelfth Series, 8 (1921), 348.

        Asks if Juan Fernandez is Crusoe's island as stated
        in a newspaper, or if the island really wasn't placed
        in the estuary of the Orinoco. Also see Armstrong,
        item 476; Freeman, item 529; Hubbard, item 561; Lynn,
        item 594; and Wainwright, item 683.

503.   Copplestone, Bennet [Frederick Harcourt Kitchin].
        "Alexander Selkirk's 'Desert Island.'" *Dead Men's
        Tales*. Edinburgh and London: William Blackwood and
        Sons, 1926. Pp. 1-21.

        Describes Juan Fernandez, the island on which Alexan-
        der Selkirk spent more than four years in exile, as an
        "earthly paradise" and compares it to Robinson Crusoe's
        desert island. On the basis of this comparison, the
        author concludes not only that Juan Fernandez was not
        Defoe's model but also that Selkirk, whom Defoe probably
        did not know, was not the original for Crusoe.

504.   Cottom, Daniel. "*Robinson Crusoe*: The Empire's New
        Clothes." *The Eighteenth Century: Theory and Inter-
        pretation*, 22 (1981), 271-86.

        Reinterprets the function of Crusoe's island, which
        appears to be a neutral stage, without a social back-
        ground and outside of time, on which man can "demystify
        his heritage of custom, prejudice, partiality, and
        superstition" and thus discover his essence. However,
        the novel suggests that when man is placed in a state
        of nature, his true being "can only appear as a dependent,
        imaginary contrast to social appearances, authorities,
        oppression, and alienation." Crusoe discovers that man
        can define his nature only in negatives and by dominating
        and exploiting others.

505.   Crowley, J. Donald. "Introduction" to *The Life and
        Strange Surprizing Adventures of Robinson Crusoe* by
        Daniel Defoe. London and New York: Oxford University
        Press, 1972. Pp. vii-xxii.

        Discusses the wide appeal of the novel, evidenced by
        its more than 700 editions, but notes that *Moll Flanders*
        is now more popular because its London environment and
        emphasis on Moll's sexual vitality are viewed as more

modern and realistic. Crowley focuses on Defoe's writing, noting that he is a careless writer who often makes
mistakes; on the other hand, his highly informative
style is effective in presenting a circumstantial
realism (albeit one without "pictorial qualities").
His style is perfectly adapted to conveying his Puritan
attitudes. Puritanism lies at the very core of Defoe's
works, and *Robinson Crusoe* is "a supreme illustration"
of the gradual secularization of religious consciousness.

*   Dahl, Erhard. *Die Kürzungen des "Robinson Crusoe" in
        England zwischen 1719 und 1819*.... (See item 1242.)

506.   Darton, Frederick J. Harvey. *Children's Books in
        England*. Second Edition. Cambridge: The University
        Press, 1960. Originally published 1932.

        Traces briefly (pp. 112-21) the influence through the
        nineteenth century of Robinson Crusoe on children's
        books. Most of the stories dealing with lonely savages,
        marooned mariners, or "rational-natural" men stem from
        Defoe's work.

507.   de la Mare, Walter. *Desert Islands and Robinson Crusoe*.
        London: Faber and Faber, 1930.

        Explores the literature, both fictional and non-
        fictional, of island adventures, focusing on *Robinson
        Crusoe*. The latter is so successful because it "taxes
        no ordinary intelligence," is highly original, and
        presents a detailed and realistic story. The continuance
        of the story in the *Farther Adventures* is one of the
        greatest mistakes in literature because it ruins our
        picture of a heroic Crusoe, replacing it with the por-
        trait of a treacherous globe-trotter.

        Reviews: Mario Praz, *Criterion*, 10 (1930-31), 195-97;
        Clennell Wilkinson, *London Mercury*, 22 (1930), 140-46.

*   Deneke, O. *Robinson Crusoe in Deutschland: Die Früh-
        drucke 1720-1780*. (See item 1245.)

508.   D'Haen, Theo. "*Robinson Crusoe* and *La Jalousie*."
        Revue des Langues Vivantes, 44 (1978), 28-36.

        Uses Barthes' terminology to contrast the *écriture*,
        or writing, of *Robinson Crusoe* and Robbe-Grillet's *La
        Jalousie*. A series of diagrams, based on Barthes, leads
        to the conclusion that *Crusoe* expresses a "colonial
        myth" typical of the bourgeoisie whereas *La Jalousie*

expresses a subversion of that very myth. Taken together, these novels express the rise and fall of the bourgeois class.

509.   Dickinson, H.T. "The Popularity of *Gulliver's Travels* and *Robinson Crusoe*." *Notes and Queries*, n.s. 14 (1967), 172.

Discovers among the loose Clavering papers in the Durham University Library a brief reference to *Robinson Crusoe* which indicates its great popularity in 1726.

510.   Dimsdale, C.D. "*Robinson Crusoe* and West Africa." *West African Review*, 31 (1960), 54–56.

Deals with Alexander Selkirk's life from the time he was marooned until his death aboard a ship off the coast of West Africa sixteen years later in 1721.

511.   Dix, E.R. "Dublin Editions of *Robinson Crusoe*." (London) *Times Literary Supplement*, 20 October 1927, p. 742.

Discovers a 1781 Dublin edition of *Robinson Crusoe* and notes a reference to a 1799 Dublin edition of the work. Also see Dix, item 512, and "Dublin Edition," item 516.

512.   ————. "The First Dublin Edition of *Robinson Crusoe* (1719)." (London) *Times Literary Supplement*, 13 October 1927, p. 715.

Locates two more copies of the first Dublin edition of *Robinson Crusoe*, a rare pirated edition of which only three copies were thought to exist. Also see "Dublin Edition," item 516, and Dix, item 511.

*   Dottin, Paul. *Daniel Defoe et ses romans*. Vol. II. (See item 1251.)

*   ————. "L'île de Robinson." (See item 1254.)

513.   ————. "Introduction" to *Robinson Crusoe Examin'd and Criticis'd* by Charles Gildon. London: J.M. Dent, 1923. Pp. 55–62.

Presents the history of Gildon's pamphlet, noting that the author was jealous of Defoe's success with *Robinson Crusoe* and angry with Defoe for attacking him in two poems, *More Reformation* and the *Pacificator*.

Dottin appends a "Life" of Gildon and explanatory notes
to this edition of Gildon's work.

514. Item Deleted.

515. Downs, Robert B. "Man Alone: Daniel Defoe's *Robinson
      Crusoe*." *Molders of the Modern Mind: III Books That
      Shaped Western Civilization*. New York: Barnes and
      Noble, 1961. Pp. 108-11.

      Finds the power of *Robinson Crusoe* to lie in Defoe's
      ability to make the uncommon common and to explore the
      isolation that is each man's fate.

516. "Dublin Edition of 'Robinson Crusoe.'" (London) *Times
      Literary Supplement*, 29 September 1927, p. 672.

      Records the purchase of a previously unknown third
      copy of the 1719 Dublin edition of *Robinson Crusoe*.
      Also see Dix, items 511 and 512.

517. Echeruo, Michael J.C. "*Robinson Crusoe, Purchas His
      Pilgrimes*, and the 'Novel.'" *English Studies in
      Africa*, 10 (1967), 167-77.

      Detects a source for *Crusoe* in *Purchas* which contains
      geographical information used by Defoe.

518. Egan, James. "Crusoe's Monarchy and the Puritan Concept
      of the Self." *Studies in English Literature*, 13
      (1973), 451-60.

      Examines Robinson Crusoe's social relationships to
      uncover evidence of his spiritual growth. Crusoe re-
      gards himself as a king, the island as his realm, and
      all who appear on the island as his subjects. The
      kingship metaphor has great significance: it implies
      distance between Crusoe and others; as "King," Crusoe
      can engage in social relationships and yet control those
      relationships. With Friday, for instance, Crusoe main-
      tains his distance and manipulates the relationship
      until, fulfilling the evangelical demands of his faith,
      he converts Friday to Christianity. The metaphor also
      implies that Crusoe is monarch over his own soul.

*   Ehnmark, Elof. *Konsten att ljuga och konsten att tala
          sanning. Om Daniel Defoe och Robinson Crusoe*. (See
          item 1266.)

519.   Elliott, Lillian E.   "Crusoe's Island."   *The Pan-*
       American Magazine, 34 (1922), 29-38.

       Covers the history of Más a Tierra, the island on
       which Alexander Selkirk was marooned; the life and ad-
       ventures of Selkirk; and the biography of Defoe. The
       latter propagates such myths as the one that says Defoe
       refused to speak a single word for twenty-eight years
       to his wife even though he still lived with her.

520.   Ellis, Frank H.   "Introduction" to *Twentieth Century*
       Interpretations of "Robinson Crusoe": A Collection of
       Critical Essays. Englewood Cliffs, N.J.: Prentice-
       Hall, 1969. Pp. 1-18.

       Divides *Robinson Crusoe* criticism into four areas for
       discussion: (1) the shift from a patronizing attitude
       towards Defoe to an attitude of respect for his artis-
       tic abilities; (2) the discovery that Robinson Crusoe
       is not a thinly veiled portrait of Defoe; (3) the reali-
       zation that *Robinson Crusoe* is a novel for adults; and
       (4) the idea that God is almost as important in the
       novel as He is in *Paradise Lost*. Ellis interpolates
       his own views into his critical surveys of each of these
       four areas.

521.   ⸺⸺, ed.   *Twentieth Century Interpretations of*
       "Robinson Crusoe": A Collection of Critical Essays.
       Englewood Cliffs, N.J.: Prentice-Hall, 1969.

       Contains a lengthy introduction by the editor (see
       item 520) and twelve items of modern criticism, all of
       which are excerpted from longer works or reprinted from
       journal articles. The contents, which follow, are
       annotated separately: Virginia Woolf, "Robinson Crusoe,"
       item 692; James Sutherland, "The Author of *Robinson*
       Crusoe," item 350; Edwin B. Benjamin, "Symbolic Elements
       in *Robinson Crusoe*," item 482; Ian Watt, "*Robinson*
       Crusoe, Individualism and the Novel," item 688; John
       Robert Moore, "*Robinson Crusoe*," item 261; E.M.W. Till-
       yard, "Defoe," item 677; William H. Halewood, "Religion
       and Invention in *Robinson Crusoe*," item 544; Roger
       Lloyd, "The Riddle of Defoe," item 592; Eric Berne,
       "The Psychological Structure of Space with Some Remarks
       on *Robinson Crusoe*," item 483; Maximillian E. Novak,
       "The Economic Meaning of *Robinson Crusoe*," item 433;
       George A. Starr, "*Robinson Crusoe* and the Myth of Mam-
       mon," item 452; and J. Paul Hunter, "The Un-sources of
       Robinson Crusoe," item 565.

522. Engelsen, Arne R. "Robinson Crusoe and the 'Assiento.'"
      Notes and Queries, n.s. 13 (1966), 305.

      Finds an anachronism in Robinson Crusoe's mention of
      the Assiento in 1659 because the Assiento did not come
      into effect until 1701.

523. Fairchild, Hoxie N. *The Noble Savage: A Study in
      Romantic Naturalism.* New York: Columbia University
      Press, 1928. Reprinted New York: Russell and Russell,
      1961.

      Sees Friday in *Robinson Crusoe* as the "Noble Savage
      of early eighteenth century 'common sense.'" The
      quaintly wholesome Friday is used by Defoe to illustrate
      the point that God gives virtue to all men but the so-
      called "civilized" man tends to abuse God's gift more
      than does the "ignorant savage."

*   Fallenbühl, Zoltán. "Dobai Székely Sámuel, a *Robinson
      Crusoe* első ismert magyar olvasója." (See item 1270.)

524. Fernsemer, O.F.W. "Daniel Defoe and the Palatine
      Emigration of 1709; a New View of the Origin of
      Robinson Crusoe." *Journal of English and Germanic
      Philology*, 19 (1920), 94-124.

      Rejects the standard theories on the origin of
      Robinson Crusoe: the Selkirk story only gave Defoe a
      few hints and outlines for the novel and there is no
      objective evidence to support the allegorical interpre-
      tation of the work. A more likely source for the story
      is the influx of 14,000 Palatine refugees into England.
      The Palatines idealistically sought a new commonwealth
      built on individual and communal effort and pervaded
      by the spirit of freedom and tolerance. Defoe was sym-
      pathetic to them and their plight triggered his imagina-
      tion, providing the impulse that led to all three parts
      of *Robinson Crusoe*.

*   Flasdieck, H.M. "Robinson Crusoe in Lichte der neueren
      Forschung." (See item 1272.)

525. Fletcher, Edward G. "Some University of Texas Copies
      of *Robinson Crusoe*, Part I." *Notes and Queries*, 164
      (1933), 4-5.

      Presents a bibliographic description of editions of
      Robinson Crusoe in the Wrenn, Stark, and Aikin collections
      at the University of Texas.

526. Foot, Michael. "The Crusoe Miracle." (London) *Observer*,
      24 July 1960, p. 20.

      The compiler was unable to read this item personally.

527. Fox, Ralph. *The Novel and the People*. London: Lawrence
      and Wishart, 1937.

      Provides a brief Marxist reading of *Robinson Crusoe*,
      calling it one of "the two greatest stories in the
      world" (the other is the *Odyssey*). Fox cites Marx's
      praise of Crusoe as an individual who is not the product
      of history but is its starting point.

528. Foxon, D.F. "More on 'Robinson Crusoe,' 1719." *Library*,
      25 (1970), 57-58.

      Checks the Rivington file of trade sale catalogs at
      the Bodleian in order to confirm Maslen's supposition
      that William Taylor was sole owner of the *Robinson
      Crusoe* copyright (see item 606).

529. Freeman, Lewis R. "Where Is Robinson Crusoe's Island?"
      Travel, 34 (1920), 27-30.

      Presents the claims of Tobago and Juan Fernandez to
      be Robinson Crusoe's island, but does not attempt to
      resolve the dispute. Also see Armstrong, item 476;
      Constant Reader, item 502; Hubbard, item 561; Lynn,
      item 594; and Wainwright, item 683.

*   Freeman, William. *The Incredible Defoe*. (See item 183.)

530. Friday [Henry C. Hutchins]. "The Yale *Robinson Crusoe*."
      Yale University Library Gazette, 8 (1934), 85-94.

      Remarks on the acquisition of the first edition, in
      three volumes, of *Robinson Crusoe* and traces the novel's
      publishing history from 1719 to 1724 when its printer,
      William Taylor, died.

*   Frosini, Vittorio. "Il vangelo di Robinson." (See item
      1275.)

531. Ganzel, Dewey. "Chronology in Robinson Crusoe." *Philo-
      logical Quarterly*, 40 (1961), 495-512.

      Challenges William Hastings' view that *Robinson Crusoe*
      is a patchwork of inconsistent detail (see item 548).
      Actually, the work contains two consistent chronologies,
      the second interpolated into the first. The interpola-

tion, a 32-page section in the Aitken edition which
focuses on Crusoe's reflections on scripture and Friday's
conversion, probably came about during revision--an
attempt to expand the story's spiritual significance--
and it reflects subtle shifts in emphasis and tone.

532. Gates, W.B. "A Note on Cooper and *Robinson Crusoe*."
      Modern Language Notes, 67 (1952), 421-22.

      Finds in *Robinson Crusoe* the source for two incidents
      in James Fenimore Cooper's *The Crater*.

533. Giles, Edward L. "Shipwrecks and Desert Islands."
      Notes and Queries, 177 (1939), 218-20.

      Discusses an anonymous tale, *The Hermit; or, The
      Unparalleled Suffering and Surprising Adventures of
      Mr. Philip Quarll, An Englishman* (1727), which was
      filched from three of Defoe's works: *Robinson Crusoe*,
      Moll Flanders, and *Colonel Jack*. In the course of the
      discussion, Giles briefly traces the history of seven-
      teenth- and eighteenth-century shipwreck stories, which
      blend fact and fiction.

534. Goebel, Julius. "The Dutch Source of *Robinson Crusoe*."
      Journal of English and Germanic Philology, 22 (1923),
      302-13.

      Reviews Lucius L. Hubbard's translation of Hendrik
      Smeek's *The Narrator of the El-Ho* from *Krinke Kresmes*
      and adds to Hubbard's introductory statement detail
      which supports Smeek's work as perhaps the major influ-
      ence on *Robinson Crusoe*. Also see Polak, item 637, and
      Hubbard, item 560.

535. Goodrick, A.T.S. "Robinson Crusoe, Imposter." *Black-
      wood's Magazine*, 183 (1908), 672-85.

      Contends that Defoe plagiarized *Robinson Crusoe*, bor-
      rowing the idea of a hermit castaway, the locale of the
      island, and many of the details from such previous
      works as the Spanish-Arabian tale of Ibn Tophail and
      Henry Nevile's *Island of Pines*. Nonetheless, Defoe's
      novel has "matchless charm" and is "the greatest romance
      the world has ever seen."

*   Gove, Philip B. *The Imaginary Voyage in Prose Fiction*.
      (See item 1100.)

536.   Grabo, Carl H. *The Technique of the Novel*. New York:
       Charles Scribner's Sons, 1928.

       Criticizes *Robinson Crusoe* as the lowest form of fic-
       tion, the episodic, simple narrative of the chrono-
       logical adventures of a single character. Defoe did
       not attempt to stir his readers' imaginations but rather
       to "allay their incredulity."

*   Gray, Christopher W. "Defoe's Literalizing Imagination."
       (See item 188.)

537.   *Greatest Yarn of All*. Avon, Conn.: Heritage Press, 1973.

       Unseen by the compiler, this item--apparently on *Robin-
       son Crusoe*--is listed in the Humanities Research Center
       Library at the University of Texas, Austin, but is
       missing from the collection.

538.   Green, Martin. *Dreams of Adventure, Deeds of Empire*.
       Boston and London: Routledge and Kegan Paul, 1980.

       Regards *Robinson Crusoe* as a novel of English im-
       perialism and supports his position by citing Lévi-
       Strauss on colonization. Green calls Defoe the inventor
       of the modern novel.

       Review: J.A. Downie, *The Scriblerian*, 14 (1982), 125-26.

539.   Greif, Martin J. "The Conversion of Robinson Crusoe."
       Studies in English Literature, 6 (1966), 551-74.

       Regards *Robinson Crusoe* as an allegorical story of
       conversion using widely recognized symbols drawn from
       contemporary religious writings. Crusoe's life on the
       island after his conversion demonstrates the rewards
       and powers of "the penitent sinner who has been saved."

540.   Griffith, Philip Mahone. "Defoe's 'Robinson Crusoe':
       Some Animadversions During the Two Hundred and Fif-
       tieth Anniversary Year, 1719-1969." *Laurel Review*,
       10 (1970), 6-14.

       Reviews the opinions on *Robinson Crusoe* held by such
       great artists as Poe, Joyce, Woolf, and Gorki and sees
       Crusoe's endurance on his island for 28 years as a
       greater symbol of human accomplishment than the first
       manned moon flight.

541.   Grundy, Isobel. "Farther Adventures of Robinson Crusoe."
       The Scriblerian, 14 (1982), 122-24.

Identifies "The Adventures of Lo Bun Sun" in Maxine
Hong Kingston's novel, *China Men*, as a "Chinesed" *Robinson Crusoe*. Her use of this story shows its "archetypal quality."

542. Gudde, Erwin Gustav. "Grimmelshausen's *Simplicius
Simplicissimus* and Defoe's *Robinson Crusoe*." *Philological Quarterly*, 4 (1925), 110-20.

Attempts to show, on the basis of internal evidence,
that Grimmelshausen's *Simplicius Simplicissimus* (1669)
is a more important source for *Robinson Crusoe* than
either Selkirk's story or Smeeks' *Krinke Kesmes* (see
Hubbard, item 560). The correspondences between Grimmelshausen's work and *Crusoe* include: the happenings
immediately preceding the shipwrecks; the similarities
of the deserted islands; the two characters' desperate
need for tools, utensils, and clothing; the parallels
between their religious reflections; and the psychological
development of the two men in their isolated environment.

* Gunther, M. *Entstehungsgeschichte von Defoes Robinson
Crusoe*. (See item 1288.)

543. Hadden, J. Cuthbert. "The Making of *Robinson Crusoe*."
*The Life and Strange Surprising Adventures of Robinson
Crusoe* by Daniel Defoe. New York: The Heritage Press,
1930. Pp. v-x.

Presents a detailed account of the life of Alexander
Selkirk, upon whose adventures Defoe based his novel.

544. Halewood, William H. "Religion and Invention in
Robinson Crusoe." *Essays in Criticism*, 14 (1964),
339-51. Reprinted in Ellis, item 521.

Objects to the critical position that views Robinson
Crusoe as Defoe in goatskins. Defoe's conscious artistry
and his distance from Crusoe are apparent in the way
religion is treated in the novel. Lacking a human
antagonist as a source of conflict, Defoe substitutes
Crusoe's religious soul as antagonist, objectifying it
and even giving it lines to speak. Defoe skillfully
develops an ironic "discontinuity between religion and
action" in *Robinson Crusoe* that informs the entire book.

545. Hardy, Barbara. *The Appropriate Form*. London: Athlone
Press, 1964.

Calls *Robinson Crusoe* a "development novel," following
the progress of a prodigal son who defies paternal advice,

suffers, repents, and is rewarded. In the novel,
Providence is an informing principle invoked to mark
the successful resolution of difficulties. Although
some of the novel's moral implications are dubious,
they provide the novel with its theme and its unity.

546. Hardyman, J. Trenchard. "Shipwrecks and Desert Islands."
      Notes and Queries, 177 (1939), 268-69.

      Adds further background information on shipwreck
      stories to Giles, item 533.

*   Hartog, Curt H. "Aggression, Femininity, and Irony in
      Moll Flanders." (See item 746.)

547. ———. "Authority and Autonomy in *Robinson Crusoe*."
      Enlightenment Essays, 5, no. 2 (Summer 1974), 33-43.

      Not seen by the compiler, but noted in the *Philo-
      logical Quarterly* bibliography for 1974, p. 667.

548. Hastings, William T. "Errors and Inconsistencies in
      Defoe's *Robinson Crusoe*." *Modern Language Notes*, 27
      (1912), 161-66.

      Points out in *Robinson Crusoe* errors in chronology
      and contradictions in statements about Crusoe's life
      on his island. Chronological mistakes make it impossible
      to determine just when Crusoe's shipwreck took place
      and exactly how long he was on the island. Contradic-
      tions about Crusoe's life are mostly taken from Gildon's
      contemporary attack on Defoe (see item 513).

549. ———. "Misprints in Defoe." *Nation* (New York),
      18 May 1911, p. 501.

      Notes several misprints that have been perpetuated
      in the text of *Robinson Crusoe* and suggests several
      emendations.

550. Häusermann, Hans W. "Aspects of Life and Thought in
      Robinson Crusoe." *Review of English Studies*, 11
      (1935), 299-312, 439-56.

      Surveys systematically the conclusions about *Robinson
      Crusoe* drawn by such scholars as Dottin and Huebner
      which emphasize the influence of Puritanism on Defoe's
      artistic conception. Defoe's Puritan religious beliefs
      permeate the novel; they explain most of Crusoe's
      actions and attitudes and even account for the sober,

simple style of the book. Defoe's life as a middle-
class merchant helps to explain the "money morality"
that to modern readers sometimes seems in conflict
with expressed religious attitudes.

551. Hayden, Lucy K. "The Black Presence in Eighteenth-
     Century British Novels." *College Language Association
     Journal*, 24 (1981), 400-15.

     "Justifies" Crusoe's racism by noting that he evolves
     from "master" to "father" in his relationship with
     Friday; also points out that in several works, Defoe
     denounced slavery.

552. Hearne, John. "The Naked Footprint: An Inquiry Into
     Crusoe's Island." *Review of English Literature*, 8
     (1967), 97-107.

     Calls *Robinson Crusoe* "a profound and magical work"
     which represents the first fictional coming to terms
     with the active creation of new wealth. Defoe perceives
     that modern man is totally alone and only the exploita-
     tion of nature for profit can give meaning to his exis-
     tence.

*   Heidenreich, Helmut. "Der spanische *Robinson Crusoe*."
     (See item 1291.)

553. Henderson-Howat, G.M.D., and Francis Watson. "Robinson
     Crusoe." *History Today*, 10 (1960), 51.

     Identifies John Poyntz's *The Present Prospects of the
     Famous and Fertile Island of Tobago* (1683) as the main
     source for *Robinson Crusoe*.

*   Herting, [No Initials]. "Die Idioten- und Geistekranken-
     fürsorge des Robinson dichters Defoe." (See item 1292.)

554. Hill, Christopher. "Robinson Crusoe." *History Work-
     shop: A Journal of Socialist Historians*, 10 (1980),
     7-24.

     Sees Defoe as a political radical who invented the
     novel to satisfy the needs of a new fiction-reading
     public. He is a conscious artist whose irony is inten-
     tional.

*   Hirn, Yrjö. *Ön i varldshavet*. (See item 1295.)

555. Hoffman, Margit. "The J.A. Ahlstrand Collection of
     Robinsonades at the Royal Library in Stockholm."

Otium et Negotium: Studies in Onomatology and Library Science Presented to Olof von Feilitzen. Ed. Folke Sandgren. Stockholm: Kungl, 1973. Pp. 142-50.

Describes briefly some of the "representative" titles among the 130 in the Ahlstrand Collection of Robinsonades in fifteen languages.

556. Holmes, Arthur F. "Crusoe, Friday, and God." *Philosophy Forum*, 11 (1972), 319-39.

Describes the effect of religious faith on personal fulfillment by explaining "the Crusoe theory" of individuality and then setting up his own contrasting model. The Crusoe theory contains these four assertions: (1) man is by nature an isolated consciousness; (2) man is by nature rational; (3) the individual is self-contained and self-sufficient; and (4) the natural state of man is one of isolation, not community. These assertions, however, are incorrect because "no man is an island"; the individual is immersed in social history, coming into existence and finding fulfillment "by virtue of his internal relatedness to the community and the social processes in which he takes part." Individual fulfillment is connected to religion because religion integrates man's values around his God and gives man new directions and motivations. Religious conversion, such as Crusoe experiences, "brings past processes to concrete fulfilment."

557. Honig, Edwin. "Crusoe, Rasselas, and the Suit of Clothes." *University of Kansas City Review*, 18 (1951), 136-42.

Contends that eighteenth-century prose writers oversimplified both the psychology of their characters and the problems the latter faced; both *Crusoe* and *Rasselas* "have about them the aura of some idyllic pastoral, edited by a prejudice for the commonplace."

*   Hortelano Pastor, Santiago. "'Robinson Crusoe' y España." (See item 1296.)

558. Howe, Irving. "*Robinson Crusoe*, Epic of the Middle Class." *Tomorrow*, 8 (June 1949), 51-54.

Distinguishes between the way Robinson Crusoe looks at himself and his environment and the way Romantics and moderns view them. Crusoe neither indulges in introspection nor views his surroundings as having

independent value; he has a "bourgeois outlook" on
everything and is best characterized as "unimaginatively
inventive."

559. Howe, Raymond F. *"Robinson Crusoe*: A Literary Accident."
      English Journal, 16 (1927), 31-35.

      Denigrates Defoe's literary reputation: the only work
      of any merit written by Defoe was *Robinson Crusoe* and
      it was "a literary accident," its theme and method dic-
      tated by "circumstances" and not artistic genius.

560. Hubbard, Lucius L. *A Dutch Source for Robinson Crusoe:*
      the Narrative of the El-ho "Sjouke Gabbes" by Hendrik
      Smeeks (1708). Translated from the Dutch and Compared
      with the Story of Robinson Crusoe. Ann Arbor: George
      Wahr, 1921.

      Argues that Defoe was more indebted to *Sjouke Gabbes*
      as a source for *Robinson Crusoe* than he was to Woodes
      Rogers or Alexander Selkirk. Not only are the frameworks
      for the two stories similar--an isolated person on an
      island demonstrating self-dependence in attempting to
      survive by mastering nature--but many details demonstrate
      that Defoe knew and used Smeeks' tale in writing *Robinson*
      Crusoe. For example, Sjouke's hut and Crusoe's habita-
      tion are similar in many details and the language
      describing the protagonists' hunting and fishing ex-
      ploits likewise is similar. Hubbard employs marginal
      notes in his translation of *Sjouke Gabbes* to point out
      additional parallels. Also see Polak, item 637, and
      Goebel, item 534.

      Reviews: Julius Goebel, *Journal of English and Germanic*
      Philology, 22 (1923), 302-13; Joseph Wood Krutch,
      Literary Review, 9 September 1922, p. 12; (London)
      Times Literary Supplement, 3 August 1922, p. 16;
      Arthur H. Nethercot, *Modern Language Notes,* 39 (1924),
      235-41; *New York Times Book Review,* 19 March 1922,
      pp. 5, 21; Hermann Ullrich, *Literaturblatt für*
      germanische und romanische Philologie, 44 (1923),
      18-22; W. van Maanen, *English Studies,* 5 (1923),
      136-39.

561. ————. "Is Tobago Robinson Crusoe's Island?" Re-
      printed from the Trinidad *Guardian* of February 20,
      1927, by The Trinidad Publishing Company, 1927.

      Believes that Tobago is not--as is often thought--
      the model for Crusoe's island; the real and fictional

places are quite different physically. Also see Armstrong, item 476; Constant Reader, item 502; Freeman, item 529; Lynn, item 594; and Wainwright, item 683.

562.   ————. "Some Inferences from the Dog Episode in
       Robinson Crusoe." Reprinted from the Trinidad
       Guardian of February 20, 1927, by Trinidad Publishing
       Co., 1927.

       A copy of this article is owned by the University of
       Texas at Austin (Humanities Research Center Library)
       but could not be located for the compiler to read prior
       to the publication of this bibliography.

563.   ————. "Text Changes in the Taylor Editions of
       Robinson Crusoe with Remarks on the Cox Edition."
       Papers of the Bibliographic Society of America, 20
       (1926), 1-76.

       Investigates the following: the succession of the Taylor editions of *Robinson Crusoe*; the derivation or
       provenance of the several editions *inter sese*; the
       reason for duplicate "editions"; the editorial source
       or sources of text changes; notes on the Cox edition
       of 1719; and the final Taylor edition of 1722. This
       highly technical article is accompanied by five useful
       explanatory tables.

*   Hübener, Gustav. "Der Kaufmann Robinson Crusoe." (See
       item 1298.)

*   Huebner, Walter. "Die Weltbücher von Robinson und Gulliver und ihre geistesgeschichtliche Bedeutung."
       (See item 1300.)

564.   Hunter, J. Paul. "Friday as a Convert: Defoe and the
       Accounts of Indian Missionaries." *Review of English
       Studies*, n.s. 14 (1963), 243-48.

       Defends Defoe from charges of psychological ineptitude in the scene in which Friday asks why God, if He
       is so powerful, did not simply kill the devil. The
       question has often been said to be too sophisticated
       for a real savage to ask, but Hunter discovers that
       John Eliot, a famous New England missionary, was asked
       exactly the same question by the Indians. Friday's
       behavior is important in the novel because his conversion is the proof of Crusoe's religious sincerity.

565.   ————.   *The Reluctant Pilgrim: Defoe's Emblematic
       Method and Quest for Form in "Robinson Crusoe."*
       Baltimore: The Johns Hopkins Press, 1966. Sections
       are reprinted in Byrd, item 132; Ellis, item 521;
       and Shinagel, item 28.

       Reassesses traditional views of *Robinson Crusoe* by
       defining "several kinds of Puritan subliterary
       materials," suggesting relationships between Puritan
       ways of thinking and the emerging prose fiction of
       the early eighteenth century, and applying the insights
       gained to a detailed critical reading of the novel.
       Hunter believes that while Selkirk's story and similar
       real-life adventures may have provided some detail for
       Defoe's story, the tale's real inspiration is idealogical:
       Defoe wishes to present the familiar Christian pattern
       of "disobedience--punishment--repentance--deliverance"
       in order to stress providential goodness. In order to
       accomplish this end, Defoe draws upon traditional Puritan
       modes of thought: "guide" and "providence" literature,
       the "pilgrim allegory," common Puritan metaphors, and
       the use of spiritual emblems drawn from the things and
       events of this created world. *Robinson Crusoe* presents
       the same story of rebellion and punishment, repentance
       and salvation, which is common to all kinds of Puritan
       spiritual histories, and--also like its Puritan pre-
       decessors--the novel emphasizes God's grace.

       Reviews: Rodney M. Baine, *South Atlantic Quarterly*, 66
           (1967), 487-88; Martin C. Battestin, *College English*,
           29 (1967), 60-62; William W. Cobau, *Seventeenth-
           Century News*, 26 (1968), 52-53; William Halewood,
           Modern Philology, 66 (1969), 274-78; Barbara K.
           Lewalski, *Novel*, 1 (1967), 85-89; Francis E. Moran,
           Seventeenth-Century News, 25 (1967), 51-52; Maximil-
           lian E. Novak, *Journal of English and Germanic Phil-
           ology*, 67 (1968), 159-61; John Preston, *Review of
           English Studies*, n.s. 19 (1968), 322-23; Robert C.
           Steensma, *Western Humanities Review*, 21 (1967), 279-
           80; (London) *Times Literary Supplement*, 5 October
           1967, p. 941; F. Wölcken, *Anglia*, 87 (1969), 97-100.

566.   Hurlimann, Bettina. "Robinson." *Three Centuries of
       Children's Books in Europe*. Translated by Brian
       Alderson. Cleveland and New York: World Publishing,
       1968. Pp. 99-112. Originally published under the
       title *Europäische Kinderbücher in drei Jahrhunderten*.
       Zürich: Atlantis, 1959.

Discovers the "magic" of *Robinson Crusoe* in its
universality: Crusoe's adventures portray in half a
lifetime "the development of the human race" and offer
a permanent ideal for all ages. Crusoe is the natural
man, without technical resources, who triumphs over
adversity and attains "goodness." Hurlimann outlines
several Robinsonades, noting the ways in which they
are related to Defoe's original work.

567.   Hutchins, Henry Clinton. *Robinson Crusoe and Its Print-*
       ing, 1719-1731: A Bibliographical Study. New York:
       Columbia University Press, 1925.

       Examines and describes in great bibliographic detail
       all the known English editions of *Crusoe* published in
       Defoe's lifetime.

       Reviews: Notes and Queries, 144 (1925), 467-68; Temple
       Scott, *Saturday Review of Literature*, 28 November
       1925, p. 339; (London) *Times Literary Supplement*,
       22 October 1925, p. 695; Hermann Ullrich, *Literatur-*
       blatt, 47 (1926), cols. 281-85; Harold Williams,
       Library Association Record, 4 (1926), 24-25.

568.   ————. "Robinson Crusoe at Yale." *Yale University*
       Library Gazette, 11 (1936), 17-37.

       Describes the Defoe collection given to the Yale
       Library by Hutchins. The 650-volume collection in-
       cludes first editions, only known copies, piracies,
       French editions, and Robinsonades.

569.   ————. "Two Hitherto Unrecorded Editions of *Robinson*
       Crusoe." *Library*, Fourth Series, 8 (1928), 58-72.

       Lists first all of the known editions and piracies
       of Parts I and II of *Robinson Crusoe* through 1724 and
       then describes two newly discovered editions. The first
       is a pirated Dublin edition of Parts I and II of *Crusoe*
       issued in 1719. The second is a sixth duodecimo edition
       of Part I issued in 1722.

570.   Hymer, Stephen. "Robinson Crusoe and Primitive Accumu-
       lation." *Monthly Review*, 23 (September 1971), 11-36.

       Gives a socialist reading of *Robinson Crusoe*, seeing
       it as an allegory about the life of all men in a capi-
       talist society. Crusoe's management of his island and
       his education of Friday parallel capitalist exploitation.
       Crusoe is a great organizer and entrepreneur who takes
       advantage of situations and manipulates other people for

his own gain. He ends up wealthy, but has suffered the
pains of solitude and the vices of greed, distrust, and
ruthlessness.

*   Isernhagen, Hartwig. "Vermittlungsmodell und thematische
     Struktur: Zu *Robinson Crusoe* und *Humphry Clinker*."
     (See item 1302.)

*   Izzo, Carlo. "Su Daniel De Foe." (See item 1303.)

571. Jackson, Henry E. *Robinson Crusoe, Social Engineer.*
     New York: Dutton, 1922.

     Takes "the reader on a quest for the secret of the
     amazing popularity of *Robinson Crusoe*" in order to show
     that Defoe's novel opens "the path to permanent indus-
     trial peace." The novel is a success because Crusoe's
     self-reliance and courage appeal to almost all men.
     The modern manager and working man must adopt these
     qualities--introducing "the spirit of adventure, joy,
     self-directed activity" into work--in order to resolve
     labor-management problems.

*   Jacob, Ernst Gerhard. "Daniel Defoe, *Robinson Crusoe*."
     (See item 1308.)

*   ——. "Defoe und Robinson." (See item 1311.)

*   ——. "Der englische Robinsondichter in seiner
     medizingeschichtlichen Bedeutung." (See item 1313.)

*   ——. "Die medizingeschichtliche Bedeutung des
     Robinsondichters Daniel Defoe." (See item 1316.)

*   ——. "Robinson Crusoe und das Abendland." (See
     item 1320.)

*   James, E. Anthony. *Daniel Defoe's Many Voices.* (See
     item 211.)

572. ——. "Defoe's Narrative Artistry: Naming and
     Describing in *Robinson Crusoe*." *Costerus*, 5 (1972),
     51-73.

     Reviews the ways in which Crusoe names and describes
     things in order to show Defoe's narrative skills and
     ability to develop psychologically realistic characters.
     Crusoe's semantic habits change to parallel his growth
     and development from uncertainty to decisiveness, from
     humility to pride, from the role of prisoner to one of
     king.

573. Jefferson, Mark. "Winds in *Robinson Crusoe*." *Journal of Geography*, 11 (1912), 23-25.

    Finds "astonishing" Defoe's detailed knowledge of the nature and direction of North Atlantic winds in *Robinson Crusoe*.

574. Johnson, Abby A. "Old Bones Uncovered: A Reconsideration of *Robinson Crusoe*." *College Language Association Journal*, 17 (1973), 271-78.

    Interprets *Robinson Crusoe* "as an expression of historic white attitudes on race." Crusoe's racial biases are apparent in his descriptions of negroes, his sale of the faithful Xury, and his enslavement of Friday whom he strips of his name and language and whom he forces to perform the most laborious tasks on the island.

*   Kaarsholm, Preben. "Defoe's 'Robinson Crusoe' og capitalismens utvikling i England." (See item 1322.)

575. Kavanagh, Thomas M. "Unraveling Robinson: The Divided Self in Defoe's *Robinson Crusoe*." *Texas Studies in Literature and Language*, 20 (1978), 416-32.

    Regards *Robinson Crusoe* as the paradigmatic tale of man alone attempting to achieve self-awareness. "Alone, with no one to vanquish or serve, the individual glimpses but can never avow the ultimate and inevitable form of all consciousness: a perception of the self through difference, an innate schizophrenia seeking finally the victory of neither, but the endless pity of each against the other. To live the present as present, to exist within a direct, unmediated relationship to reality is a myth—the myth for which the name of Robinson Crusoe has become eponymic."

*   Kehler, Henning. "Robinson Crusoe." (See item 1323.)

576. Kennedy, G.W. "Conrad and *Robinson Crusoe*." *Conradiana*, 10 (1978), 113-22.

    Shows that when Conrad uses analogues of the Robinson Crusoe story, he does so ironically because he finds false to his moral and psychological beliefs Crusoe's pursuit of material wealth, his simple religious conversion, his easy dominance over Friday, and, above all, his psychologically unscathed emergence from twenty-eight years of solitude. Moreover, Conrad saw the myth of the triumph of the solitary man isolated from his own culture as subversive to the sense of community that is the foundation of civilized life.

577. ————. "The Uses of Solitude: Dickens and *Robinson Crusoe*." *Victorian Newsletter*, 52 (1977), 25-30.

Treats the ambiguous reaction Dickens had to *Robinson Crusoe*. On the one hand, he found the book distressingly void of humor and feeling and he objected to the lack of any psychological change in a character isolated for so long. On the other hand, Dickens was influenced greatly by *Crusoe*; he referred to it frequently in his fiction and he adapted and idealized Crusoe's isolation in such characters as Captain Cuttle, Mr. Peggotty, and Wemmick. Dickens' urban castaways, however, turn their "desert islands" into private and magical worlds in which they undergo "saving transformations."

578. Kinkead-Weekes, Mark, and Ian Gregor. *William Golding: A Critical Study*. London: Faber and Faber, 1967.

Contains a brief comparison (pp. 121-24) of Golding's *Pincher Martin and Robinson Crusoe*; the former emphasizes the realism of experience and the latter focuses on the realism of the "pure record" or of "facts."

579. Klingender, F.D. "Coleridge on *Robinson Crusoe*." (London) *Times Literary Supplement*, 1 February 1936, p. 96.

Reports on a recently discovered copy of *Robinson Crusoe*, annotated by Coleridge, which formed the source of the "Critical Notes on *Robinson Crusoe*" in Volume I of *The Literary Remains of Samuel Taylor Coleridge*. The newly found copy is important because it contains notes omitted from *The Literary Remains*; these omitted notes are reproduced here.

580. Knowles, A.S., Jr. "Defoe, Swift, and Fielding: Notes on the Retirement Theme." *Quick Springs of Sense: Studies in the Eighteenth Century*. Ed. Larry S. Champion. Athens, Ga.: University of Georgia Press, 1974. Pp. 121-36.

Corrects Tillyard's statement that *Robinson Crusoe* is the "culminating embodiment" of the retirement theme in English literature (see item 677) by concentrating on episodes in Swift (the Houyhnhnms in Part IV) and Fielding (the interpolated tales of Wilson in *Joseph*

Andrews and The Man of the Hill in *Tom Jones*) to show
that *Crusoe* stands not at the end but "nearer the middle
of a tradition that continues to develop through the
eighteenth century." Defoe regards Crusoe's predicament
on his island both as an involuntary situation with interesting economic ramifications and as an opportunity
for spiritual development.

581.   Kraft, Quentin G. "*Robinson Crusoe* and the Story of
       the Novel." *College English*, 41 (1980), 535-48.

       Attempts to prove that *Crusoe* is the first modern
       novel because it transforms "the nature of story." The
       work consists of two stories: Crusoe's tale of his ad-
       ventures and Defoe's tale of Crusoe telling his tale.
       The latter undermines the former and by so doing "trans-
       forms the allegory into a novel."

*   Kramer, Jürgen. "Fortschritt und Regression: Studien
       zur 'Dialektik der Aufklärung' in der Literatur."
       (See item 1327.)

582.   Kronenberger, Louis. "Defoe—an Island and a Plague."
       Saturday Review of Literature, 32, 15 January 1949,
       pp. 9-10, 35. This article also serves as the Intro-
       duction to the Modern Library edition of *Robinson
       Crusoe and A Journal of the Plague Year*.

       Seeks to identify the appeal of *Robinson Crusoe*. It
       probably lies in Defoe's use of a realistic method to
       describe every boy's fantasies: the narrative technique
       is realistically mundane and Crusoe is a bore, yet he
       is monarch of all he surveys, a man with a whole island
       for a toy. From the raw material of his island, Crusoe
       forges a tidy little England complete with servants.
       Defoe uses the same flat, matter-of-fact method in *A
       Journal of the Plague Year*, his most unified work, to
       create an illusion of absolute reality.

583.   Kwan-Terry, John. "Robinson Crusoe through Chinese
       Eyes." *Journal of the Australasian Universities
       Language and Literature Association: A Journal of
       Literary Criticism, Philology, and Linguistics*, 51
       (1979), 20-28.

       Compares Lin Shee's 1905 "translation" of *Robinson
       Crusoe* with Defoe's original work. See John Hay's
       negative review in *The Scriblerian*, 13 (1980), 4.

584. Laird, John. "Robinson Crusoe's Philosophy." *Philo-*
      sophical Incursions into English Literature. Cam-
      bridge: The University Press, 1946. Pp. 21-33.

      Calls the philosophy of *Robinson Crusoe* a careful and
      serious expression of the liberal thought of its age.
      Actually, the discussion that follows concentrates on
      the plot involving Crusoe's filial disobedience and his
      punishment for it on his lonely island.

585. Lannert, Gustaf L. *An Investigation into the Language*
      of "Robinson Crusoe" as Compared with that of Other
      18th Century Works. Upsala: Almqvist & Wiksells,
      1910. A section of this work appears in the Norton
      Critical edition of *Robinson Crusoe*, item 28.

      Generalizes about Defoe's language and then analyzes
      specific usages and parts of speech in *Robinson Crusoe.*
      Lannert finds Defoe's language to be highly Germanic
      and remarkably free from classical allusions and quota-
      tions. He goes on to discuss and analyze Defoe's use
      of adjectives, personal pronouns, verbs, etc.

      Review: *Zeitschrift für franzosischen und englischen*
      Unterricht, 16 (1917), 227-30.

586. Latham, Jacqueline E.M. "Coleridge and Defoe." (London)
      Times Literary Supplement, 20 February 1969, p. 186.

      Finds a source for two lines of *The Ancient Mariner*
      in Defoe's *The Farther Adventures of Robinson Crusoe.*

587. Leckie, John D. "A Spanish Robinson Crusoe." *Chambers*
      Journal, 11 (1908), 510-12.

      Discovers a source for *Robinson Crusoe* in Garcilaso de
      Vega's *Commentarios Reales* (translated into English in
      1688) which relates the adventures of a shipwrecked
      Spanish sailor, Pedro Serrano, who spent seven years on
      an isolated cay in the Caribbean Sea.

588. Leslie, Francis. "Defoe, Robin, and Crusoe." *Notes*
      and Queries, 164 (1933), 26.

      Responds to J.R. Moore's attempt to locate sources
      for the name "Robinson Crusoe" (see item 618) by sug-
      gesting that Defoe may have met a real person with a
      similar name. Also see Moore's refutation of this pos-
      sibility (item 619).

589. Lewis, C.S. "Correspondence." *Essays in Criticism*, 1
      (1951), 313.

      Questions Ian Watt's interpretation of the myths of
      Midas and the Rheingold. See Watt, "Robinson Crusoe
      as a Myth," item 689, and Watt's reply to Lewis, item
      687.

*   Liebs, Elke. *Die pädagogische Insel: Studien zur
      Rezeption des "Robinson Crusoe" in deutschen Jugend-
      bearbeitungen.* (See item 1330.)

590. Little, Bryan. *Crusoe's Captain: Being the Life of
      Woodes Rogers, Seaman, Trader, Colonial Governor.*
      London: Odhams Press, 1960.

      Suggests that Defoe collaborated with Woodes Rogers,
      the rescuer of Alexander Selkirk, on Rogers' *A Cruising
      Voyage Round the World.* The Introduction to the latter—
      a defense of the Earl of Oxford's plans for the South
      Sea trade—may have been written by Defoe. Little re-
      views Defoe's sources for *Robinson Crusoe*: Rogers' ad-
      ventures, Selkirk's story, Pedro Serrano's shipwreck,
      and Maese Juan's sojourn.

      Reviews: Jean Béranger, *Etudes Anglaises*, 14 (1961),
      157-58; Christopher Lloyd, *History*, 45 (1960), 265-
      66; (London) *Times Literary Supplement*, 6 May 1960,
      p. 287; Francis Watson, *History Today*, 10 (1960), 437.

591. Lloyd, Christopher. *William Dampier.* London: Faber
      and Faber, 1966.

      Details Dampier's life and travels with scattered
      references to his influence on Defoe's *Robinson Crusoe*.

592. Lloyd, Roger. "The Riddle of Defoe: Impact of the
      Evangelical Challenge." *Church Times*, 16 July 1954,
      p. 549. Reprinted in Ellis, item 521.

      Sees Defoe as an unlikely but highly effective evan-
      gelicalist in *Robinson Crusoe*, one who imaginatively
      understands the kind of religious experience which he
      never had himself.

*   Lloyd, William S. *Catalogue of Various Editions of
      Robinson Crusoe and Other Books by and Referring to
      Daniel Defoe.* (See item 13.)

593. Loofbourow, John W. "Robinson Crusoe's Island and the
      Restoration *Tempest.*" *Enlightenment Essays*, 2 (1972),
      201-07.

Uncovers a source for Robinson Crusoe's island in the Dryden-Davenant musical version of Shakespeare's *Tempest*. "Defoe's symbolic cave and garden no longer exemplify, as in *The Tempest*, the 'natural' correspondence between microcosm and macrocosm under the control of 'right reason.' Rather, they are emblems of generic ambivalence, suggesting man's need and incapacity both for isolation and for community."

* Luithien, Gerda. *Der Realismus des Robinson Crusoe*. (See item 1334.)

* Luthi, Albert. *Daniel Defoe und seine forsetzungen zu Robinson Crusoe*. (See item 1335.)

594. Lynn, W.T. "Robinson Crusoe's Island." *Notes and Queries*, Tenth Series, 6 (1906), 225.

Corrects recent newspaper accounts which refer to Juan Fernandez as the island setting for *Robinson Crusoe*. Actually, Crusoe's adventures took place on an uninhabited island in the West Indies near the mouth of the Orinoco. See Armstrong, item 476; Constant Reader, item 502; Hubbard, item 561; and Wainwright, item 683.

595. MacCarthy, Desmond. "Crusoe's Example." *Listener*, 23 (1940), 1169-70.

Finds in Robinson--"a brave coward" full of apprehensive caution--an appropriate symbol of fortitude and resolution for the modern Englishman in a time of war.

596. MacDonald, Robert H. "The Creation of an Ordered World in *Robinson Crusoe*." *Dalhousie Review*, 56 (1976), 23-34.

Keys on several archetypal images--such as Crusoe's expulsion from his "womb-cave"--in order to demonstrate that "the hero's conquest of the outer space of his island parallels the exploration of the inner space of the self." On the island he progresses from spiritual ignorance to psychic integration, discovering himself and the divine.

597. McDowell, Tremaine. "An American Robinson Crusoe." *American Literature*, 1 (1929), 307-09.

Points out a number of parallels in diction and episode between *Robinson Crusoe* and an anonymously published American novel, *The Female American* (1767). The latter work shows the poverty of literary imagination in

eighteenth-century America; instead of writing an original work, the author typically chooses to imitate a
British novel.

598.   Mack, James D.   "*Robinson Crusoe.*" *Notes and Queries*,
       n.s. 8 (1961), 31.

       Requests information on the edition of *Robinson Crusoe*
       published in London in 1815 by Joseph Mawman.

599.   McKerrow, R.B.   "Bibliographical Terms." (London) *Times
       Literary Supplement*, 29 October 1925, p. 719.

       Refers to H.C. Hutchins' *Robinson Crusoe and Its
       Printing* (item 567) to discuss the technical differences
       between "editions" and "issues" of a work. Also see
       "Bibliographical Terms," item 485.

600.   MacLaine, Allan H.   "Robinson Crusoe and the Cyclops."
       Studies in Philology, 52 (1955), 599-604.

       Adds the *Odyssey* to the list of sources for *Robinson
       Crusoe*. Crusoe's "castle" on his island is patterned
       after Homer's description of Cyclops' cave.

601.   MacLulich, T.D.   "Crusoe in the Backwoods: A Canadian
       Fable?" *Mosaic*, 9, ii (1976), 115-26.

       Conducts an analysis of two Canadian classics--Mrs.
       Traill's *The Backwoods of Canada* and Mrs. Moodie's
       Roughing It in the Bush--by examining them in light of
       Robinson Crusoe's experience, which forms the central
       fable for much English-Canadian literature. Although
       Crusoe's experience does not fit perfectly with that of
       Traill and Moodie, there is considerable overlap in
       their adventures as lonely exiles in a strange land
       attempting to transform that land into "home." Also
       see Clara Thomas, item 674.

602.   Makeham, J.   "Cassell's Illustrated *Robinson Crusoe.*"
       Notes and Queries, Twelfth Series, 3 (1917), 194.

       Responds to Williams, item 691, by listing some of
       the artists involved in the production of Cassell's
       edition of *Crusoe*. See Cassell, item 497.

*   Mann, William E.   *Robinson Crusoé en France: Etude sur
       l'influence de cette oeuvre dans la littérature fran-
       çaise.* (See item 1336.)

603. Mannoni, O. *Prospero and Caliban: the Psychology of Colonization.* Translated by Pamela Powesland. New York: Praeger, 1956.

Applies psychoanalytic theory to Robinson Crusoe whose story, which comes from Defoe's unconscious, "recounts the long and difficult cure of a misanthropic neurosis." Also emerging from Defoe's unconscious is the attitude toward colonialism demonstrated in the relationship between Crusoe and Friday. The first part of *Robinson Crusoe* is highly symbolic, revealing many of Defoe's unconscious attitudes.

604. Martzoeff, C.L. "Robinson Crusoe—A Study in the New Geography." *Journal of Geography*, 10 (1912), 295-97.

Lists a number of incidents in *Robinson Crusoe* in which Crusoe "wrestles with nature" to establish a civilized order on his island.

605. Maslen, Keith I. "Edition Quantities for *Robinson Crusoe*, 1719." *Library*, Fifth Series, 24 (1969), 145-50.

Analyzes a newly discovered Bowyer printing ledger in order to find out how many copies of *Robinson Crusoe* were printed in 1719. Maslen speculates that probably 1,000 copies for each of the six 1719 editions were printed.

606. ———. "The Printers of *Robinson Crusoe*." *Library*, Fifth Series, 7 (1952), 124-31.

Examines the type and ornaments of the second and *two* third editions of *Robinson Crusoe* in order to show which parts were printed by William Bowyer and which by Hugh Meere and Henry Parker. Maslen denies that William Taylor, who published all three early editions of *Crusoe*, was also a printer, taking issue in this matter with Hutchins, item 569, and Hubbard, item 563. Also see Foxon, item 528.

607. Masuda, Izuru. "Style and Structure of *Robinson Crusoe*." *Anglica*, 4 (1962), 19-43.

Outlines the plot of *Robinson Crusoe* by breaking it into a prologue, three distinct episodes, and an epilogue. Each of these sections has its own motif. In the prologue, for example, the motif is the opposition of Crusoe's father to his son's going to sea.

*   Maynadier, G.H. "Introduction" to *Robinson Crusoe*.
        (See item 246.)

608.   Mégroz, Rudolphe L. "Alexander Selkirk." (London)
        Times Literary Supplement, 16 July 1938, p. 480.

        Provides biographical data on Selkirk, who lived at
        Largo, married a Frances Condis, and moved to London.

609.   ————. *The Real Robinson Crusoe*. London: Cresset
        Press, 1939.

        Tells the story of Alexander Selkirk's life. An ap-
        pendix attempts to refute the tale that Selkirk met with
        Defoe in Bristol and gave him "personal papers" which
        were the basis for *Robinson Crusoe*.

        Review: (London) *Times Literary Supplement*, 6 May 1939,
        p. 259.

610.   Meyers, Jeffrey. "Savagery and Civilization in *The Tem-
        pest*, *Robinson Crusoe*, and *Heart of Darkness*." *Con-
        radiana*, 2, iii (1970), 171-79.

        Finds Rousseau's doctrine of the purity of natural
        man very close to the views expressed by Defoe thirty-
        five years earlier in *Robinson Crusoe*. Friday is de-
        picted as possessing a primitive honor lacking in
        "civilized" man. Defoe's views of nature—that its
        order reflects heavenly order—also is close to Rousseau's
        attitude toward the natural world.

611.   Mezciems, Jenny. "Gulliver and Other Heroes." *The Art
        of Jonathan Swift*. Ed. Clive T. Probyn. New York:
        Barnes and Noble, 1978. Pp. 189-208.

        Locates Swift's art as standing between Pope's and
        Defoe's; Swift's "sympathies are with the poet but he
        insists on performing alongside the prose hack." Al-
        though in form they are similar, a striking contrast
        between Swift's *Gulliver's Travels* and Defoe's *Robinson
        Crusoe* is that the former has no heroic protagonist even
        though it abounds in heroic allusions and the latter
        does have a hero but without a heroic background.
        Crusoe heralds the new novel with its theme of a hero
        at first at odds with society but eventually being
        integrated into it. *Gulliver* concludes with its pro-
        tagonist alienated from society.

612.   Michel-Michot, Paulette. "The Myth of Innocence."
        Revue des Langues Vivantes, 28 (1962), 510-20.

Begins with a discussion of how William Golding's
Lord of the Flies (1954) is a modern answer to R.M.
Ballantyne's *The Coral Island* (1858) which shows innocence living in harmony with nature. The boys on
Ballantyne's island are civilized products of a British
empire built by the creative energy symbolized by Crusoe. The latter represents the middle class's rise to
power and its strong puritanism.

613. Mish, Charles C. "Early Eighteenth-Century Best
      Sellers in English Prose Fiction." *Papers of the
      Bibliographical Society of America*, 75 (1981), 413-18.

      Places about 400 pieces of best-selling prose fiction
      published between 1700 and 1740 in four categories;
      Part I of *Robinson Crusoe* is the eighth leading "best-
      seller" in its category and Part II of the same work
      is tenth.

614. Moffat, James. "The Religion of Robinson Crusoe."
      Contemporary Review, 115 (1919), 664-69.

      Distills from the moralizing passages in *Robinson
      Crusoe* some generalizations about Defoe's religious
      beliefs, which he identifies as the same as Crusoe's.
      The main ingredient in Defoe's religion is a belief in
      Providence.

615. Moore, Catherine E. "Robinson and Xury and Inkle and
      Yarico." *Modern Language Notes*, 19 (1981), 24-29.

      Accepts the view that the main theme of *Robinson
      Crusoe* is the hero's spiritual journey; his early re-
      lationship with Xury demonstrates that at the beginning
      of this journey, Crusoe is guilty of the sin of in-
      gratitude. Perhaps the Crusoe-Xury story had as its
      source the Inkle-Yarico anecdote, which illustrates in
      a similar way the same theme and which appeared in
      Spectator, number 11, in 1711.

616. ———. "Robinson Crusoe's Two Servants: The Measure
      of His Conversion." *A Fair Day in the Affections:
      Literary Essays in Honor of Robert B. White, Jr.*
      Eds. Jack M. Durant and M. Thomas Hester. Raleigh:
      Winston, 1980. Pp. 111-18.

      Suggests that Crusoe's treatment of Friday is morally
      superior to his treatment of Xury, his first servant
      whom he sells into slavery, because his own spiritual
      condition changes. At the time of his dealings with
      Xury, Crusoe is estranged from God, but by the time he

meets Friday, he has been saved. "Xury is Crusoe's
lost opportunity; Friday is the fulfillment of his
Christian duty."

617.   Moore, John Robert. "A Defoe Allusion in *Gulliver's
       Travels*." *Notes and Queries*, 178 (1940), 79-80.

       Views the first paragraph of *Gulliver's Travels* as a
       burlesque of *Robinson Crusoe*, reflecting Swift's dislike
       of Defoe.

618.   ———. "Defoe, Robin and Crusoe." *Notes and Queries*,
       164 (1933), 26.

       Attempts to locate sources for the name "Robinson
       Crusoe" and suggests Dampier's *A New Voyage*; less likely
       but possible is the remembrance of an old schoolmate,
       Timothy Crusoe. Also see Leslie, item 588, and Moore,
       item 619.

619.   ———. "Defoe, Robin and Crusoe." *Notes and Queries*,
       164 (1933), 249.

       Replies to Leslie, item 588, by pointing out that
       Leslie's guidebook source for the existence of a real
       Robinson Crusoe was in fact lifted from Defoe's novel
       itself. Also see Moore, item 618.

620.   ———. "Defoe, Selkirk, and John Atkins." *Notes and
       Queries*, 179 (1940), 436-38.

       Shows that John Atkins, a friend and literary col-
       laborator of Defoe, had a personal knowledge of Alexander
       Selkirk and may even have been present at his death.
       The bulk of the article traces Atkins' service aboard
       the *Swallow*, sister ship to Selkirk's ship, the *Wey-
       mouth*, in 1720/21.

621.   ———. "*The Tempest* and *Robinson Crusoe*." *Review
       of English Studies*, 21 (1945), 52-56.

       Constructs an outline of the episode in *Robinson
       Crusoe* in which the hero is delivered from his island
       and points out that it is identical to the analogous
       parts of *The Tempest*. Thus, Shakespeare's play is an
       important source for Defoe's novel.

*   Mummendy, Richard. *Defoe: Robinson Crusoe. Der Ur-
       Robinson*. (See item 1346.)

622. Napier, Elizabeth R. "Objects and Order in *Robinson
      Crusoe*." *South Atlantic Quarterly*, 80 (1981), 84-94.

      Argues that in his incessant and nearly obsessive
      arranging of his possessions, Crusoe is imitating God's
      order. Thus, there is no conflict between Crusoe's
      materialistic impulses and his spiritual aims; the former
      is a means to the latter.

623. Nettleton, G.R. "Robinson Crusoe--Sheridan's Drury Lane
      Pantomime--I." (London) *Times Literary Supplement*,
      25 December 1943, p. 624.

      Presents the first full discussion of Sheridan's
      pantomime, *Robinson Crusoe; or, Harlequin Friday*, which
      opened on 29 January 1781 as an after-piece to *The Win-
      ter's Tale* and which was performed twenty eight times in
      the following year. The libretto by Thomas Becket runs
      twenty pages in octavo and outlines the twelve scenes
      of the pantomime; the libretto is summarized by Nettle-
      ton. Also see Nettleton, item 624; Boas, item 487; and
      Rosenfeld, item 653.

624. ————. "*Robinson Crusoe*--Sheridan's Drury Lane Panto-
      mime--II." (London) *Times Literary Supplement*, 1 Jan-
      uary 1944, p. 12.

      Continues his discussion (see item 623 for the first
      part of this two-part article) of Sheridan's *Robinson
      Crusoe; or, Harlequin Friday*. Nettleton draws evidence
      from newspapers, reviews, diaries, and memoirs, among
      other sources, to prove that Sheridan authored the
      pantomime.

625. Nicholls, Norah. "Some Early Editions of Defoe."
      Bookman, 80 (1931), 42-43.

      Describes early editions of a number of Defoe's works
      and distinguishes between genuine and spurious printings.
      For example, the author notes that two editions of *Jure
      Divino* came out the same day, July 20, 1706, but only
      one was genuine. Also see Lloyd, item 13.

626. Nicolaisen, W.F.H. "Desert Island Onomastics." *Liter-
      ary Onomastic Studies*, 5 (1978), 110-51.

      Regards Robinson Crusoe's failure to provide names for
      places on his desert island as an indication of his
      fearful refusal "to observe that the natural scene on
      his island composes a landscape." There is only "a

geography conceived in moral terms," which eliminates
the need for "toponymic structuring."

*   Nordon, Pierre. *"Robinson Crusoe*: unité et contradic-
        tions." (See item 1352.)

*   Nourrisson, Paul. *Jean-Jacques Rousseau et Robinson
        Crusoe*. (See item 1353.)

627.   Novak, Maximillian E. "Crusoe the King and the Political
        Evolution of His Island." *Studies in English Litera-
        ture*, 2 (1962), 337-50.

        Regards the *Surprising Adventures* and the *Farther Ad-
ventures of Robinson Crusoe* as a single work concerned
with the political evolution of society in the state of
nature. Defoe depicts the development of society from
anarchy to an acceptance of law and limitations on
freedom. He bases this aspect of his work on the early
history of Bermuda.

*   ———. *Economics and the Fiction of Daniel Defoe.*
        (See item 433.)

628.   ———. "Imaginary Island and Real Beasts: The Imagina-
        tive Genesis of *Robinson Crusoe*." *Tennessee Studies
        in Literature*, 19 (1974), 57-78.

        Contends that *Robinson Crusoe* is in part derived from
Defoe's imaginative reshaping of the materials he worked
with as a journalist in the years preceding that novel's
publication in 1719. The carry-over from his journalism
to his fiction "is not so much a matter of specific incidents as it is of general images and feelings."
Defoe's journalistic interests in storms, shipwrecks,
wild beasts, and exiles are reflected in *Robinson Crusoe*.

629.   ———. "Robinson Crusoe and Economic Utopia." *Kenyon
        Review*, 25 (1963), 474-90.

        Reads *Robinson Crusoe* as an illustration of Defoe's
basic economic concepts. In his novel, Defoe reverses
the historical process of specialization and suggests a
form of economic primitivism in which man is shown
living under natural economic conditions. By returning
to the primitive, Defoe is better able to emphasize his
major economic themes: (1) labor and invention create
things of use, and (2) the value of things depends on
their utility. Defoe's views of the effect of labor

upon nature are influenced heavily by John Locke's
ideas. On the question of the rest of society, however,
Defoe deviates from Locke; by having Crusoe express conviction that the island belongs to him, Defoe is concur-
ring with Grotius and Pufendorf, who believe that
islands belong to whoever first seizes them, and not
with Locke, who believes that labor alone creates and
establishes a right to property.

630.   ————. "Robinson Crusoe's Fear and the Search for
        Natural Man." *Modern Philology*, 58 (1961), 238-45.

Notes that when *Robinson Crusoe* was first published,
a popular topic of discussion among intellectuals was
man's condition in the state of nature, that state
being defined as one in which the individual is isolated
and "abstracted from both society and religion." In
Defoe's day there were three major opinions on natural
man: (1) through his reason, such a man could attain
the same moral and intellectual condition as did men
in society; (2) he would be savage and brutal, but would
have greater freedom and happiness along with fewer
vices than did civilized man; and (3) because man is
basically a social creature, he would feel insecure in
the state of nature and thus would be unhappy and living
in constant fear of death. Crusoe is a paradigm of
the latter, the "timid" natural man, one who lives in
anxiety and is eager to give up his solitude for the
comparative security of the social state.

631.   ————. "Robinson Crusoe's 'Original Sin.'" *Studies
        in English Literature*, 1 (1961), 19-29.

Suggests that the "original sin" against his father
and God that troubles Robinson Crusoe so much "is his
refusal to follow the 'calling' chosen for him by his
father." Crusoe is led to his "sin" by his lack of
economic prudence, his inability to steadfastly pursue
a profession, his distaste for a bourgeois life, and
his love of travel. Crusoe does not disobey his parents
in the name of economic freedom but because he is romantic and adventurous.

*   ————. "'Simon Forecastle's Weekly Journal': Some
        Notes on Defoe's Conscious Artistry." (See item 286.)

632.   ————. "The Wild Man Comes to Tea." *The Wild Man
        Within*. Eds. Edward Dudley and Maximillian E. Novak.

Pittsburgh: University of Pittsburgh Press, 1972. Pp. 183–221.

Studies eighteenth-century primitivism by focusing on the 1724 discovery of Peter the "wild boy." Defoe wrote the longest contemporary treatise (*Mere Nature Delineated*) on Peter, but even before that his profound interest in primitivism is demonstrated in *Robinson Crusoe*. Of course, unlike Peter, Crusoe does not emerge from the wild to enter civilization, but rather returns to the wild where he gains inner peace through shedding "civilized" discontents and reaching "an understanding of the teleological scheme of the universe and his place in it."

*   Otsuka, Hisao. "Human Type in 'Robinson Crusoe.'" (See item 1355.)

633.   Parker, George. "The Allegory of *Robinson Crusoe*." *History*, 10 (1925), 11–25.

Reiterates an old argument (and one that almost all modern critics reject as absurd) that *Robinson Crusoe* is an allegory of Defoe's life; for example, the author argues that Crusoe's pet goats represent Defoe's publications and that the mysterious footprint in the sand is *The Shortest Way with the Dissenters*.

633A. Parker, Gillian. "Crusoe through the Looking Glass." *The English Novel and the Movies*. Eds. Michael Klein and Gillian Parker. New York: Ungar, 1981. Pp. 14–27.

Not reviewed by the compiler.

*   Partamyan, R. "Robinzon v Armyanskoi Literature." (See item 1359.)

634.   Pearlman, E. "Robinson Crusoe and the Cannibals." *Mosaic*, 10 (1976), 39–55.

Combines Freudianism and Marxism to provide a reading of *Robinson Crusoe* as a depiction of the neurotic basis of both middle-class individualism and colonialism. Crusoe himself is a paradigm of the colonizer: unable to succeed in his own land, he moves to an undeveloped area in which the technological advantages of his culture enable him to enslave the indigenous population and exploit the land; he is even willing to justify massacre if it will aid him in achieving his aims.

635. Peck, H. Daniel. "*Robinson Crusoe*: The Moral Geography
of Limitation." *Journal of Narrative Technique*, 3
(1973), 20-31.

Rejects the views of *Robinson Crusoe* which see the
island as the "utopia of the Protestant Ethic," a symbolic setting for the "evolution of society in the state
of nature," or a moral testing ground for Crusoe's
religious beliefs. Instead, the island is a real--not
mythic or symbolic--place which emphasizes the importance
of environment to the development of self. The island
experience teaches Defoe the virtues of a "bounded" life;
without a significant "center," a person wastes his
energies in useless activities and never comes to terms
with himself.

*   Petersen, Ulrich Horst. "Om Robinson Crusoe." (See
item 1360.)

636. Peterson, Spiro. "A Correction." *Johnsonian Newsletter*,
18 (December 1958), 11-12.

Corrects the introduction to the Augustan Reprint
Society edition of Fielding's *Voyages of Mr. Job Vinegar*
which says that the *Voyages* contain Fielding's only
reference to *Robinson Crusoe*; in fact, Fielding mentions
both that novel and "Mrs. Veal" in *Tom Jones*.

*   Pienaar, W.J.B. *English Influences in Dutch Literature
and Justus Van Effen as Intermediary.* (See item 1008.)

*   Pilgrim, Konrad. "Zu Defoes Weltverständnis im 3. Teil
von *Robinson Crusoe*. (See item 1361.)

*   Pire, G. "Jean-Jacques Rousseau et *Robinson Crusoe*."
(See item 1364.)

637. Polak, Léon. "A Source of Defoe's *Robinson Crusoe*."
Notes and Queries, Eleventh Series, 9 (1914), 486.

Notes that one source for *Robinson Crusoe* is Hendrik
Smeeks' work. Also see Goebel, item 534, and Hubbard,
item 560.

638. Poling, James. *The Man Who Saved Robinson Crusoe.* New
York: Norton, 1967.

Tells the story of Alexander Selkirk and his rescuer,
Woodes Rogers, and reiterates the obvious by arguing
that Selkirk was the model for Robinson Crusoe on his
island.

639.   Pollard, Alfred W. "Robeson Cruso." *Library*, Third
       Series, 4 (1913), 204-20.

       Turns up a mysterious 1719 edition of *Robinson Crusoe*
       (spelled "Robeson Cruso"). This edition, Pollard argues,
       is too badly printed to be designed for London sale and,
       most importantly, is earlier than the supposed first
       edition issued by William Taylor in 1719. Pollard is
       at a loss to explain this edition unless it was a piracy
       from stolen proofs of Taylor's edition designed for
       itinerant peddlers in the country or unless Defoe had
       the book set up as he wrote it and then revised it; the
       first theory seems more probable than the second.

*   Praviel, A. "Le père de 'Robinson': Daniel De Foe."
       (See item 1368.)

*   Prica, Zora. *Defoes Robinson Crusoe und Robert Poltocks
       Peter Wilkins.* (See item 1370.)

*   Price, Martin. *To the Palace of Wisdom: Studies in
       Order and Energy from Dryden to Blake.* (See item 796.)

640.   Purves, William L. "Authorship of *Robinson Crusoe*."
       Athenaeum, 11 May 1903, pp. 563, 595-96.

       Believes that Harley was the author of both *Crusoe*
       and *Memoirs of a Cavalier* and that Defoe acted only as
       editor.

641.   ———. "The 'O' Edition of *Robinson Crusoe*." *Athen-
       aeum*, 11 April 1903, pp. 465-66, 498.

       Studies the textual differences between the "official"
       first edition of *Crusoe* and a version which may have
       been printed earlier by Defoe himself.

642.   Quennell, Peter. "Crusoe's Island." *Horizon*, 9 (Spring
       1967), 66-83.

       Reviews both Alexander Selkirk's life and Defoe's
       reshaping of Selkirk's island adventure for *Robinson
       Crusoe*. The essay is accompanied by photographs of
       Juan Fernandez Island, the place where Selkirk was
       marooned, and several illustrations reprinted from
       early editions of *Crusoe*.

643.   Rasmussen, Kirk G. "Robinson Crusoe: A Motif of Initia-
       tion." *Proceedings of the Utah Academy of Science,
       Arts, and Letters*, 47 (1970), 19-24.

This item is listed in Abernethy, item 1, but has not been seen by the compiler.

644. Rathburn, Robert C. "The Makers of the British Novel." *From Jane Austen to Joseph Conrad: Essays Collected in Memory of James T. Hillhouse.* Eds. Robert C. Rathburn and Martin Steinmann, Jr. Minneapolis: University of Minnesota Press, 1958. Pp. 3-22.

Lauds *Robinson Crusoe* as the first unified novel, "complete in theme and not arbitrarily limited by historical time and circumstances." Defoe's success is in great part due to his ability to create a believable persona: Crusoe is the average middle-class man in abnormal circumstances. Defoe's ability to found the unusual on realistic detail made the novel thereafter "a story of real life."

* Reckwitz, Erhard. *Die Robinsonade: Themen und Formen einer literarischen Gattung.* (See item 1290.)

645. Rexroth, Kenneth. "Robinson Crusoe." *Saturday Review*, 51, 9 November 1968, p. 18.

Rejects the notion that Defoe was a primitive or naive writer. He was a conscious artist who skillfully used his "elaborate structure of verity" to plumb psychological depths. Crusoe's story, which can be read on various levels, is one of "spiritual realization."

* Richard, Elie. "Robinson Crusoe et Daniel de Foe." (See item 1376.)

646. Richardson, Humphrey. *The Sexual Life of Robinson Crusoe.* Paris, 1955.

An intensive interlibrary loan search failed to turn up a copy of this work, listed by Payne, item 21.

647. Robertson, J. Minto. "The True Story of Alexander Selkirk." *Chamber's Journal*, August 1941, pp. 485-88.

Presents a concise biography of Alexander Selkirk, whose adventures as a castaway were the source for *Robinson Crusoe*.

648. Robins, Harry F. "How Smart Was Robinson Crusoe?" *Publications of the Modern Language Association*, 67 (1952), 782-89.

Contests those views of Robinson Crusoe which regard him as an ingenious man who makes do with very little

equipment. In fact, Crusoe is not very inventive, and
he has a huge variety of supplies which he fails to use
to his advantage. Crusoe's ineptitude and ignorance are
part of the realism of the novel, besides which Defoe
had to find ways to keep Crusoe on the island in order
to fully exploit its fictional potential.

649. Rogers, Pat. "Crusoe's Home." *Essays in Criticism*,
      24 (1974), 375-90.

Reinterprets *Robinson Crusoe* and concludes that it is
neither a tale of primitive man in the state of nature
nor a paradigm of the capitalist exploitation of nature
for profit; rather, it is a book about the domestic
side of bourgeois life. Crusoe's energies are constant-
ly turned toward domestic chores, many of them traditionally female tasks, such as cooking, sewing, tending
goats, and expanding living accommodations. Crusoe
likes his "home" on the island so much that he waits
five years to sail the island's coastline, and he always
expresses relief when he returns to his domicile from
his infrequent explorations. Crusoe is *homo domesticus*
and his narrative is the epic of home-making.

650. ————. *Robinson Crusoe*. Unwin Critical Library. Lon-
      don: George Allen and Unwin, 1979.

Studies the novel from a great variety of perspectives.
The seven chapters that form the *corpus* of the book are
titled: Preliminary; Travel, Trade, and Empire; Religion
and Allegory; Social and Philosophic Themes; Literary
Background; Structure and Style; and Critical History.
Six appendices follow: Woodes Rogers' Narratives of
Selkirk, Richard Steele's Narrative of Selkirk, The
Illustrations of *Robinson Crusoe*, Table of Dates, Gazet-
eer, and Biographical Index. The book also includes a
map of Crusoe's voyages, a bibliography, and a general
index. The opening chapter presents a brief biography
of Defoe, a detailed history of editions and imitations
of *Crusoe*, and a section on the composition of the
novel. Chapter Two treats Defoe's great interest in
geography and travel, and it shows how "discovery and
commercial expansion" influenced his work. Chapter
Three deals with the prevailing spiritual motif of
Crusoe. Chapter Four blends the views of Rogers and
other critics on such topics as "The Middle Station,"
"Economic Ideas," "Self-Preservation and Self-Help,"
and "Solitude and Retirement." In Chapter Five, Rogers
traces Defoe's use and modification of literary prece-

dents, his contributions to the development of the
modern novel, the nature of the readership of the novel,
and the view of *Crusoe* by Defoe's contemporaries. Chapter Six studies the relationship of the three parts of
the extended novel and focuses on "the meaning of the
footprint," emphasizing Hunter's emblematic reading
(item 564) and Brooks' structuralist interpretation
(item 399). The final chapter surveys the critical
history of *Crusoe*.

Review: Jeanne Devoize, *Etudes Anglaises*, 35 (1982),
214-15.

651. Rogers, Stanley R.H. *Crusoes and Castaways*. London:
Harrap, 1932.

Reviews the writing of *Robinson Crusoe*, summarizes its
plot, and surveys the most important Robinsonades before
presenting several actual castaway stories beginning
with that of Alexander Selkirk.

652. Roorda, Gerridina. *Realism in Daniel De Foe's Narratives of Adventure*. Wageningen: H. Veenman & Zonen,
1929. Reprinted by Norwood Editions, 1976.

Explores Defoe's realistic techniques in *Robinson
Crusoe*, *The Farther Adventures of Robinson Crusoe*,
Captain Singleton, and *A New Voyage round the World*,
concluding that there is "a signal falling off in realistic effect after the island episode in *Robinson Crusoe*." The latter is remarkably realistic in its incident, scene, action, and characterization and is perfectly adapted to the tastes of its middle-class,
Puritan audience. *The Farther Adventures* is not as
realistically successful; the reader is told too much
and not shown enough, there are many errors in fact,
a disparity between Crusoe's age and his personality
exists, and minor characters are portrayed clumsily.
In *Captain Singleton*, Defoe simply did not know enough
about the scenes he utilized or the habits and speech
of mariners to make his story credible. The realistic
value of *A New Voyage* is almost nonexistent because
"the book contains no vivid representation of any
person, thing, or scene." Thus, Defoe's vaunted realism, at least in his adventure narratives, is seriously
flawed, except in *Robinson Crusoe*.

Review: A.W. Secord, *Modern Language Notes*, 45 (1930),
480.

653. Rosenfeld, Sybil. "*Robinson Crusoe*." (London) *Times Literary Supplement*, 4 March 1944, p. 120.

Notes a performance of Sheridan's *Robinson Crusoe* pantomime in 1790. Also see Nettleton, items 623 and 624, and Boas, item 487.

*   Rosenkranz, A. "Kreuznach--die Heimatstadt von Robinson Crusoe's Vater?" (See item 1380.)

654. Ross, Angus. "Introduction" to *The Life and Adventures of Robinson Crusoe of York, Mariner* by Daniel Defoe. Baltimore: Penguin, 1965. Pp. 7-21.

Listed by Payne (item 21), this item was not seen by the compiler.

*   Rovetto, Matteo. "Influence ou coïncidence entre *Robinson Crusoe* de Defoe et l'*île des esclaves* de Marivaux." (See item 1383.)

654A. Sankey, Margaret. "Meaning through Intertextuality: Isomorphism of Defoe's *Robinson Crusoe* and Tournier's *Vendredi* ou les limbes du Pacifique." *Australian Journal of French Studies*, 18 (1981), 77-88.

The compiler did not personally review this item.

*   Sanov, V. "Taina Robinzona Kruzo." (See item 1385.)

*   Sarnetski, D.H. "Daniel Defoe: Robinson Crusoe." (See item 1386.)

*   Scholte, J.H. "Robinsonades." (See item 1390.)

*   Schonhorn, Manuel. "Defoe: The Literature of Politics and the Politics of Some Fictions." (See item 320.)

*   Schou, Søren. "Robinsons to verdener: Om Defoes *Robinson Crusoe*." (See item 1391.)

655. Schrock, Thomas S. "Considering Crusoe: Part I." *Interpretation*, 1 (1970), 76-106.

Rejects the common view of *Robinson Crusoe* as a work deeply infused with Protestant religious impulses, seeing in it instead a pronounced anti-religious drift which is in keeping with early modern secular political philosophy. Crusoe never even confesses, let alone does penance for, his most serious sins; at best, his religious

feelings are spurious and eventually they completely
vanish. (Also see item 656.)

656. ———. "Considering Crusoe: Part II." *Interpretation*,
      1 (1970), 169-232.

      Continues a study of *Robinson Crusoe* as reflective of
      early modern secular political philosophy (also see
      item 655). Crusoe delivers himself from moral restraint
      in order to free himself to manipulate others and
      thereby the world. In his exploitation of Friday, he
      follows the pattern of Hobbes' "commonwealth by acquisi-
      tion." Shrock views Crusoe as a vicious, exploitive
      tyrant who prefigures the worst tyrants of the twentieth
      century.

*   Schutt, J.H. "Hermann Ullrich: a Bibliography." (See
      item 24.)

*   Secord, Arthur W. "Introduction" to *A Journal of the
      Plague Year and Other Pieces* by Daniel Defoe. (See
      item 862.)

*   ———. *Studies in the Narrative Method of Defoe*.
      (See item 327.)

657. Seeber, Edward D. "Oroonoko and Crusoe's Man Friday."
      Modern Language Quarterly, 12 (1951), 286-91.

      Discovers in Aphra Behn's *Oroonoko* many details sim-
      ilar to those used by Defoe to describe Friday. For ex-
      ample, neither Behn's Oroonoko nor Defoe's Friday have
      negroid features or curly hair.

658. Seeley, John. "Some Green Thoughts on a Green Theme."
      Tri-Quarterly, 23/24 (1972), 576-638.

      Sees Robinson Crusoe as "a brilliant portrait of the
      English colonial mind, from whence the resourceful
      Yankee sprang." For Crusoe, nature exists to be put
      in order so that it can serve mankind. In the process
      of ordering his domain, Crusoe is regenerated both
      physically and spiritually.

659. Seidel, Michael. "Crusoe in Exile." *Publications of
      the Modern Language Association*, 96 (1981), 363-74.

      Presents a reading of *Robinson Crusoe* as "narrative
      allegorical history" which "fulfills a traditional
      narrative pattern of sustained risk, trauma, and re-

turn ... allegorically analogous to patterns in biblical
history, various national histories, and spiritual and
personal 'lives.'" Because exiles suffer "domestic
withdrawal," Crusoe allegorically reconstructs a home
from his island. There also is "an interplay" between
Crusoe's twenty-eight years of exile (1659 to 1686) and
the years of the restored Stuart rule up to the Glorious
Revolution of 1688.

*   Sgard, Birgitta. "Un aspect de la révolution romantique:
       La traduction de *Robinson Crusoe* par Pétrus Borel."
       (See item 1395.)

660.   Sheppard, Alfred T. "Robinson Crusoe in the Euston
       Road." *Bookman*, 81 (1931), 8-9.

       Describes R. Ridgill Trout's collection of Crusoe
       materials, which may be the largest in the world.

*   Shinagel, Michael. *Robinson Crusoe: An Authoritative
       Text, Backgrounds and Sources, Criticism.* (See item
       28.)

661.   Shugrue, Michael F. "The Sincerest Form of Flattery:
       Imitation in the Early Eighteenth-Century Novel."
       South Atlantic Quarterly, 70 (1971), 248-55.

       Lists some of the borrowings from *Robinson Crusoe* in
       Mrs. Penelope Aubin's first novel, *The Strange Adventures
       of the Count de Vinevil and His Family* (1721); in all
       seven of her novels, Mrs. Aubin consciously used situa-
       tions, details, and stylistic techniques taken directly
       from Defoe.

662.   Siegel, Sally D. "Everyman's Defoe: Paradox as Unity
       in *Robinson Crusoe.*" *Thoth*, 14 (1974), 51-56.

       Suggests an "inclusive interpretation" of *Robinson
       Crusoe*: Defoe reconciles "the balance sheet" and
       religion by showing that Crusoe's growing fortune is
       God's reward for his piety.

*   Smit, E.M. "Een collectie betreffende *Robinson Crusoe*
       in de biblioteek der rijksuniversiteit te Groningen."
       (See item 1398.)

663.   Smith, J. Harry. "Theology of Robinson Crusoe." *Holborn
       Review*, 47 (1925), 37-47.

       Finds the theology of *Crusoe* within the framework of
       Unitarian beliefs.

664. Snodgrass, A.E. "The Source of Defoe." *Cornhill Maga-*
      zine, 159 (1939), 541-49.

      Assigns the source of *Robinson Crusoe* to William
      Dampier whose many adventures and writings provided
      Defoe with details not only for *Crusoe* but for several
      other works as well.

665. Spacks, Patricia Meyer. *Imagining a Self: Autobiog-*
      raphy and Novel in Eighteenth-Century England. Cam-
      bridge, Mass.: Harvard University Press, 1976.

      Compares "the concern with imaginative growth" that
      permeates Cowper's *Memoir* with that same concern in
      Robinson Crusoe. The conventions employed by Defoe
      are the same as those used by Cowper because both lit-
      eral and fictional spiritual autobiography stress the
      same thing: the notion that the imagination's proper
      function is to draw men toward God. (This chapter
      originally appeared as an article--see item 666.) Also
      see Starr, item 453.

666. ————. "The Soul's Imaginings: Daniel Defoe, William
      Cowper." *Publications of the Modern Language Associa-*
      tion, 91 (1976), 420-35. Included as Chapter 2 of
      Spacks' *Imagining a Self*, item 665.

      Charts Crusoe's progress to self-understanding by
      tracing his emotional and imaginative development. At
      first, "Crusoe dwells in false images which lead him to
      mistaken assessments of his own position," but later
      his imagination is subordinated to God's purposes and
      becomes "a salvationary force."

*   Spearman, Diana. *The Novel and Society*. (See item 342.)

*   Starr, George A. *Defoe and Spiritual Autobiography*.
      (See item 453.)

667. ————. "Escape from Barbary: A Seventeenth Century
      Genre." *Huntington Library Quarterly*, 29 (1965),
      35-52.

      Compares *Robinson Crusoe* with the stories of escapes
      from Barbary, noting that Defoe uses some of the same
      material such as the Sallee episode.

*   Staverman, Werner H. "Een Nederlandse Bron van de
      'Robinson Crusoe.'" (See item 668.)

668.   ————. "Robinson Crusoe in Holland. On the Two Hun-
        dredth Anniversary of the Death of Daniel Defoe."
        English Studies, 13 (1931), 49-58.

        Names Defoe the creator of the modern novel but says
        Defoe wrote *Robinson Crusoe* "as a journalist" and so
        was unaware of his achievement. Staverman comments on
        the novel's influence in Europe and notes the many
        translations into Dutch and French printed in Holland
        during the eighteenth century.

*   ————. *Robinson Crusoe in Nederland*. (See item 1404.)

669.   Stein, William Bysshe. "Robinson Crusoe: The Trickster
        Tricked." *Centennial Review*, 9 (1965), 271-88.

        Contends that *Robinson Crusoe* has never been properly
        assessed as a novel consciously designed to demonstrate
        to the bourgeoisie its economic importance and reconcile
        its materialistic ambitions with its spiritual values.
        Defoe, ironically and deliberately, exposes the hypocrisy
        of the budding capitalist, showing that Crusoe's success
        stems from his immoral and materialistic ambitions.
        Defoe depicts Crusoe as an illogical, cowardly buffoon.
        Readers have been misled in their interpretations of
        Crusoe because Defoe never acknowledged its comic irony
        and because the two further volumes of the story, written
        out of greed, distort the comedy of the first work.

*   Stockum, Th. C. van. "Robinson Crusoe, Vorrobinsonaden
        und Robinsonaden." (See item 1405.)

670.   Streeter, Harold Wade. *The Eighteenth Century English
        Novel in French Translation: A Bibliographical Study*.
        New York: Institute of French Studies, Inc., 1936.

        Treats in detail the translations, popularity, and
        influence of *Robinson Crusoe* and *Moll Flanders* in France.
        The latter may have influenced Prévost's *Manon Lescaut*,
        but the former definitely exerted a strong influence on
        a variety of writers throughout the eighteenth century.
        In fact, *Crusoe* exerted more influence in France than
        any other English novel until the 1741 translation of
        Pamela.

*   Stukasa, I. [Afterword to] *Robinson Crusoe*. (See item
        1406.)

671.   Sullivan, Tom R. "The Uses of a Fictional Formula:
        The Selkirk Mother-Lode." *Journal of Popular Culture*,
        8 (1974), 35-52.

      Attributes the popularity of the Robinsonade to its
timeless appeal to the spirit of individualism and to
its depiction of man in confrontation with his environment. Alexander Selkirk's story and Defoe's version of
it in *Robinson Crusoe* captured the important values of
the age, just as later J.M. Barrie and William Golding
were to write Robinsonades which reflected the values of
their ages.

*   Sutherland, James. *Defoe*. (See item 350.)

*   ————. "Introduction" to *Robinson Crusoe and Other
Writings* by Daniel Defoe. (See item 353.)

672. Swados, Harvey. "Afterword" to *Robinson Crusoe* by
Daniel Defoe. New York: Signet, 1961. Pp. 299-316.

      Calls Defoe "an aging Cockney hack ... who became a
great novelist almost in spite of himself." In *Robinson
Crusoe*, he provided a "gentle" introduction to the
exotic and he created a manual for the domestication
of nature. His skill lies in his ability to make the
abnormal appear normal.

673. ————. "Robinson Crusoe--The Man Alone." *Antioch Re-
view*, 18 (1958), 25-40. Reprinted in *12 Original
Essays on Great English Novels*. Ed. Charles Shapiro.
Detroit: Wayne State University Press, 1960. Pp. 1-21.
Also reprinted in Swados, *A Radical's America*. Bos-
ton: Little, Brown, and Company, 1962. Pp. 133-54.

      Contends that *Crusoe* reveals a lot about the "problem
of human loneliness." Crusoe--like Defoe--is actively
engaged in a solitary endeavor to achieve economic
security; the novel gains power from this parallel between author and protagonist. The realism of the novel
also is enhanced by Defoe's ability to normalize the
abnormal and to describe extraordinary people and events
in ordinary language.

674. Thomas, Clara. "Robinson Crusoe and the Precious King-
dom." *Journal of Canadian Fiction*, 1 (1972), 58-64.

      Suggests two mythic understructures for *Robinson Cru-
soe*: (1) the myth of "man's retreat from the world and
subsequent redemption in solitude and in nature," and
(2) the myth of "the exiled, alienated man." Crusoe's
story is the "fable of all the colonization and expansion of the Protestant era," and as such spoke for
generations of characters who came to Canada.

675. Thompson, T.A. "The Theology of *Robinson Crusoe*." *Hol-born Review*, 67 (1925), 37-47.

The compiler was unable to obtain a copy of this article (noted in Dottin's *Life and Strange Surprising Adventures*, item 164).

676. Thornburg, Thomas R. "Robinson Crusoe." *Ball State University Forum*, 15, iii (1974), 11-18.

Praises *Robinson Crusoe*, in part, for its "fascinating boredom," its mundane, true-to-life account of a middle-class, unenthusiastic, humdrum outcast who struggles to make a place for himself. That struggle is the source of the novel's greatness.

677. Tillyard, E.M.W. "Defoe." *The Epic Strain in the English Novel*. London: Chatto and Windus; Fairlawn, N.J.: Essential Books, 1958. Pp. 25-50. Ellis, item 521, reprints pp. 31-50.

Sees in *Robinson Crusoe* an expression of the energy and the attitudes of the new Puritan-dominated middle class. "Crusoe is Everyman, abounding in Original Sin ..., yet he is one of the Elect" whom God has mysteriously reserved to be saved. His island home symbolizes the "human state of isolation." Tillyard believes *Robinson Crusoe* to be an epic, but one which is limited by the "middle-class ethos whose choric expression it was."

Reviews: *Listener*, 59 (1958), 949-50; J. Loiseau, *Etudes Anglaises*, 12 (1959), 82; Mark Schorer, *Modern Language Notes*, 74 (1959), 643-44; (London) *Times Literary Supplement*, 2 May 1958, p. 242; J.M.S. Tompkins, *London Magazine*, 5 (1958), 75-78.

678. Toliver, Harold. *Animate Illusions: Explorations of Narrative Structure*. Lincoln: University of Nebraska Press, 1974.

Discovers the structural coherence of *Robinson Crusoe* to lie in its foreshadowings and in its use of the middle-class mercantile propensity for ordering events. In order to give form to his material, Defoe often foreshadows what is to come, as he does when Crusoe's father predicts that if Crusoe leaves home he will be miserable. Crusoe orders his life by imposing on its random events "a regular periodicity of production and demand." He constructs chronologies of his actions and prudently plans his production and consumption through a series of "five-year-plans."

* Triscuizzi, Leonardo. *Cultura e mito nei Robinson Crusoe.* (See item 1410.)

679. Tsuchiya, Shizuko. "*Robinson Crusoe* as a Moral Fable." *Collected Essays by Members of the Faculty*, No. 11. Kyoritsu, Japan: Kyoritsu Women's Junior College, 1968. Pp. 68-89.

Attempts to resolve the apparent conflict between spiritual and economic values in *Robinson Crusoe* by arguing that Puritans believe that involvement in the pursuit of wealth satisfies God's design for man. Crusoe regards his economic success as proof of God's blessing.

* Uchida, Takeshi. "Robinson Crusoe: a Reconsideration." (See item 1411.)

* Ullrich, Hermann. *Defoes Robinson Crusoe: die Geschichte eines Weltbuches.* (See item 1412.)

* ————. "Nachwort." (See item 1415.)

* ————. "Der Robinson-mythus." (See item 1416.)

* ————. "Robinson und Robinsonaden in der Jugend-literatur." (See item 1417.)

* ————. "Zu den Quellen des 'Robinson.'" (See item 1419.)

* ————. "Zum Robinsonproblem." (See item 1421.)

* ————. "Zur Bibliographie der Robinsonaden. Nachträge und Ergänzungen zu meiner Robinson-Bibliographie." (See item 1422.)

* ————. "Zur Robinson-Literatur." (See item 1423.)

* ————. "Zur Textgeschichte von Defoes Robinson Crusoe." (See item 1424.)

* ————. "Der zweihundertste Geburtstag von Defoes Robinson." (See item 1425.)

* Urnov, D.M. *Robinzon i Gulliver.* (See item 1429.)

680. Van Patton, Nathan. "An Eskimo Translation of Defoe's 'Robinson Crusoe.' Gothaab, Greenland, 1862-1865." *Papers of the Bibliographical Society of America*, 36 (1942), 56-58.

Discovers in the first periodical published in Greenland, *Atuagagdiutit*, a serialized translation by J. Kjer
of *Robinson Crusoe* which ran from October 16, 1862, until
January 13, 1865.

681. Villani, Sergio. "Paul Valéry's Angel, Caligula and
      Robinson Crusoe." *Revue du Pacifique: Etudes de
      Littérature Française*, 2 (1976), 42-49.

      Discusses the way in which Paul Valéry uses Robinson
      Crusoe as one of the symbolic heroes who populate his
      Comedy of the Intellect. The image of Robinson is
      associated with revolt and creativity.

682. W., W. "Robinson Crusoe." *Academy*, 63 (1902), 159-60.

      Expresses surprise that Defoe, "a grimy political
      journalist and servant-girls' novelist," could create
      a masterpiece like *Robinson Crusoe*. The author suggests
      that the book's power lies in its simplicity and its
      humdrum details.

*   Wackwitz, Friedrich. *Entstehungsgeschichte von D. Defoes
      Robinson Crusoe*. (See item 1433.)

*   Wagner, Hermann. *Robinson und die Robinsonaden in unser
      Jugendliteratur*. (See item 1434.)

683. Wainwright, John B. ["Robinson Crusoe's Island."]
      Notes and Queries, Twelfth Series, 8 (1921), 415-16.

      Informs "Constant Reader," item 502, that Defoe
      placed Crusoe's island near the Orinoco but that it is
      often confused with Juan Fernandez because the latter
      is where Selkirk, Defoe's source for Crusoe, was ac-
      tually marooned. Also see Armstrong, item 476; Hubbard,
      item 561; and Lynn, item 594.

684. Watson, Francis. "Robinson Crusoe: An Englishman of
      the Age." *History Today*, 9 (1959), 760-66.

      Reviews the background of *Robinson Crusoe*--Selkirk's
      adventure, Defoe's interest in travel, etc.--and says
      that the novel's success rests on its realistic depic-
      tion of the religious and mercantile traits of "a true-
      born Englishman" of Defoe's era.

685. ————. "Robinson Crusoe: Fact and Fiction." *Listener*,
      62 (1959), 617-19.

      Wanders through a good deal of background material
      trying to discover just how a masterpiece like *Robinson*

Crusoe emerged, finally attributing the book's success
to Defoe's ability to "become" Crusoe and feel and think
like him.

686. Watson, Harold F. *The Sailor in English Fiction and
Drama, 1550-1800.* New York: Columbia University
Press, 1931.

Notes Defoe's sources for *Robinson Crusoe*: Knox, Dampier, Le Comte, Ogilby, etc.

687. Watt, Ian. "Correspondence." *Essays in Criticism*, 1
(1957), 313.

Replies to C.S. Lewis's remarks on the myths of Midas
and the Rheingold (see item 589) by saying that he was
not trying to interpret the myths, only to briefly note
that they show gold as a symbol of wealth without work.
See Watt, "Robinson Crusoe as Myth," item 689.

*   ————. "Defoe as Novelist." (See item 464.)

688.   ————. *The Rise of the Novel: Studies in Defoe,
Richardson, and Fielding.* London: Chatto and Windus;
Berkeley and Los Angeles: University of California
Press, 1957. Sections of this work appear under diverse
titles in Byrd, item 132; Elliott, item 738; Ellis,
item 521; Hunter, item 41; and Kelly, item 38.

Contains detailed discussions of *Robinson Crusoe* and
Moll Flanders. Crusoe reflects two significant aspects
of his age: its emerging economic principles and its
Puritan religious code. With his "book-keeping conscience" and his subordination of personal relationships
to economic values, he embodies "economic individualism";
with his minute examination of almost every aspect of
his life for its religious significance, he reflects a
major tendency of contemporary Puritanism. "*Robinson
Crusoe* is certainly the first fictional narrative in
which an ordinary person's daily activities are the
centre of continuous literary attention." However,
rather than being classed with other novels, the work
belongs with the great Western myths such as *Faust, Don
Juan*, and *Don Quixote*. In *Moll Flanders*, Defoe identifies so completely with his protagonist that the work
appears more like a genuine autobiography than a novel.
Moll reflects Defoe's own inability to comprehend the
incompatibility of Puritan piety and middle-class
economic aspirations. There is no irony in this conflict;
it simply reflects Defoe's own shallow morality. In

fact, *Moll Flanders* is ethically neutral because it
makes formal realism, an ethically neutral mode of
presentation, an end rather than a means. Such moral
neutrality is the reason that Defoe is usually not regarded as the founder of the novel; it remained for
Richardson to organize Defoe's realistic narrative into
a coherent plot with a controlling moral intention.

Reviews: A.J. Farmer, *Etudes Anglaises*, 11 (1958), 57-
58; John Holloway, *Spectator*, 15 March 1958, p. 353;
Daniel F. Howard, *Kenyon Review*, 21 (1959), 317-20;
Irving Howe, *Partisan Review*, 25 (1958), 145-50;
Maurice Johnson, *College English*, 20 (1958), 152;
Alan D. McKillop, *Modern Philology*, 55 (1958), 208-
10; B. Evan Owen, *Contemporary Review*, 191 (1957),
315; V.S. Pritchett, *New Statesman*, 53 (1957), 355-
56; Mark Roberts, *Essays in Criticism*, 8 (1958), 428-
38; R.A. Scott-James, *Time and Tide*, 38 (1957), 227;
F.K. Stanzel, *Anglia*, 76 (1958), 334-36; (London)
Times Literary Supplement, 15 February 1957, p. 98;
Robert Weimann, *Zeitschrift für Anglistik und Amerikan-
istik*, 8 (1960), 315-17; F. Wölcken, *Archiv für das
Studium der neueren Sprachen*, 196 (1959), 214-15;
Charles B. Woods, *Modern Language Notes*, 72 (1957),
622-24; *Yale Review*, 46, no. 4 (1957), xviii-xxiv.

689.   ————. "Robinson Crusoe as Myth." *Essays in Criticism*, 1 (1951), 95-119. Reprinted in Shinagel,
item 28, and in *Eighteenth-Century English Literature:
Modern Essays in Criticism*. Ed. James L. Clifford.
New York: Oxford University Press, 1959. Pp. 158-79.

Shows that *Robinson Crusoe* deserves the status of
myth, and then asks the question, "But the myth of what?"
The answer is, the modern myth of economic man, which
Watt views as "rational, asocial, and anti-tradition-
al...." Crusoe, whom Defoe created by accident in his
desire to glorify labor, stands for the "individual
self-interest" which eliminates altruistic action.

Review: Arthur Secord, *Philological Quarterly*, 31 (1952),
265-66.

*   Weimann, Robert. "Robinson Crusoe: Wirklichkeit und
Utopie im neuzeitlichen Roman." (See item 1438.)

690.   Wells, Charles. "Defoe and Selkirk at Bristol."
Academy, 69 (1905), 1357-58.

Questions the traditional story that Defoe personally

met with Alexander Selkirk in Bristol and that Selkirk
either told him his story or gave him his papers.

691. Williams, Aneurin. "Cassell's Illustrated *Robinson
      Crusoe*." *Notes and Queries*, Twelfth Series, 3 (1917),
      110.

      Inquires about the illustrators and engravers who did
      the woodcuts for Cassell's nineteenth-century edition
      of *Crusoe*. See Makeham, item 602, and Cassell, item
      497.

*   Winqvist, Margareta. *Den engelske Robinson Crusoes
      sällsamma öden och äventyr genom svenska språket.*
      (See item 1442.)

*   Winter, Michael. *Compendium Utopiarum.* (See item 1443.)

692. Woolf, Virginia. "Robinson Crusoe." *The Nation and the
      Athenaeum*, 38 (1925-26), 642-43.

      Seeks to discover how any novel with no introspection
      or feeling for nature can be as great as is *Robinson
      Crusoe* and concludes that the book's greatness lies in
      its concreteness, in its massive accumulation of every-
      day facts.

693. ————. "Robinson Crusoe." *The Second Common Reader.*
      New York: Harcourt Brace Jovanovich, 1932. Pp. 50-58.
      Reprinted in Ellis, item 521.

      Focuses solely on the realistic effects produced by
      Robinson Crusoe's unimaginative descriptions, presenta-
      tion of minute detail, and seriousness in even trivial
      matters. These elements make the story move "on with
      magnificent downright simplicity."

694. Wright, Terence. "'Metaphors for Reality': Mind and
      Object and the Problem of Form in the Early Novel."
      Durham University Journal, 38 (1976), 239-48.

      Contrasts *Robinson Crusoe* with *Pilgrim's Progress* in
      order to demonstrate the new path Defoe was taking in
      fiction; both books deal with "travel to salvation,"
      but for Bunyan, liberation comes with death and for
      Defoe it is a rediscovery of this world and one's place
      in it. Defoe's works focus on "everyday reality" as
      seen by characters whose emotions are "basically in-
      stinctual."

*   Yamaguchi, Katsumasa. "Overstatement to Understatement:
         Defoe-Swift Oboegaki." (See item 1447.)

695.   Zimmerman, Everett. "Defoe and Crusoe." *ELH: Journal
         of English Literary History*, 38 (1971), 377-96.

         Begins by citing Gildon's attempt to reduce Robinson
         Crusoe "to a sign for Defoe's muddles and pretensions"
         and moves on to discuss the relationship between language
         and emotion in the novel. Language is used to repress
         ‛the "fearsome inner energies" which cause Crusoe to
         turn to writing for its own sake instead of using it to
         communicate with others. Objects also are used by Crusoe
         to control and define his emotions--thus, he collects
         apparently unneeded things. Just as Crusoe's real emo-
         tions are disguised and controlled, so are Defoe's real
         feelings masked, which leads to "disharmonies" in
         Robinson Crusoe; Defoe returns to these "disharmonies"
         in *The Farther Adventures* in an attempt to resolve them.

*   Zupancic, Peter. "'My Man Friday': Zum Motiv des edlen
         Wilden in der Robinsonade." (See item 1449.)

696.   Zweig, Paul. *The Adventurer*. New York: Basic Books and
         London: Dent, 1974.

         Redefines *Robinson Crusoe* as an anti-adventure novel,
         undermining the old ethos of adventure and reflecting
         the way in which the Enlightenment "socialized" the
         adventurer tale. Crusoe is the hero of "rational in-
         dividualism" who survives his island experience because
         he lacks traditional courage and dislikes risks. In
         the eighteenth century, venturesome heroes were replaced
         by ordinary people like Crusoe, Gulliver, and Candide
         whose stories praise domestic life instead of heroic
         action.

                    C. *Captain Singleton* (1720)

*   Baker, J.N.L. "The Geography of Daniel Defoe." (See
         item 1075.)

697.   Blackburn, Timothy C. "The Coherence of Defoe's *Captain
         Singleton*." *Huntington Library Quarterly*, 41 (1978),
         119-36.

Contends that *Captain Singleton* is designed to drama-
tically illustrate the political philosophy of Locke's
Two Treatises of Government. In the novel, Madagascar
and Africa are seen as states of nature and piracy is
viewed as a state of war. Defoe has Singleton progress
from nature to reason to civil society and from innocence
to rebellion to repentance.

*   Bonner, Willard H. *Captain William Dampier, Buccaneer-*
       Author. (See item 488.)

*   Braga, Thomas. "Daniel Defoe and the Portuguese." (See
       item 397.)

698.   Breitkreuz, Harmut. "White Flag as a Token of Peace."
       American Notes and Queries, 11 (1972), 40.

Notes that the white flag that traditionally is a
sign of surrender or truce in war is used in *Captain
Singleton* as a sign of peace.

*   Colaiacoma, Paola. "*Captain Singleton* fra *Robinson
       Crusoe* e *Moll Flanders.*" (See item 1238.)

699.   D., F. "*Treasure Island* and *Captain Singleton.*" *Notes
       and Queries,* 186 (1944), 51.

Wishes to have an analogy between a passage in
Treasure Island and one in *Captain Singleton* explained.

*   Eddy, William A. *Gulliver's Travels: A Critical Study.*
       (See item 1094.)

700.   Garnett, Edward. "Preface" to *The Life, Adventures, and
       Piracies of the Famous Captain Singleton.* London:
       Dent and New York: Dutton, 1906. Pp. vii–xiv.

Explains that Captain Singleton, like *Moll Flanders*
and *Colonel Jack,* was unpopular in the nineteenth century because "Defoe's plain and homely realism soon
grew to be thought vulgar by people who themselves
aspired to be refined and genteel." However, Defoe's
portrayals of "low life" are as artistically perfect
as any descriptions of the elite in English fiction.
His realism derives from his use of matter-of-fact details to suggest "the actuality of whatever he is
describing."

*   Izzo, Carlo. "Su Daniel De Foe." (See item 1303.)

701. Kumar, Shiv K. "Introduction" to *The Life, Adventures,
      and Pyracies of the Famous Captain Singleton* by Daniel
      Defoe. London and New York: Oxford University Press,
      1969. Pp. vii–xviii.

      Provides sources (travel literature accounts of
      pirates, and the story of Captain John Avery) for the
      novel and contends that basic Puritan religious beliefs
      infuse its values. Kumar also explores the novel's
      characterization, noting that it lacks "psychological
      sophistication." A few remarks on Defoe's use of detail
      follow.

702. Maynadier, G.H. "Introduction" to *Captain Singleton*
      by Daniel Defoe. New York: Sproul, 1903. Pp. vii–
      xiv.

      Contends that in writing *Captain Singleton*, Defoe
      borrowed from himself, reworking parts of his *Enter-
      prizes of Captain Avery* and *Robinson Crusoe*. Although
      Defoe shows a remarkable knowledge of distant lands,
      he is unable to create realistic characters.

703. Naish, Charles E. "Defoe and Africa." *Notes and
      Queries*, Twelfth Series, 8 (1921), 251.

      Notes Defoe's accuracy about African geography in
      Captain Singleton and asks if perhaps an atlas published
      by Abraham Ortelius in Antwerp in 1574 might not be
      Defoe's source.

*   Roorda, Gerridina. *Realism in Daniel De Foe's Narra-
      tives of Adventure*. (See item 652.)

704. Schonhorn, Manuel. "Defoe's *Captain Singleton*: A Re-
      assessment with Observations." *Papers on Language
      and Literature*, 7 (1971), 38–51.

      Objects to the common critical view held by Secord
      (see item 327) and others that in *Captain Singleton*
      Defoe was faithfully imitating authentic records of
      actual pirates. In fact, Defoe's novel is quite "un-
      piratical." The major difference between authentic
      pirate narratives and Defoe's work is that whereas the
      former are full of violent adventures, the latter is
      almost devoid of violence; the displacement of aggression
      in Defoe's protagonists is due to their author's deep
      mercantile interests which cause him to translate his
      pirates into "complete English tradesmen."

705. Scouten, Arthur H. "The Derelict Slave Ship in Mel-
      ville's *Benito Cereno* and Defoe's *Captain Singleton*."
      Colby Library Quarterly, 12 (1976), 122-25.

      Warns against seeing Defoe as an influence on Mel-
      ville; rather, because they are in different stages of
      the Puritan tradition, these two authors treat the same
      subject differently. Melville shows that Benito Cereno
      cannot recover from his burden of guilt, whereas Defoe
      stresses the redemptive value of labor.

706. Scrimgeour, Gary J. "The Problem of Realism in Defoe's
      Captain Singleton." *Huntington Library Quarterly*, 27
      (1963), 21-37.

      Argues that realism in Defoe is subordinated to his
      major fictional interest: "man's mastery over the
      material world." Thus, in *Captain Singleton*, Defoe
      does not use available sources on the geography and
      life of Africa but prefers to ignore them so that the
      facts will not interfere with his advocacy of gold and
      ivory trade with Africa. He sets his story in unknown
      areas of Africa so that he need not bother authenticating
      the flora and fauna but instead can focus on trade pos-
      sibilities. In Defoe's work, both aesthetics and
      reality are subordinated to commerce.

*   Secord, Arthur W. *Studies in the Narrative Method of
      Defoe*. (See item 327.)

707. Sutherland, James. "Introduction" to *The Life, Adventures
      and Piracies of the Famous Captain Singleton* by Daniel
      Defoe. London: Dent and New York: Dutton, 1963. Pp.
      v-xi.

      Generalizes about the historical context of *Captain
      Singleton*, Defoe's knowledge of piracy, and the author's
      fictional techniques. Sutherland finds Quaker William
      the best-drawn and most interesting figure in the novel.

*   Walton, James. "The Romance of Gentility: Defoe's
      Heroes and Heroines." (See item 461.)

D. *Memoirs of a Cavalier* (1720)

708. Aitken, George A. "Introduction" to *Memoirs of a
      Cavalier* by Daniel Defoe. London: Dent, 1908. Pp.
      vii-xx.

      Unseen by the compiler, this piece deals with the
      authorship of *Cavalier* according to Payne, item 21.

709. Boulton, James T. "Introduction" to *Memoirs of a
      Cavalier* by Daniel Defoe. London: Oxford University
      Press, 1972. Pp. vii-xv.

      Emphasizes Defoe's verisimilitude, which is based on
      experience and research; this facet of Defoe's art is
      exemplified by the fact that 187 of the 193 names men-
      tioned in the works are authentic. Boulton also ex-
      plores Defoe's sources, especially those for Swedish
      affairs.

710. Burke, John J., Jr. "Observing the Observer in His-
      torical Fictions by Defoe." *Philological Quarterly*,
      61 (1982), 13-32.

      Agrees with Sir Walter Scott's view of Defoe's im-
      portance as an historical novelist. Although "he did
      not establish the classical form of the historical novel,
      he certainly advanced one form of it by combining auto-
      biographical forms and historical subject matter, by
      mixing fact and fiction." Defoe's principal interest
      in historical fiction--manifested in *Memoirs of a
      Cavalier* and *A Journal of the Plague Year*--lies in the
      responses to history of individuals, like the cavalier
      and H.F., who are changed for the better by their "his-
      torical experiences."

*   "Defoe as a Soldier." (See item 153.)

711. Maynadier, G.H. "Introduction" to *Memoirs of a Cavalier*
      by Daniel Defoe. New York: Sproul, 1903. Pp. ix-
      xxiii.

      Believes that Defoe wrote the *Memoirs*, basing it on
      his travels throughout England and his vast reading in
      history. The manner is Defoe's and a statement in his
      The Scots Nation and Union Vindicated apparently refers
      to a manuscript version of the *Memoirs*.

*   Purves, William L. "Authorship of *Robinson Crusoe*."
      (See item 640.)

E. *Moll Flanders* (1722)

712. Aldrich, Pearl G. "Daniel Defoe: The Father of the Soap
      Opera." *Journal of Popular Culture*, 8 (1974), 767-74.

      Contends that *Moll Flanders* founds soap opera. The
      modern soap opera audience and Defoe's audience are
      similar: "non-analytical people, mostly women, who ac-
      cept passivity as a way of life...." The heroines of
      soap opera and Defoe's heroine are similar, too, as are
      the disasters which affect them. The main difference is
      in language: the soaps' language is derived from popular
      psychology, while Defoe draws his language from popular
      religion.

713. Allende, Nora A. de. "Social Context in *Moll Flanders*,
      Pamela, and *Tom Jones*." *Revista de Literaturas Modern-
      as*, 8 (1969), 81-126.

      The compiler was unable to read this item.

714. Alter, Robert. "A Bourgeois Picaroon." *Rogue's Progress:
      Studies in the Picaresque Novel*. Harvard Studies in
      Comparative Literature, 26. Cambridge, Mass.: Harvard
      University Press, 1964. Pp. 35-57. Reprinted in
      Elliott, item 738.

      Discusses Moll Flanders in the context of picaresque
      fiction. Alter sees her as "quasi-picaresque" and an
      "anti-heroine." Like the picaroon, she is outspoken,
      imaginatively nimble, and protean in her use of disguise,
      but unlike the picaro, she does not rejoice in her
      rogueries for their own sakes; rather, she possesses
      the typical middle-class concern for economic stability.
      Money is her sole motivating force, and her main desire
      in life is to be a "gentlewoman." In addition, the book
      is fundamentally religious, which is antithetical to
      the picaresque novel. Therefore, it is "misleading ...
      to call *Moll Flanders* a picaresque novel"; actually,
      the novel derives from the English criminal biography.

      Review: B.J. Randall, *College English*, 26 (1964), 65.

715. Angel, Shelly G. "*Moll Flanders* as Feminist Literature."
      *Proceedings of the Conference of College Teachers of
      English of Texas*, 39 (1974), 56-61.

      Classifies *Moll Flanders* as "definitely feminist litera-
      ture" because Moll is a "real" woman who uses all her
      resources to struggle against her involuntary place in

society. There actually are two Molls in the story:
Moll the actor, who is essentially feminine, and Moll
the narrator, who is essentially masculine. Also see
Bordner, item 723.

*   Backscheider, Paula. "Defoe's Women: Snares and Prey."
       (See item 387.)

716. Baine, Rodney M. "The Cancelled Passage in *Moll Flan-
       ders*." *Papers of the Bibliographical Society of
       America*, 66 (1972), 55-58.

       Points out that in *Moll Flanders* there are two con-
       tradictory passages which tell how James, Moll's Lan-
       cashire husband, secures passage aboard the ship which
       is to take Moll to Virginia. The second of these pas-
       sages is a revision of the first which was meant to be
       cancelled but for some unknown reason was not. The
       first version does not conform to details found elsewhere
       in the narrative while the second is constant with them.

716A. Bartmann, Susanna. "Defoe's Daydream: Becoming Moll
       Flanders." *Visible Language*, 14 (1980), 283-305.

       The compiler was unable to locate a copy of this
       article.

717. Bateson, Henry. "Queries on *Moll Flanders*." *Notes and
       Queries*, 160 (1931), 86.

       Identifies "Whitney and the Golden Farmer," mentioned
       in *Moll Flanders*, as highwaymen who were hanged. See
       W.R.D., item 729.

718. Beberfall, Lester. "The Picaro in Context." *Hispania*,
       37 (1954), 288-92.

       Places Moll Flanders in the picaro tradition, seeing
       her as similar to Aleman's Guzman in her progress from
       wickedness to virtue. For an opposing view, see
       Alter, item 715.

719. Bell, Robert H. "Moll's Grace Abounding." *Genre*, 8
       (1975), 267-82.

       Explores some of the difficulties that Defoe unknowingly
       encounters in his efforts to yoke together two popular
       genres of his day, spiritual autobiography and criminal
       biography. The two forms are essentially incompatible
       because as a criminal Moll is too egocentric and morally
       blind to develop spiritually. She constantly manipulates

someone who loves her and then "shams religious scru-
ples to mimic middle class morality." Moll is a thoroughly unreliable narrator in her repentant self-delusions
and illusions, but she is fully convincing in her all-
too-human assertions that she is better than she appears
to be. Also see Starr, item 453.

720. Bishop, John P. "Moll Flanders' Way." *The Collected
      Essays of John Peale Bishop*. Ed. Edmund Wilson. New
      York and London: Charles Scribner's Sons, 1948. Pp.
      47-55.

      Exonerates Moll by claiming that she is fundamentally
      decent and is forced by circumstances into her life of
      sin. Bishop sees *Moll* as the epitome of the middle-
      class novel. The essay is primarily an "appreciation,"
      a musing on the author's reaction to the novel, rather
      than a rigorously critical piece.

721. Bjornson, Richard. *The Picaresque Hero in European
      Fiction*. Madison: University of Wisconsin Press,
      1977.

      Finds *Moll Flanders* ambiguous because Defoe allows
      Moll to honestly describe her dishonesty but casts
      suspicion on her religious convictions; the reader
      realizes that Moll is unreliable but also recognizes
      that her casuistical arguments often seem to coincide
      with those of the author and society in general. The
      morality of the novel is ambiguous in another way: al-
      though Defoe condemns sin and crime, he argues that
      necessity often drives people like Moll to such wicked-
      ness and he attacks self-righteous people who condemn
      others when their own virtue has never been tested.
      The novel was so popular because Moll's dreams of pros-
      perity, respectability, and marital felicity were
      identical to the dreams of its middle- and lower-class
      readers.

721A. Blewett, David. "Changing Attitudes Toward Marriage
      in the Time of Defoe: The Case of Moll Flanders."
      Huntington Library Quarterly, 44 (1981), 77-88.

      Not seen by the compiler.

*   ————. *Defoe's Art of Fiction*. (See item 395.)

722. Booth, Wayne C. *The Rhetoric of Fiction*. Chicago:
      University of Chicago Press, 1961. Pp. 316 and 318-28

are reprinted in Kelly, item 38, as "Troubles with
Irony in Cavalier Literature."

Argues that it is impossible to measure the conscious
irony in both *The Shortest Way with the Dissenters* and
Moll Flanders because the reader is not warned "that
irony is at work" and there are no clearly expressed
norms within the texts.

722A. Borck, Jim Springer. "One Woman's Prospects: Defoe's
     Moll Flanders and the Ironies in Restoration Self-
     Image." *Forum* (Houston), 17 (1979), 10-16.

     The compiler did not review this work.

723. Bordner, Marsha. "Defoe's Androgynous Vision: In *Moll
     Flanders* and *Roxana*." *Gypsy Scholar*, 2 (1975), 76-93.

     Argues that in order to show "the quickness and sharp-
     ness of the female sex," Defoe had to portray Moll
     Flanders and Roxana with masculine traits because the
     traditional feminine role did not offer any way to
     demonstrate female capabilities. The masculine princi-
     ple of aggressive self-interest, however, results in
     both heroines' spiritual hardening. While Moll is able
     to reawaken her femininity and eventually repent, Roxana
     retains her masculine spirit to the end and remains
     unrepentant. Also see Angel, item 715.

724. Brooks, Douglas. "*Moll Flanders* Again." *Essays in
     Criticism*, 20 (1970), 115-18.

     Defends his earlier article on parallels and repeti-
     tions in *Moll Flanders* (item 725) against Sherbo's
     criticism (item 808). Brooks restates his belief that
     Defoe is at pains to pattern his novels through echoes
     and parallels and therefore is a more conscious artist
     than he often is credited with being.

725. ————. "*Moll Flanders*: An Interpretation." *Essays
     in Criticism*, 19 (1969), 46-59.

     Points out how the latter part of *Moll Flanders*
     echoes, parallels, and repeats a number of phrases and
     incidents in the earlier part of the novel and contends
     that Defoe consciously employs this method to give the
     book a solid structure and a meaningful theme. Many of
     these repeated elements show Moll's reflection on her
     past sins as she moves toward the expiation of her
     guilt and her ultimate repentance. See Sherbo, "Defoe's
     Limited Genius," item 808.

*   Brown, Lloyd W. "Defoe and the Feminine Mystique." (See
        item 122.)

726.   Chaber, Lois A. "Matriarchal Mirror: Women and Capital
        in *Moll Flanders*." *Publications of the Modern Language
        Association*, 97 (1982), 212-26.

        Reads *Moll Flanders* as "the typical bourgeois novel"
        seen from a feminist perspective. Moll's role as a
        female criminal who co-opts what are the "essentially
        criminal practices of a burgeoning capitalist patriarchy"
        exposes the evils of emergent capitalism as well as
        those of women's oppression.

727.   Chandler, Frank W. *The Literature of Roguery*. 2 Vols.
        New York: Houghton Mifflin, 1907. Reprinted New York:
        Burt Franklyn, 1958.

        Remarks on Defoe throughout both volumes, but Vol. II
        contains a fifteen-page section exclusively devoted to
        his novels of roguery. He modifies his picaresque
        predecessors by adding realistic detail and an interest
        in a single character to the basic picaresque model.
        However, he has no insight into human psychology and
        thus his characters lack motivation and his novels fail
        to convey realistic human emotions.

*   Colaiacoma, Paola. "*Captain Singleton* fra *Robinson
        Crusoe* e *Moll Flanders*." (See item 1238.)

728.   Columbus, Robert R. "Conscious Artistry in *Moll Flan-
        ders*." *Studies in English Literature*, 3 (1963), 415-
        32.

        Objects to the many critics who believe that plot in
        Moll Flanders is totally subordinate to other aspects
        of the work. Defoe structures his novel upon Moll's
        limitations: her vacillations, vanity, avarice, and
        desire to dominate her environment. Through plot,
        Defoe shows "Moll's psychic transformations," as she
        "moves from innocence to guilt, from love to material
        idolatry, from natural morality to natural amorality."

*   Crowley, J. Donald. "Introduction" to *The Life and
        Strange Surprizing Adventures of Robinson Crusoe* by
        Daniel Defoe. (See item 505.)

729.   D., W.R. "Queries on *Moll Flanders*." *Notes and Queries*,
        158 (1930), 423.

Wants information on several statements in *Moll Flanders*: what goods were prohibited from importation, who were "Whitney and Golden Farmer," and where is Bugby's Hole? See Bateson, item 717, and Wanklyn, item 820.

730. Davies, William H. "Moll Flanders." *New Statesman*, 23 June 1923, p. 330.

Remarks that Defoe's ability to create realistic figures is due to his total focus on character and his omission of details of appearance, architecture, geography, and the like. His style enhances his presentation of character because of its beautiful clarity and simplicity.

731. Day, Robert Adams. "Speech Acts, Orality, and the Epistolary Novel." *The Eighteenth Century: Theory and Interpretation*, 21 (1980), 187-97.

Concentrates on Richardson but comments on Defoe as well. *Moll Flanders* is seen as a precursor to *Clarissa*; both novels are highly original because their authors are not profoundly influenced by "oral-based traditional narrative."

Review: *The Scriblerian*, 13 (1981), 99.

*   Desvignes, Lucette. "Vues de la terre promise: Les Visages de l'Amérique dans *Moll Flanders* et dans *L'Histoire de Manon Lescaut*." (See item 1246.)

732. Dollerup, Cay. "Does the Chronology of *Moll Flanders* Tell Us Something About Defoe's Method of Writing?" *English Studies*, 53 (1972), 234-35.

Contends that the chronology of *Moll Flanders* is "femininely inexact" because while Defoe checked Moll's age whenever she was married or began a long affair, he did not calculate time elapsed in minor episodes.

733. Donoghue, Denis. "The Values of *Moll Flanders*." *Sewanee Review*, 71 (1963), 287-303.

Finds Defoe and his characters "morally obtuse." They accept Christian values only when those values do not conflict with their commercial interests, and they sacrifice both conscience and feeling at the altar of commerce. For example, after Xury proves loyal, Crusoe sells him into slavery, and when Moll's criminal accomplice is arrested, she thinks only of her own safety. Moll excuses her sins by citing "necessity" and regards virtue as possible only when one's economic goals have

been reached. The great flaw in *Moll Flanders* is that
it ignores the two-thirds of life to which the analogies
of trade are irrelevant and it never offers a glimpse
of human action as "genial, charitable, or selfless."

734. Donovan, Robert Alan. "The Two Heroines of *Moll Flan-
      ders*." *The Shaping Vision: Imagination in the English
      Novel from Defoe to Dickens*. Ithaca, N.Y.: Cornell
      University Press, 1966. Pp. 21-46. Part of this
      material is reprinted in Kelly, item 38.

      Attributes the irony in *Moll Flanders* to Defoe's suc-
      cess "in putting himself in ... [Moll's] place and seeing
      with her eyes." Thus, Moll's remarks are completely
      sincere and at the same time reflect "Defoe's ordinary
      mental processes." The novel's "substance" is revealed
      through the narrator's consciousness, which both reveals
      and *is* the subject of the novel. This method results in
      an irony which controls and gives shape and coherence
      to the novel.

*   Dottin, Paul. *Daniel Defoe et ses romans*. Vol. III.
      (See item 1251.)

735. Drew, Elizabeth. "Daniel Defoe, 1660?-1731: *Moll Flan-
      ders*." *The Novel: A Modern Guide to Fifteen English
      Masterpieces*. New York: Norton, 1963. Pp. 23-38.

      Calls Defoe the father of the novel: when he employed
      his factual, plain style in a fictional autobiography,
      "he created the modern novel." Because Moll lives by
      expediency and not principle and because there is no
      evidence that Defoe saw things differently than his
      narrator, *Moll Flanders* has no moral life; however, it
      is "bursting with life, and with the energy and deter-
      mination to make life worth living."

736. Edwards, Lee. "Between the Real and the Moral: Prob-
      lems in the Structure of *Moll Flanders*." *Twentieth
      Century Interpretations of "Moll Flanders*." Ed.
      Robert C. Elliott. Englewood Cliffs, N.J.: Prentice-
      Hall, 1970. Pp. 95-107.

      Attempts to answer the question, Is Defoe technically
      skillful enough to integrate his moral concerns with
      literal authenticity in *Moll Flanders*? Edwards con-
      cludes that the "moral structure and the structure of
      reality remain divorced because Defoe has failed to
      coordinate the two aspects of his narrative purpose.

He has created two perspectives without a narrative
adequate to contain both of them." His failure to integrate these perspectives has resulted in the unre-
solvable critical debates over the novel's ironies, debates which dominate modern commentary on the book.

*   Elissa-Rhais, Roland. "Une influence anglaise dans
          Manon Lescaut, ou une source du réalisme." (See
          item 1268.)

737.   Elliott, Robert C. "Introduction." *Twentieth Century
          Interpretations of "Moll Flanders."* Englewood Cliffs,
          N.J.: Prentice-Hall, 1970. Pp. 1-9.

          Comments briefly on Defoe's life and art and then
          presents a summary of the critical debate over the irony
          of *Moll Flanders.*

738.   ————, ed. *Twentieth Century Interpretations of "Moll
          Flanders."* Englewood Cliffs, N.J.: Prentice-Hall,
          1970.

          Contains the following items, all of which are anno-
          tated individually under the authors' names: Robert C.
          Elliott, "Introduction" (item 737); Virginia Woolf,
          "Defoe" (item 827); Ian Watt, "Defoe as Novelist" (item
          464); Dorothy Van Ghent, "On *Moll Flanders*" (item 819);
          Maximillian E. Novak, "Conscious Irony in *Moll Flanders*:
          Facts and Problems" (item 786); Howard L. Koonce, "Moll's
          Muddle: Defoe's Use of Irony in *Moll Flanders*" (item
          763); Cesare Pavese, "Preface to *Moll Flanders*" (item
          792); Robert Alter, "A Bourgeois Picaroon" (item 714);
          George A. Starr, "*Moll Flanders*" (item 452); Lee Ed-
          wards, "Between the Real and the Moral: Problems in the
          Structure of *Moll Flanders*" (item 736).

739.   Erickson, Robert A. "Moll's Fate: 'Mother Midnight'
          and *Moll Flanders.*" *Studies in Philology,* 76 (1979),
          75-100.

          Studies Moll's "governess" (or, her "Mother Midnight,"
          a cant term for a midwife-bawd) in order to trace Moll's
          development and her discovery of her true psychological
          identity. Erickson presents a brief historical overview
          of midwifery and its language and suggests that it
          serves as a metaphor for thievery in the novel. Moll
          eventually arrives at the level of practical competence
          and knowledge of the world which she admired in her
          "governess," at which point she becomes her own "Mother
          Midnight."

740. Faletti, Heidi E. "The Picaresque Tradition of the
      Erotic." *Human Sexuality in the Middle Ages and Ren-*
      aissance. Ed. Douglas Radcliffe-Umstead. University
      of Pittsburgh Publications on Middle Ages and Renais-
      sance, No. 4. Pittsburgh: University of Pittsburgh
      Press, 1978. Pp. 167-82.

      Finds Moll Flanders to be an example of the plight of
      women with no mercantile skills in a capitalist society.
      Without such skills, Moll must achieve her goal--becoming
      a "gentlewoman"--through prostitution and thievery even
      though she reflects certain aspects of Puritan propriety.
      Also see Wilson, item 825.

741. Faller, Lincoln B. "The Myth of Captain James Hind: A
      Type of Primitive Fiction before Defoe." *Bulletin of*
      the New York Public Library, 79 (1976), 139-66.

      Traces the mythologizing of the life of Captain James
      Hind, a highwayman who, like Whitney and the Golden
      Farmer, was the subject of several highly romanticized
      narratives which made him "larger than life but less
      than a man." Such criminal biographies transformed
      "truths into seeming fiction" and it is against them
      that Defoe was reacting when in *Moll Flanders* he reversed
      the trend of the popular literature of roguery by
      creating a fiction that was seemingly true.

*   Földényi, László F.A. "A magabiztos meghasonlottság
      regénye Defoe 'Moll Flanders'--e; a történelen és a
      regénye iróniája." (See item 1274.)

742. Forster, E.M. *Aspects of the Novel.* New York: Harcourt,
      Brace, 1927. A section of this work is reprinted in
      Kelly, item 38.

      Regards *Moll Flanders* as the supreme example of the
      novel of character--"nothing matters but the heroine."
      Forster views Moll's "reflections" as "just" and her
      repentance as "sincere." She is portrayed as completely
      natural and realistic.

742A. Gaba, Phyllis R. *"Moll Flanders* in Hebrew." *Scriblerian,*
      12 (1980), 167-68.

      Not seen by the compiler.

743. Gaskin, Bob. "Moll Flanders: Consistency in a Psycho-
      path." *Lamar Journal of the Humanities,* 6 (1980),
      5-18.

Rejects the usual approaches to Moll's character as
"not to the point"; the apparent inconsistencies or
ironies in her character can be explained away if one
views her, in modern clinical terms, as a psychopath.
Looked at in this way, Moll is a consistent and realistic
character.

*   Gifford, George E., Jr. "Daniel Defoe and Maryland."
        (See item 829.)

*   Goetsch, Paul. "Defoes *Moll Flanders* und der Leser."
        (See item 1284.)

744.   Goldberg, M.A. "*Moll Flanders*: Christian Allegory in
        a Hobbesian Mode." *University Review* (Kansas City),
        33 (1967), 267-78.

        Finds the Christian allegory of Moll Flanders' road to
        repentance strangely modified by Hobbesian materialism.
        Virtue, principles, and honor are luxuries which Moll
        cannot afford, and so she discounts them and concen-
        trates on those external, concrete objects--like gold--
        which can make her secure. Once that security is at-
        tained, Moll can indulge in the luxury of virtue. In
        the world as presented by Moll, "necessity is the only
        law."

745.   Hammond, Brean S. "Repentance: Solution to the Clash
        of Moralities in *Moll Flanders*." *English Studies*,
        61 (1980), 329-37.

        Rejects those views of *Moll Flanders* which explain
        the conflict between material and spiritual values as
        a consequence of Defoe's mentality or as a result of
        his conscious irony. Defoe believed that an absolute
        moral code was fine for one who could afford it, but
        that an expedient moral code was inevitable for one
        who faced a disaster like starvation. Thus Moll whores
        and steals to live and tries to palliate, even vindicate,
        her sins, but when she is affluent she reverts to an ab-
        solute moral code and sincerely repents.

746.   Hartog, Curt H. "Aggression, Femininity, and Irony in
        Moll Flanders." *Literature and Psychology*, 22 (1972),
        121-38.

        Applies psychoanalytic theory in order to show that
        Defoe's use of the feminine point of view in *Moll Flan-
        ders* enables him to express aggression without seeming
        to and while pretending to disapprove of it. A comparison

of *Moll* with *Robinson Crusoe* demonstrates how the different treatment of aggression in the two novels results in a different kind of reader involvement in each.

747. Hatfield, Theodore M. "*Moll Flanders* in Germany."
      Journal of English and Germanic Philology, 32 (1933),
      51-65.

      Compares the first German translation of *Moll Flanders*--
      by Johann Mattheson in 1723--to the third London edition.
      Hatfield notes that this novel virtually disappears in
      Germany during the eighteenth and nineteenth centuries.

748. Hibbett, Howard S. "Saikaku and Burlesque Fiction."
      Harvard Journal of Asiatic Studies, 20 (1957), 53-73.

      Compares *Moll Flanders* with Ihara Saikaku's *Ichidaionna*
      (1686), finding the former more suspenseful and the
      latter livelier. Where Saikaku's characters are ex-
      travagant or funny, Defoe's are convincing.

749. Higdon, David Leon. "The Chronology of *Moll Flanders*."
      English Studies, 56 (1975), 316-19.

      Believes that the verisimilitude of *Moll Flanders* is
      enhanced by its "remarkably consistent time scheme."

750. ————. "Defoe's *Moll Flanders*." *Explicator*, 29 (1971),
      item 55.

      Credits Defoe with subtle irony in having Moll say
      she has slept with thirteen men but allowing her to
      tell of only six; the omission of seven lovers emphasizes
      Moll's duplicity as an unreliable narrator and confirms
      the promiscuity which she repeatedly denies.

751. ————. "A Poetics of Fictional 'Time Shapes.'" *Buck-
      nell Review*, 22 (1976), 50-68.

      Places the narrative structure of *Moll Flanders* in
      the category of "retrospective time." In the novel,
      time does not function to unfold character gradually
      but rather "boldly juxtaposes opposed states of being."
      Moll herself is well aware of her "before" and "after"
      states of being separated by her conversion.

752. ————. *Time and English Fiction*. London: Macmillan,
      1977. Parts of this material originally appeared in
      Higdon's "The Chronology of *Moll Flanders*," item 749,
      and "The Critical Fortunes and Misfortunes of Defoe's
      Roxana," item 871.

Finds a remarkably consistent time scheme in *Moll
Flanders* and provides a chart outlining it. Moll lives
continually in the present--although her egocentricity
does not allow her to remark on important historical
events such as the plague and the Great Fire of London--
until her conversion enables her to link past, present,
and future as a coherent unit. Her view of time is a
reflection of her character. The time scheme of *Roxana*,
also schematized in a chart, reveals a symmetry lacking
in Defoe's other works. The novel is arranged in six
major episodes that trace Roxana's movement from passive
innocence to active guilt.

753. Hocks, Richard. "Defoe and the Problem of Structure:
      Formal 'Ropes' and Equivalent Technique." *Literatur
      in Wissenschaft und Unterricht*, 3 (1970), 221-35.

      Looks for structural elements that give coherence to
      Moll Flanders, rejecting most of the usually cited
      devices and symbols in favor of Defoe's use of a par-
      ticular value system which views "human fallibility as
      intrinsically worthwhile and interesting." Defoe is
      in touch with the middle-class ethos which "is both
      critical and *self*-critical"; the reflection of this
      dual view in *Moll Flanders* makes Defoe the "authorita-
      tive root" of "critical realism" and gives the novel
      whatever coherence it has.

754. Howson, Gerald. "The Fortunes of Moll Flanders."
      *Thief-Taker General: The Rise and Fall of Jonathan
      Wild*. London: Hutchinson and New York: St. Martin's
      Press, 1970. Pp. 156-70.

      Provides information on a Moll King who may have been
      the model for Defoe's Moll Flanders. Defoe may have
      met her in Newgate to interview her for a pamphlet for
      Applebee's series of criminal true confessions.

755. ———. "Who Was Moll Flanders?" (London) *Times
      Literary Supplement*, 18 January 1968, pp. 63-64.
      Reprinted in Kelly, item 38.

      Finds a possible source for Moll Flanders in Moll
      King, a pickpocket whom Defoe might have met in Newgate
      in 1721. This material appears in Chapter XVI of Howson's
      Thief-Taker General, item 754.

756. Hunter, J. Paul. "Introduction" to *Moll Flanders* by
      Daniel Defoe. New York: Crowell, 1970. Pp. xi-xxi.

Sketches "the critical vicissitudes" of *Moll Flanders*, placing it "in the context of Defoe's career and times." *Moll* was a popular novel at first, running through five editions in two years, but by the end of the eighteenth century, it had diminished in popularity, and Defoe was considered a one-book novelist, famous only because of his *Robinson Crusoe*. *Moll* was critically resurrected in the late nineteenth century and has continued to gain popularity since. The interest in crime and criminals shown in *Moll* and in other Defoe works reflects the fascination of the public with these subjects and demonstrates Defoe's awareness of the public taste. Defoe adds significance to the public's expectations by showing that Moll in many ways is like us, sharing the acquisitive values of respectable society.

/5/. Itkovic, Edward. "Daniel Defoe: The Father of Soap Opera." *Journal of Popular Culture*, 8 (1975), 767-74.

Regards *Moll Flanders* as the "mother" of soap opera; however, *Moll* is fictional religious biography and the soap operas are fictional psychological biography. There are many similarities of theme, structure, plot, characterization, and language in Defoe's novel and the modern soap opera.

* Jackson, Wallace. "*Roxana* and the Development of Defoe's Fiction." (See item 874.)

* James, E. Anthony. *Daniel Defoe's Many Voices*. (See item 211.)

758. Jesson, David N. "Moll Flanders, a True-Born Peripatetic." *Pucred*, 1 (1972), 5-8.

Parodies scholarly inquiry with a humorously overwritten commentary on Moll's trip to Stone in Cheshire.

759. Johnson, C.A. "Two Mistakes of Geography in *Moll Flanders*." *Notes and Queries*, n.s. 9 (1962), 455.

Points out two mistakes in geography made by Moll when she places Stone and Burford in the wrong areas.

760. Jones, A.G.E. "The Banks of Bath." *Notes and Queries*, n.s. 5 (1958), 277-83.

Substantiates his claim that the beginnings of banking were laid in Bath in the early eighteenth century by citing Moll Flanders' reference to a bank draft.

761. Karl, Frederick R. "Moll's Many-Colored Coat: Veil and
      Disguise in the Fiction of Defoe." *Studies in the
      Novel*, 5 (1973), 86-97.

      Finds that eighteenth-century novelists, especially
      Defoe, conceived of character in terms of disguises,
      hidden origins, misleading identities, assumed roles,
      etc., which indicates that they sensed major social
      changes that they wished to capture artistically. Thus,
      Defoe employs protean characters like Moll Flanders and
      Roxana who mirror their era by continually reshaping
      themselves in efforts to gain identity.

*   Kelly, Edward, ed. *Moll Flanders: An Authoritative
      Text, Backgrounds and Sources, Criticism.* (See item
      38.)

762. Kettle, Arnold. "In Defence of 'Moll Flanders.'" *Of
      Books and Humankind: Essays and Poems Presented to
      Bonamy Dobrée.* Ed. John Butt. London: Routledge and
      Kegan Paul, 1964. Pp. 55-67. Reprinted in Hunter,
      item 41, and Kelly, item 38.

      Takes issue with Watt's view of *Moll Flanders* as ex-
      pressed in *The Rise of the Novel* (item 688). Moll's
      character confuses Watt, as well as such earlier critics
      as Leslie Stephens and F.R. Leavis, precisely *because*
      she is so psychologically real: she remembers things
      haphazardly, is "an incurable self-deceiver," and
      doesn't think of herself as a criminal--all realistic
      traits which show Defoe's absorption into the characters
      he invents. The vitality of *Moll* as a work of art is
      due to its heroine being both "splendid and contemptible,"
      both "unusually honest and extraordinarily dishonest" at
      the same time. The "whole nature of Defoe's book" is
      determined by Moll's desire to be free in a man's world.

763. Koonce, Howard L. "Moll's Muddle: Defoe's Use of Irony
      in *Moll Flanders.*" *ELH: A Journal of English Literary
      History*, 30 (1963), 277-88, 390-91. Reprinted in
      Elliott, item 521.

      Disagrees with Watt's view that *Moll* is not consciously
      ironic (see item 688). Defoe certainly is not obtuse,
      and so he is well aware of the ironic disparity between
      Moll's pious professions and her criminal activities.
      He forces her to wander "into a thoroughly disarming
      moral muddle" which makes *her* an ingratiating character
      and makes the *novel* an ironic structure. Also see
      Elliott, item 737, and Novak, item 786.

764. Krier, William J. "A Courtesy Which Grants Integrity:
     A Literal Reading of *Moll Flanders.*" *ELH: A Journal
     of English Literary History*, 38 (1971), 397-410.

     Questions the standard approach of seeing *Moll Flan-
     ders* only through its irony and contends that it is
     more fruitful to explore the novel's "consistencies--
     consistencies which present not only a sensitive and
     subtle rendering of character, but a highly complex
     organization of statement as well." These "consisten-
     cies" include Moll's radical shift from the typical
     feminine social situation to a typical masculine one
     and her discovery of a sense of responsibility.

*   Legouis, Pierre. "Marion Flanders, est-elle une victime
     de la société?" (See item 1329.)

765. Lerenbaum, Miriam. "Moll Flanders: 'A Woman on her
     own Account.'" *The Authority of Experience: Essays
     in Feminist Criticism*. Eds. Arlyn Diamond and Lee R.
     Edwards. Amherst: University of Massachusetts Press,
     1977. Pp. 101-17.

     Correlates the stages in Moll's aging process with
     crises in her life to show how Defoe depicts Moll's
     roles as young woman, wife, mother, thief, and pioneer.
     Defoe concludes each stage and begins the next with
     episodes in which Moll falls psychosomatically ill but
     recovers to begin a wholly new career with verve and
     optimism. Her ability to weather her crises is a
     tribute to her resilient femininity.

766. Lieberman, Marcia R. "Sexism and the Double Standard
     in Literature." *Images of Women in Fiction: Feminist
     Perspectives*. Ed. Susan Koppelman Cornillon. Bowling
     Green, Ohio: Bowling Green University Popular Press,
     1972. Pp. 328-40.

     Regards Moll Flanders as the "quintessential female"
     because she adopts the strategy of disguise but is not
     destroyed by it; she retains her own personality and
     her sense of self-worth.

767. MacCarthy, Sir Desmond. "Defoe." *Criticism*. New York
     and London: Putnam, 1932. Pp. 216-22.

     Emphasizes the "contradictory elements" in Defoe's
     nature: he possesses a superb honesty of vision but
     also has "a taste for devious devices." Thus, the
     preface to *Moll Flanders* caters to prurient interests
     while it allays the scruples of the moral reader.

768. McClung, M.G. "A Source for Moll Flanders' Favourite
      Husband." *Notes and Queries*, n.s. 18 (1971), 329-30.

      Locates a source for the Lancashire gentleman-highway-
      man--Moll's favorite husband--in a Samuel Kempton who,
      when offered a choice between transportation and hanging,
      chose the latter, saying that he would rather be hanged
      than sold for a slave.

769. McCoy, Kathleen. "The Femininity of Moll Flanders."
      Studies in Eighteenth-Century Culture, 7. Ed. Roseann
      Runte. Madison: University of Wisconsin Press, 1978.
      Pp. 413-22.

      Spends half the article reviewing critical discussions
      of Moll Flanders' femininity and then turns to her own
      analysis of the subject. McCoy believes that discussions
      of Moll's gender are misleading because Moll is more the
      product of her class than of her gender. Her character
      derives from lower-middle-class dissenting ideas and
      not from traditional concepts of femininity.

770. McCullough, Bruce. "The Conquest of Realistic Incident."
      Representative English Novelists: Defoe to Conrad.
      New York: Harper and Row, 1946. Pp. 3-22.

      Generalizes about Defoe's realism and then analyzes
      Moll Flanders to support the general remarks. Defoe
      was not original in pretending that his novels were
      "histories," but he added a great deal to the develop-
      ment of prose fiction through his "technique of circum-
      stantial narration which enabled him to secure an un-
      paralleled appearance of credibility and validity in
      the depiction of wholly imaginary events." This method
      is best illustrated in *Moll Flanders*, which presents its
      title character as a fully realized human being charac-
      teristic of her epoch. The art of this novel, which is
      seriously limited by its lack of a framing action and by
      its lack of drama, lies in its apparent artlessness; the
      novel reads as though it were written by a real Moll
      Flanders rather than a skilled author.

771. Macey, Samuel L. *Clocks and the Cosmos: Time in Western
      Life and Thought.* Hamden: Archon, 1980.

      Claims that the materialist desire for watches during
      the horological revolution is exemplified by Moll Flan-
      ders, who often associates gentility with gold watches
      and who always mentions the number of watches she has
      on hand when she assesses her wealth.

772. ————. "The Time Scheme in *Moll Flanders*." *Notes and Queries*, n.s. 16 (1969), 336-37.

Rejects two proposed time schemes for *Moll Flanders* (on the grounds that they are anachronistic) in favor of one which has Moll telling her story to Defoe in 1721-22 instead of 1683/84 or 1694. Macey bases his view on the existence of a real Moll King (see Howson, item 755.)

773. McMaster, Juliet. "The Equation of Love and Money in *Moll Flanders*." *Studies in the Novel*, 2 (1970), 131-44.

Finds conscious irony in Defoe's portrait of Moll, whose moralizing cannot conceal the way in which her mercenary values engulf all others so that friendship becomes a profitable business partnership, courtship becomes negotiation over settlements, lovemaking becomes an exchange of coins and purses, and tenderness becomes the payment of a reckoning. Defoe has given us an ironic and consistent picture of a woman who is a prostitute and thief by vocation, not necessity.

774. Main, Charles F. "The German Princess; or Mary Carleton in Fact and Fiction." *Harvard Library Bulletin*, 10 (1956), 166-85.

Associates the journalistic accounts of the notorious Mary Carleton with the later realistic fiction written by Defoe. Although Main does not mention it, some of Mary's adventures are later paralleled in Defoe's *Moll Flanders*.

775. Martin, Terence. "The Unity of *Moll Flanders*." *Modern Language Quarterly*, 22 (1961), 115-24. Reprinted in Kelly, item 38.

Finds the unity of *Moll Flanders* in three areas: the presence of Moll in all of the episodes, the psychological progression of the book, and "a formal pattern of circumstance shaped coherently by the episodes which make up Moll's experience." The latter is the focus of this study, emphasizing the episodic pattern of theft which gives the book coherence. Moll consistently seeks the relative security of her early life, first through sex and finally, when her age prevents her using sex for economic gain, theft.

*   Mauriac, François. "En relisant *Moll Flanders*. Quand
       le romancier s'anéantit dans un personnage." (See
       item 1340.)

776.   ————. *Mémoires Intérieurs*. Translated by G. Hopkins.
       New York: Farrar, Straus, and Cudahy, 1961.

       Lauds Defoe for his ability to "become" Moll Flanders:
       "Nowhere else in the whole history of the novel is there
       an instance of a male author merging himself so com-
       pletely with a female character."

777.   Maynadier, G.H. "Introduction" to *Moll Flanders* by
       Daniel Defoe. New York: Sproul, 1903. Pp. vii-xv.

       Suggests that a real person may have been the inspira-
       tion for Defoe's Moll, "as vital a character as Defoe
       ever created." She is a psychologically realistic
       character whose vividness demonstrates a creative ability
       which is "unfortunately rare in Defoe's fiction."

778.   Michaelson, L.I. "Defoe and Dickens: Two London Jour-
       neys." *Dickensian*, 74 (1978), 103-07.

       Compares a passage from *Moll Flanders* with one from
       Oliver Twist to show how both Defoe and Dickens use
       realistic details (street names and the like) but
       still "create" a London which reflects the psychological
       states of their characters.

779.   Michie, J.A. "The Unity of *Moll Flanders*." *Knaves and
       Swindlers: Essays on the Picaresque Novel in Europe*.
       Ed. Christine J. Whitbourn. Oxford: Oxford University
       Press, 1974. Pp. 75-92.

       Aims at showing that *Moll Flanders* is more strongly
       unified than hitherto has been recognized. There are
       two logically unified patterns in the novel: (1) a plot
       sequence which develops Moll's desire, expressed in the
       opening scenes, to become a gentlewoman, and (2) a series
       of events and reflections which illustrate Moll's spiri-
       tual changes as she pursues her materialistic goals.
       The conflict between Moll's professed piety and her con-
       tinued criminal activity "is no doubt a reflection of
       the ambiguity inherent in the mercantile society" of
       Defoe's age.

       Review: Dorothy H. Lee, *Seventeenth-Century News*, 33
       (1975), 49-50.

780.   Miller, Stuart. *The Picaresque Novel*. Cleveland: Case
        Western Reserve University Press, 1967.

        Uses eight works, including *Moll Flanders*, to define
        the picaresque novel, which depicts a chaotic world
        totally without structure. At first glance, *Moll Flan-
        ders* seems not to fit this pattern because it demon-
        strates poetic justice rather than chaos, but the
        Preface is ironically designed to reveal a naive editor
        who does not understand the story he edits. The chaos
        that the novel demonstrates is at odds with its contra-
        dictory conclusion, imposed artificially to show Moll's
        "conversion," which implies a providential order in the
        universe.

        Reviews: *Bulletin of Hispanic Studies*, 47 (1970), 75-77;
        Peter H. Dunn, *Journal of Aesthetics and Art Criticism*,
        27 (1969), 474-75; Hugh A. Harter, *Novel*, 3 (1969),
        85-86; Robert D. Spector, *Books Abroad*, 42 (1968),
        442; Philip Stevick, *Criticism*, 10 (1968), 254-56.

781.   Mitchell, Juliet. "Introduction" to *The Fortunes and
        Misfortunes of the Famous Moll Flanders* by Daniel
        Defoe. Harmondsworth and New York: Penguin Books,
        1978.

        Not seen by the compiler.

*   Monk, Samuel Holt. "Introduction" [to *Colonel Jack*].
        (See item 833.)

782.   Monteser, Frederick. *The Picaresque Element in Western
        Literature*. Studies in the Humanities, No. 5. Uni-
        versity, Alabama: University of Alabama Press, 1975.

        Looks for a picaresque source for *Moll Flanders* and
        finds it in Andrés Pérez's *La Pícara Justina*. Other
        sources for the novel include Defoe's personal experiences
        in Newgate and his production of criminal confessions
        and biographies for *Applebee's Journal*.

783.   Morrissey, L.J., and Barry Slepian. "Fanny and Moll."
        Notes and Queries, n.s. 11 (1964), 61.

        Notes several parallels between Moll Flanders and
        Fanny Hill: each is left on her own at fourteen, each
        mistakes a prostitute for a gentlewoman because of her
        nice clothes, each has a favorite lover to whom she
        returns at the end, and each reforms and retires rich.

784.   Murray, Douglas. "Emblems in *Pilgrim's Progress* and
       Moll Flanders: The Movement Toward Isolation."
       Enlightenment Essays, 10 (1979), 60-64.

       Defines "emblem" as an object which images spiritual
       truths and discusses Moll's Newgate experience as an
       emblem of hell itself as well as of her "captivity to
       sin." Such emblems, however, are rare in *Moll* because
       it is a secular work depicting "a world separated from
       God."

785.   Needham, J.D. "Moll's 'Honest Gentlemen.'" *Southern
       Review: An Australian Journal of Literary Studies*,
       3 (1969), 366-74.

       Believes that an analysis of the ambiguities of Moll's
       idiom helps reveal the irony of *Moll Flanders*; the
       meanings of certain key words are not the same for
       Defoe as they are for Moll. For example, in *The Com-
       pleat English Gentleman*, Defoe defines "honest" and
       "honour" in their traditional senses, but Moll uses
       these terms to conceal some very dishonest and dis-
       honorable conduct. She refers, for instance, to her
       governess having children "honestly taken care of" which
       can be translated as "straightforwardly murdered."
       Further ironies arise when Moll applies the term "gen-
       tleman" to Jemmy, her highwayman husband. For his
       irony, Defoe depends a great deal on contemporary
       idiomatic usage.

*   Nolting-Hauff, Ilse. "Die betrugerliche Heirat: Realis-
       mus und Pikareske in Defoes *Moll Flanders*." (See
       item 1351.)

786.   Novak, Maximillian E. "Conscious Irony in *Moll Flan-
       ders*." *College English*, 26 (1964), 198-204. Re-
       printed in Elliott, item 38, and Hunter, item 41.

       Sides with Van Ghent (item 819) and Koonce (item 763)
       in viewing *Moll Flanders* as an ironic novel, but unlike
       them argues that it can be demonstrated that Defoe is
       consciously ironic. Novak lists thirteen areas (morality;
       repentance; sex, love, and marriage; children; etc.) in
       which he believes that Defoe's irony may be measured.
       The essence of the novel's irony is to be found in
       Moll's "blindness" which causes her to regard herself
       as a Christian penitent although she actually remains
       "only dimly aware that she operates on a level of
       natural law," seeking security and self-preservation
       through any means necessary.

787.   ————. "Defoe's 'Indifferent Monitor': The Complexity
        of *Moll Flanders*." *Eighteenth-Century Studies*, 3
        (1970), 351-65. Parts of this essay are reprinted
        in Kelly, item 38.

        Approaches the debate on whether or not Defoe was a
        conscious artist and ironist by looking at his manipu-
        lation of language. Defoe consistently employs specific
        linguistic devices in order to obtain complexities of
        meaning. These devices include repeated phrases (often
        italicized) such as "and the like" and "as I call'd it"
        which are used for ironic understatement and puns (often
        based on contemporary slang) which enable Defoe "to
        convey subtle meanings playing underneath Moll's narra-
        tive." Moll also justifies her own criminal behavior
        through linguistic manipulation: she refers to other
        criminals as "they" in order to separate herself from
        them, and she creates vivid fictions to add a moral
        coloring to her immoral actions.

*   ————. "Freedom, Libertinism, and the Picaresque."
        (See item 436.)

788.   ————. "Moll Flanders' First Love." *Papers of the
        Michigan Academy of Science, Arts, and Letters*, 46
        (1961), 635-43.

        Illustrates the view that Defoe frequently is detached
        and ironic in his portrayal of Moll by examining the
        first episode of *Moll Flanders*. In this section of the
        novel Defoe clearly is depicting a clever, vain, and
        self-interested servant girl destined to fall into sin.
        Because Moll is guided by her economic interests and
        dominated by self-love, the reader can never accept
        anything she says without questioning her motives.
        Moll's "first love" is herself, and Defoe is fully
        aware of this fact.

*   Oda, Minoru. "Moll's Complacency: Defoe's Use of Comic
        Structure in *Moll Flanders*." (See item 1354.)

789.   Olsen, Alexandra Hennessey. "Chaucer and the Eighteenth
        Century: The Wife of Bath and Moll Flanders." *Chaucer
        Newsletter*, 1 (1979), 13-15.

        Makes a case for Chaucer's influence on Defoe: both
        the Wife of Bath and Moll Flanders have had five hus-
        bands, are not interested in sex, and view marriage as
        a financial arrangement.

790. Olshin, Toby. "'Thoughtful of the Main Chance': Defoe
      and the Cycle of Anxiety." *Hartford Studies in Litera-
      ture*, 6 (1974), 117-28.

      Accounts for the unity of *Moll Flanders* and its "strik-
      ing intensity of effect" by seeing it as a dramatization
      of the anxiety-satiety cycle common to orally fixated
      people. The novel is not at all ironic; Moll's vacilla-
      tions between piety and sinful actions parallel the
      movement from anxiety to satiety to anxiety, etc., in the
      orally fixated. *Roxana* follows the same pattern, except
      that it ends in anxiety whereas *Moll* ends in satiety.

791. Parker, Alexander A. *Literature and the Delinquent:
      The Picaresque Novel in Spain and Europe, 1599-1753.*
      Edinburgh: University of Edinburgh Press, 1967.

      Allies *Moll Flanders* with the picaresque novel on
      three grounds: (1) Moll has disreputable origins;
      (2) she desires to be a gentlewoman; and (3) she sinks
      into infamy but experiences a religious conversion.
      The novel is flawed because Moll's conversion is not
      psychologically motivated and the work lacks a serious
      moral purpose. *Colonel Jack*, also viewed as a picaresque
      novel, has the same flaws as does *Moll*. In Defoe's
      works necessity leads to delinquency and therefore com-
      passion is shown for the unfortunate.

792. Pavese, Cesare. "Preface to *Moll Flanders*." *American
      Literature: Essays and Opinions*. Berkeley and Los
      Angeles: University of California Press, 1970. Pp.
      203-06. Reprinted in Elliott, item 38.

      Remarks that much of the power of *Moll Flanders* de-
      rives from Defoe's ability to reduce "to its most
      elementary form the tragedy of existence." Pavese sees
      the ironic basis of the novel in the conflict between
      Moll's examination of her conscience and her detailed
      concern with her financial condition. In spite of this
      conflict, and Moll's resolution of it in favor of money,
      Moll is an attractive character who gains sympathy be-
      cause she undergoes so many tribulations.

*   Peterson, Spiro. "The Matrimonial Theme of Defoe's
      Roxana." (See item 882.)

793. Peterson, William H. "Gide and Defoe." *Notes and
      Queries*, 197 (1952), 202-03.

      Finds that Gide's *Les Caves du Vatican* was greatly in-
      fluenced by the picaresque tale as exemplified in *Moll*

Flanders and *Robinson Crusoe*. Gide greatly admired both of these novels, considering them to be illustrations of the isolation of the individual and "the unmotivated action which asserts the freedom of the individual."

794. Piper, William Bowman. "*Moll Flanders* as a Structure of Topics." *Studies in English Literature*, 9 (1969), 489-502.

Observes that the title page to *Moll Flanders* suggests that the work is structured around three topics: sexual adventures, criminal adventures, and Virginia adventures. However, Defoe typically digresses from this topical framework, producing a fortuitous "expressive effect." Understanding Moll to be writing her own story, the reader finds her failure to impose order on her narration parallel to her failure to impose order on her life; Moll settles for "the brief appearance of truth" in her human dealings and for "the brief appearance of order" in her narrative of those dealings.

795. Preston, John. "Moll Flanders: 'The Satire of the Age.'" *The Created Self: The Reader's Role in Eighteenth-Century Fiction*. New York: Barnes and Noble and London: Heinemann, 1970. Pp. 8-37.

Places *Moll Flanders* in the context of "reader response" criticism. The novel "is overall an oblique criticism of a presumed reader": Moll's conduct makes us question our conduct; she forces us to confront our own dishonesty and to come to grips with it. Because Moll cannot really describe how she felt, the reader is forced "to supplement her story from his own experience." Defoe wishes to change our thinking about social principles and motives; his novels "are a kind of conscience" for society.

796. Price, Martin. *To the Palace of Wisdom: Studies in Order and Energy from Dryden to Blake*. New York: Doubleday, 1964. Pp. 264-71 and 274-75 are reprinted in Kelly, item 38, and pp. 263-76 are reprinted in Byrd, item 132.

Believes that the depth of Defoe's characters stems from their consciences, which are troubled by the conflicting demands of spiritual salvation and commercial gain. There is no consistent irony in Moll's character, but she has all the ambiguities of the Puritan faith, ambiguities compounded because she is a once-

dedicated servant to the Lord who has turned to the
false worship of wealth, power, and success. Crusoe
experiences many of the same conflicts but they are
resolved on his island which is a utopia of the Protestant ethic where he may work without distraction and
with no danger of inordinate desires leading to dishonesty.

797. Quennell, Peter. "Daniel Defoe." *The Singular Prefer-*
      ence. London: Collins, 1952. Pp. 125-31. Reprinted
      in *English Critical Essays of the Twentieth Century*.
      Second Series. London: Oxford, 1958. Pp. 209-15.

      Calls Defoe the "prophet" of that class of people,
      created by capitalism, for whom conformity is virtue
      and economic security is happiness. His fictional
      characters are distinguished by their passion for re-
      spectability and their persistence in "getting ahead."
      Moll Flanders, with her pretensions to gentility,
      epitomizes this kind of character.

798. Rader, Ralph W. "Defoe, Richardson, Joyce, and the
      Concept of Form in the Novel." *Autobiography, Biog-*
      raphy, and the Novel: Papers Read at a Clark Library
      Seminar, May 13, 1972. Eds. William Matthews and
      Ralph W. Rader. Los Angeles: Clark Memorial Library
      and University of California at Los Angeles, 1972.
      Pp. 31-72.

      Presents a complex argument defining the form of *Moll*
      Flanders which is a "simulated naive incoherent auto-
      biography" designed to exploit the interest aroused by
      true stories. Of course, an actual true story is
      likely to be boring, but the writer of pseudo-biography
      has to avoid that pitfall. Defoe does so by including
      a number of sensational incidents—a kidnapping by
      gypsies, conversion in the face of execution, incest—
      along with minor events. He points up the minor, such
      as when Moll is given the horse to hold and walks off
      with it, and plays down the important, such as when Moll
      does not reveal for three years her incestuous rela-
      tionship with her brother. Thus, "the usual is moved
      ... toward the unusual, and the unusual is moved ...
      toward the usual." In this manner, the form of *Moll*
      Flanders forces the reader to construe its content as
      real; the reader thinks of the incidents as if they
      were not invented but merely reported.

799. Reed, Walter L. "*Moll Flanders* and the Picaresque:
      The Transvaluation of Virtue." *An Exemplary History*

of the Novel: The Quixotic Versus the Picaresque.
Chicago: The University of Chicago Press, 1981. Pp.
93-116.

Establishes a context for *Moll Flanders* by discussing
the literary culture of Defoe's time and the expectations
that such a culture created in the contemporary reader.
Moll Flanders is situated between two polarities of
prose fiction of its day: the idealizing romance and
the picaresque tale. The romantic formulas that are
invoked, however, are not conventionally resolved;
for example, Moll mentions her orphanhood among the gyp-
sies but when questioned about it, cannot remember anything specifically of interest. While the novel de-
values romantic conventions, at the same time it re-
values the picaresque formulas by elevating them; Defoe
removes the traditional comic element of the picaresque
and makes the form more serious and more ironic. *Moll
Flanders* chronicles its protagonist's attempts to define
and protect her personal worth, moving from a view of
value as purely economic to a view of it as the ethical
content of one's life.

800. Rexroth, Kenneth. "Afterword." *The Fortunes and Mis-
      fortunes of the Famous Moll Flanders* by Daniel Defoe.
      New York: Signet, 1964. Pp. 303-13.

      Focuses on Defoe's realistic technique which enabled
      him to create "an absolutely convincing archetype" in
      Moll Flanders. The novel is a harshly moral one, and
      Defoe was fully aware that he was showing a parallel
      between the morality of a whore and that of the new
      capitalist middle class.

*   Richetti, John J. "The Portrayal of Women in Restora-
      tion and Eighteenth-Century English Literature."
      (See item 886.)

801. Rodway, A.E. "*Moll Flanders* and *Manon Lescaut*." *Essays
      in Criticism*, 3 (1953), 303-20.

      Believes that in order to steer a middle course be-
      tween the popular romances and burlesques of his day,
      Prévost turned to Defoe as a realistic model. In addi-
      tion to the verbal parallels which suggest Defoe's
      direct influence on Prévost, other obvious similarities
      exist; for example, both authors show great emotional
      sympathy for characters--Prévost's Manon Lescaut and
      Defoe's Moll Flanders--whom they are intellectually
      bound to condemn.

802.   Rogal, Samuel J.   "The Profit and Loss of Moll Flanders."
       Studies in the Novel, 5 (1973), 98-103.

       Contends that Defoe records so many of Moll's business
       transactions that they could be entered into a mer-
       chant's ledger.   Rogal then constructs such a ledger,
       showing all of Moll's receipts and payments and con-
       cludes that her "net profit from life" was £4,047.

803.   Rogers, Henry N., III.   "The Two Faces of Moll."
       Journal of Narrative Technique, 9 (1979), 117-25.

       Agrees with G.A. Starr (item 453) that Moll is a sin-
       cere penitent by the end of *Moll Flanders*.   She is a
       reflective narrator who looks over and judges her past
       conduct in the light of her newly awakened spiritual
       awareness.

804.   Rogers, Pat.   "Moll's Memory."   *English*, 24 (1975),
       67-72.

       The compiler was unable to read this article, listed
       in the *MLA Bibliography* for 1975, item 4737.

805.   Sacks, Sheldon.   *Fiction and the Shape of Belief: A
       Study of Henry Fielding With Glances at Swift, John-
       son, and Richardson*.   Berkeley and Los Angeles: Uni-
       versity of California Press, 1964.

       Praises Defoe's genius even though he did not add
       anything "new" to the novel as did Richardson and
       Fielding.   Although *Moll Flanders* "is not organized
       as a coherent action" (Sacks' definition of "novel"),
       Defoe remains an influential figure in the development
       of the novel form because of his abilities in presen-
       tation and characterization.

       Reviews: Martin C. Battestin, *College English*, 27 (1966),
          654; Benjamin Boyce, *South Atlantic Quarterly*, 64
          (1965), 568-69; Frank Brady, *Journal of General Edu-
          cation*, 17 (1966), 332-35; George A. Cevasco, *Library
          Journal*, 90 (1965), 249-50; William B. Coley, *Yale Re-
          view*, 55 (1965), 126-30; George P. Elliott, *Hudson Re-
          view*, 18 (1965), 433-41; C.T.P., *American Book Col-
          lector* (1966), 5; and Ronald Paulson, *Journal of
          English and Germanic Philology*, 65 (1966), 602-04.

*   [Schorer, Mark.]   "Surprising Adventures."   (See item
       450.)

806.   ————. "A Study in Defoe: Moral Vision and Structural
        Form." *Thought*, 25 (1950), 275-87. Reprinted as
        the "Introduction" to the Modern Library edition of
        Moll Flanders, item 45. Also reprinted as "Moll
        Flanders" in Byrd, item 132.

        Calls *Moll Flanders* "our classic revelation of the
        mercantile mind": everything can be weighed, measured,
        handled, paid for in gold, or expiated by a prison term.
        The story is an "allegory of an impoverished soul--the
        author's." This moral weakness--the novel "has no real
        moral life"--is at the heart of the story's realism;
        Defoe's guile and moral imperception ideally reflect
        what a criminal like Moll would be like.

807.   ————. "Technique as Discovery." *Hudson Review*, 1
        (1948), 67-87. Reprinted in *Critiques and Essays on
        Modern Fiction, 1920-51*. Ed. John W. Aldridge. New
        York: Ronald Press, 1952. Pp. 67-82.

        Condemns *Moll Flanders* as "the true allegory of an
        impoverished soul--the author's." The novel is the
        classic revelation of the "mercantile mind," that kind
        of mind which deals only in things and never in ethics.

808.   Sherbo, Arthur. "Defoe's Limited Genius." *Essays in
        Criticism*, 19 (1969), 351-54.

        Rejects Brooks' argument (item 724) that the parallels
        and repetitions of *Moll Flanders* are intentional. Many
        of them also occur in *Roxana* and they merely reflect the
        limits of Defoe's novelistic skills.

809.   —   . "Moll Flanders: Defoe as Transvestite?"
        Studies in the Eighteenth-Century Novel. East Lansing:
        Michigan State University Press, 1969. Pp. 136-67.

        Disagrees with some widely accepted critical views of
        conscious artistry in *Moll Flanders*, particularly the
        positions taken by Robert Alter, Arnold Kettle, and
        Dorothy Van Ghent. Sherbo finds Defoe to be a shoddy
        artist whose repetitions reflect his "lack of imagina-
        tion." Although Defoe is capable of achieving some fine
        effects, his artistry is vastly overrated.

810.   ————. "Moll's Friends." *Studies in the Eighteenth-
        Century Novel*. East Lansing: Michigan State University
        Press, 1969. Pp. 168-76.

        Takes issue with the standard view of Moll Flanders
        as tough and self-reliant and with the image of her as

a victim of society. In reality, Moll consistently
laments her friendlessness and helplessness, and whenever she is in real difficulty, someone appears to
rescue her. Such situations occur so frequently that
a major motif emerges: it is not who you are or what
you have, but who you know that really counts in life.

811. Shinagel, Michael. "The Maternal Theme in *Moll Flan-
       ders*: Craft and Character." *Cornell Library Journal*,
       7 (1969), 3-23. Reprinted in Kelly, item 38.

       Identifies a "maternal theme" which enables Defoe to
       reveal Moll's character. The mixture of "warm kisses
       and cold cash" in Moll's relationship with her son,
       Humphrey, typifies her view of all her children and
       shows her to be a thoroughly materialistic person, bent
       on achieving "a secure state of affluence." The con-
       tradictions between Moll's professed feelings for her
       offspring and her actions are a result more of Defoe's
       narrative lapses than of any consistent attempt to pre-
       sent conscious irony.

812. Sieber, Harry. *The Picaresque*. The Critical Idiom
       Series. London: Methuen, 1977.

       Disagrees with the view that *Moll Flanders* is not a
       picaresque novel (see Alter, item 714). There are many
       basic similarities between the Spanish picaresque and
       Defoe's fiction: Moll's definition of morality, her
       association of poverty and criminality, her desire for
       upward social mobility, and her status as an outsider,
       among other things, echo the basic themes of Spanish
       picaresque, although Defoe probably owes more to the
       traditional criminal biography than to the picaro tale.

813. Singleton, Robert R. "Defoe, Moll Flanders, and the
       Ordinary of Newgate." *Harvard Library Bulletin*, 24
       (1976), 407-13.

       Discovers two real-life models for the chaplain who
       attempts to get Moll to confess in Newgate.

*   Smith, Leroy W. "Daniel Defoe: Incipient Pornographer."
       (See item 889.)

814. Spadaccini, Nicholas. "Daniel Defoe and the Spanish
       Picaresque Tradition: The Case of *Moll Flanders*."
       *Ideologies and Literature: A Journal of Hispanic and
       Luso-Brazilian Studies*, 2 (1978), 10-26.

Examines the elaboration in *Moll Flanders* of two aspects of the traditional picaresque: the relationship
between delinquency and autobiography and the exploration of the interrelated themes of freedom, survival,
and disillusionment. That there is a direct influence
of the picaresque on Defoe is suggested by his ownership
of Francisco López de Ubeda's *La picara Justina* and the
parallel between it and the "Preface" to *Moll Flanders*.

815.   Item deleted.

*   Starr, George A. *Defoe and Casuistry*. (See item 452.)

*   ————. *Defoe and Spiritual Autobiography*. (See item
        453.)

816.   ————. "Introduction." *The Fortunes and Misfortunes
        of the Famous Moll Flanders*. London and New York:
        Oxford University Press, 1971. Pp. vii-xxii.

        Notes the standard debate over the irony of the novel,
        but then goes on to other considerations. *Moll Flanders*
        "is akin to tales of obsession by Hogg or Hawthorne or
        Melville.... We are drawn into the quest of a heroine
        who in some degree escapes the bounds of everyday moral,
        social, and psychological laws." In spite of this,
        Moll still strikes the reader as a realistic figure.
        Starr also discusses Defoe's sources and the temporal
        setting of the book (which "hovers in a timeless fic-
        tional once-upon-a-time"). He approaches Defoe's in-
        tentions by trying to determine the readership of *Moll*.
        Starr concludes his discussion with remarks on Defoe's
        use of language. For information on the edition itself,
        see item 39.

817.   Strange, Sallie Minter. "Moll Flanders: A Good Cal-
        vinist." *South Central Bulletin*, 36 (1976), 152-54.

        Responds to those views of *Moll Flanders* which see the
        novel as structurally ironic or as philosophically con-
        fused by postulating a consistent Calvinistic basis for
        the work. Modern readers usually fail to see "the
        interdependence of Moll's ethical nature, her actions,
        and her experience, which together make up the Calvin-
        istic idea of man." Read in this way, the novel is
        straightforwardly clear and consistent.

*   Streeter, Harold Wade. *The Eighteenth-Century English
        Novel in French Translation: A Bibliographical Study*.
        (See item 670.)

*   Sutherland, James R. *Daniel Defoe: A Critical Study.*
      (See item 349.)

818. Taube, Myron. "Moll Flanders and Fanny Hill: A Com-
      parison." *Ball State University Forum*, 9, ii (1968),
      76-80.

      Points out the similarities and differences between
      Fanny Hill and Moll Flanders. Both are orphaned young,
      both come to London to make their fortunes, both are
      seduced early, both are prostitutes with aspirations
      for gentility, etc. On the other hand, there is a vast
      difference between the fictional worlds in which the
      two reside. Moll's world is harshly realistic, mirroring
      the commercial world of middle-class England, whereas
      Fanny's world is an unreal, arcadian one of sexual de-
      lights.

*   Vaid, Sudesh. *The Divided Mind: Studies in Defoe and
      Richardson.* (See item 371.)

819. Van Ghent, Dorothy. "On *Moll Flanders.*" *The English
      Novel: Form and Function.* New York: Rinehart and Co.,
      1953. Pp. 33-43. Reprinted in Byrd, item 132;
      Elliott, item 738; and Hunter, item 41.

      Views the structure of *Moll Flanders* as "a hierarchy
      of ironies" and dismisses as irrelevant the debate over
      whether or not these ironies are conscious or uncon-
      scious on Defoe's part because we cannot know his in-
      tentions or his sincerity. We do know, however, that
      the novel yields itself to analysis as an ironic struc-
      ture, and we also know that the novel's greatness is,
      at least in part, due to Defoe's thorough understanding
      of Moll. Also see Novak, "Conscious Irony," item 786.

*   Walton, James. "The Romance of Gentility: Defoe's
      Heroes and Heroines." (See item 461.)

820. Wanklyn, C. "Queries on *Moll Flanders.*" *Notes and
      Queries*, 159 (1930), 15.

      Locates Rugby's Hole, mentioned in *Moll Flanders*, for
      W.R.D., item 729.

821. Watson, Francis. "Moll, Mother of the Group." *Guardian*,
      6 February 1965, p. 8.

      Unseen by the compiler.

822. Watson, Tommy G. "Defoe's Attitude toward Marriage and
      the Position of Women Revealed in *Moll Flanders*."
      Southern Quarterly, 3 (1964), 1-8.

      Finds Defoe remarkably sympathetic to the plight of
      a single woman in the commercially oriented society of
      his day. His comments on marriage in *Moll Flanders* and
      several of his non-fiction tracts serve as a vehicle for
      criticizing a society that precludes women from the
      economic marketplace while demanding that they have
      money to survive.

*   Watt, Ian. "Defoe as Novelist." (See item 464.)

823. ————. "The Recent Critical Fortunes of *Moll Flanders*."
      Eighteenth-Century Studies, 1 (1967), 109-26.

      Traces and analyzes the trends of ten years (1956-66)
      of criticism of *Moll Flanders*, emphasizing discussions
      of unity and irony.

*   ————. *The Rise of the Novel*. (See item 688.)

824. Weinstein, Arnold. *Fictions of the Self: 1550-1800*.
      Princeton: Princeton University Press, 1981.

      Claims that Moll Flanders is one of the most fully
      realized characters in literature, partly because
      Defoe does not stop at erotic adventures or at a youth-
      ful and happy marriage but goes far beyond that in por-
      traying "a vigorous old lady bent on affirmation at all
      costs." Moll is "authentic," refusing to fake her
      emotions; even her disguises reflect her real character,
      her genuine "self." Defoe's greatest accomplishment
      is his creation of a realistic figure able to grasp and
      share the fullness of her entire life.

*   Weisgerber, Jean. "Aspects de l'espace romanesque."
      (See item 1440.)

*   ————. "A la recherche de l'espace romanesque: *Lazar-
      illo de Tormès, Les Aventures de Simplicius Simplicis-
      simus*, et *Moll Flanders*." (See item 1441.)

825. Wilson, Bruce L. "'Sex and the Single Girl' in the
      Eighteenth Century: An Essay on Marriage and the
      Puritan Myth." *Journal of Women's Studies in Litera-
      ture*, 1 (1979), 195-219.

      Uses *Moll Flanders* to illustrate "the typical plight
      of single women in the eighteenth century: How is one

to gain economic security and any recognition of individual worth or human dignity in a male-oriented
society where marriage is the only 'genteel' possibility
for a women [sic], but where it is arranged on purely
business principles?" Moll's methods to attain her
goals are identical to those of males, but are articula-
ted in Puritan religious terms. Also see Faletti, item
740.

826. Winsor, Kathleen, Louis Kronenberger, and Lyman Brison.
      "Moll Flanders." *Invitation to Learning: English and
      American Novels*. Ed. George D. Crothers. New York:
      Basic Books, 1966. Pp. 3-14.

      Takes from the tapes of the CBS radio show, *Invitation
      to Learning*, a wide-ranging discussion of *Moll Flanders*
      which emphasizes Moll's lack of hypocrisy in her repen-
      tance and Defoe's skills in realistic social analysis
      and criticism.

*   Winterich, John T. "How This Book Came to Be." (See
      item 382.)

827. Woolf, Virginia. "Defoe." *The Common Reader*. New
      York: Harcourt, Brace, and World, 1925. Pp. 89-97.
      Reprinted in Byrd, item 132; Elliott, item 738;
      Hunter, item 41; and Kelly, item 38.

      Calls *Moll Flanders* one of "the few English novels
      which we can call indisputably great" because in it
      Defoe "deals with the important and lasting side of
      things and not with the passing and trivial." Defoe
      appreciates the social position of the downtrodden and
      comprehends courage, resourcefulness, and tenacity.
      He is one of the "great plain writers."

                      F. *Colonel Jack* (1722)

*   Blewett, David. *Defoe's Art of Fiction*. (See item
      395.)

828. ————. "Jacobite and Gentleman: Defoe's Use of
      Jacobitism in Colonel Jack." *English Studies in
      Canada*, 4 (1978), 15-24.

      Makes two points about Jacobitism in *Colonel Jack*:
      (1) it is part of Defoe's didactic purpose in the novel,

and (2) it is important in the characterization of the
hero. Defoe consistently opposed Jacobitism, and in
Colonel Jack he presents it as a lost cause appealing
only to the politically naive or deluded. Defoe uses
the latter idea in characterizing Jack; by showing him
to be a Jacobite, Defoe depicts him as naive, deluded,
and unthinking.

*   Bonner, Willard H. *Captain William Dampier, Buccaneer-
       Author.* (See item 488.)

*   Dupas, Jean-Claude. "La Passion de l'or chez Defoe."
       (See item 1264.)

829.   Gifford, George E., Jr. "Daniel Defoe and Maryland."
       Maryland Historical Magazine, 52 (1957), 307-15.

       Suggests that the Maryland backgrounds in *Colonel
       Jack* and *Moll Flanders* may have been derived from the
       experience of Defoe's niece, Elizabeth Maxwell.

830.   H., A. "Note" to *The History and Remarkable Life of
       the Truly Honorable Colonel Jack.* London: Hamish
       Hamilton, 1947. Pp. v-viii.

       Explains Defoe's lack of popularity in the nineteenth
       century as due to his choice of "thieves and whores"
       as heroes and heroines and to his omission of "pathetic
       sentiment." Defoe's characters are matter-of-fact crea-
       tures who evaluate their actions in monetary not emo-
       tional terms. Even the morals drawn by Defoe are
       "severely practical" ones which argue that necessity
       causes crime. Colonel Jack is typical of Defoe's pro-
       tagonists--he is "a rogue with a conscience, and with
       ambitions to be honest."

831.   Hartveit, Lars. "A Chequer-Work of Formulae. A Reading
       of Defoe's *Colonel Jack.*" *English Studies*, 63 (1982),
       122-33.

       Identifies Colonel Jack as a picaro who encounters
       "various formulae which represent real as well as ideal
       ways of organizing society." Defoe combines the con-
       ventions of the picaresque (adventure, enterprise, prog-
       ress, strategic skill) with the conventions of Defoe's
       own society (acquiescence, consolidation, endurance,
       patience) to trace Jack's career from that of mercantile
       adventurer to that of benevolent landowner.

832. McBurney, William H. "Colonel Jacque: Defoe's Defini-
      tion of the Complete English Gentleman." *Studies in
      English Literature*, 2 (1962), 321-36.

      Observes that in *Colonel Jacque*, Defoe begins by fol-
      lowing the established pattern of a criminal biography
      but abruptly shifts into a story of the educational
      development of one who was born a gentleman. Colonel
      Jacque follows the educational steps outlined later in
      Defoe's *Compleat English Gentleman*: education, wealth,
      travel, "conversation," and a happy conjugal life. The
      focus on these middle-class goals is in part the reason
      for the novel's great contemporary appeal.

*   Mohr, Hans-Ulrich. "Texts als funktionale Äquivalente:
      Mandevilles *Fable of the Bees* und Defoes *Col. Jack*."
      (See item 1344.)

833. Monk, Samuel Holt. "Introduction." *The History and
      Remarkable Life of the Truly Honorable Col. Jacque,
      Commonly Call'd Col. Jack*. London and New York:
      Oxford University Press, 1965. Pp. ix-xxiii.

      Makes some general remarks on Defoe's life and career
      and then focuses on *Colonel Jack*. The novel "reveals an
      unusually large number of the author's convictions."
      For instance, it illustrates "Defoe's beliefs that
      gratitude is natural to all men" and his view that
      poverty justifies theft (Jack's early crimes are ex-
      cused on the grounds of necessity and ignorance). Jack
      is a sentimental figure who anticipates the good-hearted
      rake of later literature (Bevil, Tom Jones, Charles
      Surface). Monk is one of the few critics to point out
      that Defoe's use of detail is sporadic and that he
      often is quite vague in his use of physical description
      and detail. For information on the text, see item 49.

834. Moore, John Robert. "Defoe's Use of Personal Ex-
      perience in *Colonel Jack*." *Modern Language Notes*,
      54 (1939), 362-63.

      Believes that the accusation of horse theft levelled
      at Defoe in *A Hue and Cry after Daniel De Foe and His
      Coventry Beast* (1711) was the source for the horse
      stealing incident in *Colonel Jack*.

835. Novak, Maximillian E. "Colonel Jack's 'Thieving
      Roguing' Trade to Mexico and Defoe's Attack on Econ-
      omic Individualism." *Huntington Library Quarterly*,
      24 (1961), 349-53.

Dissects the final episode in *Colonel Jack* to illustrate Defoe's theory of commercial morality. Defoe
objects to Jack's economic individualism, for in his
attempt to benefit himself by entering into the for-
bidden trade with Mexico, Jack adversely affects the
public good. Therefore, Defoe punishes his hero by
destroying his dream of great wealth.

836. Prideaux, W.F. "Defoe's *Colonel Jacque.*" *Notes and
Queries*, Tenth Series, 8 (1907), 87.

Inquires about the whereabouts of a first edition of
Colonel Jack.

837. ————. "Defoe's *Colonel Jacque.*" *Notes and Queries*,
Tenth Series, 8 (1907), 411-12.

Provides bibliographical information on the first
edition of *Colonel Jack*, suggesting that perhaps the
novel was not first published in December 1722 as believed but in 1723.

838. Singleton, Robert R. "English Criminal Biography,
1651-1722." *Harvard Library Bulletin*, 18 (1970),
63-83.

Describes the genre of criminal biography: such works
often are comic, they usually do not attempt a realistic
time scheme, and they generally use real place names
and realistic personal names. The genre influenced
Defoe's criminal biographies, especially *Colonel Jacque*
which has several significant parallels to the robber
Ralph Wilson's autobiography. Defoe's knowledge of
literature about criminals is demonstrated by his mention of four real criminals, three of whom were the
subjects of biographies, in *Moll Flanders*.

*   Starr, George A. *Defoe and Casuistry.* (See item 452.)

839. ————. "'Only a Boy': Notes on Sentimental Novels."
Genre, 10 (1977), 501-27.

Defines the sentimental novel as an anti-*Bildungsroman*
in which the central character cannot grow up and find
his or her place in society. *Colonel Jack* is such a
novel, not because of its thirty-three instances of
weeping and two swoonings but because its protagonist
remains infantile throughout with his incessant craving
for devotion and avoidance of responsibility.

840.   T., R.E.   "R. Bilcliffe." *Notes and Queries*, 193 (1948),
          215.

          Asks for particulars on R. Bilcliffe, Speaker of the
          Quaker meeting house in White Hart Court, Lombard Street,
          in Defoe's *Captain Jack* [sic].

*   Walton, James. "The Romance of Gentility: Defoe's
          Heroes and Heroines." (See item 461.)

841.   Woodcock, George. "*Colonel Jack* and *Tom Jones*: Aspects
          of a Changing Century." *Wascana Review*, 5 (1970), 67-
          73.

          Compares Defoe and Fielding in order to show the dif-
          ferences in the periods in which the two men wrote. The
          story of Colonel Jack's clawing his way up the economic
          ladder suggests an age of economic development and a
          class consolidating its social gains. Tom Jones's rise
          to fortune reflects a less vigorous, more settled age
          which is in some ways stagnant.

                  G. *Journal of the Plague Year* (1722)

842.   Aitken, G.A. "Introduction" to *A Journal of the Plague
          Year* by Daniel Defoe. London: J.M. Dent and New York:
          E.P. Dutton, n.d.

          Establishes a context for Defoe's *Journal*, which Aitken
          sees as the author's masterpiece. Defoe's didactic pur-
          pose is advanced by his narrative's appearance of truth,
          attained through trivial details and the saddler's fre-
          quent expressions of doubt concerning the anecdote he
          is telling.

843.   Baker, Ronald L., and Richard C. Frushell. "Defoe's
          'Blow-bladder Street' in *A Journal of the Plague Year*."
          Journal of American Folklore, 87 (1974), 160-62.

          Explores various accounts of how "Blow-bladder Street,"
          mentioned by H.F. in *A Journal of the Plague Year*, got
          its unusual name.

844.   Bastian, F. "Defoe's *Journal of the Plague Year* Recon-
          sidered." *Review of English Studies*, n.s. 16 (1965),
          151-73.

Reviews the debate over the authorship and authenticity
of *The Journal of the Plague Year* from Gough's remarks
in 1780 to Bell's attacks in 1924 and then goes on to
investigate the "historical reality" of the characters
mentioned in the *Journal* and to discuss Defoe's sources
and the uses he made of them. Bastian concludes that
H.F., the supposed author of the *Journal*, "can be identi-
fied with Defoe's uncle, Henry Foe, with complete cer-
tainty." The three main sources for the book are *Orders
Conceived and Published by the Lord Mayor and Aldermen
of the City of London concerning the Infection of the
Plague, 1665*; the *Bills of Mortality* from 1665; and
Loimologia by Dr. Nathaniel Hodges. The *Journal* uses
its sources in such a way that it stands closer to our
idea of history than of fiction.

*   Bergmeir, F. "Ein Beitrag zur Quellenuntersuchung von
        Daniel Defoes 'Journal of the Plague Year.'" (See
        item 1223.)

845.   Birrell, Augustine. "Daniel Defoe." *The Nation and the
        Athenaeum*, 7 May 1927, pp. 147-48.

        Generalizes about *A Journal of the Plague Year*,
        branding it a "fake" and finding its power in the
        descriptions of the various plague victims' behavior.

846.   Blair, Joel. "Defoe's Art in *A Journal of the Plague
        Year*." *South Atlantic Quarterly*, 72 (1973), 243-54.

        Finds the art in *A Journal of the Plague Year* in the
        book's "artlessness." But the work only appears to be
        haphazard and unplanned; actually it is highly complex
        in its treatment of man confronting "inexplicable evil."
        It is a disturbing and unsettling book because it does
        not resolve its major conflicts, a characteristic that
        adds to its realism.

847.   Burgess, Anthony. "Introduction" to *A Journal of the
        Plague Year* by Daniel Defoe. Harmondsworth and
        Baltimore: Penguin, 1966. Pp. 6-19.

        Finds Defoe's art in his artlessness: "Defoe was our
        first great novelist because he was our first great
        journalist, and he was our first great journalist because
        he was born, not into literature, but into life." The
        apparent simplicity of Defoe's style "is a product of
        great craft." The novel's truth is both the truth of
        the historian and the deeper truth of the creative
        imagination.

*   Burke, John J., Jr. "Observing the Observer in His-
        torical Fictions by Defoe." (See item 710.)

848.   Flanders, W. Austin. "Defoe's *Journal of the Plague
        Year* and the Modern Urban Experience." *The Centennial
        Review*, 16 (1972), 328-48. Reprinted in Byrd, item
        132.

        Studies the *Journal of the Plague Year* not as an his-
        torical document or a part of the debate over the
        plague's providential nature but rather as a literary
        work which embodies the "eighteenth-century psychological
        and social experience common to all of Defoe's fic-
        tion...." Life in London under plague conditions serves
        as a metaphor for the ills of urban life: growing ag-
        gression and violence, the fear of economic collapse,
        and a sense of alienation and isolation. Defoe's per-
        ceptions of urban life are remarkably modern and thus
        give the *Journal* immediacy to the modern reader.

*   Füger, Wilhelm. "Der betrunkene Pfeifer: Ein Beitrag
        zur Quellenkunde und Erzählmode von Defoes *Journal
        of the Plague Year*." (See item 1276.)

*   Gergmeier, F. "Ein Beitrag zur Quellenuntersuchung von
        Daniel Defoes *Journal of the Plague Year*." (See item
        1283.)

*   Hess, G. "La peste di Londra." (See item 1293.)

849.   Hopkins, Kenneth. "Introduction" to *A Journal of the
        Plague Year* by Daniel Defoe. London: The Folio
        Society, 1960. Pp. 5-8.

        Calls the *Journal* "the most finished example of
        Defoe's peculiar talent for telling fiction in the guise
        of truth"; there is no more vivid account of an his-
        torical event in English literature.

*   Jacob, Ernst Gerhard. "Der englische Robinsondichter
        in seiner medizingeschichtlichen Bedeutung." (See
        item 1313.)

*   ————. "Die medizingeschichtliche Bedeutung des
        Robinsondichters Daniel Defoe." (See item 1316.)

*   ————. ["Postscript" to] *Ein Bericht vom Pestjahr*.
        (See item 1318.)

850. Johnson, Clifford. "Defoe's Reaction to Enlightened
      Secularism: A Journal of the Plague Year." Enlighten-
      ment Essays, 3 (1972), 169-77.

      Shows that A Journal of the Plague Year is important
      both in the history of science and in the tradition of
      English piety. To Defoe, Christian piety was consistent
      with an avid interest in experimental science. The ar-
      tistic power of the Journal, however, does not come from
      its scientific information but from its theological
      fervor.

851. Jones, A.G.E. "The Great Plague in Croydon." Notes and
      Queries, n.s. 3 (1956), 332-34.

      Provides background information on the Great Plague,
      with references to Defoe's Journal of the Plague Year.

852. Kay, Donald. "Defoe's Sense of History in A Journal of
      the Plague Year." Xavier University Studies, 9 (1970),
      1-8.

      Checks facts given by Defoe in A Journal of the Plague
      Year against Pepys' Diary and finds that they match.
      Defoe usually is accurate in his use of statistics,
      time, and location, and he makes them vivid through
      his artistic imagination.

853. Keys, T. "The Plague in Literature." Bulletin of the
      Medical Library Association, 32 (1944), 35-56.

      Surveys literary descriptions of the plague from
      Thucydides to Defoe, remarking on Defoe's vividness and
      realism in describing its effects.

*   Kozul, André. "Notes sur le journal de l'année de la
      peste de Daniel Defoe." (See item 1325.)

*   Kronenberger, Louis. "Defoe--an Island and a Plague."
      (See item 582.)

854. Landa, Louis. "Introduction" to A Journal of the Plague
      Year by Daniel Defoe. New York and London: Oxford
      University Press, 1969. Pp. ix-xxxix.

      Shows that Defoe was long obsessed by the idea of the
      plague; his fears were crystallized by the 1720 epidemic
      in Marseilles which precipitated ten essays and one
      tract from him in the two years between the epidemic
      and the appearance of the Journal in 1722. The Great

Plague of 1665, the subject of the *Journal*, provided an
opportunity for Defoe to express many of his opinions
on social, religious, economic, and philosophic issues.
He is particularly interested in the religious implications of the plague, which is ambivalently viewed as on
the one hand a divine visitation and on the other a
natural calamity. Defoe also glances at various medical
theories about the plague, but for the most part he con-
fines himself to discussions of those theories current
at the time of the Great Plague. The success of the
Journal lies in Defoe's ability to fuse historical fact
with imaginative interpretation.

855. Maynadier, G.H. "Introduction" to *A Journal of the
      Plague Year* by Daniel Defoe. New York: Sproul, 1904.
      Pp. ix-xii.

      Rates *A Journal of the Plague Year* as Defoe's finest
      artistic achievement because of its unified "combina-
      tion of recollection, tradition, imagination, and
      statistics."

*   Moore, John Robert. "Defoe's Workshop." (See item
      267.)

856. Nicholson, Watson. *The Historical Sources of Defoe's
      Journal of the Plague Year*. Boston: The Stratford
      Co., 1919. Reprinted Port Washington, N.Y.: Kennikat
      Press, 1966.

      Classifies the *Journal of the Plague Year* as an
      authentic history rather than a fiction. Defoe's
      sources included Hodges' *Loimologia*, Kemp's *Brief Trea-
      tise*, Vincent's *God's Terrible Voice in the City*,
      Thomson's *Loimotomia*, and several historical accounts
      of earlier plagues in other countries. Twelve appen-
      dices contain excerpts from these sources. Nicholson
      also argues that Defoe also drew details from accounts
      of survivors and his own childhood memories of the
      plague.

857. Novak, Maximillian E. "Defoe and the Disordered City."
      Publications of the Modern Language Association, 92
      (1977), 241-52.

      Contends that *A Journal of the Plague Year* presents
      "a different view of human life under the stress of the
      plague" than did earlier works which treated the plague
      as divine visitation or which emphasized the problems
      of civil disorder created by the plague. Defoe's book

presents the human suffering, pity, and fellowship
brought about by the epidemic. It is unusual in this
and in its concern with the poor of London, with whom
H.F., the tale's narrator, deeply sympathizes. No narrator before H.F. demonstrates such depths of sympathy
for the human condition and thus Defoe's work initiates
a direction for those many humane novels of feeling and
pathos which followed it.

858.   Plumb, J.H. "Daniel Defoe and *The Journal of the Plague*
       Year." *Men and Places*. London: The Cresset Press,
       1963. Pp. 275-80. Also published in *Men and Centuries*.
       Boston: Houghton Mifflin, 1963.

       Zeroes in on a discussion of *A Journal of the Plague*
       Year after briefly surveying Defoe's life and career.
       The *Journal* is a terrifying reading experience because
       it is so accurate and vivid.

       Reviews: John Brooks, *Listener*, 69 (1963), 286-89;
       Betty Kemp, *New Statesman*, 65 (1963), 681-82; (London)
       Times Literary Supplement, 29 March 1963, p. 214.

859.   Rocks, James E. "Camus Reads Defoe: *A Journal of the*
       Plague Year as a Source of *The Plague*." *Tulane*
       Studies in English, 15 (1967), 81-87.

       Points out that Camus listed Defoe's *Plague Year* in
       his notebooks when he started work on *The Plague* and
       then presents a series of parallels between the two
       works which includes: isolation in a closed city; re-
       volt against authority; and religion as solace in a
       time of crisis.

860.   Rynell, Alarik. "Defoe's *Journal of the Plague Year*,
       the Lord Mayor's *Orders* and O.E.D." *English Studies*,
       50 (1969), 452-64.

       Shows that some of the *O.E.D.*'s attributions to Defoe
       give a misleading picture of his usage. These errors
       come about because the *O.E.D.* cites as Defoe's the Lord
       Mayor's *Orders* on the plague which Defoe had simply
       quoted verbatim in the *Journal of the Plague Year*;
       actually the *Orders* were written 57 years before the
       Journal.

861.   Schonhorn, Manuel. "Defoe's *Journal of the Plague Year*:
       Topography and Intention." *Review of English Studies*,
       n.s. 19 (1968), 387-402.

       Takes a "topographical" approach to the *Journal* in
       order to overcome the limitations of the two most common

approaches--viewing the work as distorted history or
seeing it as historical fiction--both of which over-
simplify and negate Defoe's artistry in blending together fact and fancy. In order to set the stage for
his depiction of the horrors of the plague, Defoe had
to do much more than merely go fifty years into the
past; he had to recreate a Jacobean London which had
ceased to exist when the Great Fire of 1666 destroyed
373 of the 448 acres within the walls of the ancient
city. Defoe is careful not to err in his imaginative
reconstruction of London; as one means to avoid error,
he emphasizes those edifices and locations in and around
the city which were the same in 1665 as they were in
1721 when he wrote the *Journal*. A list of the *Journal*'s
topographical references is appended to this article.

*   [Schorer, Mark.] "Surprising Adventures." (See item
        450.)

862.   Secord, Arthur W. "Introduction" to *A Journal of the
        Plague Year and Other Pieces* by Daniel Defoe. New
        York: Doubleday Doran, 1935. Pp. vii-xxxv.

        Listed by Payne (item 21) but unread by the compiler.

*   Starr, George A. *Defoe and Casuistry*. (See item 452.)

863.   Vickers, Peter. "Daniel Defoe's *Journal of the Plague
        Year*: Notes for a Critical Analysis." *Filología
        Moderna*, 13 (1973), 161-70.

        Regards the *Journal of the Plague Year* as a master-
        piece because of its artful use of the saddler as "mor-
        tal man, a member of society, and extra-society man who
        enjoys God's protection." The saddler reminds one of
        Robinson Crusoe; the latter acts out a solitary drama
        amidst nature while the former is isolated within
        society. The *Journal* functions as "a protracted bib-
        lical parable."

864.   Zimmerman, Everett. "H.F.'s Meditations: *A Journal of
        the Plague Year*." *Publications of the Modern Language
        Association*, 87 (1972), 417-23.

        Approaches the *Journal of the Plague Year* through the
        conflicts and growing anxieties of H.F., the narrator,
        whose psychological complexities make the work "more
        like a novel than like either history or the seven-
        teenth-century pious writings that lie in its background."

The story's unity derives from H.F.'s attempts to understand morality, or its lack, in a time of plague.

H. *Roxana* (1724)

*   Backscheider, Paula. "Defoe's Women: Snares and Prey."
        (See item 387.)

865.   Baine, Rodney M. "Roxana's Georgian Setting." *Studies
        in English Literature*, 15 (1975), 459-71.

        Provides a chronology to show that the title page of
        Roxana is misleading in its reference to the "Time of
        Charles II" as the period in which the novel is set.
        In fact, most of Roxana's adventures and triumphs occur
        during the reign of George I. Internal evidence, in-
        cluding details of dress, support this thesis. The
        historical period that frames the action is important
        if one is to savor the ironies and appreciate the satire
        of the work. The discrepancy is not Defoe's however,
        but is due to the bookseller who inserted the title-
        page as a "bill-of-fare" designed to entice its readers
        into a purchase. Also see item 866.

*   Blewett, David. *Defoe's Art of Fiction*. (See item
        395.)

866.   ———. "*Roxana* and the Masquerades." *Modern Language
        Review*, 65 (1970), 499-502.

        Suggests that although the masquerade scenes in *Roxana*
        supposedly are set in King Charles II's time, they
        really are slightly veiled attacks on contemporary
        masquerades which were said to be the cause of immorality.
        Also see item 865.

*   Bordner, Marsha. "Defoe's Androgynous Vision: In *Moll
        Flanders* and *Roxana*." (See item 723.)

*   Brown, Lloyd W. "Defoe and the Feminine Mystique."
        (See item 122.)

867.   Cagle, William R. "A 'Lost' Edition (1745) of Defoe's
        Roxana." *Book Collector*, 11 (1962), 483-84.

        Locates in the Huntington Library a 1755 edition of
        Roxana which contains a sequel by an unknown hand.

868. Castle, Terry J. "'*Amy*, who knew my Disease': A Psycho-
      sexual Pattern in Defoe's *Roxana*." *ELH: A Journal of
      English Literary History*, 46 (1979), 81-96.

      Presents a Freudian analysis of *Roxana* based on the
      scene in which Roxana watches her maid, Amy, make love.
      Amy is a surrogate mother, the perfect friend, and a
      version of Roxana herself.

869. Cather, Willa. "Introduction" to *Roxana, or the Fortu-
      nate Mistress* by Daniel Defoe. New York: Knopf, 1924.

      Accuses Defoe of a meanness of spirit which is exem-
      plified in *The Complete British Tradesman*, "one of the
      ... most sordid books ever written." Although Defoe
      lacks all of the most valuable gifts of a writer--he
      has, for example, no imagination or depth of feeling--
      his verisimilitude is so persuasive that he gains a place
      among the immortals in literature.

870. Cohan, Steven. "Other Bodies: Roxana's Confession of
      Guilt." *Studies in the Novel*, 8 (1976), 406-18.

      Views the subordinate characters in *Roxana* as psycho-
      logical surrogates for the protagonist who uses them to
      "cushion her ego from assuming the blame for her ac-
      tions." Roxana's manipulation of these characters
      "makes them adhere closely to her most secret fantasies"
      and this illuminates the inner psychological conflict
      that she refuses to articulate. Once she orders Amy to
      leave, Roxana must deal with her fears and her wishes
      on her own.

*   Dottin, Paul. "Les sources de la *Roxana* de Daniel de
      Foë." (See item 1257.)

*   Elistratova, A.A. *Shchastlivaya Kurtizanka, ili Roksana*.
      (See item 1269.)

*   Gasquet, Emile. "*Roxana* de Defoe: Tensions et ruptures."
      (See item 1281.)

871. Higdon, David L. "The Critical Fortunes and Misfor-
      tunes of Defoe's *Roxana*." *Bucknell Review*, 20 (1972),
      67-82.

      Reviews briefly the history of *Roxana* criticism and
      then presents his own views of the novel's structure
      and theme. Not enough credit has been given Defoe for
      the structure of *Roxana*, which possesses great logical,

thematic, and aesthetic design. Thematically the novel
records Roxana's struggle to maintain a sense of self in
the face of forces which attempt to take it from her; the
work forecasts "the bleak alienation of the self in an
economic world." For an expanded version of this material, see Higdon's *Time and English Fiction*, item 752.

*   ————. *Time and English Fiction*. (See item 752.)

872.   Hume, Robert D. "The Conclusion of Defoe's *Roxana*:
         Fiasco or Tour de Force?" *Eighteenth-Century Studies*,
         3 (1970), 475-90.

         Objects to appraisals of *Roxana* as an inferior *Moll
         Flanders*. The former is a different kind of novel than
         Moll, is structurally superior to it, and has an artis-
         tically defensible ending. Unlike the earlier novels,
         Roxana is not a success story but rather a carefully
         controlled, gradually developing story of ruin, the
         abrupt ending of which is a logical conclusion to the
         action and avoids the anti-climactic details which
         Defoe generally added to his novels.

873.   Jack, Jane. "Introduction" to *Roxana, The Fortunate
         Mistress* by Daniel Defoe. London: Oxford University
         Press, 1964. Pp. vii-xiii.

         Calls *Roxana* "an unromantic romance" because of
         Defoe's ability to lie "like the truth." The book is
         not a picaro tale because the characters reflect bour-
         geois attitudes. Jack believes that Defoe's sympathetic
         portrayal of Roxana is due to his identification with
         her attitudes, and this identification is reflected in
         "the tension between sympathy and reprobation which is
         evident throughout the book."

874.   Jackson, Wallace. "*Roxana* and the Development of Defoe's
         Fiction." *Studies in the Novel*, 7 (1975), 181-94.

         Opposes the conclusions of McKillop (see item 424)
         and Shinagel (see item 332) that Defoe's fiction shows
         no artistic development; in fact, the progression of
         Defoe's artistic self-discovery can be traced from
         Robinson Crusoe through *Moll Flanders* to *Roxana*. The
         latter depicts Roxana's fate--trapped between her fear
         of exposure from without and her terrible guilt within--
         in a psychologically realistic manner matched in the
         eighteenth century only by Richardson.

*   James, E. Anthony. *Daniel Defoe's Many Voices*. (See
        item 211.)

875.   Jenkins, Ralph E. "The Structure of *Roxana*." *Studies
        in the Novel*, 2 (1970), 145-58.

        Makes an allegorical interpretation of the structure
        of *Roxana*, a novel which "shows a conscious artistry,
        a command of structure, and a clarity of moral judgment"
        unequalled in Defoe's other novels. The work's struc-
        ture is built around two actions, the debauching of Amy
        which begins Roxana's moral decline and the murder of
        Susan which culminates it. Roxana commits moral suicide
        by sacrificing others to her self-interest and by pre-
        ferring the vices of avarice, vanity, and adultery to
        love, responsibility, and repentance.

876.   Kestner, Joseph A., III. "Defoe and Madame de La Fay-
        ette: *Roxana* and *La Princesse de Monpensier*." *Papers
        on Language and Literature*, 8 (1972), 297-301.

        Finds in *La Princesse de Monpensier* a source for the
        masked ball and Roxana's Turkish dress in *Roxana*.

877.   Kropf, C.R. "Theme and Structure in Defoe's *Roxana*."
        Studies in English Literature, 12 (1972), 467-80.

        Denies the frequent complaint that Roxana is incom-
        plete and lacks thematic control. The novel has a sym-
        metrical structure as Roxana moves from poverty to
        riches and as she proceeds up the social scale in her
        relationships with the merchant and then the lord and
        then the king and down the scale again from king to
        lord to merchant. There is a sense of thematic com-
        pletion given the novel as Roxana degenerates from a
        religious and proper young lady to an unregenerate
        whore facing certain damnation. In fact, the double
        movement of progressive financial security accompanied
        by gradual spiritual degeneracy gives the novel a com-
        plexity of structure and theme superior to most of
        Defoe's other works.

878.   Novak, Maximillian E. "Crime and Punishment in Defoe's
        Roxana." *Journal of English and Germanic Philology*,
        65 (1966), 445-65.

        Presents four ways in which *Roxana* is Defoe's greatest
        achievement in the novel: (1) the narrative point-of-
        view; (2) the work's moral complexity; (3) the investi-
        gation of the individual conscience and passions; and

(4) the use of a single action to focus all the moral
and social implications of Roxana's career. Roxana is
not, as often stated, an upper-class Moll Flanders; she
lacks Moll's warmth and humor, she does not think well
of herself and destroys her own rationalizations about
her conduct, and she sinks into despair in her knowledge
of her moral decay. Defoe's true genius is shown in
Roxana by his ability to explore previously unplumbed
psychological depths and to create a disturbing and
realistic moral complexity in his plot.

*   ————. "Freedom, Libertinism, and the Picaresque."
(See item 436.)

879.   Oda, Minoru. "Allegory and History: A Study of Daniel
Defoe's *Roxana*." *Memoirs of Osaka Gakugei University*, A, No. 15 (1966), pp. 62-87.

Sees Roxana's life as realistically portrayed (because
it parallels Defoe's life) as opposed to the unrealistic
portrayals of the lives of Crusoe, Colonel Jack, and
Moll, all of whom are aided by "God's mercy" without
deserving it.

*   Olshin, Toby. "'Thoughtful of the Main Chance': Defoe
and the Cycle of Anxiety." (See item 790.)

880.   Peterson, Spiro. "A 'Lost' Edition (1745) of Defoe's
Roxana." *Book Collector*, 7 (1958), 295.

Asks for information on a 1745 edition of *Roxana*
which was enlarged by an anonymously written sequel.

881.   ————. "A 'Lost' Edition (1745) of Defoe's *Roxana*."
Notes and Queries, n.s. 3 (1956), 44.

Seeks information on a 1745 edition of *Roxana* enlarged
by an anonymously written sequel referred to by Godwin
and Lamb.

882.   ————. "The Matrimonial Theme of Defoe's *Roxana*."
Publications of the Modern Language Association, 70
(1955), 166-91.

Places Roxana's ideas on marriage in the context of
the matrimonial laws of Defoe's day. The author brings
forth several characters—Roxana, the Fool Husband, the
Landlord, and Amy—to point out the defects of current
marriage and divorce procedures. *Moll Flanders* and
Roxana form a primitive sequence-novel on domestic
relations.

883. Pettigrove, Malcolm C. "The Incomplete English Gentle-
      woman: Character and Characterization in *Roxana*."
      Studies in the Eighteenth Century, 4 (1979), 123-46.

      Unseen by the compiler (who failed to locate a journal
      of this name), the above item is reviewed by Susan Staves
      (item 26), who says that it views Roxana as vacillating
      between the model of a virtuous gentlewoman and that of
      a progressively degenerate sinner.

884. Raleigh, John Henry. "Style and Structure and Their
      Import in Defoe's *Roxana*." *University of Kansas City
      Review*, 20 (1953), 128-35.

      Links Defoe's style—which is midway between the
      high style and the vernacular—with the theme of *Roxana*;
      the plainness of style perfectly reflects "the prosaic
      quality of the people and experience" in the novel. The
      author gives examples of several of Defoe's rhetorical
      techniques, including his use of strong adjectives re-
      inforced with adverbial superlatives, his movement into
      baroque prose when treating moral issues, his employment
      of interpolated vignettes, and his frequent summaries,
      both concise and extended.

885. Ray, J. Karen. "The Feminine Role in *Robinson Crusoe*,
      Roxana, and *Clarissa*." *Emporia State Research Studies*,
      24 (1976), 28-33.

      Identifies a common theme in the three novels men-
      tioned in the title: they all demonstrate a rejection
      of the secondary position of women in eighteenth-century
      society. In *Crusoe*, woman is a symbol of maternal,
      restrictive society from which the hero flees. Roxana
      seeks financial and social independence outside the
      realm circumscribed for women and Clarissa rejects the
      traditional psychological domination of the male.

886. Richetti, John J. "The Portrayal of Women in Restora-
      tion and Eighteenth-Century English Literature." *What
      Manner of Woman: Essays on English and American Life
      and Literature*. Ed. Marlene Springer. New York: New
      York University Press, 1977. Pp. 65-97.

      Calls Moll Flanders and Roxana "female impersonators"
      who, as male creations, are untouched by female ex-
      perience.

887. Rogers, Katherine. "Afterword" to *Roxana, The Fortunate
      Mistress* by Daniel Defoe. New York and London: Signet,
      1979.

Calls *Roxana* a "primitive" book which blurs distinctions between factual, moral, and fictional works because the novel form was not yet fully developed as a definable genre. Defoe argues for female independence in *Roxana*, but it is not clear if these arguments are sincere or are Roxana's rationalizations for her actions. *Review*: *The Scriblerian*, 15 (1982), 56.

888. Sloman, Judith. "The Time Scheme of Defoe's *Roxana*." *English Studies in Canada*, 5 (1979), 406-19.

Explores *Roxana* from the perspective of Defoe's use of time. Distortions of time demonstrate the character of Roxana, who, as she ages, is obsessed with dates, which she confuses, distorts, and forgets; her use of time reflects her "personal needs."

889. Smith, LeRoy W. "Daniel Defoe: Incipient Pornographer." *Literature and Psychology*, 22 (1972), 165-78.

Claims that five of Eberhard and Phyllis Kronhausen's identifying characteristics of hard-core pornography appear in Defoe's *Moll Flanders* and *Roxana*. Defoe has many of the attitudes and prejudices about sex and women that eventually led to the Victorian conflict between public prudery and private pornography.

890. Snow, Malinda. "Diabolic Intervention in Defoe's *Roxana*." *Essays in Literature*, 3 (1976), 52-60.

Applies the Puritan conception of diabolic intervention in human affairs to the relationship between Roxana and her maid, Amy, who "argues according to diabolic method" in order to convince Roxana that she should receive the landlord as a lover. Roxana, in turn, helps corrupt Amy, who also beds the landlord and possibly murders Roxana's daughter.

*   Starr, George A. *Defoe and Casuistry*. (See item 452.)

*   ————. *Defoe and Spiritual Autobiography*. (See item 453.)

891. ————. "Sympathy v. Judgement in Roxana's First Liaison." *The Augustan Milieu: Essays Presented to Louis A. Landa*. Eds. Henry K. Miller, Eric Rothstein, and George S. Rousseau. Oxford: Clarendon Press, 1970. Pp. 59-76.

Focuses solely on the initial episodes of *Roxana*--
Roxana's seduction by the landlord--in order to show
how Defoe establishes "tonal and thematic patterns" that
run throughout the book while simultaneously eliciting
reader sympathy for Roxana who must choose between
starvation for herself and her five children or survival by becoming the landlord's whore. Defoe does not
attempt to determine the rights and wrongs of this
question; instead, he presents it as a complex and ambiguous issue.

892. Stephanson, Raymond. "Defoe's *Roxana*: The Unresolved
      Experiment in Characterization." *Studies in the
      Novel*, 12 (1980), 279-88.

      Attributes the controversial ending of *Roxana* to De-
      foe's inability to resolve a narrative problem he poses
      for himself: he is interested in tracing Roxana's moral
      and psychological disintegration, but his first-person
      method does not let him conclude satisfactorily because
      Roxana obviously cannot objectively present her own
      mental breakdown.

893. Taylor, S. Ortiz. "Episodic Structure and the Picaresque
      Novel." *Journal of Narrative Technique*, 7 (1977),
      218-25.

      Develops a diagram to explain the pattern of picaresque
      novels. Such novels begin with "Entry" accompanied by
      an optimistic tone; next is "Error or Fate" and a pes-
      simistic tone; following is "Expulsion" with either a
      cynical or exulting tone; and, finally, there is "Time
      Lapse" with its introspective tone. This structural
      diagram is illustrated by *Roxana* which follows the pat-
      tern perfectly.

*   Uphaus, Robert W. "Defoe, Deliverance, and Dissimula-
      tion." (See item 458.)

*   Vaid, Sudesh. *The Divided Mind: Studies in Defoe and
      Richardson*. (See item 371.)

*   Walton, James. "The Romance of Gentility: Defoe's
      Heroes and Heroines." (See item 461.)

894. Williams, Orlo. "Roxana." *Some Great English Novels:
      Studies in the Art of Fiction*. St. Clair Shores,
      Mich.: Scholarly Press, 1970. Pp. 120-48. Originally
      published London: Macmillan, 1926.

Calls Defoe's works "narratives"--as opposed to the
"novels" of Richardson and Fielding--but sees *Roxana* as
approximating the novel form (a term which is not defined). Although Defoe's ostensibly moral purpose in
it is suspect, *Roxana* is a highly believable "great
story," done with originality and skill. Roxana herself is a thoroughly realistic character not a "mere
mouthpiece" for abstract ideas, and her views on matri-
mony logically present a legitimate feminist opinion of
marriage in the eighteenth century.

895. Zimmerman, Everett. "Language and Character in Defoe's
Roxana." *Essays in Criticism*, 21 (1971), 227-35.

Supports Douglas Brooks (item 724) in his dispute
with Arthur Sherbo (item 808) over parallel passages in
Defoe. A close study of the language of *Roxana* shows
that the protagonist's materialism is a defense against
metaphysical terrors and that she is a psychologically
complex character. Metaphoric patterns emerge in the
novel which reveal the central character's mind to be
a confused one that does not fully comprehend its own
stratagems.

V

MISCELLANEOUS WRITINGS

A. General

896. Bosse, Malcolm J. "Introduction" to *The Consolidator*
by Daniel Defoe. New York and London: Garland, 1972.
Pp. 5-9.

Outlines the work and provides a key to identify the
thinly disguised contemporary figures who appear in
the narrative. This work, with its "vigorous prose" and
"mastery of detail," anticipates the later novels.

897. Curtis, Laura Ann. "Introduction." *The Versatile
Defoe: An Anthology of Uncollected Writings by Daniel
Defoe*. Totowa, N.J.: Rowman and Littlefield, 1979.
Pp. 1-33.

Presents Defoe as a protean figure of great versatility whose varied experience writing about politics,
religion, economics, commerce, history, sociology, and
psychology prepared him to become a great and realistic
novelist. Defoe's interests are such that to know his
works is to know the consciousness of early eighteenth-
century England itself. Moreover, Defoe is a vitally
important figure of his age because he contributes to
"the emergence of political stability" and "the notion
of modernity" (the systematic effort to improve man's
living conditions through exploiting nature). Curtis
also illuminates Defoe's character by comparing his relationship with Harley to the latter's relationship
with Swift. A lengthy and forthright exploration of
Defoe's duplicity is balanced by a discussion of Defoe's
principles and enduring loyalties "to his religious
and social origins."

898.   Damrosch, Leopold, Jr. "Defoe as Ambiguous Impersona-
          tor." *Modern Philology*, 71 (1973), 153-59.

          Discusses the ambiguity of the narrative method em-
          ployed in *A True Relation of the Apparition of One Mrs.
          Veal*, *The Poor Man's Plea*, and letter eight of *The Com-
          plete English Tradesman*, concluding that it is impossible
          to tell if Defoe speaks straightforwardly or is ironic
          in these works. Such ambiguity also appears in his
          fiction.

*   Freeman, William. *The Incredible De Foe*. (See item
          183.)

*   Horsley, L.S. "Rogues or Honest Gentlemen: The Public
          Characters of Queen Anne Journalists." (See item 205.)

899.   Merrett, Robert James. *Daniel Defoe's Moral and Rhe-
          torical Ideas*. ELS Monograph Series, No. 19. Vic-
          toria, B.C.: University of Victoria Press, 1980.

          Depicts Defoe as a "deliberate thinker" and "provoca-
          tive teacher" whose didactic concerns cause him to
          subordinate individual elements of his works to his
          moral aims. Even his novels are geared more to ad-
          vancing moral ideas than to entertaining. The book
          concentrates more on the overtly didactic works, like
          Conjugal Lewdness, than it does on the fiction.

*   Moore, John Robert. "Defoe's Lampoons: *A Speech of a
          Stone Chimney-Piece*." (See item 982.)

900.   ———. "Milton Among the Augustans: The Infernal
          Council." *Studies in Philology*, 48 (1951), 15-25.

          Notes Milton's reputation among the Augustans and
          then discusses the Infernal Council from *Paradise Lost*
          as greatly influential on Augustan political satirists.
          Defoe's frequent use of debates and formal conversations
          in his political tracts probably stems in part from
          Milton's Infernal Council which Defoe greatly admired.

*   Rothman, Irving N. "Defoe's Census of *The Family In-
          structor* and *The Political History of the Devil*."
          (See item 1013.)

*   Shinagel, Michael. *Daniel Defoe and Middle-Class Gen-
          tility*. (See item 332.)

901. Trent, W.P. "Defoe Tracts." *Notes and Queries*, Tenth
Series, 6 (1906), 47.

   Asks for help in locating seven Defoe pieces listed
   in Lee's list.

B. Essays, Periodicals, and Tracts

902. Alkon, Paul K. "Defoe's Argument in *The Shortest Way
with the Dissenters*." *Modern Philology*, 73 (1976),
512-23.

   Contrasts the *Shortest Way with the Dissenters* with
   Swift's *Modest Proposal* and Sacheverell's *Political
   Union* in order to analyze its satiric method (or lack
   of it) and to uncover the nature of its argument. Defoe
   raises the question, "Is it morally permissible to enact
   a cruel law for a worthy end if that law might never have
   to be applied?" Although Defoe's answer to the question
   is "no," it takes a close reading to discover it; the
   difficulty of the task is due to Defoe's method of en-
   trapping the unwary Anglican into choosing a vicious
   course of action which he thinks is virtuous. Defoe's
   ultimate aim, of course, is to rouse the sleeping
   Anglican conscience about the plight of the Dissenters.

903. Alsop, J.D. "Defoe and His Whig Paymasters." *Notes
and Queries*, 28 (1981), 225-26.

   Traces the devious way that Defoe was paid by Sunderland for infiltrating Mist's *Journal*; Sunderland was
   careful to keep Defoe's name out of all official records.

904. ———. "New Light on Nathaniel Mist and Daniel Defoe."
Papers of the Bibliographical Society of America, 75
(1981), 57-60.

   Shows that Sunderland arranged for Mist to be arrested
   to allow Defoe to infiltrate Mist's *Journal*.

905. Anderson, Paul B. "A Reply to John Robert Moore."
Philological Quarterly, 21 (1942), 419-23.

   Responds to Moore's attack on Anderson's scholarship
   (see item 979) and admits that *A Trip through London*
   (1728) contains material taken from Defoe's *The Great
   Law of Subordination*. Also see Moore, "A Rejoinder,"
   item 991.

906.   Baine, Rodney M. "The Apparition of Mrs. Veal: A
       Neglected Account." *Publications of the Modern Lan-
       guage Association*, 69 (1954), 523-41.

       Reprints the text of a hitherto neglected account by
       the Reverend Mr. Payne of the apparition of Mrs. Veal.
       Payne's work, a longer and more detailed account than
       Defoe's, prefaced the 1766 edition of Charles Drelin-
       court's *Christian's Consolidator against the Fears of
       Death*. Comparing the two versions, Baines notes that
       Defoe's earlier work serves as a narrative model for
       Payne and other later reporters of Mrs. Bargrave's
       story.

907.   ————. "Defoe and Mrs. Bargrave's Story." *Philological
       Quarterly*, 33 (1954), 388-95.

       Argues that Defoe did not write "The Apparition of
       Mrs. Veal" but merely edited and published Mrs. Bar-
       grave's account.

       Review: Arthur W. Secord, *Philological Quarterly*, 34
       (1955), 282.

*   Baker, J.N.L. "The Geography of Daniel Defoe." (See
       item 1075.)

908.   Baring-Gould, Sabine. *Cornish Characters and Strange
       Events*. London: John Lane, 1909.

       Notes briefly a pamphlet, "A Remarkable Passage of an
       Apparition," which was included with some copies of the
       second edition of Defoe's *Duncan Campbell* in 1720 and
       seems to suggest (it is difficult to know what the
       author means exactly) that this account of an appari-
       tion has some connection (as a source?) with Defoe's
       Apparition of Mrs. Veal.

*   Béranger, Jean. "Defoe pamphlétaire, 1716-1720."
       (See item 1220.)

909.   Bergholz, H. "Defoe's 'Review.'" (London) *Times Liter-
       ary Supplement*, 18 June 1938, p. 424.

       Provides data about extant copies of Defoe's *Review*
       in British public libraries. Suggests that perhaps
       No. 81 never existed. See Secord, item 1020.

910.   Black, Stephen A. "Defoe's 'The Shortest Way.'"
       American Notes and Queries, 5 (1966), 51-52.

Rejects the view that the irony of "The Shortest Way
with the Dissenters" can be discovered only by means
of external information; the analogies which begin and
end the tract disclose its ironic purpose.

911. Boardman, Michael M. "Defoe's Political Rhetoric and
the Problem of Irony." *Tulane Studies in English*,
22 (1977), 87-102.

Defines three types of ironic political pamphlet
written by Defoe: systematic irony, sarcasm, and
polemic. In all three types, Defoe was highly successful in convincing the reader that a sane and sensible
author stands behind the mad or biased speaker. This
success makes the failure of *The Shortest Way with the
Dissenters* all the more puzzling. The work is bereft
of the kind of internal clues which might identify
it to the reader as ironic, and thus the persona is
taken precisely for what he seems to be: a rabid rabble-
rouser. Also see Boyce, item 914, and Novak, item 999.

912. Bond, Donovan H., and W. Reynolds McLeod, eds. *News-
letters to Newspapers: Eighteenth-Century Journalism*.
Morgantown, West Virginia: School of Journalism, West
Virginia University, 1977.

Makes passing mention of Defoe in several of the
essays which comprise this volume. Perhaps the most
enlightening is Robert V. Hudson's view that Benjamin
Franklin was in some ways "a disciple" of Defoe.

913. Bond, Richmond P., ed. *Studies in the Early English
Periodical*. Chapel Hill: University of North Carolina
Press, 1957.

Calls Defoe's *Review* "the most considerable monument
of essay journalism" and remarks that his journalistic
performance is "the most remarkable single achievement
in the history of professional journalism." These
comments by the editor are followed by scattered
references to Defoe in the six essays that comprise
this volume.

*   Booth, Wayne C. *The Rhetoric of Fiction*. (See item
722.)

914. Boyce, Benjamin. "*The Shortest Way*: Characteristic
Defoe Fiction." *Quick Springs of Sense: Studies in
the Eighteenth Century*. Ed. Larry S. Champion. Athens,
Ga.: University of Georgia Press, 1974. Pp. 1-13.

Rejects the view, advanced by Novak (item 999) that
The Shortest Way with the Dissenters is rhetorically
"extraordinarily clever." The work is more confusing
than clever, more puzzling than ironic; its end result
is to offend both High Churchman and Dissenter. The
problem with the pamphlet is its fictional speaker who
seems completely villainous at times but who expresses
some of Defoe's own most cherished beliefs. The didactic interjections of Defoe's views on Occasional Con-
formity, for example, are inconsistent with the speaker's
character and therefore negate the intended irony.
Later, Defoe was able to successfully utilize similar
inconsistencies to develop the complex characters of
his fictions. Also see Boardman, item 911.

915. Bretherton, Ralph H. "The Apparition of Mrs. Veal."
      Gentlemen's Magazine, n.s. 291 (1901), 531-43.

      Suggests that Defoe pretended that the Veal story was
      true in order to "puff"--and thus aid the sales of--
      Drelincourt's *Book of Consolation Against the Fears of
      Death*.

916. Burch, Charles Eaton. "Defoe's Connections with the
      Edinburgh Courant." *Review of English Studies*, 5
      (1929), 437-40.

      Reviews briefly Couper's remarks (item 924) on Defoe's
      1710 legal interest in the *Courant* and then goes on to
      argue from internal evidence that Defoe actually began
      writing for the paper in October 1708 and continued
      until December 1709. Several articles contain ex-
      pressions common to Defoe's known work; moreover, the
      sentiments in these articles are firmly behind Godolphin's
      policies, and Defoe was sent into Scotland at this time
      to advance those policies.

*   ————. "Defoe's First *Seasonable Warning* (1706)."
          (See item 1166.)

917.   ————. "Defoe's 'Some Reply to Mr. Hodges and Some
          Other Authors.'" *Notes and Queries*, 193 (1948), 72-74.

      Dates Defoe's *A Fourth Essay at Removing National
      Prejudices: with some Reply to Mr. H(o)dges and Some
      Other Authors* between November 4 and November 14, 1706.
      The pamphlet was written primarily against Hodges'
      Essay Upon the Union, which opposed the union with
      England, and the "other authors" of the title were

given only cursory treatment. Also see Burch's "The Authorship of 'A Letter Concerning Trade,'" item 1164.

918. ————. "Notes on the Contemporary Popularity of Defoe's *Review*." *Philological Quarterly*, 16 (1937), 210-13.

Cites evidence to show that Defoe's *Review* was extremely popular. Wilson and Lee emphasized its popularity, Leslie in *The Rehearsal* bemoaned its wide readership among the masses, Ward noted its influence on the lower classes, and Swift complained about its impact on shaping the public's attitudes.

ʎ   ————. "An Unassigned Defoe Pamphlet in the Defoe-Clark Controversy." (See item 1168.)

*   ————. "Wodrow's List of Defoe's Pamphlets on the Union." (See item 1169.)

*   Churchill, R.C. *English Literature of the Eighteenth Century*. (See item 137.)

919. Cole, G.D.H. *Politics and Literature*. London: The Hogarth Press, 1929.

Calls Defoe "the principal founder of modern journalism" because he is the first author to deliberately write for the bourgeois public on political matters. Because of his public, Defoe--unlike Swift--conceals his cleverness and appears in the guise of a plain, blunt, commonsensical man.

920. Constantine, J. Robert. "The Negro in Defoe's *Religious Courtship*." *Negro History Bulletin*, 17 (1953), 85.

Identifies Defoe as "one of the very earliest friends of the Negro" and illustrates his point by outlining the positive portrait of Negum, the Negro in *Religious Courtship*.

921. Cook, Richard I. "Defoe and Swift: Contrasts in Satire." *Dalhousie Review*, 43 (1963), 28-39.

Compares Defoe's *Shortest Way with the Dissenters* with Swift's *Modest Proposal*, noting that Defoe was not as successful as Swift in terms of conveying a satiric intent through irony because Defoe's work "is not so much an ultra-subtle satire as it is an astute and skilful imitation."

922.   ———. "'Mr. *Examiner*' and 'Mr. *Review*': The Tory
        Apologetics of Swift and Defoe." *Huntington Library
        Quarterly*, 29 (1966), 127-46.

        Attributes the differences in the political essays of
        Defoe and Swift to the distinct nature of their respec-
        tive audiences: Defoe wrote for the commercial middle
        class and Swift for the country squiredom. Unlike
        Swift, Defoe attempted to exploit his own life and per-
        sonality for rhetorical effect in the *Review* essays.

923.   ———. "Swift and Defoe." *Jonathan Swift as a Tory
        Pamphleteer*. Seattle: University of Washington Press,
        1967. Pp. 93-113.

        Compares Swift and Defoe as propagandists for Harley's
        ministry, showing that their differences in method are
        related to their distinct audiences. Swift's audience
        was the rural gentry, basically sympathetic to the
        Tories, whereas Defoe's readers came from the urban com-
        mercial middle class, basically suspicious of the Tories.
        Swift implies that his status as a gentleman entitles
        him to a hearing, especially since as a gentleman he is
        a friend to the great and an inside observer of secret
        affairs. Defoe, on the other hand, assumes that his
        native wit and practical experience entitle him to a
        hearing, but in order to establish these credentials,
        he must reveal a great deal of himself to his readers.
        Therefore, Defoe is highly autobiographical, intimate,
        and down-to-earth in the political pieces he wrote in
        support of Harley's administration.

924.   Couper, W.J. *The Edinburgh Periodical Press*. Stirling:
        Eneas Mackay, 1908.

        Establishes that Defoe obtained in 1710 the sole
        legal right to print the *Courant*, but that in fact he
        only published two issues, those of March 20 and March
        23. It is likely that Defoe wrote for the *Courant*
        prior to obtaining a financial interest in it.

925.   ———. "The Writings and Controversies of James
        Clark, Minister at Glasgow, 1702-1724." *Records of
        the Glasgow Bibliographical Society*, 11 (1933), 73-95.

        Devotes Section IV of this essay to a review of the
        controversy between Defoe and Clark over the Union.
        Defoe attributed the 1706 civil disorders in Glasgow
        to a sermon by Clark, who defended himself and precipi-
        tated a pamphlet war.

926. Curry, Frank. "Defoe's *Weekly Review*." *Notes and Queries*, Eleventh Series, 8 (1913), 448-49.

Urges publication of Defoe's *Review*; the artistry of it and its information on affairs between 1704 and 1713 make it a valuable work, of which only one complete copy, and that in private hands, exists. See Matthews, item 975.

927. Curtis, Laura Ann. "An Answer to a Question that Nobody Thinks of, viz. But What If the Queen Should Die?" *The Versatile Defoe: An Anthology of Uncollected Writings by Daniel Defoe*. Totowa, N.J.: Rowman and Littlefield, 1979. Pp. 75-79.

Outlines the problems which led Defoe to write this pamphlet concerning Queen Anne's successor. Sees the tract as unusual in that Defoe employs an inflammatory tone, unlike the ironic indirection which he uses in other pamphlets on the same topic. This work illustrates his talent for close reasoning from "strong and simple basic premises" and it shows his mastery of such rhetorical devices as the repetitive refrain, "And what if the Queen should die?"

928. ———. "A Brief Deduction of the Original, Progress, and Immense Greatness of the British Woollen Manufacture." *The Versatile Defoe: An Anthology of Uncollected Writings by Daniel Defoe*. Totowa, N.J.: Rowman and Littlefield, 1979. Pp. 171-78.

Views this pamphlet as illustrative of Defoe's wide range of knowledge in English history, world geography, manufacturing, and political and economic theory. The tract reveals Defoe's economic view that a favorable balance of trade is the key to national power. The *Brief Deduction* also demonstrates Defoe's mastery of prose, showing how he is able to successfully adapt his style to both his subject matter and his audience.

929. ———. "A Case Study of Defoe's Domestic Conduct Manuals Suggested by *The Family, Sex and Marriage in England, 1500-1800*." *Studies in Eighteenth-Century Culture*. Vol. 10. Ed. Harry C. Payne. Madison: University of Wisconsin Press, 1981. Pp. 409-28.

Uses Lawrence Stone's 1977 book on the family to provide a context for several of Defoe's domestic tracts, especially *The Family Instructor* and *Religious Courtship*. Curtis questions Stone's assumption that the

urban upper-middle class and the squirarchy held common
beliefs on domesticity. Defoe's works, which reflect
decidedly Lockean attitudes, are aimed at the latter
group as well as at the Nonconformist middle class.
He depicts a patriarchal family unit with a strong emphasis on family prayer.

930.   ———. "A Declaration of Truth to Benjamin Hoadley."
        The Versatile Defoe: An Anthology of Uncollected
        Writings by Daniel Defoe. Totowa, N.J.: Rowman and
        Littlefield, 1979. Pp. 57-62.

        Presents the historical context for this pamphlet,
        one of nine in which Defoe impersonated a Quaker speaker.
        Curtis explores Defoe's views of the Quakers, whom he
        both admired and mocked, and concludes that in this
        essay he used them "to personify the principle of peace
        and thus to comment upon partisan violence from a posi-
        tion most dramatically opposed to such violence."

931.   ———. "An Essay Upon Loans." *The Versatile Defoe:*
        An Anthology of Uncollected Writings by Daniel Defoe.
        Totowa, N.J.: Rowman and Littlefield, 1979. Pp.
        228-33.

        Concludes that Defoe is "avant-garde in economics"
        even though he often expresses conservative notions
        about borrowing money. Here he successfully uses bib-
        lical allusion to argue in favor of a national debt.
        He employs a variety of images to present an accurate
        and concise history of public financing.

932.   ———. "The Family Instructor." *The Versatile Defoe:*
        An Anthology of Uncollected Writings by Daniel Defoe.
        Totowa, N.J.: Rowman and Littlefield, 1979. Pp. 419-
        22.

        Comments on a passage from the 1715 and 1718 versions
        of *The Family Instructor* which treats the patriarch's
        handling of a headstrong son and wife. The work is
        valuable as a study of contemporary marriage values in
        the "squirarchy." It shows Defoe's appeal to classes
        other than the merchant class and reflects his ability
        to change his style to fit his audience.

933.   ———. "The Freeholder's Plea against Stock-Jobbing...."
        The Versatile Defoe: An Anthology of Uncollected Writings
        by Daniel Defoe. Totowa, N.J.: Rowman and Littlefield,
        1979. Pp. 243-50.

Discusses three of Defoe's pamphlets: *The Freeholder's Plea* (1701), *The Villainy of Stock-Jobbers* (1701), and *The Anatomy of Exchange Alley* (1719); all three works show the evils of stock speculation and reflect Defoe's concern with the effects of such speculation on the nation as a whole. These essays are not among Defoe's best, but they represent "a goldmine of inspired individual passages" and they offer insight into Defoe's economic principles and techniques of argumentation.

934. ————. "King William's Affection to the Church of England Examined." *The Versatile Defoe: An Anthology of Uncollected Writings by Daniel Defoe*. Totowa, N.J.: Rowman and Littlefield, 1979. Pp. 37-42.

Provides the historical background for an understanding of *King William's Affection*, which is viewed as an ironic companion piece to *The Shortest Way with the Dissenters*, and then analyzes the tract. *King William's Affection* is logically and ironically complex in the way in which Defoe has the argument gradually turn against the speaker. The essay's conclusion is a prime example of Defoe's forceful plain style.

935. ————. "A Letter from a Gentleman at the Court of St. Germains." *The Versatile Defoe: An Anthology of Uncollected Writings by Daniel Defoe*. Totowa, N.J.: Rowman and Littlefield, 1979. Pp. 118-31.

Gives information on the Sacheverell Affair (1710) because it is "only against this complex but exciting historical background [that] ... the rhetorical brilliance of the *Letter* [can] be understood and appreciated." Although the *Letter* purports to be written by a supporter of the Pretender in France, it really demonstrates an acceptance of the principles of the Revolution Settlement and it is designed "to frighten moderates of all factions with the danger of a restoration of Roman Catholicism in England...." The pamphlet illustrates Defoe's moderate and commonsensical political position which he advocates through the voice of a plain-speaking, honest persona (the publisher who introduces the *Letter*) in contrast with the devious voice of a Jacobite gentleman. Defoe is able to brilliantly adapt his style to fit the personalities as well as the politics of these two speakers.

936. ————. "Reasons Why This Nation Ought to Put a Speedy End to This Expensive War." *The Versatile Defoe: An*

Anthology of Uncollected Writings by Daniel Defoe.
Totowa, N.J.: Rowman and Littlefield, 1979. Pp. 89-
98.

Details the intricacies of the peace negotiations that
culminated in the Treaty of Utrecht (1713) in order to
put this highly successful (three editions in eighteen
days) pamphlet (1711) into perspective. In *Reasons Why*,
Defoe assumes the voice of a country gentleman and uses
innuendo to a greater extent than he does in his other
political tracts. Although superficially *Reasons Why*
and *The Review* seem to reflect different political views,
Defoe's principles of foreign policy remain constant;
he has been misunderstood because extremists oversimplified his position. Any apparent wavering in
principle is due to Defoe's use of various rhetorical
strategies to make his point.

937. ————. "Religious Courtship." *The Versatile Defoe:*
An Anthology of Uncollected Writings by Daniel Defoe.
Totowa, N.J.: Rowman and Littlefield, 1979. Pp. 449-
53.

Shows Defoe's advocacy of the newly emerging marriage
code which allowed a child of either sex to exercise a
veto over marital arrangements made by the parents.
The pamphlet's style shows Defoe's ability to alter his
style for a particular audience, in this case the
"squirarchy." Sections of *Religious Courtship*, especially the "necklace scene," anticipate the ideas and
techniques of *Roxana*.

938. ————. "A True Account of the Proceedings at Perth."
The Versatile Defoe: An Anthology of Uncollected
Writings by Daniel Defoe. Totowa, N.J.: Rowman and
Littlefield, 1979. Pp. 320-26.

Emphasizes the force of Defoe's imagination in writing
this 76-page pamphlet on the "petering out of the Jacobite
rebellion of 1715." The work purports to record the
speeches made in a great council of the rebels who were
debating whether to fight or retreat, and Defoe so
accurately handles both the details and the shifting
narrative of each speaker that "A True Account" was considered an eyewitness report even by some of the par-
ticipants. To emphasize the wickedness of disloyalty
and treachery, Defoe bases his fictional meeting of
rebel leaders on the Miltonic Infernal Council. To this
common Augustan device, Defoe adds humor in his portrait

of The Pretender as gloomily inept; such humor is used by Defoe for the "polemical purpose of attracting reasonable Jacobites back to the Hanoverian fold."

939. ————. "Two Andrew Moreton Pamphlets: 1. The Protestant Monastery; 2. Augusta Triumphans." *The Versatile Defoe: An Anthology of Uncollected Writings by Daniel Defoe*. Totowa, N.J.: Rowman and Littlefield, 1979. Pp. 397-401.

Selects for discussion two of the five pamphlets on social reform that Defoe wrote under the pseudonym, "Andrew Moreton." These works tempt the reader to compare them technically with the *Essay upon Projects*, written almost thirty years earlier, but such a comparison is fruitless because Defoe consistently altered his style and narrative method for the audience he was addressing; he always was aware of "the age, temper, and social class" of both his audience and persona. *The Protestant Monastery* (1726), which discusses contempt for old people and treats child-rearing, demonstrates Defoe's skill in developing and manipulating a persona. *Augusta Triumphans* (1728), a lively pamphlet on wife-beating and street crime, shows Defoe's interest in crime.

* Damrosch, Leopold, Jr. "Defoe as Ambiguous Impersonator." (See item 898.)

940. "Daniel Defoe as Journalist." (London) *Times Literary Supplement*, 8 July 1939, p. 412.

Remarks on the A.W. Secord edition of Defoe's *Review* which is worth reprinting because it reveals Defoe to be the first great journalist; this edition is a sound and useful one.

941. Davis, Andrew McFarland. *A Bibliographical Puzzle*. Cambridge: The University Press, 1910. Reprinted from *Publications of The Colonial Society of Massachusetts*, 13 (1910), 2-15.

Determines that *News from the Moon*, one of the pamphlets from the colonial currency arguments of 1720-21, is a slightly altered version of No. 15, Vol. VII, of Defoe's *Review*, dated April 29, 1710. Defoe's original work is reprinted here. Why a Defoe piece on an unrelated topic should have been of use in a colonial currency debate is a mystery.

*   Dobrée, Bonamy. *English Literature in the Early
        Eighteenth Century, 1700-1740.* (See item 160.)

942.   Downie, J.A. "Mr Review and His Scribbling Friends:
        Defoe and the Critics, 1705-1706." *Huntington
        Library Quarterly,* 41 (1978), 345-66.

        Theorizes that Defoe's *Review* reached its highest
        circulation in 1705 and 1706. The large number of
        literary attacks on Defoe and his journal in those years
        attests to its wide-ranging influence which gradually
        dwindled until it terminated in 1713.

*   Dupas, Jean-Claude. "Defoe et le récit de la mort:
        The Apparition of Mrs. Veal." (See item 1263.)

*   Einhoff, Eberhard. *Emanzipatorische Aspekte im Frauen-
        bild von "The Review," "The Spectator," und "The
        Female Spectator."* (See item 1267.)

943.   Escott, T.H.S. *Masters of English Journalism.* London:
        Fisher Unwin, 1911.

        Not seen by the compiler, but listed by Sen, item 328.

944.   Ewald, William Bragg. *The Newsmen of Queen Anne.* Ox-
        ford: Basil Blackwell, 1956.

        Arranges a number of journalistic essays from Queen
        Anne's reign into thematic groups: Eloped, Lost, Run
        Away; Insurance and Lotteries; Education; Aids to
        Beauty; Crime and Criminals; etc. The latter includes
        a statement of plundering shipwrecks from Defoe's *Review
        of the State of the British Nation.* A "Descriptive List
        of Periodicals," which concludes this collection,
        describes both the journals for which Defoe wrote and
        comments he made on other journals.

945.   Ewing, Dessagene C. "The First Printing of Defoe's
        Family Instructor." *Papers of the Bibliographical
        Society of America,* 65 (1971), 269-72.

        Examines Defoe's first full-length didactic work, the
        1715 *Family Instructor.* The work was printed in New-
        castle to conceal Defoe's authorship and is full of
        errors, including a pagination mistake which suggests
        a later insertion by Defoe, probably made to reinforce
        his point about the importance of family worship.

946. Firth, C.H. "Defoe's *True Relation of the Apparition of Mrs. Veal.*" *Review of English Studies*, 7 (1931), 1-6.

Prints a letter of 9 October 1705 which tells essentially the same story as Defoe's *True Relation* and thus provides an important source for the latter.

947. Fletcher, Edward G. "The London and Edinburgh Printings of Defoe's *Review*, Volume VI." *University of Texas Studies in English*, 14 (1934), 50-58.

Arranges in tabular form a comparison of the London and Edinburgh editions of Volume VI of Defoe's *Review*.

948. ————. "Some Notes on Defoe's *Review.*" *Notes and Queries*, 166 (1934), 218-21.

Records a series of miscellaneous notes and questions which arose when the author examined copies of Defoe's *Review* in the Boston Public Library, The Harvard Library, and the Aiken collection in the University of Texas Library.

949. Frost, William. "Religious and Philosophical Themes in Restoration and Eighteenth-Century Literature." *Dryden to Johnson*. Ed. Roger Lonsdale. London: Barrie and Jenkins, 1970. Pp. 399-433.

Regards *The Shortest Way with the Dissenters* as "brilliant," seeing it as "a classic paradigm of all such propositions." Frost identifies the "ingredients" of the paradigm as: Doctored History, Stimulation of Paranoia, Invocation of Group Enthusiasm, Defense of Violence as Preventative Medicine, Loaded Analogy, Frank Appeal to Blood Lust, The Argument that Much Smaller Offences Are Treated More Severely, The Argument that What Separates Us Is So Small that It's No Cruelty to the Opposition to Force Them to Join Us, The Argument that What Separates Us Is So Great that It's Intolerable for Us to Have to Endure Their Dissent, and The Call to Immediate Action.

950. Gardiner, Dorothy. "What Canterbury Knew of Mrs. Veal and Her Friends." *Review of English Studies*, 7 (1931), 188-97.

Identifies several Canterbury residents who knew Mrs. Veal and Mrs. Bargrave, thus providing authenticity and background for Defoe's *Apparition of Mrs. Veal*.

951. Graham, Walter. *The Beginnings of English Literary
      Periodicals: A Study of Periodical Literature, 1665–
      1715.* New York: Oxford University Press, 1926.

      Contains scattered remarks on Defoe as a journalist
      and a short section on the *Review*; the latter concen-
      trates on the history of "Advice from the Scandalous
      Club" which eventually became the *Little Review*.

952. ————. "Defoe's *Review* and Steele's *Tatler*—The Ques-
      tion of Influence." *Journal of English and Germanic
      Philology*, 33 (1934), 250–54.

      Points out the *Review*'s specific influences on the
      Tatler. The "piquant personalities" of the latter
      derive from the Scandal Club of the *Review*; Defoe used
      the court device or vision device to convey his ideas
      as did both Addison and Steele. The *Review* and *Tatler*
      both aimed at reform of the same things; and Defoe's
      development of a more natural dialogue form was imitated
      by Steele.

953. ————. *English Literary Periodicals.* New York: Thomas
      Nelson and Sons, 1930.

      Refers to Defoe throughout in a general way; the only
      specific remarks note that Defoe's *Little Review* is the
      best example of the pure question-answer serial.

*   Gray, Christopher W. "Defoe's Literalizing Imagination."
      (See item 188.)

954. Greenough, Chester N. "Defoe in Boston." *Publications
      of the Colonial Society of Massachusetts* (Transactions,
      1930–1933), 28 (1935), 461–93.

      Presents the first Defoe work printed in America, a
      May 2, 1710, item from the *Review* titled "News From the
      Moon," which was published in Boston on March 13, 1721.

955. ————. "Defoe's Review." (London) *Times Literary
      Supplement*, 15 February 1934, p. 108.

      Wishes to find a copy of Vol. IX, No. 81, of the
      Review. See Harris, item 957.

956. Hanson, Laurence. *Government and the Press, 1695–1763.*
      London: Humphrey Milford, 1936.

      Refers to Defoe throughout, emphasizing his role as a
      governmental voice in the *Review* and his efforts to
      undermine opposition journals.

957. Harris, L.J. "The Missing Number of Defoe's *Review*."
     Library, 28 (1973), 329-32.

   Locates a copy of No. 81, Vol. IX, of Defoe's *Review*
   in the St. David's University College, Lampeter, library.
   This copy is the only one known to exist. It deals with
   trade in the light of the Treaty of Utrecht and is a
   companion piece to numbers 80 and 82. See Greenough,
   item 955.

958. Healey, George Harris. "Defoe's Handwriting." (Lon-
     don) *Times Literary Supplement*, 19 December 1952,
     p. 837.

   Says that the manuscript for the December 31, 1709,
   Review is not in Defoe's easily recognized handwriting.

959. Higenbottam, Frank. "The Apparition of Mrs. Veal to
     Mrs. Bargrave at Canterbury, 8th of September, 1705:
     Two New Contemporary Manuscript Accounts." *Archaeo-
     logica Cantiana*, 73 (1959), 154-66.

   Prints two letters--from "E.B." (September 13, 1705)
   and from Stephen Gray (November 3, 1705)--which relate
   the famous Veal/Bargrave incident and which predate
   Defoe's account. A bibliography of versions of the
   stories and articles on Defoe's essay is appended.

960. Hindle, C.J. "Defoe's Review." (London) *Times Literary
     Supplement*, 26 April 1934, p. 303.

   Locates two items needed by Newton (see item 996.)

961. Hobman, D.L. "Defoe the Journalist." *Fortnightly*, No.
     1029 (September 1952), 203-07.

   Sees Defoe as "a humanitarian in the best tradition
   of liberal journalism." He advocated reforms far in
   advance of his time, denouncing the slave trade, opposing
   persecutions for witchcraft, and championing women's
   rights.

962. Horsley, L.S. "Contemporary Reactions to Defoe's *Short-
     est Way with the Dissenters*." *Studies In English
     Literature*, 16 (1976), 407-20.

   Believes that the *Shortest Way* failed because of its
   "successful" (i.e., consistent) use of irony throughout.
   Defoe confused his readers because he omitted the
   various obvious clues that lesser satirists used to
   signal that irony was being used. The result was that
   Defoe created a vivid, memorable, and disturbing specimen

of High Church extremism which accurately reflected
much of the extremist position and emphasized its dan-
gerous potential.

*   Ivanyi, B.G. "Defoe's Prelude to the *Family Instructor*."
        (See item 1183.)

*   Izzo, Carlo. "Su Daniel De Foe." (See item 1303.)

963.   Jackson, Alfred. "Defoe, Ward, Brown, and Tutchin,
        1700-1703." *Notes and Queries*, 162 (1932), 418-23.

        Reprints from various London newspapers advertisements
        for several responses to Defoe's *Shortest Way with the
        Dissenters*. Included here are government announcements
        describing Defoe and offering a reward for his capture.
        Defoe's arrest and punishment in the pillory are also
        announced.

*   Jacob, Ernst Gerhard. *Daniel Defoe, Essay on Projects
        (1697): eine wirtschafts- und sozialgeschichtliche
        Studie*. (See item 1306.)

*   ————. "Die medizingeschichtliche Bedeutung des
        Robinson dichters Daniel Defoe." (See item 1316.)

964.   James, E. Anthony. "Defoe's Autobiographical Apologia:
        Rhetorical Slanting in *An Appeal to Honour and Jus-
        tice*." *Costerus*, 4 (1972), 69-86.

        Dissects Defoe's prose style in *An Appeal to Honour
        and Justice* to demonstrate how every aspect of the work
        is calculated to make the author appear "innocent and
        upstanding, sympathetic and pathetic, talented and
        available [for political service]." Defoe manages to
        vindicate his conduct to his enemies and ingratiate
        himself with the politically powerful at the same time.

965.   Kennedy, Joyce D. "Defoe's *An Essay upon Projects*: The
        Order of Issues." *Studies in Bibliography*, 23 (1970),
        170-75.

        Establishes the sequence and dating of seven pre-
        viously undated issues of Defoe's *Essay on Projects* by
        investigating the history of their printer, Thomas
        Cockerill.

966.   L'Ami, C.E. "The Philosophy of Journalism." *Dalhousie
        Review*, 29 (1949), 314-26.

Regards Defoe as the earliest exponent of the journalistic philosophy that the electors are superior to the elected, a philosophy which leads to the press setting itself up as an entirely free agent which cultivates contempt toward government.

967. Landon, Richard. "Introduction" to *A System of Magick* by Daniel Defoe. East Ardsley, Wakefield: EP Publishing; distributed through Totowa, N.J.: Rowman and Littlefield, 1973. Pp. v-x.

Provides textual information: only three editions preceded this one; suggests sources: Sir Walter Raleigh's *History of the World*, Rochard Brovet's *Pandemonium*, and the *Bible*; and discusses the text: *A System of Magick* "is the story ... of how the Devil seduced mankind into willing co-operation with him."

968. Law, Marie Hamilton. "The Indebtedness of *Oliver Twist* to Defoe's *History of the Devil*." *Publications of the Modern Language Association*, 40 (1925), 892-97.

Discovers significant parallels between Dickens' exploration of the effect of sin on the individual in *Oliver Twist* and Defoe's philosophy of sin expounded in the *History of the Devil*. It is known that Dickens read the Defoe book while he was writing *Oliver Twist* and it may have influenced his portrait of Fagin as satanic.

969. Leranbaum, Miriam. "'An Irony Not Unusual': Defoe's *Shortest Way with the Dissenters*." *Huntington Library Quarterly*, 37 (1974), 227-50.

Calls Defoe's *Shortest Way* a "banter" or a hoax and not a satire. Leranbaum lists the conventions of satire and shows that Defoe either does not use them or uses them in different ways than does a satirist. The *Shortest Way* is not a botched satire but is an excellent imitation of militant High-Church propaganda.

970. Lindsay, W.B. "Defoe's *Review*--Forerunner of Modern Journalism." *English Journal*, 16 (1927), 359-63.

Believes Defoe to be the father of modern journalism because he originated the different departments common to the modern newspaper: his *Review* contained the lead article; the editorial; the literary commentary; and the social, or society, section.

*   Macaree, David. "The Flyting of Daniel Defoe and Lord
       Belhaven." (See item 1148.)

971.   McEwen, Gilbert D. "The Influence of Locke's *Two
       Treatises of Government* upon Two Augustan Pamphleteers."
       *Translations of the Samuel Johnson Society of the
       Northwest*. Vol. 6. Ed. Thomas R. Cleary. Calgary:
       Samuel Johnson Society of the Northwest, 1974. Pp.
       27-33.

       Demonstrates Locke's influence on both Humphrey Mack-
       worth's *A Vindication of the Rights of the Commons of
       England* and Defoe's reply to it, *The Original Power of
       the Collective Body of the People of England Examined
       and Asserted.* Even though the two authors were on
       different sides of the 1701 controversy over the arrest
       of a group of Kentish freeholders who petitioned Commons
       to support King William's war efforts, both of them
       argued by invoking Locke's appeals to natural law, the
       preservation of the constitution, the maintaining of
       separation of powers, the observance of the rights of
       the individual, and the use of reason to settle political
       issues.

972.   McLeod, W.R., and V.B. McLeod, compilers. *Anglo-Scottish
       Tracts, 1701-1714: A Descriptive Checklist.* Lawrence:
       University of Kansas Library, 1979.

       The compiler did not review this work personally.

973.   ————. *A Graphical Directory of English Newspapers and
       Periodicals: 1702-1714.* Morgantown, West Virginia:
       West Virginia School of Journalism, 1982.

       Lists all known copies of newspapers for the period
       covered, including Defoe's journalistic endeavors.

       Review: The Scriblerian, 15 (1982), 62.

974.   Marr, George S. *The Periodical Essayists of the Eigh-
       teenth Century.* New York: D. Appleton, 1924.

       Believes that Defoe's *Advice from the Scandal Club*
       ushers in the essay periodical and, specifically, an-
       ticipates the *Tatler*. The idea of the "club" adds
       verisimilitude to the essay form.

975.   Matthews, Albert. "Defoe's *Weekly Review*." *Notes and
       Queries*, Eleventh Series, 9 (1914), 95-96.

       Contains information on little-known, but bibliographically interesting, partial sets of the *Review* in response to Curry, item 926.

* Meier, T.K. "Defoe and Rivington." (See item 1187.)

976. Miller, E. Arnold. "Some Arguments Used by English Pamphleteers, 1697-1700, Concerning a Standing Army." *Journal of Modern History*, 18 (1946), 306-13.

Sums up the arguments for and against King William's plan to maintain a standing army after the Peace of Ryswick in 1697. Defoe wrote three pamphlets in support of the king, arguing that the army would not be harmful to the constitution because parliament would control it, that a militia lacks the intensive training of a professional army, and that a militia would cause delays in defending England should it be attacked.

* Minet, William. "Daniel Defoe and Kent: A Chapter in Capel-le-Ferne History." (See item 1051.)

977. Moore, John Robert. "Daniel Defoe, Ambidextrous Mercury." *Periodical Post Boy*, 11 (1952), 1-2.

Points out that Indiana University has purchased *Mercurius Politicus* (May 1716-December 1719) and *Mercurius Britannicus* (1716). Although the *Politicus* is a Tory journal and the *Britannicus* is a Whig publication, Defoe wrote them both. The ostensible Toryism of the former actually is designed to discourage any further Jacobite attempts at rebellion.

* ————. *Daniel Defoe: Citizen of the Modern World.* (See item 255.)

978. ————. "Daniel Defoe: King William's Pamphleteer and Intelligence Agent." *Huntington Library Quarterly*, 34 (1971), 251-60.

Traces Defoe's career as an intelligence agent and propagandist for King William and discusses Defoe's first known publication as an accepted spokesman for the government. A copy of this tract, *Reflections upon the Late Horrid Conspiracy Contrived by the French Court, to Murther His Majesty in Flanders ...* (1692), is held by the Huntington Library.

* ————. "Daniel Defoe: Precursor of Samuel Richardson." (See item 256.)

*   ————. "Defoe Acquisitions at the Huntington Library."
         (See item 258.)

979.   ————. "Defoe and the Eighteenth-Century Pamphlets on
         London." *Philological Quarterly*, 20 (1941), 38–45.

         Replies to an article by Paul B. Anderson on Thomas
         Gordon's and John Motteley's respective shares in *A Trip
         through London* (1728). Moore points out that no less
         than five pages of this pamphlet were plagiarized from
         Defoe's *The Great Law of Subordination*. See Anderson's
         reply, item 905.

980.   ————. "Defoe's 'Essay upon Projects': An Unrecorded
         Issue." *Notes and Queries*, 200 (1955), 109–10.

         Locates in the Special Collections of the Indiana
         University Libraries an unrecorded issue of the first
         edition of the *Essay upon Projects* and explains the ap-
         pearance of this issue. Moore also presents details
         concerning the printers of the first four issues of this
         edition.

981.   ————. "Defoe's Hand in *A Journal of the Earl of Marr's
         Proceedings* (1716)." *Huntington Library Quarterly*,
         17 (1954), 209–28.

         Presents the history of *A Journal of the Earl of Marr's
         Proceedings*. The original work was put together by Marr
         and his followers in order to justify Marr's conduct in
         the rebellion of 1715 and the supplanting of Bolingbroke
         in James's favor. Defoe got hold of the work, added his
         own introduction, and then rewrote the *Journal* to divert
         the attack from Bolingbroke to the entire Jacobite
         leadership. Defoe's forged versions of the document
         completely supplanted the original and eventually helped
         lead to Marr's downfall.

982.   ————. "Defoe's Lampoon: A Speech of a Stone Chimney-
         Piece." *Boston Public Library Quarterly*, 9 (1957),
         137–42.

         Reconstructs from fragments in *The Review* for 1711 and
         The Present State of the Parties in Great Britain (1712)
         two versions of a piece by Defoe that is no longer
         extant.

983.   ————. "Defoe's 'Lost' *Letter to a Dissenter*." *Hunt-
         ington Library Quarterly*, 14 (1951), 299–306.

Identifies a 1688 tract, *A Letter to a Dissenter*, as Defoe's first known publication and shows how it was confused with the Marquis of Halifax's tract of the same title. Moore presents a historical context for Defoe's argument that James II's dispensing power is a covert means to subvert the constitution.

Review: George Harris Healey, *Philological Quarterly*, 31 (1952), 263-64.

984.   ————. "Defoe's Persona as Author: *The Quaker's Sermon.*" *Studies in English Literature*, 11 (1971), 507-16.

Discovers at the Huntington Library a previously unknown Defoe tract, *The Quaker's Sermon*, which is significant as another of Defoe's attacks on Sacheverell, defenses of Marlborough, and uses of a persona. Defoe wrote as a Quaker in six other tracts but nowhere more effectively or earnestly than here.

985.   ————. "Defoe's Political Propaganda in *The Dumb Philosopher.*" *Huntington Library Quarterly*, 4 (1940), 107-17.

Gives a new interpretation for *The Dumb Philosopher*, a Defoe tract which purports to tell the story of a mute servingman who left at his death seventeen prophecies. There has been great disagreement over the meaning of these prophecies, but Moore contends that reading them in a contemporary context reveals them as thinly disguised pieces of political propaganda on a veriety of subjects ranging from Alberoni's candidacy for the papacy to the South Sea Bubble.

986.   ————. "Defoe's 'Queries upon the Foregoing Act': A Defense of Civil Liberty in South Carolina." *Essays in History and Literature Presented by Fellows of The Newberry Library to Stanley Pargellis*. Ed. Heinz Bluhm. Chicago: The Newberry Library, 1965. Pp. 133-55.

Offers a thoroughly detailed context for Defoe's "Queries upon the Foregoing Act" (1706) by tracing the history of the Dissenters in South Carolina, a state in which Defoe was interested because he admired its fundamental constitution with its support for political freedom and religious toleration. Consequently, when the South Carolina Act of Exclusion was passed in 1704, disenfranchising the state's Dissenters, Defoe was dis-

tressed, although he remained publicly silent on the
subject until December 25, 1705, when his *Review* article
appeared opposing the Act. Shortly thereafter, Defoe's
tract on the topic, *Party-Tyranny*, was published. Because
the tract was thirty pages long, Defoe felt that for the
hasty reader he needed a more succinct way to present
his views; therefore, he had the Act reprinted and supplemented with a two-page appendix presenting his negative position on the Act in twenty questions. (The
twenty "Queries" are reprinted here, accompanied by a
brief argument assigning them to the Defoe canon.)

987.   ————. "Defoe's *Some Seasonable Queries*: A Chapter
        Concerning the Humanities." *Newberry Library Bulletin*,
        6 (1965), 179–86.

Discovers in the Newberry Library a previously unknown
Defoe tract of four pages entitled *Some Seasonable
Queries, On the Third Head, viz. A General Naturalization.* The pamphlet probably dates sometime in early
1697 and is designed to persuade Parliament to support
King William's naturalization policy for Protestant
foreigners.

988.   ————. "Introduction" to *An Essay on the Regulation
        of the Press* by Daniel Defoe. Luttrell Reprints,
        No. 7. Oxford: Blackwell, 1948. Pp. v–xvi.

Presents the historical context for this rare tract
in which Defoe proposes that the law should clearly
define the parameters of publication so that authors
would not be at the mercy of their judges' whims.
Defoe also suggests that an author should be allowed
to publish anything as long as he is willing to abide
by the legal consequences of his actions.

989.   ————. "Lydia Languish's Library." *Notes and Queries*,
        202 (1957), 76.

Finds moral parallels in Defoe's *Religious Courtship*
and *The Family Instructor* with the episode of Lydia
Languish's library in Sheridan's *The Rivals*.

990.   ————. "A Rare Tract by Daniel Defoe." *Indiana Quar-
        terly for Bookmen*, 1 (1945), 9–17.

Summarizes Defoe's tract, *The Fears of the Pretender
Turn'd into the Fears of Debauchery* (1715), in which
Defoe attacks Sir Richard Steele and licentiousness on
the stage. Moore praises Defoe for being way ahead of

his time as a political analyst and prophet, an economist, a sociologist, a journalist, and a theorist on
education.

991. ————. "A Rejoinder." *Philological Quarterly*, 21
      (1942), 424.

      Responds to Paul B. Anderson's defense of his scholar-
      ship (see item 905) which Moore had attacked in an earlier
      article (see item 979).

992. Morgan, William T. "Defoe's *Review* as a Historical
      Source."

      Provides background on Defoe's *Review* as part of a
      review article on Secord's edition (see item 70).
      Morgan points out that the *Review*'s 5,600 pages provide
      invaluable reference material for the historian because
      Defoe touched on so many facets of early eighteenth-
      century life, particularly on the economic and political.

993. ["Mrs. Veal."] *Notes and Queries*, 160 (1931), 38.

      Refers to Firth's discovery (see item 946) of a
      letter which confirms that Mrs. Veal and her friends
      really existed.

994. Mullett, Charles F. "The English Plague Scare of 1720-
      23." *Osiris*, 2(1936), 484-516.

      Mentions briefly Defoe's *Due Preparations for the
      Plague* and provides detailed background for it through
      discussions of proposed preventions and remedies current
      in the early eighteenth century.

995. Murray, John J. "Defoe: News Commentator and Analyst
      of Northern European Affairs." *Indiana Quarterly for
      Bookmen*, 3 (1947), 39-50.

      Compares Defoe with modern foreign correspondents
      and concludes that in spite of lacking a research staff
      and rewrite men, he is at least their equal. Even
      though he often missed the significance of events, he
      occasionally showed great insight, as he did in fore-
      seeing the obstacles confronting any invader of Russia.
      His writings throw considerable light upon England's
      diplomatic relations with Sweden, Russia, Poland, and
      Denmark during the Great Northern War (1700-1721).

996. Newton, Theodore F.M. "Defoe's *Review*." (London)
      Times Literary Supplement, 19 April 1934, p. 282.

      Asks for information on the existence of several rare
      periodicals needed as background for a study of Defoe's
      Review. Also see Hindle, item 960.

997. ————. "William Pettis and Queen Anne Journalism."
      Modern Philology, 33 (1935), 169-86; 279-302.

      Surveys two periodicals, *Heraclitus ridens* (1703-04)
      and the *Whipping Post* (1705), both of which frequently
      and violently attacked Defoe for everything from standing
      in the pillory to publishing his *Dyet of Poland*.

998. Nicholson, Marjorie H. "Introduction." *The Best of
      Defoe's "Review": An Anthology*. Ed. William L. Payne.
      New York: Columbia University Press, 1951. Pp. ix-
      xxi.

      Contends that Defoe's *Review* gives us a more realis-
      tic, well-rounded, and "modern" view of the early
      eighteenth century than do the *Tatler* and *Spectator*.
      Defoe was a more serious moralist than Addison and
      Steele, and his essays are more interesting than theirs--
      even if less "charming"--because they deal with topics
      important to modern readers.

999. Novak, Maximillian E. "Defoe's *Shortest Way with the
      Dissenters*: Hoax, Parody, Paradox, Fiction, Irony, and
      Satire." *Modern Language Quarterly*, 27 (1966), 402-17.

      Responds to those like Ian Watt (see item 688) who
      contend that Defoe did not practice irony; Novak be-
      lieves that the *Shortest Way with the Dissenters* is a
      clever blend of "fiction, satire, parody, hoax, and
      paradox which are the ingredients of the best ironic
      works of the Augustan Age." In fact, Defoe was "addic-
      ted" to paradox and irony, frequently employed them in
      his tracts, and was arrested in 1703 and 1713 because
      his irony went unperceived by the majority of his readers.

*   ————. "Defoe's Use of Irony." (See item 285.)

1000. ————. "Introduction" to *Conjugal Lewdness; or, Matri-
      monial Whoredom. A Treatise concerning the Use and
      Abuse of the Marriage Bed* (1727) by Daniel Defoe.
      Gainesville, Fla.: Scholars' Facsimiles and Reprints,
      1967. Pp. v-xiv.

Regards this treatise as an extremely important item
in the Defoe canon. First, it is a straightforward
treatment of sex, love, and marriage, the central theme
of *Moll Flanders*, *Colonel Jack*, and *Roxana*. It shows
how Defoe turned fiction "away from romance to the
realities of sex and marriage in common life." Second,
the book vividly delineates a side of eighteenth-century
life about which almost nothing is known. Finally, the
work is stylistically "brilliant," showing a variety
unusual in Defoe and demonstrating that he had not lost
his creative powers even near the end of his career and
life.

* ————, *"Two Arguments Never Brought Yet*: An Addition
to the Defoe Canon." (See item 1193.)

* ————. "The Wild Man Comes to Tea." (See item 632.)

1001. Oldham, Ellen M. "Problems of a Defoe Cataloger."
Boston Public Library Quarterly, 7 (1955), 192–206.

Discusses various editions, issues, and variants of
three items in the Trent collection of Defoe's works
held by the Boston Public Library: *Essay upon Projects*,
The Experiment, and *A New Test of the Church of
England's Loyalty*.

1002. Parsons, Coleman O. "Ghost-Stories Before Defoe."
Notes and Queries, 201 (1956), 293–98.

Traces the history of ghost-stories up to Defoe's
Mrs. Veal and briefly discusses the latter. Defoe's
work embodies the eight devices developed by his
predecessors but is more believable because of its
reportorial style and wealth of circumstantial detail.
The story is an important one in the history and development of the modern short story.

1003. Patterson, Paul B. "Harley, Defoe, Trapp and the
Faults on Both Sides Controversy." *Albion*, 11
(1979), 128–42.

Argues that Harley, Defoe, and Trapp perpetrated an
elaborate hoax in the *Faults on Both Sides* controversy;
this argument is based on the assumptions that Harley
wrote *Faults* and that Trapp's *Most Faults on One Side*
was a party pamphlet. (Both these assumptions are
seriously challenged in an unsigned review in *The
Scriblerian*, 13 [1980], 27.)

1004.   Payne, William L. *Index to Defoe's Review.* New York:
        Columbia University Press, 1948.

        Provides a subject index for the *Review* along with an
        appendix of "Authors and Translators, Books, Pamphlets,
        and Plays Named in Advertisements in the *Review*" and a
        list of "Booksellers Named in Advertisements in the
        Review."

        Reviews: Donald F. Bond, *Modern Philology*, 48 (1950),
        133-34; Louis Landa, *Philological Quarterly*, 28
        (1949), 387-88; J.R. Moore, *South Atlantic Quarterly*,
        48 (1949), 320-21; *Philological Quarterly*, 29 (1950),
        271; (London) *Times Literary Supplement*, 9 April
        1949, p. 239; *Year's Work in English Studies* (1948),
        209.

1005.   ————. *Mr. Review: Daniel Defoe as Author of the Re-
        view.* New York: King's Crown Press, 1947.

        Develops a portrait of Defoe drawn from his opinions
        in the *Review* on authorship, journalism, economics,
        and social relationships. Defoe's views of writing
        consistently emphasize clarity, the means to which is
        the plain style; plainness of expression is not just
        an artistic aim with Defoe, however--it is a part of
        his very nature and he functions as the "plain dealer"
        with his opinions of trade, church controversy, and
        politics. Defoe's concept of journalism is dominated
        by his sense of responsibility to his material, his
        readers, and posterity; his strong ethical sense is
        behind his belief that the press should be regulated
        to promote peace in the nation and prevent the abuse
        of the printed word. As an economist, Defoe anticipates
        the *laissez faire* philosophy with his belief in high
        wages, no workhouses, competition, and expansion of
        trade; on the other hand, he was a mercantilist in his
        eagerness for a favorable balance of trade, his em-
        phasis on the value of bullion and coin, his approval
        of colonial charters and trade, and his hatred of
        speculation. Defoe was an inveterate "giver-of-advice,"
        and the last chapter of this study surveys his views
        concerning women, love, marriage, the roles of wife
        and husband, and the relationship of parents and
        children. A valuable index enables one to look up
        Defoe's opinions on a variety of topics from the colonies
        to the woolen industry.

        Reviews: John R. Moore, *South Atlantic Quarterly*, 46
        (1947), 584-85; Arthur W. Secord, *Modern Language*

Notes, 63 (1948), 564-65; Oscar Sherwin, *Modern Language Quarterly*, 9 (1948), 363, 365; (London) *Times Literary Supplement*, 30 August 1947, p. 443.

1006. Perry, John J. "The Date of Publication of Defoe's *Atalantis Major*." *Notes and Queries*, 25 (1978), 38-39.

Corrects Moore's dating of *Atalantis Major* from "before 28 December 1710" to "after the eleventh of January 1710/11," citing a letter to Harley as evidence.

1007. ————. "Introduction" to *Atalantis Major* by Daniel Defoe. Augustan Reprint Society, No. 198. Los Angeles: Clark Memorial Library and University of California Press, 1979. Pp. iii-xii.

Provides political and biographical background for the pamphlet. The reliability of this material is seriously questioned in an unsigned review in *The Scriblerian*, 12 (1979), 50.

1008. Pienaar, W.J.B. *English Influences in Dutch Literature and Justus Van Effen as Intermediary*. Cambridge: The University Press, 1929.

Shows the influence of Defoe's *Review* on the *Tatler* which, in turn, influenced Van Effen's paper, *Le Misanthrope*, "the first moralist periodical on the continent." Van Effen's preface to his translation of *Robinson Crusoe* (1720-21) served to explain and popularize that novel in Europe.

1009. Poston, Lawrence, III. "Defoe and the Peace Campaign, 1719-1713: A Reconsideration." *Huntington Library Quarterly*, 27 (1963), 1-20.

Reviews Defoe's foreign policy writings from 1710 to 1713 in order to refute some of the negative generalizations made about his work for Harley. Although often inconsistent on the surface, Defoe actually was true to his own political principles in his writings that pointed toward the Treaty of Utrecht. His main concern is for a balance of power because it was a prerequisite for orderly and uninterrupted trade. His ideas on this subject can be traced back to 1706, before he began working for the Harley administration.

1010. Powell, Lawrence F. "Defoe and Drelincourt." (London) *Times Literary Supplement*, 7 February, 1929, p. 98.

Corrects several bibliographical errors concerning
the relationship of Defoe's "A True Relation of the
Apparition of one Mrs. Veal" to Drelincourt's "The
Christian Defence against the Fears of Death."

1011. Price, E.J. "The Projects of Daniel Defoe." *Congrega-
       tional Quarterly*, 29 (1951), 145-52.

       Outlines Defoe's *Essay upon Projects*, presenting his
       ideas on taxation, banking, highways, insurance, edu-
       cation, etc. The *Essay* is an "amazing combination of
       imagination, ingenuity, audacity, and sound common-
       sense."

1012. Reeve, Juliet. "Daniel Defoe and the Quakers."
       Friends Intelligencer, 103 (1946), 282-84.

       Notes that although Defoe was usually friendly to
       Quakers, his *A Friendly Epistolary.Way of Reproof from
       one of the People Called Quakers* (1715) was considered
       very negative by the Quaker community in England.

1013. Rothman, Irving N. "Defoe's Census of *The Family In-
       structor* and *The Political History of the Devil*."
       Notes and Queries, n.s. 23 (1976), 486-92.

       Prints a census of library holdings of Defoe's *Family
       Instructor* and *The Political History of the Devil* in 71
       libraries and provides some bibliographic data on them.

1014. ———. "Defoe's *The Family Instructor*: A Response to
       the Schism Act." *Papers of the Bibliographical
       Society of America*, 74 (1980), 201-20.

       Provides a comprehensive bibliographical description
       of the first edition of Defoe's *Family Instructor* and
       assesses the purpose and success of the work. It forms
       part of the opposition to the Schism Act by providing
       a family instructor that teaches the principles of
       catechism without being sworn to the Anglican Church.

*   Schonhorn, Manuel. "Defoe: The Literature of Politics
       and the Politics of Some Fictions." (See item 320.)

1015. ———. "Introduction" to *Daniel Defoe and Others:
       Accounts of the Apparition of Mrs. Veal*. Augustan
       Reprint Society, No. 115. Los Angeles: Clark Memorial
       Library and University of California Press, 1965.
       Pp. i-iv.

Concludes after surveying the various accounts contained in this volume that Defoe's piece is by far the best: it "has all the strengths and none of the weaknesses of the correspondents." Particularly effective are Defoe's use of certain details to add credibility and his omission of others which might cast suspicion on the validity of Mrs. Bargrave's tale.

1016. Schwoerer, Lois G. "Chronology and Authorship of the Standing Army Tracts, 1697-1699." *Notes and Queries*, n.s. 13 (1966), 382-90.

Attempts to establish authorship for several pamphlets on the standing army controversy, including three by Defoe. These are: *Some Reflections on a pamphlet lately published*; *An Argument showing that a standing army, with consent of Parliament is not inconsistent with a free government*; and *A Brief Reply to the History of Standing Armies in England*.

1017. Scouten, Arthur H. "At that Moment of Time: Defoe and the Early Accounts of the Apparition of Mistress Veal." *Ball State Teachers College Forum*, 2, No. 2 (1961-62), 44-51.

Identifies six versions of the Veal story that preceded Defoe's account and shows how Defoe drew upon all six in his own essay.

1018. ———. "An Early Printed Report on 'The Apparition of Mrs. Veal.'" *Review of English Studies*, n.s. 6 (1955), 259-63.

Uncovers in the New York Public Library a copy of the *Loyal Post* for Monday, December 24, 1705, in which the Veal-Bargrave incident is reported. This discovery supports the view that Defoe did not invent the story but simply retold a tale that was attracting a lot of contemporary attention.

1019. ———. "*The Loyal Post*: A Rare Queen Anne Newspaper and Daniel Defoe." *Bulletin of the New York Public Library*, 59 (1955), 195-97.

Discovers an account of the Veal story published six months prior to Defoe's version and which could be a source for the latter.

1020. Secord, Arthur W. "Defoe's 'Review.'" (London) *Times Literary Supplement*, 20 July 1938, p. 508.

Responds to Bergholz, item 909, by providing information to show that No. 81 of Defoe's *Review* actually did
exist, although there is no copy extant.

1021. ———. "A September Day in Canterbury: the Veal-
Bargrave Story." *Journal of English and Germanic
Philology*, 54 (1955), 639-50.

Believes that there is confusion in discussing "The
Apparition of Mrs. Veal" because commentators like
Baine (item 907) do not distinguish between Mrs. Bargrave's story and Defoe's retelling of it. The story
was a hoax that possibly came about from some difficulties Mrs. Bargrave had with her husband, and Defoe
simply dressed up the story, trying to exploit its
popularity, and attempted to convince his readers of
its truth as he did with almost everything he wrote.

*   Senba, Yutaka. "Defoe no yūreijitsuwa to sono model"
[Defoe's Ghost Story and Its Model]. (See item 1394.)

1022. Sherwin, Oscar. "Defoe Reviews World War II." *Journal
of the History of Ideas*, 5 (1944), 359-68.

Quotes Defoe's *Review* on the War of the Spanish Succession and finds there universal truths applicable to
World War II: the evil of rumor in wartime, the necessity of patience and realistic goals if victory is to
be achieved, and the necessity for a balance of power
in order to prevent the ascending of tyrannical super-
powers.

1023. Sill, Geoffrey M. "Introduction" to *Street-Robberies
Consider'd: The Reason of Their Being So Frequent*
by Daniel Defoe. Stockton, N.J.: Carolingian Press,
1973. Pp. i-viii.

Sees *Street Robberies Consider'd* as "a good condensa-
tion of the major themes and techniques used by Defoe
in his longer works." Its literary value is in its
use of "an assimilating consciousness" to integrate the
book's various elements. Defoe does not view criminals
as being "naturally" wicked; rather they are products
of a socioeconomic system, and their criminal acts are
learned skills used by those who have no talents or
goods to market.

1024. ———. "Rogues, Strumpets, and Vagabonds: Defoe on
Crime in the City." *Eighteenth-Century Life*, 2
(1976), 74-78.

Uses *Street-Robberies Consider'd: The Reason of their being so Frequent* to identify Defoe's attitudes toward crime. Defoe saw London as both a blessing in providing economic opportunities and a curse in setting large numbers of people free from social controls and into lives of crime. He believed that antisocial behavior followed a pattern: it begins with the necessity of survival, grows with the accumulation of wealth, and culminates in a freedom and selfhood in which the individual is alienated from society.

1025. Skarda, Patricia L., and Nora Crow Jaffe, eds. *The Evil Image: Two Centuries of Gothic Short Fiction and Poetry.* New York: New American Library, 1981.

Includes Defoe's "Apparition of Mrs. Veal" and remarks that it is part of the occult background used later by the Gothic novelists for terrifying psychological effects.

1026. Stevens, David H. *Party Politics ánd English Journalism, 1702-1742.* Menasha, Wisconsin: George Banta, 1916.

Details Defoe's journalistic efforts on behalf of both Queen Anne and George I. Defoe entered the field of political journalism with the *Review* when Godolphin had Harley enlist his services in 1702. Although Defoe was never as publicly powerful as Addison or Swift, he stood above them in the amount of political work he did and in the secret political influence he exerted.

*   Sutherland, James R. *Daniel Defoe: A Critical Study.*
         (See item 349.)

*   ————. *Defoe.* (See item 350.)

1027. Titlebaum, Richard. "Some Notes Toward a Definition of Defoe's Demonology." *Unisa English Studies*, 14 (1976), 1-7.

Concludes that Defoe's works on demonology—*A System of Magick, The Political History of the Devil,* and *The History and Reality of Apparitions*—represent "the consummation of Defoe's thinking on religion." His novels are illuminated by a knowledge of his "theology of the Devil": his belief in a spiritual universe divided between God and Satan; his belief in the influence on man of magicians, witches, and incubi; and his conviction that Satan controls the events of history in order to damn mankind.

1028.   van Maanen, W. "Defoe and Swift." *English Studies*,
        3 (1921), 65-69.

        Speculates that a reference to "pillory" in Swift's
        Tale of a Tub may have been an oblique reference to
        Defoe, one which precipitated several negative remarks
        on Swift in Defoe's *Consolidator*.

*   Voisine, Jacques. "Review of *La pensée réligeuse et
        morale de George Eliot*." (See item 1431.)

1029.   Walker, Hugh. *The English Essay and Essayists*. Lon-
        don: Dent and New York: Dutton, 1915.

        Rates Defoe as more the disciple than the master of
        Steele in the essay form because "Defoe was too strenu-
        ous a man of affairs to have the temperament of the
        essayist" and he lacked the charm and lightness of touch
        that characterized Steele. Yet, some of the *Review*
        essays remain of interest as literary pieces and the
        Applebee's Journal work, *The Instability of Human
        Greatness*, is Defoe's masterpiece in the essay form.

*   Warner, G.F. "An Unpublished Political Paper by Daniel
        Defoe." (See item 1207.)

1030.   Wasserman, George R. "John Norris and the Veal-
        Bargrave Story." *Modern Language Notes*, 75 (1960),
        648-51.

        Examines the similarities between Defoe's *A True
        Relation of the Apparition of Mrs. Veal* and John
        Norris's poem, "Friendship in Perfection" (1687),
        noting that Mrs. Veal's remarks on conversation are
        analogous to Norris's remarks on policy.

1031.   Watson, Francis. "Daniel Defoe: The Father of Modern
        Journalism." *Bookman* (London), 80 (1931), 16-18.

        Offers several reasons for Defoe's journalistic
        genius: (1) a simple but vivid prose style; (2) an
        ability to unerringly select appropriate details;
        (3) a mastery of a wide variety of subjects; (4) a
        profound knowledge of his public; and (5) a talent
        for adapting his style to his audience and the journal
        for which he was writing.

1032.   Williams, Otho Clinton. "Introduction" to *A Vindica-
        tion of the Press* by Daniel Defoe. Augustan Reprint
        Society, No. 29. Los Angeles: Clark Memorial Library
        and University of California Press, 1951. Pp. i-v.

Assigns the tract to Defoe on the basis of internal evidence and the authority of W.P. Trent. Williams also speculates about the motives behind the work and comments on Defoe's conventional remarks about writers and writing.

1033. Wright, Herbert G. "Defoe's Writings on Sweden." *Review of English Studies*, 16 (1940), 25-32.

Reviews several Defoe pamphlets which treat the Swedish king Charles XII. Defoe reveals his Protean nature in these tracts because early (in *The History of the Wars*, 1715) he eulogizes the king but later (*What if the Swedes Should Come?*, 1717) he discredits Charles and denounces the Jacobites, some of whom apparently supported the idea of a Swedish invasion of England.

* Zimmerman, Everett. *Defoe and the Novel*. (See item 472.)

C. Histories, Memoirs, and Journals,
Both Real and Fictional

* Adams, Percy G. *Travelers and Travel Liars, 1660-1800*. (See item 1070.)

* Alkon, Paul K. *Defoe and Fictional Time*. (See item 384.)

1034. Avery, Emmett L. "The Great Storm of 1703." *Research Studies*, 29 (1961), 38-49.

Presents details of the terrible storm of 1703, discusses its influences on "the cleric and the moralist," and analyzes Defoe's work (*The Storm*, 1704) on the subject. Defoe's use of realistic detail in *The Storm* is that work's great strength and is a precursor of the inventive mingling of reality and imagination that is shown later in *Robinson Crusoe* and *A Journal of the Plague Year*.

1035. Backscheider, Paula R. "Introduction" to *A Short Narrative of the Life and Actions of his Grace John, D. of Marlborough* by Daniel Defoe. Augustan Reprint Society, No. 168. Los Angeles: Clark Memorial Library and University of California Press, 1974. Pp. i-xv.

Sketches briefly Marlborough's career and discusses
his relationship to the Harley administration. Defoe's
Short Narrative and his other 1711 political pamphlets
were designed to serve Harley's varying purposes, first
by shoring up Marlborough's prestige when it was important for the French to think that he was solidly
supported by the government and then gradually to dis-
associate him, when he was no longer needed, from the
ministry's "business of peace." The *Short Narrative*
"serves as a kind of barometer for the age," demonstrating the shifting fortunes of Whig and Tory. Backscheider also points out that many of the opinions and
techniques expressed in this pamphlet anticipate Defoe's
later fiction.

1036.   Baer, Joel H. "'The Complicated Plot of Piracy':
        Aspects of English Criminal Law and the Image of
        the Pirate in Defoe." *The Eighteenth Century: Theory
        and Interpretation*, 23 (1982), 3-26.

Demonstrates Defoe's detailed knowledge of piracy
and the laws surrounding it to show how well pirates
suited him as subjects; their stories brought together
many of his favorite topics: travel, trade, crime,
colonization, national security, and the isolation of
the human soul. Moreover, because pirates embodied
certain contradictions--"cunning thief and generous
lord of the sea, anarchist and nation builder, destruc-
tive demon and pioneer of commerce"--they serve Defoe
as symbols of Satan's temptations and our own spiritual
weaknesses.

1037.   ———. "Introduction." *"The Life and Adventures of
        Capt. John Avery" (1709?) and Charles Johnson, "The
        Successful Pyrate" (1713)*. Augustan Reprint Society,
        Nos. 203-04. Los Angeles: Clark Memorial Library and
        University of California Press, 1980. Pp. i-xiv.

Suggests that the two works reprinted here are sources
for Defoe's piratical writings. Defoe was fascinated
by pirates because to him they demonstrated an evolving
community, a paradigm of the development of society in
general.

*   Baine, Rodney M. "Daniel Defoe and Captain Carleton's
        Memoirs of an English Officer." (See item 1159.)

*   ———. "Daniel Defoe and Robert Drury's *Journal*."
        (See item 1160.)

1038. ————. "Daniel Defoe and *The History and Reality of Apparitions.*" *Proceedings of the American Philosophical Society*, 106 (1962), 335-47.

Outlines Defoe's beliefs in the supernatural as they appeared in his *Essay on the History and Reality of Apparitions* (1727). Defoe believed in both heavenly and what he called "intermediate" spirits, but he rejected the possibility of the revenant (the ghost of a dead person revisiting the earth to communicate with the living). In telling his ghost stories, Defoe used traditional narrative methods to obtain suspense; he employed minute, even inconsequential, details for purposes of verisimilitude; and he frequently interrupted dialogue to interject editorial commentary.

*   ————. "Defoe and the Angels." (See item 110.)

*   Bastian, F. "Defoe and Guy Miege." (See item 1162.)

*   Bonner, Willard H. "Moll, Knapton, and Defoe: A Note on Early Serial Publication." (See item 1081.)

1039. Boulton, James T. "Preface" to *"Memoirs of an English Officer (The Military Memoirs of Captain George Carleton)"* with *"The History of the remarkable Life of John Sheppard"* and *"The Memoirs of Major Alexander Ramkins, a Highland Officer."* London: Gollancz, 1970. Pp. 7-19.

Discusses the blend of fact and fiction in the three works contained in this volume and remarks on Defoe's ability to provide authenticating details which convince the reader that these "memoirs" are true stories told by real people. Each of the "heroes" of these three narratives have qualities that Defoe admired: they are men of action with ingenuity, resourcefulness, and adaptibility.

*   Callender, Geoffrey. "The Authorship of *The History of the ... Pirates* (1724)." (See item 1170.)

*   "Captain Carleton." (See item 1171.)

1040. Chaplin, Holroyd. "Defoe on the Vicar of Baddow." *Notes and Queries*, Tenth Series, 5 (1906), 428.

Asks for the full story of the "Vicar of Baddow," alluded to in Defoe's *History of the Devil*, Part II, Chapter iv.

1041. Clark, Paul O. "Lapponia, Lapland, and Laputa."
       Modern Language Quarterly, 19 (1958), 343-51.

       Discovers Johannes Schefferus' *History of Lapland*
       (1704) to be the source for the Lapland references in
       Defoe's *History of the Life and Adventures of Mr.
       Duncan Campbell* (1720). In turn, the Lapland material
       in *Duncan Campbell* is the source for Swift's conception
       of Laputa in *Gulliver's Travels* (1726).

1042. Curry, Frank. "De Foe and Napoleon Bonaparté." *Notes
       and Queries*, Eleventh Series, 7 (1913), 405-06.

       Discovers in an 1837 edition of Defoe's *The History
       of the Devil* a passage in which "Napolean Bonaparte"
       has been substituted for "the great King George."
       Also see Jonas, item 1049.

1043. Curtis, Laura Ann. "The Military Memoirs of Captain
       George Carleton." *The Versatile Defoe: An Anthology
       of Uncollected Writings by Daniel Defoe*. Totowa,
       N.J.: Rowman and Littlefield, 1979. Pp. 300-08.

       Believes that Defoe wrote the *Memoirs* although Carle-
       ton may have seen it through the press and made some
       changes in it. (On the matter of attribution, see
       Baine, item 1159; Hargevik, items 1179 and 1180; Hart-
       mann, items 1181 and 1182; Secord, item 1197; and
       Williams, item 1210.) The second section, devoted to
       the military exploits of the Earl of Peterborough from
       1705 to 1707 during the War of the Spanish Succession,
       is the *raison d'être* of the work. Curtis believes
       that Peterborough hired Defoe to glorify him, and
       Defoe succeeded so well that only in this century has
       Peterborough's "bloated military reputation" been
       deflated to more realistic proportions.

1044. ————. "Minutes of the Negotiation of Monsr. Mesnager
       at the Court of England during the Four Last Years
       of the Reign of Her Late Majesty Queen Anne." *The
       Versatile Defoe: An Anthology of Uncollected Writings
       by Daniel Defoe*. Totowa, N.J.: Rowman and Little-
       field, 1979. Pp. 341-49.

       Finds the *Minutes* "as exciting as a modern spy
       thriller" because of Defoe's ability to shape and point
       up his material by blending history and fiction for the
       polemical purpose of defending Harley from charges of
       treason. The work purports to be written by the French
       negotiator of the treaties that ended the War of the

Spanish Succession, but the book immediately was judged to be a forgery and was attributed to Defoe. Although some critics, like Sutherland, see the *Minutes* as part translation of Mesnager and part Defoe's fiction, Curtis views it as coming entirely from Defoe's pen. The work reflects Defoe's great personal loyalty to Harley and is a sincere attempt to show that he acted in good faith and for the best interests of England.

1045. ————. "The Storm: or a Collection of the Most Remarkable Casualties and Disasters which Happened in the Late Dreadful Tempest, Both by Sea and Land." *The Versatile Defoe: an Anthology of Writings by Daniel Defoe*. Totowa, N.J.: Rowman and Littlefield, 1979. Pp. 279 85.

Views this pamphlet as significant for two reasons: (1) it launches Defoe's career as a reporter and historian of contemporary events and (2) it is the first elaborate, factual eyewitness report in English literature of a recent natural phenomenon. Defoe records his own observations of the great storm of November 26-27, 1703, and those of numerous other viewers (which he obtained through advertisements in several newspapers). Defoe's methods, especially his strict fidelity to fact, anticipate his techniques in his later histories and memoirs as well as those in the *Journal of the Plague Year*.

1046. Gove, Philip B. "Robert Drury." *Notes and Queries*, 178 (1940), 150-51.

Lists editions of *Robert Drury's Journal* and collects here "relevant references" to it and the debate over its authorship. Much of this material appears in Gove's *The Imaginary Voyage*, item 1100.

1047. Hardyman, J. Trenchard. "Origin and Death of Robert Drury." *Notes and Queries*, 177 (1939), 47.

Accepts the biographical data of *Robert Drury's Journal* as true and asks for corroboration of details in it.

* Hargevik, Steig. *The Disputed Assignment of "Memoirs of an English Officer" to Daniel Defoe*. Parts 1 and 2. (See items 1179 and 1180.)

* Hartmann, Cyril H. "Introduction" to *Memoirs of Captain Carleton*. (See item 1181.)

*   ————. [On the Memoirs of Captain Carleton.] (See
            item 1182.)

1048.   Healey, George Harris. "Another Defoe Item." *Notes
            and Queries*, 195 (1950), 195.

            Discovers for Payne, item 1060, a copy of Defoe's
            *Proposals for Printing by Subscription a Compleat His-
            tory of the Union* which is bound in with the copy of
            the *History* in the Library of the University of London.

1049.   Jonas, Alfred Charles. "De Foe and Napoleon Bona-
            parte." *Notes and Queries*, Eleventh Series, 7
            (1913), 514.

            Finds in a 1793 edition of Defoe's *The History of
            the Devil* a passage in which "the great King George"
            has been replaced by "his most Christian Majesty
            Louis XIV." See Curry, item 1042.

1050.   Maynadier, G.H. "Introduction" to *Mr. Duncan Campbell*
            by Daniel Defoe. New York: Sproul, 1903. Pp. xi-xxi.

            Provides background on Campbell, a deaf and dumb seer
            of Defoe's time, and notes several references to him
            in the *Tatler* and *Spectator*.

1051.   Minet, William. "Daniel Defoe and Kent: A Chapter in
            Capel-le-Ferne History." *Archaeologia Cantiana*, 31
            (1914), 61-74.

            Demonstrates that Mrs. Veal was a real person and
            argues that Defoe wrote Drury's *Journal*.

*   Moore, John Robert. *Daniel Defoe: Citizen of the
            Modern World*. (See item 255.)

*   ————. *Defoe in the Pillory and Other Studies*. (Con-
            tains section of Defoe's *History of the Pirates*.)
            (See item 261.)

*   ————. "Defoe, Thoresby, and 'The Storm.'" (See item
            264.)

1052.   ————. "Defoe's 'History of the Pirates': Its Date."
            Notes and Queries, 179 (1940), 6-7.

            Adduces evidence to prove that the earliest possible
            date for Volume 2 of Defoe's "A General History of the
            Pirates" is 1728, making it one of the latest of his
            works.

1053.   ————. *Defoe's Sources for "Robert Drury's Journal."*
         Indiana University Publications, Humanities Series
         No. 9. Bloomington: Indiana University Press, 1943.

Investigates Defoe's sources for this fiction which
appears to be substantially true. The germinal idea
was a 1705 newspaper account of a boy who had escaped
from Madagascar after natives there massacred all his
companions. Defoe elaborated this story into a fictional narrative, drawing details from Robert Knox's
Ceylon, Robert Everard's *Relation*, and the *Atlas Geo-
graphus*. Defoe also drew upon his conversations with
pirates for details about Madagascar. The map that
accompanies the narration was adapted for the book,
but Defoe did not adhere to its details in writing the
Journal.

Reviews: Rae Blanchard, *Modern Language Notes*, 59
    (1944), 201-02; Willard Hallam Bonner, *Modern Lan-
    guage Quarterly*, 4 (1943), 512-13; H.C. Hutchins,
    Philological Quarterly, 23 (1944), 160-61; Gwyn
    Jones, *Modern Language Review*, 39 (1944), 90; *Notes
    and Queries*, 185 (1943), 349-50.

*   ————. "Evidence for Defoe's Authorship of *The Memoirs
         of Captain Carleton*." (See item 1189.)

1054.   ————. "Further Notes on Defoe's Sources for 'Robert
         Drury's Journal.'" *Notes and Queries*, 188 (1945),
         268-71.

Attacks Secord's arguments in "Defoe and Robert
Drury's Journal," item 1066. Moore refutes Secord's
premises that Defoe *must* have drawn his firsthand
information from Drury himself and that Flacourt and
Ogilby *must* have been Defoe's source for his knowledge
of Madagascar. Moore also says Secord is wrong in re-
fusing to accept Defoe's authorship of the "History of
the Pirates," the notes for which are "so obviously"
used again for Drury's journal. Also see Secord,
"Robert Drury and Robert Drury's Journal," item 1067.

1055.   ————. "Introduction" to *A Brief History of the Poor
         Palatine Refugees* by Daniel Defoe. Augustan Reprint
         Society, No. 106. Los Angeles: Clark Memorial Library
         and University of California Press, 1964. Pp. i-ix.

Provides historical data on the Palatine refugees
(about 10,000 people from the area around Heidelberg),
presents publishing information of the tract, and discusses characteristic Defoe techniques in the work.

1056.   ————. "Scott's *Antiquary* and Defoe's *History of Apparitions*." *Modern Language Notes*, 59 (1944), 550-51.

Finds in Defoe's *History of Apparitions* a source for the scene in Scott's *Antiquary* in which Edie and the Adept dig for buried treasure.

1057.   Novak, Maximillian E. "Defoe, Thomas Burnet, and the 'Diestical' Passages of Robert Drury's *Journal*." *Philological Quarterly*, 42 (1963), 207-16.

Accepts Defoe's role as the "transcriber" of *Robert Drury's Journal* and attempts to reconcile it with the work's "diestical" passages. The attack on the literal truth of the Bible seems incompatible with Defoe's often expressed belief that scripture is "God speaking to Men, even in every Word." This apparent paradox can be resolved by assessing the influence of Thomas Burnet on Defoe and by outlining the latter's attitudes toward natural man and natural religion. Finally, it must be noted that while Defoe was not a deist, he always was willing--as was Burnet--to apply reason to religion.

1058.   ————. "Introduction" to *Of Captain Mission* (1728) by Daniel Defoe. Augustan Reprint Society, No. 87. Los Angeles: Clark Memorial Library and University of California Press, 1961. Pp. i-iv.

Notes that this work, although called a "history," is actually a fiction which comments on the injustice and hypocrisy of contemporary English society. The piece also is interesting for its portrayal of a Communist utopia by Defoe, who generally is viewed as an early exponent of *laissez-faire*. Defoe uses the same techniques here as he does in his longer fictions: the narrator pretends to work from a manuscript, real events and persons are worked into the plot, and the hero has an intellectual mentor.

1059.   Pafford, H.H.P. "Defoe's *Proposals* for Printing the *History of the Union*." *Library*, Fifth Series, 11 (1956), 202-06.

Reproduces from the August 5, 1707, *Review* an announcement that Defoe planned to publish by subscription "a Compleat History of the Union." Pafford traces the evolution of this proposal.

1060. Payne, William L. "Another Defoe Item." *Notes and Queries*, 194 (1949), 326.

Refers to an item in Defoe's *Review* for August 5, 1707, which announces the publication of "Proposals for Printing by Subscription a Compleat History of the Union" and asks for information on the "Proposals," which may have been bound in with the first edition (1709) of the *History*.

1061. ————. "Defoe Not Guilty." *Notes and Queries*, 18 (1971), 46.

Refutes charges of plagiarism leveled at Defoe in a 1705 pamphlet, *The Republican Bullies*, which says that parts of Defoe's *The Storm* (1704) were taken from Dr. Ralph Bohun's *A Discourse Concerning the Origins and Properties of Wind* (1671).

1062. Playfair, Edward. "The Master of 'a Peculiar Talent.'" (London) *Times Literary Supplement*, 15 May 1969, pp. 535–36.

Pleads for a fully annotated modern edition of Defoe's *History of the Union between England and Scotland* (last printed in 1786), an important account of the statesmanship and skilled negotiations that went into forming the Union. The work still reads well because of Defoe's passionate, personal involvement in the events of the day and because of his ability to shape his diffuse and repetitious material.

* Rothman, Irving N. "Defoe's Census of *The Family Instructor* and *The Political History of the Devil*." (See item 1013.)

1063. Russell, John R. "Preface" to *An Account of the Conduct and Proceedings of the Pirate Gow*. New York: Burt Franklin, 1970. Pp. v–viii.

Quotes extensively from William Lee's biography attesting to Defoe's authorship of the tract and to its authenticity.

1064. Ryan, A.P. "Defoe." (London) *Times Literary Supplement*, 26 May 1972, p. 605.

Corrects the review of Sutherland's *Daniel Defoe* in the April 28, 1972, issue of the (London) *Times Literary Supplement* by noting that the *Storm* by Defoe deserves

to be remembered as a brilliant feat of on-the-spot
reporting.

1065.   Schonborn, Manuel R. "Defoe's Pirates: A New Source."
        Review of English Studies, n.s. 14 (1963), 386-89.

        Supplements Secord's study of Defoe's sources (item
        327) by providing a hitherto undetected source for
        the incident of the merchant vessel's theft in *Captain
        Singleton*. This scene is based on an actual event in
        the life of pirate Henry Every, an event recorded in a
        twenty-eight-page pamphlet on the trials of pirates
        Joseph Dawson and Edward Forseith.

*   Secord, Arthur W. "Captain Carleton." (See item 1197.)

1066.   ————. "Defoe and *Robert Drury's Journal*." *Journal
        of English and Germanic Philology*, 44 (1945), 66-73.

        Accepts Defoe's part in writing *Robert Drury's Jour-
        nal* and investigates *how* Defoe might have written it.
        Did Defoe revise Drury's long manuscript, did he write
        from notes and oral accounts given him by Drury, or
        did he invent the whole story? Because the *Journal's*
        brief account of Drury's second voyage is pure fiction
        and because there are a number of errors in the account
        of his other adventures, it seems likely that Defoe
        used a factual framework within which he invented
        freely. Also see Moore's *Defoe's Sources*, item 1053;
        Secord's *Robert Drury*, item 1067; and "*Robert Drury's
        Journal*," item 1068.

*   ————. "Defoe in Stoke Newington." (See item 325.)

1067.   ————. "Robert Drury and 'Robert Drury's Journal.'"
        Notes and Queries, 189 (1945), 178-80.

        A rejoinder to Moore's "Further Notes," item 1054.
        Secord defends his position on "Drury's Journal,"
        saying that he considers that work "a framework of
        fact within which Defoe invented freely." Secord says
        that he never denied Defoe's authorship of the *History
        of the Pirates*, but that whether he did or not fails
        to affect his argument in any way. Furthermore, he
        states that his suggestion that Defoe may have gotten
        information from Drury is supported by the fact that
        Defoe had to have gotten information from pirates or
        ex-pirates and Drury was one of them; besides, Defoe
        would have had to know of Drury to name his book after

him. Secord goes on to respond to details of Moore's critique. Also see Secord's "Defoe and Robert Drury's Journal," item 1066.

1068.   ————. *"Robert Drury's Journal" and Other Studies.* Champaign: University of Illinois Press, 1961.

Publishes posthumously four studies, the first three of which are relevant to Defoe, left finished but unpolished by Professor Secord at his death in 1957. The first of these, *"Robert Drury's Journal,"* traces Drury's life and seafaring adventures and argues that he probably wrote an account of them on which the journal is based. "Thirteen Years on Madagascar," the second essay, studies life on the island, the genealogy of its inhabitants, and the Malagasy language in order to demonstrate that Drury was the principal source of information for the Madagascar material in the *Journal* and that Defoe simply put Drury's manuscript into a more literary form. The third essay, "The Origins of Defoe's *Memoirs of a Cavalier*," credits Defoe with the invention of the historical novel; the *Memoirs* shows Defoe's movement from fictitious propaganda to fiction with only incidental propaganda. Defoe pieces together his novel from previously printed biographies, memoirs, and histories, especially the *Swedish Intelligencer*, Ludlow's *Memoirs*, and Whitelock's *Memorials*.

Reviews: L.R. Christie, *English Historical Review*, 78 (1963), 387; Jane H. Jack, *Modern Language Review*, 58 (1963), 463; C.J. Rawson, *Notes and Queries*, 208 (1963), 157-58; F. Wölcken, *Review of English Studies*, n.s. 14 (1963), 303-05.

*   ————. *Studies in the Narrative Method of Defoe.* (See item 327.)

1069. Wilkie, Everett C., Jr. "Eidous' Translation of Defoe's *A General History of Discoveries and Improvements*." *Papers of the Bibliographical Society of America*, 74 (1980), 67-70.

Shows that Eidous' *Histoire des principales découvertes faites dans les arts et les sciences* (1767) is not really an original work but rather a sloppy translation of Defoe's *A General History of Discoveries and Improvements in Useful Arts* (1726-27).

*   Williams, Harold. "Captain Carleton." (See item
       1210.)

D. Trade, Travel, Voyages, and
Imaginary Voyages

1070.   Adams, Percy G. *Travelers and Travel Liars, 1660-*
       1800. Berkeley and Los Angeles: University of Cal-
       ifornia Press, 1962.

       Deals both with authentic travel accounts that include
       lies and pseudo-voyages that try to convince the reader
       of their truth. Defoe--called "the supreme creator of
       literary hoaxes"--is mentioned frequently and in detail.
       The section on "Fireside Travelers" concentrates on
       Robert Drury's Journal and compares Defoe with the
       French travel hoaxer, François Coreal. Some mention
       is made of Defoe's manipulation of travel literature
       in his fiction.

1071.   Andrews, J.H. "A Case of Plagiarism in Defoe's 'Tour.'"
       Notes and Queries, n.s. 6 (1959), 399.

       Finds evidence of Defoe's typical carelessness and
       haste in a passage from Edmund Gibson which finds its
       way into the *Tour* in a place where it makes no sense.

1072.   ————. "Defoe and the Source of His *Tour.*" *Geo-*
       graphical Journal, 126 (1960), 268-77.

       Determines that the *Tour* was based on travels made
       more than a decade before the book was published, hence
       Defoe had tô supply his material from memory and pub-
       lished sources. Although his firsthand knowledge of
       England was extraordinary, it was not as extensive as
       he pretended. Andrews lists a variety of sources pos-
       sibly used by Defoe.

1073.   ————. "Defoe's 'Tour' and Macky's 'Journey.'" *Notes*
       and Queries, n.s. 7 (1960), 290-92.

       Suggests that Defoe's *Tour* "was written as a deliberate
       attempt to capture Macky's market by producing a better
       book of the same kind." Like Macky, Defoe adopts the
       epistolary convention, mixes personal narrative and
       objective guidebook description, and promises not to
       record anything he has not personally seen. The latter

statement, however, is fallacious; in fact, Defoe borrows and paraphrases heavily from Macky.

1074. Atkinson, A.D. "Goldsmith Borrows." (London) *Times Literary Supplement*, 25 January 1947, p. 51.

Cites a passage from Goldsmith's *Life of Richard Nash* which is plagiarized from Letter VI of Defoe's *Tour Through England and Wales*.

*   Baine, Rodney. "Daniel Defoe's Imaginary Voyages to the Moon." (See item 1161.)

1075. Baker, J.N.L. "The Geography of Daniel Defoe." *Scottish Geographical Magazine*, 47 (1931), 257-69.

Examines Defoe's use of geography in *The Storm*, *Robinson Crusoe*, *Captain Singleton*, and the *New Voyage round the World* in order to demonstrate his discrimination in selecting the facts that he blended with his fiction and sometimes altered altogether in the interest of enhancing his story. Defoe relied on the best geographical authorities available for the details that he often used to add realism to his works.

1076. Barringer, George M. "Defoe's *A Tour Thro' the Whole Island of Great Britain*." *Thoth*, 9 (1968), 3-13.

Views the *Tour* as more than a guidebook and a study of English commerce, as it generally is treated; the work is above all a patriotic tribute to Great Britain.

*   Bastian, F. "Daniel Defoe and the Dorking District." (See item 112.)

1077. ————. "Defoe's Tour and the Historian." *History Today*, 17 (1967), 845-51.

Seeks to show how Defoe put together his *Tour thro' the Whole Island of Great Britain*. He did draw upon his own travels and observations, but he also drew upon earlier writings (often plagiarizing from them) and at times resorted to pure, although informed, invention. In spite of this non-factual material, the *Tour* is full of useful information about eighteenth-century England and about Defoe's life. Also see Andrews, item 1072.

1078. Batten, Charles L., Jr. *Pleasurable Instruction: Form and Convention in Eighteenth-Century Travel Literature*. Berkeley and Los Angeles: University of California Press, 1978.

Places Defoe in the tradition of English travel
literature, noting that he designs his *Tour thro' the
Whole Island of Great Britain* as an artistic work of
"pleasurable instruction." He holds the *Tour* together
with the "central fiction" of an itinerary which he
pretends he follows but which actually combines personal
observation with materials taken from other travel
works. Following the "rules" of good travel writing,
Defoe remains impersonal throughout, keeping autobiographical materials at a minimum in order to focus
on the geographical purpose of his book.

1079. Black, William George. "Glasgow Cross and Defoe's
       Tour." *Notes and Queries*, Eleventh Series, 8 (1913),
       349.

       Asks if a sentence--"In the centre stands the cross"
       --which appears in the eighth edition of the *Tour* also
       appears in the first. See G., item 1097; Curry, item
       1085; and J.F.R., item 1111.

1080. Blunden, Edmund. "Defoe's Great Britain." *Votive
       Tablets*. Freeport, N.Y.: Books for Libraries Press,
       1967. Pp. 101-06. Originally published London,
       1932.

       Depicts Defoe's "earthly paradise" as presented in
       his *Tour thro' the Whole Island of Great Britain*.
       Defoe's enthusiasm is kindled more by a market or
       workshop than by the beauties of antiquity or nature.

1081. Bonner, Willard H. "Moll, Knapton, and Defoe: A Note
       on Early Serial Publication." *Review of English
       Studies*, 10 (1934), 320-23.

       Points out that although Defoe is well-known for
       his journalistic endeavors and his pamphleteering ac-
       tivities, he is less well-known for his publishing of
       geographico-trade serials. His *General History of the
       Principle Discoveries and Improvements* (1726-27) ap-
       peared in four monthly numbers and was designed to
       cater to the age's tremendous interest, shared by Defoe,
       in geography, trade, and travel.

1082. Bosse, Malcolm J. "Introduction" to *The Four Years
       Voyages of Captain George Roberts* by Daniel Defoe.
       New York: Garland, 1972.

       Points out that *Captain Roberts* is similar to Defoe's
       fiction in its detail, "fatalistic belief in Providence,"

and "view of nature as hostile but controllable." The work succeeds because of the "brute power of data" contained in it.

* Burch, Charles E. "The Authorship of 'A Letter Concerning Trade from Several Scots Gentlemen That Are Merchants in London,' Etc. (1706)." (See item 1164.)

* Cather, Willa. "Introduction" to *Roxana, or the Fortunate Mistress* by Daniel Defoe. (See item 869.)

1083. Cole, G.D.H. "Introduction" to *A Tour Through England and Wales* by Daniel Defoe. London: Dent and Sons and New York: Dutton, 1968. Pp. vii-xvii.

Finds Defoe's *Tour* the most graphic book on the economic and social condition of England at the beginning of the eighteenth century. The *Tour* also shows Defoe in his role as apologist for the English middle class.

1084. ————. "Introduction" to *A Tour thro' the Whole Island of Great Britain* by Daniel Defoe. 2 Vols. London: Peter Davies, 1927. Reprinted London: Frank Cass and New York: Augustus M. Kelley, 1968.

Presents a highly generalized overview of the work, emphasizing its value to economic historians, and asserts (without supporting evidence) that Defoe borrowed heavily from previous works, especially Macky's *A Journey through England in Familiar Letters*.

1085. Curry, Frank. "Glasgow Cross and Defoe's *Tour*." *Notes and Queries*, Eleventh Series, 8 (1913), 492-93.

Lists editions of Defoe's *Tour* which are not in the works of his biographers and provides evidence to show that Defoe was responsible for the Scottish section of the book. See Black, item 1079; G., item 1097; and J.F.R., item 1111.

1086. Curtis, Laura Ann. "A Brief State of the Inland or Home Trade, of England." *The Versatile Defoe: An Anthology of Uncollected Writings of Daniel Defoe*. Totowa, N.J.: Rowman and Littlefield, 1979. Pp. 208-11.

Shows how Defoe is able to present the argument of a special interest group—in this case, the shopkeepers, who were trying to eliminate competition from

peddlers—and at the same time develop an economic
theory relating to the whole system of production and
distribution in England. Although *A Brief State* is
one of Defoe's best-written and most lucid arguments,
it also demonstrates his limitations as an economist
(especially showing his "lack of insight about production").

1087.   ————. "The Complete English Tradesman." *The Versa-*
         tile Defoe: An Anthology of Uncollected Writings by
         Daniel Defoe. Totowa, N.J.: Rowman and Littlefield,
         1979. Pp. 377-80.

Regards this book as "significant ... for expressing
Defoe's theory of style and his instinctive grasp of
decorum...." In a lively and charming manner, Defoe
outlines an entire lifestyle for the beginning tradesman, advising him to practice self-restraint and to be
frugal; Defoe also provides practical information on
merchandising, keeping books, writing business letters,
and so on. In both his pamphlets and novels, trade is
a metaphor for social stability.

1088.   ————. "Some Thoughts upon the Subject of Commerce
         with France." *The Versatile Defoe: An Anthology of*
         Uncollected Writings by Daniel Defoe. Totowa, N.J.:
         Rowman and Littlefield, 1979. Pp. 151-57.

Calls this work, which treats the commercial portions
of the Treaty of Utrecht, "an important contribution
to a pamphlet controversy ... which has great interest
in the history of economic thought." Defoe's intermediate position between free trade and mercantile
protection "earned him the unmerited epithet of a
turncoat." His clear and forceful argument in favor of
trade with France—expressed through the persona of a
plainspoken honest man—shows that he was ahead of his
time as a statistician and economist. We know today
that Defoe's statistics were more accurate than those
of his opponents in this economic controversy.

1089.   Davies, Godfrey. "Daniel Defoe's *A tour thro' the*
         whole island of Great Britain." *Modern Philology*,
         48 (1950), 21-36.

Classifies the kinds of changes made in the *Tour* over
the years by its editors and demonstrates that only
the first edition can safely be said to be Defoe's.
Davies also discovers in the first volume of the *Tour*

the previously unidentified source for the "Diary of the Siege of Colchester."

1090. Davies, H. Neville. "Defoe and the Swallows." (London) *Times Literary Supplement*, 27 February 1969, p. 211.

Notes an earlier account than Garnett's (item 1099) of the lunar migration of birds theory. Defoe is only mentioned in passing.

*   Downie, J.A. "Eighteenth-Century Scotland as Seen by Daniel Defoe." (See item 170.)

1091. Duff, E. Gordon. "Defoe's Novels Issued in Paris." *Notes and Queries*, Tenth Series, 7 (1907), 389.

Seeks bibliographical information on his copy of *A New Voyage round the World*, issued in forty-four parts of two leaves each and printed in various type sizes and faces.

*   Earle, Peter. "The Economics of Stability: The Views of Daniel Defoe." (See item 174.)

1092. Easson, Angus. "Defoe and the Swallows." (London) *Times Literary Supplement*, 6 March 1969, p. 241.

Points out that others held a theory of bird migration similar to that which Defoe propounded in his *Tour of Great Britain*, thus implying that Defoe may not have been as original as Garnett (item 1099) supposes.

1093. Eaves, T.C. Duncan, and Ben D. Kimpel. *Samuel Richardson: A Biography*. Oxford: Clarendon Press, 1971.

Makes many scattered references to Defoe, the most important of which treat Richardson's revisions of Defoe's *Tour thro' the Whole Island of Great Britain* and *The Complete English Tradesman*. Many of the specific changes made by Richardson are recorded in Eaves and Kimpel's footnotes.

1094. Eddy, William A. *Gulliver's Travels: A Critical Study*. Princeton, N.J.: Princeton University Press, 1923.

Notes briefly in passing that in his *Consolidator*--which represents him at his worst--Defoe anticipates Swift's device of creating tongue-twisting languages for his imaginary lands. Defoe, particularly in *Captain*

Singleton, employs a method also used by Swift: "surrounding a few important lies with a multitude of in-
significant truths" in order to disarm the reader and
trick him into accepting the lies.

1095. Fishman, Burton J. "Defoe, Herman Moll, and the Geog-
       raphy of South America." *Huntington Library Quarter-
       ly*, 36 (1973), 227-38.

       Regards the *New Voyage round the World* as a serious
       plan to establish colonies in Chile and Argentina for
       purposes of trade. In the *New Voyage*, Defoe apparently
       believed that there existed a 360-mile route across the
       Andes from Beldiva to Camarones Bay. The source for
       his geographical error is a map of Chile by Herman
       Moll, the most famous cartographer of the day; the
       fact that Defoe made such an error based on Moll's map
       demonstrates his careful attention to factual detail
       even in his fiction.

1096. Fussell, Paul. *The Rhetorical World of Augustan Human-
       ism*. London: Oxford, 1965.

       Mentions Defoe's *Tour* as a work which emphasizes the
       modern and the idea of progress, concluding that there-
       fore it is not "humanistic." Fussell's brief remarks
       provoke a response from Pat Rogers at item 1113.

1097. G. "Glasgow Cross and Defoe's *Tour*." *Notes and Queries*,
       Eleventh Series, 8 (1913), 416-17.

       Replies to Black, item 1079, that the sixth edition
       of the *Tour* contains the words, "In the centre stands
       the cross." G. suggests that the omitted words in
       Glasgow Facies is due to the author's source for the
       quotation from the *Tour*. See Curry, item 1085, and
       J.F.R., item 1111.

1098. Garnett, Richard. "Defoe and the Swallows." (London)
       Times Literary Supplement, 13 February 1969, pp. 161-
       62.

       Discusses contemporary theories concerning the migra-
       tion of birds and shows how Defoe's views, expressed in
       Tour ... of Great Britain, flew in the face of the day's
       "experts" and are remarkably modern and accurate. In
       spite of Defoe's accurate account of bird migration,
       the most learned zoologists continued to hold mistaken
       views of the subject for nearly a hundred years. Defoe's
       commonsensical attitude and use of accurate detail in

advancing it is typical of his later work in fiction.
See the following responses, all in the (London) *Times
Literary Supplement*, to this article: Davies, item 1090;
Easson, item 1092; Garnett, item 1099; Lindsay, item
1104; Moseley, item 1108; Newbury, item 1109; and Seeley,
item 1122.

1099. ————. "Defoe and the Swallows." (London) *Times
Literary Supplement*, 3 April 1969, p. 369.

Confirms his earlier supposition (see item 1098) that
Charles Morton's book on bird migration was current by
1686.

1100. Gove, Philip B. *The Imaginary Voyage in Prose Fiction:
A History of Its Criticism and a Guide for Its Study
with an Annotated Check List of 215 Imaginary Voyages
from 1700 to 1800.* London: The Holland Press, 1961.
Originally published 1941.

Refers to Defoe throughout and emphasizes *Crusoe* in
a section on the Robinsonade. The latter explains how
the conception of the Robinsonade developed and how it
has been variously defined. Gove covers the European
criticism of imaginary voyages--especially that in
German--in great detail. The annotated checklist of
imaginary voyages which concludes the book contains
bibliographic information on *Captain Singleton*, *Consolidator*, *Robert Drury's Journal*, *A New Voyage* round
the World, and *Robinson Crusoe*.

1101. Hackos, JoAnn T. "The Metaphor of the Garden in
Defoe's *A Tour thro' the Whole Island of Great
Britain*." *Papers in Literature and Language*, 15
(1979), 247-62.

Sees Defoe as a more aware and sophisticated aes-
thetician than he generally is given credit for. He
understood that formal realism depended on an artistic
rearrangement of nature, and he clarifies this concept
through the use of a garden metaphor in his *Tour*. He
also uses this metaphor to express his views on trade;
he sees the tradesman as an artist "methodizing" the
natural resources of Britain for its future prosperity.

1102. Jack, Jane H. "*A New Voyage round the World*: Defoe's
Roman à Thèse." *Huntington Library Quarterly*, 24
(1961), 323-36.

Regards Defoe's *A New Voyage* as a *roman à thèse* designed to gain support for the author's plan to colonize

the east coast of South America. Defoe's optimistic
conception of human nature, his view of the positive
nature of a life of unceasing activity is symbolized
by the idea of a colony. Everything in *A New Voyage*
is secondary to his colonization scheme, thus subordina-
ting dramatic action to the points he wishes to make.

1103.   Jarvis, R.C. "Fielding, Dodsley, Marchant, and Ray."
        Notes and Queries, 189 (1945), 90-92; 117-20; 139-41.

        Refers frequently to Defoe's *Tour*, into the fourth
        edition of which was incorporated Dodsley's "Succinct
        History of the Rebellion"; this material continued to
        appear in the *Tour* until the ninth edition of 1779.

1104.   Lindsay, Jack. "Defoe and the Swallows." (London)
        Times Literary Supplement, 20 February 1969, p. 186.

        Adds to Garnett's essay on bird migration (item
        1098) the views of Joseph Priestley. Also see Davies,
        item 1090; Easson, item 1092; Moseley, item 1108;
        Newbury, item 1109; and Seeley, item 1122.

*   M., P.D. "Daniel De Foe and Martock, Somerset." (See
        item 231.)

1105.   McVeagh, John. "Defoe and the Romance of Trade."
        Durham University Journal, 70 (1978), 141-47.

        Denies that Defoe is only an unimaginative recorder
        of details and facts. On the contrary, even his
        writings on trade are infused with imagination. The
        trader is an adventurous hero who advances himself
        through a process of self-discovery and self-fulfillment,
        and in this he has much in common with the heroes and
        heroines of Defoe's fiction.

1106.   Moir, Esther. "A Planted Garden: Celia Fiennes and
        Daniel Defoe." *The Discovery of Britain*. London:
        Routledge and Kegan Paul, 1964. Pp. 35-46.

        Compares Defoe's *Tour* with *The Journeys of Celia
        Fiennes*: "between them they bring to life the England
        they found." The two authors have a lot in common,
        particularly their distaste for antiquities and
        natural scenery and their preference for busy indus-
        trial towns. Both Defoe and Fiennes, who wax rhap-
        sodic over mines and marketplaces, depict a bustling,
        prosperous England.

1107. Moore, John Robert. "Defoe and the South Sea Company."
       Boston Public Library Quarterly, 5 (1953), 175-88.

       Presents evidence to show that Defoe was not behind
       the South Sea Company as many modern historians have
       assumed. In fact, he had been out of touch with
       Harley—who got the Act through Parliament—for several
       months prior to the Act's passage, he did not approve
       of the Company and he foresaw the probability of stock-
       jobbing and the possibility of disaster. Defoe's own
       South Sea plan, very different from the 1712 Act, was
       presented in his *A New Voyage round the World* (1724).
       Also see Fishman, item 1095, and Jack, item 1102.

1108. Moseley, C.W.R.D. "Defoe and the Swallows." (London)
       Times Literary Supplement, 6 March 1969, p. 241.

       Suggests that Defoe's theory of bird migration, pre-
       sented in his *Tour* ... *of Great Britain* (see Garnett,
       item 1098), may have been based on local folklore.
       Also see Davies, item 1090; Easson, item 1092; Lindsay,
       item 1104; Newbury, item 1109; and Seeley, item 1122.

1109. Newbury, R.D.A. "Defoe and the Swallows." (London)
       Times Literary Supplement, 27 February 1969, p. 211.

       Suggests that perhaps Garnett (item 1098) gave Defoe
       too much credit for original scientific thinking in
       his theory of bird migration; the theory advanced by
       Defoe in his *Tour* ... *of Great Britain* had already
       been well-publicized by Willoughby and Derham. Also
       see Davies, item 1090; Easson, item 1092; Lindsay, item
       1104; Moseley, item 1108; and Seeley, item 1122.

1110. Nicolson, Marjorie Hope, and Nora M. Mohler. "Swift's
       'Flying Island' in the *Voyage to Laputa*." *Annals
       of Science*, 2 (1937), 405-30.

       Mentions in passing—with some citation—that Defoe's
       Consolidator may be the source of Swift's Flying Island
       in *Gulliver's Travels*.

1111. R., J.F. "Glasgow Cross and Defoe's *Tour*." *Notes and
       Queries*, Eleventh Series, 9 (1914), 32.

       Responds to Black, item 1079, Curry, item 1085, and
       G., item 1097; that he owns a first edition of Defoe's
       Tour and the words, "In the centre stands the cross,"
       do not appear.

1112. Raven, Simon. "Defoe for England." *Spectator*, 31
       (July 1959), p. 142.

       Regards Defoe as a brilliant journalist, a dedicated
       social observer, an enemy of bigotry, and a lover of
       freedom. Defoe's *Tour* is a charming and accurate por-
       trait of his England, but if he returned now he would
       find a debased England, albeit one which still protects
       individual freedom.

1113. Rogers, Pat. "Defoe and Virgil: The Georgic Element
       in *A Tour Thro' Great Britain*." *English Miscellany*,
       22 (1971), 93-106.

       Takes issue with Paul Fussell's remarks on Defoe's
       Tour as a work which emphasizes the modern and the
       idea of progress (see item 1096). In fact, the in-
       fluence of Virgil's *Georgics* is everywhere and gives
       the *Tour* an antiquarian tone and a historical context.
       To support his thesis, Rogers notes many parallel
       passages and images in the *Georgics* and the *Tour*.

1114. ————. "Defoe as Plagiarist: Camden's *Britannia* and
       A Tour thro' the Whole Island of Great Britain."
       Philological Quarterly, 52 (1973), 771-74.

       Summarizes Defoe's extensive and unacknowledged
       borrowings from Camden; this material infuses every
       section of the *Tour* except for Letter V (which deals
       with Defoe's "home territory" of London).

1115. ————. "Defoe at Work: The Making of *A Tour thro'
       Great Britain*, Volume I." *Bulletin of the New York
       Public Library*, 78 (1975), 431-50.

       Attempts to demonstrate that Volume I of Defoe's
       Tour contains much recent information and is not just
       a patchwork of old memories of forty years of traveling
       England combined with borrowings from other authors.
       At several places in the *Tour*, Defoe indicates that he
       made a special journey for purposes of the book and
       these contentions are frequently supported by the
       author's detailed knowledge of contemporary events.
       Defoe used current happenings along with secondhand
       anecdotes and borrowed information to achieve a highly
       artistic sense of "contemporaneity."

1116. ————. "Later Editions of Defoe's 'Tour.'" *Book Col-
       lector* (London), 25 (1976), 390-91.

Reports that there has never been an accurate listing of the British editions of Defoe's *Tour* and then lists the nine editions of the full work printed through 1779.

1117. ————. "Literary Art in Defoe's *Tour*: The Rhetoric of Growth and Decay." *Eighteenth-Century Studies*, 6 (1972-73), 153-85.

Sees Defoe's *Tour* as an example of its author's literary maturity. That maturity is reflected in the book's structure: a clear itinerary is maintained with the movement from county to county carefully charted; Defoe's awareness of design is shown when he calls his journey a "circuit" or "circle" and proposes beginning and ending his travels in London. Likewise, the *Tour* is stylistically sophisticated, and two kinds of sustained imagery are predominant: anthropomorphic metaphors and images connected with trade or commerce. Just as sophisticated is Defoe's rhetorical use of contrast throughout the work. The *Tour* blends Defoe's skills as a great reporter with his talent as an imaginative creator to achieve "the true English epic."

1118. ————. "The Making of Defoe's *A Tour thro' Great Britain*, Volumes II and III." *Prose Studies*, 3 (1980), 109-37.

Draws several general conclusions--based on a wealth of minute and particular knowledge of current events, architecture, rentals, weather conditions, Defoe's whereabouts, etc.--about Defoe's writing of his *Tour*. Defoe drew his information from previous authorities, his many contacts, and his own observations both as a youth and as a mature traveler. He wrote the book between November 1722 and May/June 1726, working consecutively and synthetically, although the separate volumes were basically independent productions.

1119. ————. "Samuel Richardson and Defoe's 'Tour' (1738): The Evidence of Bibliography." *Studies in Bibliography*, 28 (1975), 305-07.

Strengthens the case of Eaves and Kimpel (item 1093) that Samuel Richardson was involved in the 1738 second edition of Defoe's *Tour*.

* Roorda, Gerridina. *Realism in Daniel Defoe's Narratives of Adventure*. (See item 652.)

1120. Sale, William Merritt, Jr. *Samuel Richardson: A Bib-
       liographical Record of His Literary Career with His-
       torical Notes.* New Haven: Yale University Press,
       1936.

       Describes and comments on the four editions (the
       third through the sixth) of Defoe's *Tour* published by
       Samuel Richardson. All of these editions were exten-
       sively revised by Richardson; in the third, for example,
       he added details of antiquarian interest (largely ig-
       nored by Defoe) and greatly expanded the description
       of Scotland in order to do "some further Justice to
       that Country...."

1121. Schonhorn, Manuel. "Defoe's *Four Years Voyages of Capt.
       George Roberts* and *Ashton's Memorial.*" *Texas Studies
       in Literature and Language*, 17 (1975), 93-102.

       Uncovers a hitherto ignored source for Defoe's *Four
       Years Voyages*; this source--Philip Ashton's *Memorial*--
       gave Defoe information on the pirate Low which was not
       available elsewhere and suggested to him several inci-
       dents such as the cruelty of quartermaster John Russel.

1122. Seeley, N.J. "Charles Morton." (London) *Times Literary
       Supplement*, 13 February 1969, p. 186.

       Plans an edition of the works of Charles Morton,
       Defoe's teacher. See Garnett, item 1098.

1123. Sill, Geoffrey M. "Defoe's *Tour*: Literary Art or
       Moral Imperative?" *Eighteenth-Century Studies*, 11
       (1977), 79-83.

       Evaluates the interpretations of Defoe's *Tour* by Pat
       Rogers (see his article at item 1117) and by G.D.H.
       Cole (see his two introductions, items 1083 and 1084).
       Although Rogers' emphasis on the literary qualities of
       the *Tour* provides useful insights into it, Cole's view
       of the work as a celebration of preindustrial England
       is more fundamentally sound. The *Tour* "is a moral im-
       perative pointing the way toward England's industrializa-
       tion."

*   Singer, Helmut. *Daniel Defoe: A Tour Through England
       and Wales. Eine kulturgeschichtliche Studie.* (See
       item 1396.)

1124. Thomas, Gilbert. "Defoe's England." *Contemporary
       Review*, 136 (1929), 211-19.

Uses G.D.H. Cole's just-issued edition of *A Tour
Through England and Wales*, two-thirds of Defoe's *Tour*,
to precipitate a discussion of Defoe's skills as a
travel writer. Defoe emerges from these pages as the
first great apologist for the middle class whose chief
interest was in trade (so much so that he laments the
lack of lead mines and coal pits in the Lake district).

1125. Witcutt, W.P. "Defoe's England." *English Review*, 60
       (1935), 69-76.

       Paints a portrait of England as seen through Defoe's
       eyes in his *Tour*. Defoe's England displayed vast trade
       and manufacturing centers, independent miners, and all
       sorts of diversions, both intellectual and physical.

                            E. Letters

1126. Backscheider, Paula R. "John Russell to Daniel Defoe:
       Fifteen Unpublished Letters from Scotland." *Philo-
       logical Quarterly*, 61 (1982), 161-77.

       Prints the transcriptions of fifteen letters from the
       copybook of John Russell held by the National Library
       of Scotland. These letters, sent to Defoe between
       1710 and 1712, are the first significant additions to
       Healey's definitive 1955 edition of Defoe's letters
       (see item 90).

*   Dottin, Paul. "La Correspondance de De Foe." (See
       item 1248.)

1127. Greene, Dorothy. "Daniel Defoe's Letters." *Notes and
       Queries*, 187 (1944), 109.

       Refers to a letter by Defoe, published in *The Daily
       Post* on February 8, 1723, on rendering the River Don
       navigable.

1128. Healey, George H. "Defoe's Letters." *Notes and Queries*,
       187 (1944), 35.

       Requests information on Defoe letters for the edition
       (see item 90) he is preparing.

1129. ————. "Defoe's Letters." (London) *Times Literary
       Supplement*, 29 July 1944, p. 367.

Asks for information on any existing Defoe letters
for an edition in preparation (see items 90 and 1128).

1130. Rogers, J.P.W. "Two Unrecorded Letters by Daniel
       Defoe." *Papers on Language and Literature*, 7 (1971),
       298-99.

       Prints two brief Defoe notes--probably to Charles
       Delafaye--discovered in the Public Record Office and
       not contained in Healey's *Letters of Daniel Defoe*
       (item 90).

1131. Shipley, John B. "Daniel Defoe and Henry Baker: Some
       of Their Correspondence Again and Its Provenance."
       Bodleian Library Record, 7 (1967), 317-29.

       Reproduces a tracing found in the Bodleian Library
       of Defoe's last letter, that of August 12, 1730, to
       his son-in-law, Henry Baker. Shipley compares this
       tracing with a Rylands Library transcript and four pub-
       lished versions of the letter, concluding that the
       tracing is the most accurate. A history is given of
       both the Bodleian and Rylands letters.

1132. V., Q. ["Defoe's Letters."] *Notes and Queries*, 6
       (1900), 337.

       Notes the publication of some of Defoe's letters in
       the Historical MSS Commission's recent issue of the
       Duke of Portland's papers.

                              F. Verse

1133. A., N.M. "Defoe: The Devil's Chapel." *Notes and
       Queries*, Tenth Series, 9 (1908), 187.

       Uncovers sources for the rhyme, "Wherever God erects
       a house of prayer / The devil always builds a chapel
       there," which is attributed to Defoe. See Apperson,
       item 1134; Bayne, item 1135; McKerrow, item 1149;
       Bensly, item 1136; Hayward, item 1143; and Lloyd, item
       1146.

1134. Apperson, G.L. ["Defoe: the Devil's Chapel."] *Notes
       and Queries*, Tenth Series, 9 (1908), 255.

       Discovers several sources for the aphorism contained
       in Defoe's verse: "Wherever God erects a house of prayer /

The devil always builds a chapel there." Also see
N.M.A., item 1133; Bayne, item 1135; McKerrow, item
1149; Bensly, item 1136; Hayward, item 1143; and
Lloyd, item 1146.

1135. Bayne, Thomas. "Defoe: the Devil's Chapel." *Notes
       and Queries*, Tenth Series, 9 (1908), 255.

       Adds to N.M.A., item 1133, further sources for the
       saying that the devil always builds a chapel wherever
       God builds a house of prayer. Also see Apperson,
       item 1134; McKerrow, item 1149; Bensly, item 1136;
       Hayward, item 1143; and Lloyd, item 1146.

1136. Bensly, Edward. "Lines of Defoe." *Notes and Queries*,
       148 (1925), 301-02.

       Replies to Hayward, item 1143, by citing William Drum-
       mond of Hawthornden and George Herbert; also adds some
       prose sources for Defoe's "Wherever God erects a house
       of prayer / The devil always builds a chapel there."
       Also see Lloyd, item 1146; N.M.A., item 1133; Apperson,
       item 1134; Bayne, item 1135; and McKerrow, item 1149.

*   Burch, Charles E. "The Authorship of *A Scots Poem*
       (1707)." (See item 1165.)

1137. Campbell, Mary E. *Defoe's First Poem*. Bloomington,
       Indiana: Principia Press, 1938.

       Presents a highly detailed historical context for
       Defoe's "A New Discovery of an Old Intreague" (1691);
       reprints the text of the poem; and provides the petition
       of the 117 petitioners as well as the Lord Mayor's
       reply to it. After determining Defoe's purpose in the
       poem--"to establish William on the throne of England
       and discourage the desire for and the belief in the
       return of James"--Campbell conducts a rigorous, section-
       by-section examination of the work, tracking down even
       the most obscure allusions to people and events. She
       finds in this poem, as well as in all of Defoe's later
       writings on the subject, an undeviating defense of
       King William which suggests that Defoe's character is
       sounder and his behavior more consistent than generally
       thought.

       Reviews: R. Putney, *Philological Quarterly*, 19 (1940),
       222; D.N. Raymond, *American Historical Review*, 45
       (1940), 459-60; A.W. Secord, *Modern Language Notes*,
       55 (1940), 314-15; Rudolph Stamm, *English Studies*

(Amsterdam), 24 (1942), 25-27; Mark A. Thompson, *English Historical Review*, 60 (1945), 258-60.

*   "Daniel Defoe." (See item 149.)

*   Dobrée, Bonamy. *English Literature in the Early Eighteenth Century, 1700-1740.* (See item 160.)

*   Ellis, Frank H. "Defoe Disinformation." (See item 1178.)

1138. ————. "Introduction." *Poems on Affairs of State: Augustan Satirical Verse, 1660-1714.* Vol. 6. New Haven: Yale University Press, 1970. Pp. xxvii-xxxv.

Dismisses the charge that Defoe was "a shameless hack" and comments on the "strangeness" of Defoe's verse due to his rejection of conventional poetic diction.

1139. ————. "Notes for an Edition of Defoe's Verse." *Review of English Studies*, 32 (1981), 398-407.

Reproduces photographically the first eighteen lines of a holograph copy of Defoe's *The Vision* discovered by the author among the Nottingham Library's Harley papers. (The entire poem is reproduced typographically.) The holograph manuscript should provide an authoritative basis for future editions of Defoe's verse.

1140. Fairchild, Hoxie Neale. *Religious Trends in English Poetry.* Vol. I. New York: Columbia University Press, 1939.

Regards Defoe's verse--especially *Jure Divino*, *Reformation of Manners*, *The True-Born Englishman*, and *The Storm*--as reflections of the author's Puritan morality "permeated by a latitudinarian philosophy."

1141. Foxon, David F. "Defoe: A Specimen of a Catalog of English Verse, 1701-1750." *Library*, Fifth Series, 20 (1965), 277-97.

Lists editions, issues, and reprints of all of Defoe's verse printed in the British empire, excluding America.

1142. Friday [Henry C. Hutchins]. "*The True-born Englishman* at Yale." *Yale University Library Gazette*, 24 (1950), 132-40.

Presents a context for Defoe's *True-born Englishman*
and compares the first two authorized editions of the
poem.

1143.   Hayward, M.M.   "Lines of Defoe."   *Notes and Queries*,
        148 (1925), 262.

Inquires about a poetic source for Defoe's lines,
"Wherever God erects a house of prayer / The devil
always builds a chapel there."   See the responses by
Bensly, item 1136, and Lloyd, item 1146.   Also see
N.M.A., item 1133; Apperson, item 1134; Bayne, item
1135; and McKerrow, item 1149.

1144.   Healey, George H.   "Introduction" to *The Meditations
        of Daniel Defoe*.   Cummington, Mass.: The Cummington
        Press, 1946.   Pp. v-ix.

Identifies as Defoe's earliest known writings seven
verse meditations taken from a notebook written in
Defoe's hand and printed here for the first time.

1145.   Krapp, Robert M.   "Class Analysis of a Literary Con-
        troversy: Wit and Sense in Seventeenth Century
        English Literature."   *Science and Society*, 10 (1946),
        80-92.

Examines the late seventeenth-century literary war
between the men of sense (generally middle-class) and
the men of wit (generally aristocratic).   The leaders
of the men of sense were Sir Richard Blackmore, Samuel
Wesley, and Daniel Defoe.   The latter's *Pacificator*
speaks for the middle class and helped turn literature
away from the "airy sophistication" of aristocratic
taste.

1146.   Lloyd, Bertram.   "Lines of Defoe."   *Notes and Queries*,
        148 (1925), 353.

Responds to Hayward, item 1143, by citing a version
of Defoe's "Wherever God erects a house a prayer / The
devil always builds a chapel there" in Charles Allen's
epic poem, *Henry VIII* (1638).   Also see Bensly, item
1136; N.M.A., item 1133; Apperson, item 1134; Bayne,
item 1135; and McKerrow, item 1149.

1147.   Macaree, David.   "Daniel Defoe: A Reference Corrected."
        Notes and Queries, 19 (1972), 216-17.

Corrects a reference in Healey (*Letters*, item 90,
footnotes 1 and 5, page 162) to Defoe's "ballad,"

which Healey identifies as "The Vision." The ballad
mentioned, however, is not "The Vision" but another
poem which may or may not be by Defoe. The poem was
part of the controversy over the Union and attacks
Lord Belhaven. See Ellis, item 1178.

1148.   ————. "The Flyting of Daniel Defoe and Lord Bel-
        haven." *Studies in Scottish Literature*, 13 (1978),
        72-80.

        Traces the exchanges in doggerel verse between Defoe
        and John Hamilton, Lord Belhaven, during the last two
        months of 1706 following the latter's November 2 speech
        against the Union in the Scottish Parliament.

1149.   McKerrow, R.B. ["Defoe: The Devil's Chapel."] *Notes
        and Queries*, Tenth Series, 9 (1908), 255.

        Offers early sources for the saying, used by Defoe,
        that where God builds a church, the devil erects a
        chapel. Also see N.M.A., item 1133; Apperson, item
        1134; Bayne, item 1135; Bensly, item 1136; Hayward,
        1143; and Lloyd, item 1146.

1150.   McVeagh, John. "Rochester and Defoe: A Study in Influ-
        ence." *Studies in English Literature*, 14 (1974),
        327-41.

        Traces the influence of Rochester on Defoe. Because
        of Defoe's Puritanism, it is surprising that he would
        admire a licentious, irreligious rake like Rochester,
        but he did, and his works abound with positive references
        both to the man and his poetry. Rochester's influence
        is seen on Defoe's *Jure Divino* and in Defoe's view--in
        the novels and elsewhere--of man's fundamental in-
        security in nature and society.

1151.   Moore, John Robert. "Defoe's 'New Discovery' and
        'Pacificator.'" *Notes and Queries*, 196 (1951), 85.

        Points out (for Wilkinson, item 1157) that Defoe's
        "New Discovery" is available in the Campbell edition,
        Defoe's First Poem, item 1137. Also provides biblio-
        graphical information on Gildon's attack on Defoe,
        Dottin's edition of it, and Dottin's books on Defoe.

1152.   Peterson, Spiro. "Daniel Defoe's 'Abdy, Harvy' in 'A
        New Discovery of An Old Intreague.'" *Note and Queries*,
        197 (1952), 232-34.

Attempts to unravel the meaning of the baffling
phrase "horrid cryes for Abdy, Harvy" in Defoe's
satiric verse, "A New Discovery." An etymological
reconstruction leads the author to believe that "Abdy,
Harvy" means "abdicate by force," a meaning which adds
considerable satiric power to the verse. See Rickwood,
item 1154, and Steer, item 1156.

1153. ————. "Defoe's Yorkshire Quarrel." *Huntington
       Library Quarterly*, 19 (1955), 57-79.

Analyzes the differences between George Plaxton, a
Tory clergyman, and William Lowther, a Whig member of
Parliament and justice of the peace, in order to explain
a verse satire against Plaxton by Defoe. This work was
included as part of a letter written by George Standi-
land which was discovered in the Huntington. The
letter, two sets of verse by Plaxton, and Defoe's
verse are printed here for the first time.

*   ————. "A Sonnet not Defoe's." (See item 1194.)

1154. Rickwood, G.O. "Defoe's 'New Discovery of an Old In-
       treague.'" (Although the compiler did review this
       article personally, he misplaced the bibliographical
       data and was unable to retrieve it prior to the pub-
       lication of this bibliography.)

Supports Steer's claim as to the meaning of the words
"Abdy, Harvy" in Defoe's "A New Discovery" (see item
1156) against Peterson's "etymological reconstruction"
which finds the words a rendition of a Latin phrase
meaning to "abdicate by force" (see item 1152).

1155. Rosenberg, Albert. "Defoe's *Pacificator* Reconsidered."
       Philological Quarterly, 37 (1958), 433-39.

Laments the widespread misunderstanding of Defoe's
Pacificator and attempts to correct it through a
chronological consideration of the poem's battles between the Men of Sense and the Men of Wit. Defoe
argues for a judicious combination of wit and sense.
Also see Krapp, item 1145, and Wilkinson, item 1157.

*   Schonhorn, Manuel. "Defoe: The Literature of Politics
       and the Politics of Some Fictions." (See item 320.)

1156. Steer, Francis W. "Daniel Defoe's 'Abdy, Harvy' in
       'A New Discovery of an Old Intreague.'" *Notes and
       Queries*, 197 (1952), 305.

Disagrees with Spiro Peterson's "ingenious interpretation" of "Abdy, Harvy" in Defoe's "A New Discovery" (see
item 1152). Actually the two words are family names for
two political figures, Sir Robert Abdy and William
Harvy, whom the Tories wanted in office in place of the
Whigs. Also see Rickwood, item 1154.

*   Sutherland, James R. *Daniel Defoe: A Critical Study*.
          (See item 349.)

*   Sypher, Wylie. *Guinea's Captive Kings: British Anti-
          Slavery Literature of the XVIIIth Century*. (See
          item 359.)

1157.   Wilkinson, Andrew M. "Defoe's 'New Discovery' and 'Pac-
          ificator.'" *Notes and Queries*, 195 (1950), 496-98.

Finds that Defoe's later biographers have not read or
not read carefully Defoe's two poems the "New Discovery"
and the "Pacificator," relying instead upon Lee's statements (*Daniel Defoe*, 1869) about them. The first of
these poems is not about the Jacobite plot of 1690-91
involving Lord Preston and John Ashton but about the
1690 petition by 117 members of the Common Council of
the City of London concerning their rights in appoint-
ments and elections to public office. The "Pacificator"
is not, as Lee and others state, about an imaginary war
between Men of Sense and Men of Wit but rather is on
the very real Jeremy Collier stage controversy. See
Moore, same title, item 1151.

*   Wilkinson, Andrew M. "*Good Advice to the Ladies*: A
          Note on Daniel Defoe." (See item 1209.)

1158.   ————. "The 'Meditations' of Daniel Defoe." *Modern
          Language Review*, 46 (1951), 349-54.

Assesses Defoe's youthful religious views as they
appear in his *Meditations*. He was a Presbyterian
influenced by Richard Baxter to reject the doctrine
of predestination.

VI

DISCUSSIONS OF THE CANON

1159. Baine, Rodney M. "Daniel Defoe and Captain Carleton's *Memoirs of an English Officer.*" *Texas Studies in Literature and Language*, 13 (1972), 613-27.

Rejects *The Memoirs of an English Officer* (1728) as a Defoe work in spite of its acceptance by Trent, Hutchins, Dottin, Secord, and Moore. The use of internal evidence to prove the work is Defoe's results in unscholarly, impressionistic argument. A large number of stylistic features and ideas which are unlike Defoe's argues against the work being assigned to him, and there is no evidence to support his authorship. Also see Curtis, item 1043; Hartmann, items 1181 and 1182; Secord, item 1197; and Williams, item 1210.

1160. ————. "Daniel Defoe and Robert Drury's *Journal.*" *Texas Studies in Literature and Language*, 16 (1974), 479-91.

Excludes *Madagascar: or, Robert Drury's Journal* (1729) from the Defoe canon, rejecting the internal evidence cited by Moore and others: "not an iota of external evidence connects Defoe with it." The diestic remarks in the Preface and narrative are further evidence that Defoe had nothing to do with the work. Also see Secord, items 1067 and 1068.

* ————. *Daniel Defoe and the Supernatural.* (See item 109.)

1161. ————. "Daniel Defoe's Imaginary Voyages to the Moon." *Publications of the Modern Language Association*, 81 (1966), 377-80.

Reviews the debate over whether two imaginary voyages to the moon and a letter from the Man in the Moon should

be regarded as original Defoe works or as piracies from
The Consolidator (1705). Baine concludes that *A Journey
to the World in the Moon*; *A Second and more Strange
Voyage to the World in the Moon*; and *A Letter from the
Man in the Moon to the author of the True-born Englishman*, all dated 1705, are plagiarized from *The Consolidator* and therefore must be excluded from the Defoe canon
as independent items. Blaine also suggests that it is
unlikely that Defoe plagiarized from himself and therefore these works probably are piracies.

*   ————. "Defoe and Mrs. Bargrave's Story." (See item
           907.)

1162.   Bastian, F. "Defoe and Guy Miege." *Notes and Queries*,
           n.s. 16 (1969), 103-05.

        Explains why a Defoe piece, *A Complete History of the
        Late Revolution*, has been attributed to Guy Miege. A
        tract, *Utrum Horum?*, written to defend Miege from
        charges of plagiarism, includes the *Complete History*
        in a list of Miege's works, but it appears that *Utrum
        Horum?* itself may be by Defoe. The latter, writing in
        defense of Miege, may have listed the *Complete History*
        as Miege's because Miege provided the documents upon
        which it is based.

1163.   Bond, Clinton S. "*Street-Robberies, Considered* and the
           Canon of Daniel Defoe." *Texas Studies in Literature
           and Language*, 13 (1971), 431-45.

        Challenges the inclusion of *Street-Robberies, Con-
        sidered* (1728) in the Defoe canon. The jocular tone
        and the undermining of the speaker's character through
        cynical levity are unlike Defoe's usual practice. Many
        of the pamphlet's ideas are at odds with Defoe's known
        views during his last decade of life.

1164.   Burch, Charles E. "The Authorship of 'A Letter Concerning
           Trade from Several Scots Gentlemen That Are Merchants
           in London,' Etc. (1796)." *Notes and Queries*, 193
           (1948), 101-03.

        Argues that the journalistic techniques employed and
        the political and economic arguments advanced in *A Let-
        ter Concerning Trade* make it almost certain that the
        pamphlet is by Defoe and is the third of three responses
        to William Black's *A Short View of Our Present Trade and
        Taxes*. Black had challenged Defoe to support his con-

tention that union with England would increase Scotland's trade, and the *Letter Concerning Trade* attempts
to do just that, using techniques and information previously employed by Defoe elsewhere. Also see Burch's
"Defoe's 'Some Reply to Mr. Hodges,'" item 917.

1165. ————. "The Authorship of *A Scots Poem* (1707)."
Philological Quarterly, 22 (1943), 51-57.

Argues for the inclusion of *A Scots Poem*--an anonymously published work of eight hundred lines--in the
Defoe canon. The poem advances arguments for the
union with England which closely resemble those made
elsewhere by Defoe. Moreover, Defoe's earlier panegy-
rics on King William and the Dukes of Argyle and Hamilton are repeated by the poem's author.

1166. ————. "Defoe's First *Seasonable Warning* (1706)."
Review of English Studies, 21 (1945), 322-26.

Warns against confusing *A Seasonable Warning or the
Pope and King of France Unmasked* (1706) with Defoe's
*A Seasonable Warning and Caution against the Insinuations
of Jacobites and Papists in Favor of the Pretender.
Being a Letter from an Englishman at the Court of
Hanover* (1712) but argues that Defoe wrote the earlier
pamphlet as well as the later one. The argument in the
1706 work closely parallels Defoe's arguments on this
subject elsewhere; likewise, the remarks on Scottish
trade are similar to Defoe's views; and, finally, certain autobiographical allusions point to Defoe as author.

* ————. "Defoe's 'Some Reply to Mr. Hodges and Some
Other Authors." (See item 917.)

1167. ————. "'A Discourse Concerning the Union': An Unrecorded Defoe Pamphlet?" *Notes and Queries*, 188
(1945), 244-46.

Attempts to prove that Defoe wrote "A Discourse Concerning the Union," a reply to "A Letter Concerning the
Union, with Sir George Mackenzie's Observations and Sir
John Nisbet's Opinion on the same Subject." The controlling arguments of Defoe's other Union pamphlets are
present in the "Discourse," and it seems that Dugald
Campbell in arguing against two other pamphlets by
Defoe also referred to a third which is likely to be
the "Discourse."

1168.   ———. "An Unassigned Defoe Pamphlet in the Defoe-
         Clark Controversy." *Notes and Queries*, 188 (1945),
         185-87.

         Adduces evidence to show that Defoe was the author
         of "A Reproof to Mr. Clark and a Brief Vindication of
         Mr. Defoe," an unsigned pamphlet in the controversy
         between Defoe and the Rev. James Clark, whom Defoe
         accused of preaching insurrection against the Union of
         Scotland and England. Certain facts are mentioned in
         the pamphlet which only Defoe would know and the pamphlet
         has some striking parallels with "An Answer to a Paper
         Concerning Mr. Defoe Against His History of the Union,"
         which is known to be by Defoe.

1169.   ———. "Wodrow's List of Defoe's Pamphlets on the
         Union." *Modern Philology*, 28 (1930), 99-100.

         Discovers at the National Library of Scotland, Edin-
         burgh, five pamphlets on the Union between England and
         Scotland which Robert Wodrow, a Scotch clergyman and
         contemporary of Defoe, attributed to Defoe and suggests
         that they be admitted to the Defoe canon.

1170.   Callender, Geoffrey. "The Authorship of *The History
         of the* ... *Pirates* (1724)." *Mariner's Mirror*, 26
         (1940), 97-99.

         Praises the worth of the *History of the Pirates*,
         which created the modern conception of piracy, and—on
         the basis of Moore's arguments in *Defoe in the Pillory*
         (item 261)—assigns its authorship to Defoe.

1171.   "Captain Carleton." (London) *Times Literary Supple-
         ment*, 18 April 1929, p. 306.

         Reviews C.H. Hartmann's edition of *Memoirs of Captain
         Carleton*. The reviewer notes the controversy surround-
         ing the authenticity of the work and cites Hartmann's
         contention that the memoirs are authentic and hence not
         the work of Defoe. Also see Secord, item 1197; Hartmann,
         items 1181 and 1182; and Williams, item 1210.

*   Curtis, Laura Ann. "A Letter from a Gentleman at the
         Court of St. Germains." (See item 935.)

*   ———. "The Military Memoirs of Captain George Carle-
         ton." (See item 1043.)

*   ———. "Minutes of the Negotiation of Monsr. Mesnager
         at the Court of England during the Four Last Years

of the Reign of Her Late Majesty Queen Anne." (See
item 1044.)

1172. Downie, J.A. "Ben Overton: An Alternative Author of
A Dialogue betwixt Whig and Tory." *Papers of the
Bibliographical Society of America,* 70 (1976), 263-71.

Proposes on the basis of external and circumstantial
evidence Ben Overton as possible author of *A Dialogue
betwixt Whig and Tory.* Defoe is unlikely to have
written this 1693 tract at a time when he was a bank-
rupt; indeed, he may have been in debtor's prison at
the time the work was written.

1173. ————. "Defoe and *The Advantages of Scotland by an
Incorporate Union with England:* An Attribution Re-
viewed." *Papers of the Bibliographical Society of
America,* 71 (1977), 489-93.

Questions the inclusion of *The Advantages* in the
Defoe canon for several reasons: the author says he is
a Scotsman, Defoe denied authorship, and the style is
unlike Defoe's.

1174. ————. "'Mistakes on all Sides': A New Defoe Manuscript." *Review of English Studies,* 27 (1976),
431-37.

Reprints the text of a two-page manuscript in Defoe's
hand discovered among the Harley papers. This work,
"Mistakes on all Sides, Or, An Enquiry into the Vulgar
Errors of the State," was clearly intended for publication and so must be included in the Defoe canon.

1175. ————. "An Unknown Defoe Broadsheet on the Regulation
of the Press?" *Library,* 33 (1978), 51-58.

Locates among the Harley papers in the British Library
a tract entitled *To the Honourable C————s of England
Assembled in P————t.* The tract is accompanied by a
letter attributing it to Defoe, and this attribution
is supported by internal evidence of style and political
opinion consistent with that of Defoe. The tract, only
one copy of which is known to exist, is here reprinted.

1176. E. "Defoe: 'Royal Gin.'" *Notes and Queries,* Eleventh
Series, 5 (1912), 228.

Asks for information on a purported Defoe piece,
"Royal Gin."

1177.   Ellis, Frank H. "Defoe and *The Master Mercury*." *Notes and Queries*, n.s. 19 (1972), 28-29.

Presents evidence to suggest that Defoe may have been connected with the *Master Mercury*, a periodical which began in August 1704.

1178.   ―――. "Defoe Disinformation." *Notes and Queries*, n.s. 21 (1974), 46-47.

Corrects errors in Macaree's attempt to correct Healey (see item 1147). The most serious of these is Macaree's suggestion that Defoe wrote a ballad, "She Put Her Hand Upon His Scull," when most evidence denies this attribution. Macaree also was inaccurate in a number of small points, including his calling the ballad untitled.

*   Gove, Philip B. "Robert Drury." (See item 1046.)

1179.   Hargevik, Stieg. *The Disputed Assignment of "Memoirs of an English Officer" to Daniel Defoe*. Part 1. Stockholm Studies in English, 30. Stockholm: Almqvist & Wiksell, 1972.

Uses a statistical method of stylistic analysis to argue against Defoe's authorship of *Memoirs of an English Officer*. Hargevik uses word length, sentence length, vocabulary, word frequency, etc., accompanied by extensive tables and appendices, to conclude that this work should be excluded from the Defoe canon. See Part 2 of this study at item 1180. Also see Baine, item 1159; Curtis, item 1043; Hartmann, items 1181 and 1182; Secord, item 1197; and Williams, item 1210.

1180.   ―――. *The Disputed Assignment of "Memoirs of an English Officer" to Daniel Defoe*. Part 2. Stockholm Studies in English, 31. Stockholm: Almqvist & Wiksell, 1974.

Examines the "veracity and authenticity" of the *Memoirs*, concluding that most of the work's information is correct and that Carleton himself was the author. See Part 1 of this study at item 1179. Also see Baine, item 1159; Curtis, item 1043; Hartmann, items 1181 and 1182; Secord, item 1197; and Williams, item 1210.

1181.   Hartmann, Cyril H. "Introduction" to *Memoirs of Captain Carleton*. London: Routledge, 1929. Pp. xi-xxviii.

Revives an old controversy over the authorship of
Captain Carleton. Hartmann believes that Carleton
either wrote the work or collaborated with the author,
who may or may not be Defoe. See the following on this
issue: Hartmann, item 1182; Secord, item 1197; and
Williams, item 1210.

1182. ————. [On the *Memoirs of Captain Carleton*.] (London)
Times Literary Supplement, 19 September 1929, p. 723.

Argues that Carleton must have been the author of the
Memoirs or must have collaborated with the author since
all the facts presented in the work were not available
from other sources. Also see Hartmann, item 1181;
Secord, item 1197; and Williams, item 1210.

* Healey, George H. "Defoe's Handwriting." (See item
958.)

1183. Ivanyi, B.G. "Defoe's Prelude to the *Family Instructor*."
(London) *Times Literary Supplement*, 7 April 1966,
p. 312.

Places a pamphlet, *The Schism Act Explain'd* (1714),
in the Defoe canon. The pamphlet attacks the Schism
Bill for its abridgement of the Dissenters' rights and
its effect on the Dissenter system of education. The
pamphlet's ideas are identical to those expressed in
some of the Defoe's other works such as *Party Politics*
(1712) and the *Brief Survey of 1714*. This circumstantial evidence for Defoe's authorship is supplemented
by the author's statement that he intends to speak out
on the subject of family instruction "on another occa-
sion"; Defoe's *Family Instructor* was published in March
1715, only a few months after the appearance of *The
Schism Act Explain'd*. Also see Rothman, "Defoe's *The
Family Instructor*," item 1014.

1184. Kennedy, Joyce Deveau. "The Case for Defoe's Authorship of the *Consolidator* Pamphlets." *Huntington
Library Quarterly*, 39 (1975), 77-89.

Questions some of Rodney Baine's findings (see item
1161), specifically arguing that Defoe himself and not
literary pirates republished selections from the *Consolidator* and that these pamphlets should be treated
apart from the *Consolidator* as separate bibliographical
entities.

*   Macaree, David. "Daniel Defoe: A Reference Corrected."
            (See item 1147.)

1185.   Main, Charles F. "Defoe, Swift, and Captain Tom."
            Harvard Library Bulletin, 11 (1957), 71-79.

    Examines Defoe's claim to six works of 1710-1711: *A
    Letter from Captain Tom to the Mobb*; *Captain Tom's
    Ballad*; *The Capt. of the Mobs Declaration*; *A Rod for
    a Fools Back, in a Letter from Captain Tom, to the
    Minister of Covent Garden*; *Dialogue Between Captain
    Tom and Sir H---y D---n C---t*; and *Captain Tom's Re-
    membrance*. The first four of these Captain Tom papers
    were written by Defoe; the *Remembrance* probably is
    Defoe's; but Swift is the more likely author of the
    Dialogue. The thread that runs through Defoe's Captain
    Tom papers is that the mob is the traditional safeguard
    of English freedom.

1186.   Matthews, Albert. "Defoe and Woodward." *Nation*, 85
            (1907), 140.

    Demonstrates that Josiah Woodward did not write the
    Account of the Societies for the Reformation of Manners
    as W.P. Trent indicated in his "Bibliographical Notes
    on Defoe. II" (item 1203) and suggests that if Wood-
    ward did not write the tract, perhaps Defoe did. See
    Trent's reply, item 1205.

1187.   Meier, T.K. "Defoe and Rivington." *Notes and Queries*,
            n.s. 15 (1968), 145.

    Seeks information on Defoe's relationship with Charles
    Rivington, who published four of Defoe's works, in
    order to ascertain if Defoe really wrote the pamphlet,
    An Humble Proposal (1729).

1188.   Moore, John Robert. "The Canon of Defoe's Writings."
            Library, Fifth Series, 11 (1956), 155-69. Republished
            as a pamphlet--London: Oxford University Press, 1956.

    Notes the difficulties--due to Defoe's writing methods
    and his habit of publishing anonymously or pseudony-
    mously--in assigning works to the Defoe canon and
    points out some of the more egregious errors in such
    attributions. Moore lists four "special approaches"
    to assessing Defoe's authorship: (1) tracts which are
    hard to read or printed sloppily are usually not Defoe's
    because he was sensitive to readers' needs; (2) detailed
    knowledge about Defoe's relations with his publishers

helps to identify and date Defoe's works; (3) an awareness of historical backgrounds of writings assigned to
Defoe can provide evidence for excluding them from the
canon; and (4) Defoe frequently repeated favorite quota-
tions, ideas, and situations--recognizing them can help
identify his work.

*   ————. *Defoe in the Pillory and Other Studies.* (See
item 261.)

*   ————. "Defoe's Persona as Author: *The Quaker's Sermon.*" (See item 984.)

*   ————. "Defoe's 'Queries upon the Foregoing Act': A
Defense of Civil Liberty in South Carolina." (See
item 986.)

1189.   ————. "Evidence for Defoe's Authorship of *The Memoirs
of Captain Carleton.*" *Modern Language Notes*, 55
(1940), 430-31.

Cites an anecdote used twice in Defoe's *Tour thro' the
Whole Island of Great Britain* and repeated in *Captain
Carleton* to support Defoe's authorship of the latter.

1190.   Item deleted.

1191.   Morgan, William T. *A Bibliography of British History,
1700-1715.* 2 Vols. Bloomington: Indiana University
Press, 1937.

Assigns several of the "Captain Tom" pamphlets of
1710-1711 to Defoe. Also see Main, item 1185.

1192.   Novak, Maximillian E. "Defoe's Authorship of *A Collection of Dying Speeches* (1718)." *Philological Quarterly*, 61 (1982), 92-97.

Assigns *A Collection of Dying Speeches* to the Defoe
canon on the basis of the work's publication by William
Boreham, who published several other Defoe pieces in
1718; on stylistic mannerisms associated with Defoe,
such as paragraph beginnings and certain word combina-
tions; and on the compatibility of the ideas with those
Defoe expressed elsewhere.

1193.   ————. "*Two Arguments Never Brought Yet*: An Addition
to the Defoe Canon." *Notes and Queries*, n.s. 22
(1975), 345-47.

Presents evidence (style and subject matter) for in-
cluding in the Defoe canon a pamphlet, *Two Arguments
Never brought yet; Which Are a Full Answer to Some
Speeches, Said to be made in the House of Commons,
Against Continuing the Present Establishment of the
Army* ... (1718). The work defends the idea of a small
standing army against three speeches made in Commons
by William Shippen, Edward Jefferies, and Sir Thomas
Hanmer.

1194.   Peterson, Spiro. "A Sonnet not Defoe's." *Notes and
            Queries*, 202 (1957), 208-10.

Denies that Defoe wrote "Upon one who was bribed
while he was at Prayers in the Chapel, to vote contrary
to his Promise," a sonnet attributed to him by Lee
(*Daniel Defoe*, 1869). The extreme Tory politics of the
poem are not likely to be Defoe's even if he was at
times masquerading as a Tory. Other evidence supports
George Coningsby as the true author.

*   Purves, William L. "Authorship of *Robinson Crusoe*."
            (See item 640.)

1195.   Rogers, J.P.W. "Defoe and *The Immorality of the Priest-
            hood* (1715): An Attribution Reviewed." *Papers of
            the Bibliographical Society of America*, 67 (1973),
            245-53.

Claims that John Oldmixon, not Defoe, wrote *The Immorality of the Priesthood*. Internal evidence (allusions, method of argument, style, etc.) points to Oldmixon's authorship, as does the fact that James Roberts,
for whom Oldmixon wrote other works, published the
tract.

1196.   Rogers, Pat. "The Authorship of *Four Letters to a
            Friend in North Britain* and Other Pamphlets Attributed
            to Robert Walpole." *Bulletin of the Institute of
            Historical Research*, 44 (1971), 229-38.

Presents evidence to show that Defoe did not write
the *Four Letters*, attributed to him by Moore and
others, and that Arthur Maynwaring is a more likely
candidate. Also see Snyder, item 1199.

*   Schwoerer, Lois G. "Chronology and Authorship of the
            Standing Army Tracts, 1697-1699." (See item 1016.)

1197. Secord, Arthur W. "Captain Carleton." (London) *Times Literary Supplement*, 12 September 1929, p. 704.

Responds to the *Times* review of Hartmann's edition of *Memoirs of Captain Carleton* (see item 1171) by noting that although Captain Carleton did exist, the *Memoirs* is a fiction derived by Defoe from previously published works. The work therefore has no value as a historical source or as a realistic portrait of the Captain himself. Also see Hartmann, items 1181 and 1182; and Williams, item 1210.

* ————. "Defoe and *Robert Drury's Journal*." (See item 1066.)

* ————. *Studies in the Narrative Method of Defoe*. (See item 327.)

* Shugrue, Michael F. "Introduction" to *Selected Poetry and Prose of Daniel Defoe*. (See item 335.)

1198. Smith, G.C. Moore. "An Unrecognized Work of Defoe's?" *Review of English Studies*, 5 (1929), 64-66.

Submits that Defoe wrote *Reasons humbly offered for a Law to enact the Castration of Popish Ecclesiasticks, as the best way to prevent the Growth of Popery in England* (1700). This tract, intended to ironically show the weakening of the Protestant interest on the Continent, has several passages similar to those in Defoe's *The Danger of the Protestant Religion Consider'd* (1701).

1199. Snyder, Henry L. "Daniel Defoe, Arthur Maynwaring, Robert Walpole, and Abel Boyer: Some Considerations of Authorship." *Huntington Library Quarterly*, 33 (1970), 133-54.

Quotes Schoenbaum on the unreliability of internal evidence as proof of authorship and notes that most Defoe attributions are made precisely on these grounds. Much more reliable external evidence shows, for example, that Moore was wrong in attributing Maynwaring's *Four Letters to a Friend in North Britain* (1710) to Defoe. Also see Rogers, "The Authorship of *Four Letters*," item 1196.

1200. ————. "Daniel Defoe, the Duchess of Marlborough, and the *Advice to the Electors of Great Britain*." *Huntington Library Quarterly*, 29 (1965), 53-62.

Reprints several letters--between Harley and Godolphin
and from Halifax to the Duchess of Marlborough--that
pertain to Defoe's release from prison and subsequent
work for the administration. Snyder also reports a
draft of *Advice to the Electors of Great Britain*, usually
attributed to Defoe, in the hand of the Duchess of Marlborough; he concludes from this and from correspondence
between the Duchess and Arthur Maynwaring that the latter two co-authored the pamphlet and that Defoe had no
part in it.

1201.   ————. "The Reports of a Press Spy for Robert Harley."
         Library, Fifth Series, 22 (1967), 326-45.

         Attributes five new items to Defoe.

1202.   Trent, William P. "Bibliographical Notes on Defoe.
         I." *Nation*, 84 (1907), 515-18.

         Analyzes Lee's list of Defoe's writings and disputes
         some of his ascriptions. Identifying Defoe's works is
         made more difficult by the fact that he often wrote
         anonymously on both sides of a question. Also see Trent,
         items 1203 and 1204.

1203.   ————. "Bibliographical Notes on Defoe. II." *Nation*,
         85 (1907), 29-32.

         Assesses the sixty-one tracts assigned to Defoe by
         Crossley over and above the ascriptions made by Lee and
         confirms fifty-two of them as certainly or probably
         Defoe's. Also see Trent, items 1202 and 1204.

1204.   ————. "Bibliographical Notes on Defoe. III."
         Nation, 85 (1907), 180-83.

         Uses Lee's list of Defoe's writings as a basis for
         a final (at this point) bibliography of 289 items more
         or less certainly Defoe's. Also see Trent, items 1202
         and 1203.

1205.   ————. "Defoe and Woodward." *Nation*, 85 (1907),
         140.

         Responds to Matthews (item 1186), accepting his
         correction of Trent's ascription of the *Account of
         the Societies for the Reformation of Manners* to Joseph
         Woodward; Trent, however, is uncertain as to whether
         or not Defoe wrote the tract.

1206. Tucker, Joseph E. "On the Authorship of the *Turkish Spy*: An Etat Présent." *Papers of the Bibliographical Society of America*, 52 (1958), 34-47.

Affirms Defoe's authorship of 63 of the *Turkish Spy* letters and notes that from 1742 on these letters were published in the complete French text but without mention of Defoe.

1207. Warner, G.F. "An Unpublished Political Paper by Daniel Defoe." *English Historical Review*, 22 (1907), 130-43.

Discovers in the British Museum, among the Landsdowne papers, a previously unpublished essay in Defoe's hand and reprints it in full. The work is directed at Harley and offers advice on conduct in public office.

1208. Watt, Ian. "*Considerations upon Corrupt Elections of Members to Serve in Parliament*, 1701: By Anthony Hammond, Not Defoe." *Philological Quarterly*, 31 (1952), 45-53.

Excludes this rare pamphlet, attributed to Defoe by Lee and others, from the Defoe canon on the basis of its political attitudes and style. The work probably is by Anthony Hammond.

1209. Wilkinson, Andrew M. "Good Advice to the Ladies: A Note on Daniel Defoe." *Notes and Queries*, 195 (1950), 273-75.

Discusses and rejects the grounds upon which Dottin, in *La Vie* (item 1258), assigns the poem, "Good Advice to the Ladies," to the Defoe canon. Wilkinson concludes that since Defoe did not deny writing the poem when asked, he may indeed have written it, but his authorship cannot be affirmed on the evidence provided by Dottin.

1210. Williams, Harold. "Captain Carleton." (London) *Times Literary Supplement*, 26 September 1929, pp. 746-47.

Prints four notes written in Williams' personal copy of the *Memoirs of Captain Carleton* which support the theory that Carleton collaborated with Defoe in writing the work. Also see "Captain Carleton," item 1171; Hartmann, items 1181 and 1182; and Secord, item 1197.

*   Williams, Otho Clinton. "Introduction" to *A Vindica-
        tion of the Press* by Daniel Defoe. (See item 1032.)

VII

FOREIGN LANGUAGE MATERIAL

1211. Alekseyev, M.P. *Sibir v Romanye Defo*. Irkutsk, 1928.

1212. Angelino, Paolo. *Il problema etico-religioso nel "Robinson Crusoe."* Torino: L'Erma, 1934.

1213. Arnold, Heinz Ludwig. "Robinson Crusoe: Notizen zu einer Illusion." *Antaios*, 6 (1965), 611-20.

1214. Artizzu, Lucio. "Motivi economici e morali: nei romanzi di Daniel Defoe." *Economia e storia*, 11 (1964), 346-81.

1215. Bantaş, Andrei. [Introduction to] *Robinson Crusoe*. Burcureşti: Editura Tineretului, 1969. Pp. 5-13.

1216. Barth, Dirk. *Prudence im Werke Daniel Defoes*. Europäische Hochschulschriften, ser. XIV: Angelsächsische Sprache und Literatur, 13. Bern: H. Lang; Frankfurt on the Main: P. Lang, 1973.

1217. Beck, Richard. "Höfunder Robinson Crusoes." *Idunn*, 15 (1931), Arg., 4 Hefti, 363-75.

1218. Bellessort, André. "Les romans picaresque de Defoe." *Revue Bleue*, 58 (1920), 442-45.

1219. Béranger, Jean. "Defoe et les forces armées dans la nation." *Hommage à Emile Gasquet (1920-1977)*. Annales de la Faculté des Lettres et Sciences Humaines de Nice, No. 34. Paris: Les Belles Lettres, 1978. Pp. 119-31.

Treats Defoe's defense of a standing army.

Review: *The Scriblerian*, 13 (1981), 78-79.

1220. ———. "Defoe Pamphlétaire, 1716-1720." *Etudes Anglaises*, 14 (1961), 97-106.

1221. ———. "Du nouveau sur Defoe." *Etudes Anglaises*, 18 (1965), 44-52.

1222. ———. *Les Hommes de lettres et la politique en Angleterre de la révolution de 1688 à la mort de George Ier: Essai d'exposé et d'interprétation des attitudes et des idées dans l'action politique de De Foe, Swift, Addison, Steele, Arbuthnot, et Pope.* Vol. I. Etudes anglaises et nord-américaines. Bordeaux: Université de Bordeaux, Faculté des Lettres et Sciences Humaines, 1968.

1223. Bergmeir, F. "Ein Beitrag zur Quellenuntersuchung von Daniel Defoes 'Journal of the Plague Year.'" *Archiv für das Studium der neueren Sprachen*, 114 (1905), 87-91.

1223A. Bignami, Marialuisa. "Defoe e Salgari." *Studi inglesi: Raccolta di saggi e ricerche*. Ed. Agostino Lombardo. Bari: Adriatica, 1978. Pp. 373-83.

1223B. Birkner, Gerd. "Das Utopische in *Robinson Crusoe*." *Literatur in Wissenschaft und Unterricht*, 14 (1981), 73-90.

1224. Birnbaum, Johanna. *Die 'Memoirs' um 1700: eine Studie zur Entwicklung der realistischen Romankunst vor Richardson*. Halle, 1934.

1225. Blass, Armin. *Die Geschichtsauffassung Daniel Defoes*. Heidelberg: Carl Winters, 1931.

       Reviews: H.H. Andersen, *Philological Quarterly*, 11 (1932), 191; A. Brandl, *Archiv für das neueren Sprachs*, 161 (1932), 306; G. Hübener, *Deutsche Literaturzeitung*, 6 (1935), 1512-13; E.G. Jacob, *Anglia Beiblatt*, 43 (1932), 306-09; P. Meissner, *Englische Studien*, 67 (1932), 129-31; Rudolph Stamm, *Literary Supplement*, 18 August 1932, p. 581.

1226. Böker, Uwe. "Sir Walter Ralegh, Daniel Defoe und die Namengebung in Aphra Behns Oroonoko." *Anglia*, 90 (1972), 92-104.

1227. Borinski, Ludwig. *Der englische Roman des 18. Jahrhunderts*. Frankfort: Athenäum, 1968.

1228. ——. *Englischer Gesit in der Geschichte seiner Prosa.* Freiburg, 1951.

1229. Boucé, Paul-Gabriel. "D. Defoe: Bibliographie selective et critique." *Bulletin de la Société d'Etudes Anglo-Américaines des XVII*e *et XVIII*e *Siècles,* 1 (1975), 15-24.

1230. Brandl, Leopold. "Krinke Kesmes und Defoes *Robinson.*" *Neophilologus,* 11 (1925), 28-40.

Discovers sources for *Crusoe* in a 1708 Dutch publication.

1231. ——. "Vordcfoesche Robinsonaden in der Weltliteratur." *Germanisch-romanische Monatsschrift,* 5 (1913), 233-61.

1232. Broich, Ulrich. "Robinsonade und Science Fiction." *Anglia,* 94 (1976), 140-62.

1233. Bruggermann, Fritz. *Utopie und Robinsonade.* Weimar: Duncker, 1914.

1234. Brunner, Horst. "Kinderbuch und Idylle: Rousseau und die Rezeption des *Robinson Crusoe* im 18. Jahrhundert." *Jahrbuch der Jean-Paul-Gesellschaft,* 2 (1967), 85-116.

1235. Buisine, Alain. "Repères, marques, gisements: A propos de la robinsonnade vernienne." *La Revue des Lettres Modernes* (1978), 113-39.

1236. Calvet, J. *Les types universels dans les littératures étrangères.* Paris, 1932.

Includes Crusoe as one of the ten universal characters with which the book deals.

1237. Colaiacomo, Paola. *Biografia del personaggio nei romanzi di Daniel Defoe.* Studi e ricerche--Istituto di litteratura inglese e americana, Università di Roma, 2. Roma: Bulzoni, 1975.

1238. ——. "*Captain Singleton* fra *Robinson Crusoe* e *Moll Flanders.*" *English Miscellany,* 20 (1969), 141-61.

1239. ——, ed. *Interpretazioni di Defoe.* Rome: Savelli, 1977.

1240. Comarnescu, Petru. [Introduction to] *Robinson Crusoe*.
       Bucharest: Minerva, 1971. Pp. v-xlvi.

1241. Item deleted.

1242. Dahl, Erhard. *Die Kürzungen des "Robinson Crusoe" in
       England zwischen 1719 und 1819 vor dem Hintergrund
       des zeitgenossischen Druckgewerbes, Verlagswesens
       und Lesepublikums*. AAF 6. Frankfort: Lang, 1977.

1243. Item deleted.

1244. Degering, Klaus. *Defoes Gesellschaftskonzeption*.
       BAS 5. Amsterdam: Grüner, 1977.

1245. Deneke, Otto. *Robinson Crusoe in Deutschland: Die
       Frühdrucke 1720-1780*. Gottingische Nebenstunden,
       11. Göttingen: Deneke, 1934.

       Review: E. Schröder, *Anzeiger für deutsches Altertum
       und deutsche Literatur*, 54 (1935), 77.

1246. Desvignes, Lucette. "Vues de la terre promise: Les
       Visages de l'Amérique dans *Moll Flanders* et dans
       L'Histoire de Manon Lescaut." *Transactions of the
       Fourth International Congress on the Enlightenment*.
       Ed. Theodore Besterman. *Studies on Voltaire and the
       Eighteenth Century*, 152 (1976), 543-57.

1247. Dibelius, Wilhelm. *Englische Romankunst*. Vol. I.
       Palaestra, 92. Berlin: Mayer und Müller, 1910.

1248. Dottin, Paul. "La Correspondance de De Foe." *Etudes
       Anglaises*, 8 (1955), 330-34.

1249. ————. *Daniel de Foë*. Paris: Perrin, 1925.

       Reviews: S.B. Liljegren, *Anglia Beiblatt*, 36 (1925),
       337-43; H. Ullrich, *Englische Studien*, 60 (1926),
       364-70.

1250. ————. "Daniel De Foe et les sciences occultes."
       Revue Anglo-Américaine, 1 (1923), 102-19.

1251. ————. *Daniel Defoe et ses romans*. 3 Vols. Paris:
       Presses Universitaires; London: Milford, 1924.

       The first volume is a biography of Defoe, the second
       is a study of *Robinson Crusoe*, and the third is a
       survey of the other novels.

Reviews: R.S. Crane, Modern Philology, 23 (1925), 231-32; Louis Cazamian, Revue Anglo-Américaine (1924), 438-40; Oliver Elton, French Quarterly, 7 (1925), 89-92; S.B. Liljegren, Anglia Beiblatt, 35 (1924), 355-64; E. Pons, Revue de l'Enseignement des Langues vivantes, 42 (1925), 220-22; George Saintsbury, Litteris, 1 (1924), 123-26; W.H. Staverman, English Studies, 8 (1926), 189-93; Hermann Ullrich, Englische Studien, 60 (1926), 364-69.

1252. ———. "Daniel De Foe, mystificateur; ou, les faux Mémoires de Mesnager." Revue Germanique, 14 (1923), 269-82.

1253. ———. "De Foe et la France." English Studies, 13 (1931), 69-74.

Says that Defoe took his French geography from journals and gazettes and not from personal experience and observation.

1254. ———. "L'île de Robinson." Mercure de France, 11 (1922), 15.

1255. ———. "Les relations de voyage remaniées par Daniel Defoe." (Hommage à Paul Dottin.) Caliban, No. 3 (Special Issue). Annales publiées trimestriellement par la Faculté des Lettres et Sciences Humaines de Toulouse, N.S. 2, janvier, 1966. Pp. 15-33.

1256. ———. "Le Robinson Suisse." Mercure de France, 13 (1924), 114-26.

1257. ———. "Les sources de la Roxana de Daniel de Foë." Revue Anglo-Américaine, 4 (1927), 531-34.

1258. ———. La vie et aventures de Daniel De Foe, auteur de Robinson Crusoe. Paris: Perrin, 1925. Translated by Louise Ragan as The Life and Strange and Surprising Adventures of Daniel De Foe, item 164. Condenses the first volume of Daniel De Foe et ses romans, item 1251.

Reviews: Camille Cé, Revue de l'Enseignement des Langues Vivantes, 43 (1926), 166-67; H. Servajean, Revue Anglo-Américaine, 3 (1926), 256-57.

1259. Ducrocq, Jean. "Des littératures populistes à Defoe." Roman et société en Angleterre au XVIIIe siècle.

Eds. Jean Ducrocq, Suzy Halimi, and Maurice Lévy.
Paris: Presses Univ. Pp. 45-58.

1260. ———. "*Moll Flanders* (1722)." *Roman et société en
Angleterre au XVIIIe siècle.* Eds. Jean Ducrocq, Suzy
Halimi, and Maurice Lévy. Paris: Presses Univ.
Pp. 59-66.

1261. Item deleted.

1262. Dupas, Jean-Claude. "Defoe en Écosse voyageur et
voyeur." *Regards sur l'Écosse au XVIIIe Siècle.*
Ed. Michèle S. Plaisant. Centre de Recherches sur
le XVIIIe siècle britannique 4. Lille: Université
de Lille, 1977. Pp. 41-61.

1263. ———. "Defoe et le récit de la mort: *The Apparition
of Mrs. Veal.*" *La Mort, le fantastique, et la sur-
naturel du XVIe siècle à l'époque romantique.* Ed.
Michèle Plaisant. Lille III, 1980. Pp. 61-66.

Presents a Freudian view of the work.

1264. ———. "La Passion de l'or chez Defoe." *La Passion
dans le monde anglo-américain aux XVIIe et XVIIIe
siècles.* Bordeaux, III, 1979. Pp. 61-71.

Offers a Marxist interpretation of the role of gold
in *Colonel Jack.*

1265. Du Sorbier, Françoise. "De la potence à la biographie,
ou les avatars du criminel et de son image en Angleterre (1680-1740)." *Etudes Anglaises*, 32 (1979),
257-71.

1266. Ehnmark, Elof. *Konsten att ljuga och konsten att tala
sanning. Om Daniel Defoe och Robinson Crusoe.*
Stockholm: Sveriges Radio, 1972.

1267. Einhoff, Eberhard. *Emanzipatorische Aspekte im Frauen-
bild von "The Review," "The Spectator," und "The
Female Spectator."* Frankfort: Lang, 1980.

1268. Elissa-Rhais, Roland. "Une influence anglaise dans
Manon Lescaut, ou une source du réalisme." *Revue
de Littérature Comparée*, 7 (1927), 619-49.

Views *Moll Flanders* as a direct influence on *Manon
Lescaut.*

1269. Elistratova, A.A. *Shchastlivaya Kurtizanka, ili Roksana.* Moscow: Nauka, 1975.

1270. Fallenbühl, Zoltán. "Dobai Székely Sámuel, a *Robinson Crusoe* elsö ismert magyar olvasója." *Magyar Könyvszemle Könyvtörténeti Folyóirat/Revue pour l'Histoire du Livre*, 92 (1977), 128-33.

Treats *Robinson Crusoe* in Hungary.

1271. Fischer, Walther. "Defoe und Milton." *Englische Studien*, 58 (1924), 213-27.

1272. Flasdieck, H.M. "Robinson Crusoe in Lichte der neueren Forschung." *Deutsche Rundschau*, 214 (1928), 47-61.

1273. ———. "Zur Abwehr." *Germanisch-romanische Monatsschrift*, 18 (1930), 484-85.

1274. Földényi, László F.A. "A magabiztos meghasonlottság regénye Defoe 'Moll Flanders'--e; a történelem és a regény iróniája." *Világosság*, 16 (1975), 415-21.

1275. Frosini, Vittorio. "Il vangelo di Robinson." *Il Mondo*, 12 (1960), 9-10.

1276. Füger, Wilhelm. "Der betrunkene Pfeifer: Ein Beitrag zur Quellenkunde und Erzählmode von Defoes *Journal of the Plague Year*." *Archiv für das Studium der neueren Sprachen*, 202 (1965), 28-36.

1277. ———. "Courtiliz de Sandras, der franzosische Defoe. Zur Geschichte des franzosischen Romans im der Wende zum 18. Jahrhundert." *Neueren Sprachen*, 8 (1963), 407-16.

1278. ———. *Die Entstehung des historischen Romans aus der fiktiven Biographie in Frankreich und England; unter besonderer Berücksichtigung von Courtiliz de Sandras und Daniel Defoe.* München: Wilhelm Füger, 1965.

Reproduces the typescript of Füger's 1963 dissertation.

1279. Fusini, Nadia. "Da Calibano in poi: Per un'analisi del romanzesco." *Calibano*, 1 (1977), 37-64.

1280. Galino, M. Angeles. "El Robinsón que vió Iriarte." *Libro Español*, 1 (1958), 564-66.

1281. Gasquet, Emile. "*Roxana* de Defoe: Tensions et rup-
       tures." *Hommage à Emile Gasquet (1920-1977)*.
       Annales de la Faculté des lettres et Sciences
       Humaines de Nice, No. 34. Paris: Les Belles Let-
       tres, 1978. Pp. 221-28.

       Review: Guy Laprevotte, *Scriblerian*, 13 (1981), 79.

1282. Gerber, Richard. "Zur Namengebung bei Defoe." *Fest-
       schrift für Walter Hübner*. Eds. Dieter Riesner and
       Helmut Gneuss. Berlin: Schmidt, 1964. Pp. 227-33.

1283. Item deleted.

1284. Goetsch, Paul. "Defoes *Moll Flanders* und der Leser."
       Germanisch-romanische Monatsschrift, 30 (1980),
       271-88.

1284A. Gondebeaud, Louis. "Le Roman anglais (1700-1739):
       Suggestions pour une étude de son public." *Etudes
       Anglaises*, 34 (1981), 399-412.

1285. ————. *Le Roman "picaresque" anglais, 1650-1730*.
       Atelier de Reproduction des Thèses: Lille III.
       Paris: Honoré Champion, 1979.

       Defines *Moll Flanders* as picaresque but excludes
       Roxana, *Captain Singleton*, and *Colonel Jack* from his
       list of picaresque tales. Defoe's use of the pseudo-
       autobiography and his focus on the moral decline of
       his criminal protagonists are significant additions to
       the picaresque form.

1285A. Grossi, Marina. "*Moll Flanders* e il viaggio della
       conoscenza tra libertà e necessità." *Acme*, 33
       (1980), 407-25.

1286. Gückel, W., and E. Günther. *D. Defoes und J. Swifts
       Belesenheit und literarische Kritik*. Leipzig: Meyer
       und Muller, 1925.

       Reviews: Hermann M. Flasdieck, *Englische Studien*, 63
       (1928), 120-22; G. Hübener, *Dt. Litztg.*, N.F., 3
       (1926), 2142-44; S.B. Liljegren, *Anglia Beiblatt*,
       37 (1925), 134-35; A. Ludwig, *D. Literatur*, 28
       (1926), 556; C.S. Northrup, *Journal of English and
       Germanic Philology*, 29 (1930), 451-52.

1287. Gugliemelli, Amedeo. *Daniel De Foe*. Rovigo, Italy,
       1954.

1288. Gunther, Max. *Entstehungsgeschichte von Defoes Robinson Crusoe*. Greifswald: Abel, 1909.

Review: *Literaturblatt für germanische und romanische philologie*, 33 (1912), 105-13.

1289. Haster, Elsbeth. *Studien zur Entwicklung des realistischen Romans in England zu Anfang des 18. Jahrhunderts*. Glessen, 1943.

1290. Heckwitz, Erhard. *Die Robinsonade: Themen und Formen einer literarischen Gattung*. Amsterdam: B.R. Grüner, 1976.

Contains a lengthy section (pp. 29-114) on *Robinson Crusoe* as the Robinsonade model.

Review: Klaus Degering, *Scriblerian*, 13 (1981), 80.

1291. Heidenreich, Helmut. "Der spanische *Robinson Crusoe*." *Die neueren Sprachen*, 69 (1970), 261-71.

1292. Herting, [no first name available]. "Die Idioten- und Geistekrankenfürsorge des Robinson dichters Defoe." *Zeitschrift für Kinderforschung*, 38 (1931), [no pagination available].

Listed in this incomplete manner in the *New Cambridge Bibliography of English Literature*, col. 911.

1293. Hess, G. "La peste di Londra." *Letteratura* (Fierenza) A. no. 2 (1940), 155.

1294. Hieber, Hermann. *Bücher haben ihre Schicksale*. Stuttgart, 1959.

1294A. Higuchi, Kinzo. "Robinson Crusoe: Aru kaishaku no Kokoromi." *Eikoku Shosetsu Kenkyu Dai 13 satsu*. Tokyo: Shinozaki, 1981. Pp. 1-21.

1295. Hirn, Yrjö. *Ön i världshavet*. Helsingfors, 1928.

Analyzes *Robinson Crusoe* and the English and European criticism of it.

Review: *Literaturblatt für germanische und romanische Philologie*, 50 (1929), 9-10.

1296. Hortelano, Pastor. "'Robinson Crusoe' y España." *Vallodolid: ES*, 3 (1973), 149-62.

1297. Horten, Franz. *Studien über die Sprache Defoes.*
       Bonn, 1914.

1298. Hübener, Gustav. "Der Kaufmann Robinson Crusoe."
       Englische Studien, 54 (1920), 367-98.

       Applies the economic theories of Max Weber to Defoe's
       works. Also see Liljegren, item 1331, and Ullrich,
       item 1421.

1299. ————. "Zu Ullrichs Aufsatz 'Zum Robinson-Problem.'"
       Englische Studien, 57 (1923), 316-18.

1300. Huebner, Walter. "Die Weltbücher von Robinson und
       Gulliver und ihre geistesgeschichtliche Bedeutung."
       Neuphilologische Zeitschrift, 1, ii (1949), 33-46;
       iii (1949), 8-32.

*   Hurlimann, Bettina. "Robinson." (See item 566.)

1301. Iser, Wolfgang. *Der implizite Leser.* Munich: Wilhelm
       Fink, 1972.

1302. Isernhagen, Hartwig. "Vermittlungsmodell und thema-
       tische Struktur: Zu *Robinson Crusoe* und *Humphry
       Clinker.*" *Deutsche Vierteljahrsschrift für Literatur-
       wissenschaft und Geistesgeschichte*, 51 (1977), 181-
       207.

       Blends reader-response criticism, structuralism, and
       hermeneutics in a reply to Iser's views of *Robinson
       Crusoe* (see item 1301).

       Review: Klaus Degering, *The Scriblerian*, 13 (1981), 80.

1303. Izzo, Carlo. "Su Daniel De Foe." *Letteratura Moderne*,
       5 (1957), 542-61.

1304. Jacob, Ernst Gerhard. [Book Reviews.] *Deutsche Litera-
       turzeitung.* Juli 1950 und Dezember 1951, n.p.

       Reviews books published on Defoe between 1947 and 1950.

1305. ————. "Daniel Defoe als Sozialreformer." *Leuvense
       Bijdragen*, 40 (1950), 53-62.

1306. ————. *Daniel Defoe, Essay on Projects (1697): eine
       wirtschafts- und sozialgeschichtliche Studie.* Leipzig:
       Bernhard Tauchnitz, 1929.

       Discusses the various projects and their sources.

Reviews: Hans H. Andersen, *Modern Philology*, 29 (1931), 250-51; Paul Dottin, *Revue Anglo-Américaine*, 7 (1930), 343-44; E.L., *Revue d'Histoire Economique et Sociale*, 18 (1930), 529-30; *Philological Quarterly*, 9 (1930), 187; A.W. Secord, *Modern Language Notes*, 45 (1930), 479-80; (London) *Times Literary Supplement*, 3 July 1930, p. 555; A.C.E. Vechtman-Veth, *English Studies*, 12 (1930), 198-99.

1307. ———. "Daniel Defoe im Lichte der neueren Forschung." *English Studies*, 13 (1931), 58-68.

1308. ———. "Daniel Defoe, *Robinson Crusoe*." (Neubearbeitet mit einem Nachwort nach dem neuesten Stand der Forschung.) Leipzig, 1950.

1309. ———. "Daniel Defoe und die neuere forschung." *Die englische Sprache*, 1 (1948), Heft 2, 34-39.

Reviews twenty years of Defoe scholarship.

1310. ———. "Defoe als Kolonialpolitiker." *Uebersee- und Kolonialzeitung*, 43 (1931), n.p.

1311. ———. "Defoe und Robinson." *Archiv für das Studium der neueren Sprachen*, 186 (1949), 49-64.

1312. ———. *De Foe's Projekts, Ein Beitrag zur Characteristik De Foe's und seiner Zeit*. Leipzig, 1921.

1313. ———. "Der englische Robinsondichter in seiner medizingeschichtlichen Bedeutung." *Aktuelle Probleme aus der Geschichte der Medizin*. Ed. R. Blaser and H. Buess. Basel: S. Karger, 1966. Pp. 550-53.

Notes Defoe's interest in the treatment of insanity and presents a general study of *Journal of the Plague Year*.

1314. ———. "Der ewig junge Robinson." *Denkendes Volk*, 3 (1949), 161.

1315. ———. "Der gegenwärtige Stand der internationalen Defoe-Forschung." *Wissenschaftliche Zeitschrift der Karl-Marx-Universität Leipzig* (Gesellschafts- und Sprachwiss. Reihe Heft 5), 4 (1954-55), 517-26.

1316. ———. "Die medizingeschichtliche Bedeutung des Robinsondichters Daniel Defoe." *Wissenschaftliche*

Zeitschrift der *Karl-Marx Universität Leipzig*
(Mathematisch–Naturwissenschaftliche Reihe Heft 1),
5 (1955–56), 91–97. Reprinted in *Die medizinische
Welt*, 1 (1962), 1–20.

1317. ———. "Parlamentssouveränität und Volkssouveränität
in der Staatslehre Daniel Defoes." *Amt und Volk*, 6
(1932), 139–41. Reprinted in *Zeitschrift für
öffentliches Recht*, 13 (1933), 367–74.

1318. ———. [Postscript to] *Ein Bericht vom Pestjahr* by
Daniel Defoe. Bremen: Schünemann, 1965. Pp. 333–59.

1319. ———. "Das Problem der 'Impersonation' bei Daniel
Defoe." *Forschungen und Fortschritte* (January 1951),
n.p.

1320. ———. "Robinson Crusoe und das Abendland." *Kultur
in die lebenden Freundsprachen*, 1 (September 1949),
277–80.

1321. ———. "Zum 300 jährigen Defoe-Jubiläum (1660–1960):
Sammelbericht über neuere Defoe-Literatur." *Archiv
für das Studium der neueren Sprachen*, 197 (1960),
126–35.

Surveys Defoe scholarship from 1929 through 1960.

1322. Kaarsholm, Preben. "Defoe's 'Robinson Crusoe' og
capitalismens utvikling i England." *Poetik*, 6,
no. 2 (1974), 75–134.

Review: Ralf Pittelkow, *Poetik*, 6, no. 2 (1974), 135–
45.

1323. Kehler, Henning. "Robinson Crusoe." *De Store Romaner*.
Copenhagen: Gyldendal, 1940. Pp. 69–90.

1324. Klotz, Volker. *Die erzählte Stadt: Ein Sujet als
Herausforderung des Romans von Lesage bis Döblin*.
München: Hanser, 1969.

1325. Koszul, André H. "Notes sur le journal de l'année de
la peste de Daniel Defoe." *Bulletin de la faculté
de lettres de Strasbourg* (Fevr.-Mars 1945), 45–55.

1326. Krajewska, Wanda. "Daniel Defoe, 'The Dyet of Poland.'"
Kwartalnik Neofilologiczny, 12 (1965), 17–30.

Says that although Defoe understood Polish politics, he did not really understand the Polish governmental system.

1327. Kramer, Jürgen. "Fortschrift und Regression: Studien zur 'Dialektik der Aufklärung' in der Literatur." *Germanisch-romanische Monatsschrift*, 25 (1975), 350-70.

1328. Kuckuk, Hans-Dietrich. *Die politischen Ideen Daniel Defoes*. Kiel, 1962.

1329. Legouis, Pierre. "Marion Flanders, est-elle une victime de la société?" *Revue de l'Enseignement des Langues Vivantes*, 48 (1931), 289-99.

Takes issue with the position that Moll is the victim of society; rather, society is Moll's victim.

1330. Liebs, Elke. *Die pädagogische Insel: Studien zur Rezeption des "Robinson Crusoe" in deutschen Jugendbearbeitungen*. Stuttgart: Metzler, 1977.

Traces the German versions of *Robinson Crusoe* for children from the eighteenth century to the twentieth.

Review: Rex W. Last, *The Scriblerian*, 13 (1981), 81.

1331. Liljegren, Sten B. "Bemerkung zu Ullrichs Ausführungen." *Englische Studien*, 57 (1923), 315-16.

Also see Hübener, item 1298, and Ullrich, item 1421.

1332. ———. "Defoes Robinson." *Englische Studien*, 56 (1922), 281-86.

1333. Lombardo, Agostino. *Ritratto di Enobarbo*. N.p., 1971. Pp. 68-86.

Noted by Abernethy, item 1.

1334. Luithien, Gerda. *Der Realismus des Robinson Crusoe*. Köln: Heinrich Pöppinghaus, 1938.

1335. Luthi, Albert. *Daniel Defoe und seine Fortsetzungen zu "Robinson Crusoe," "The Farther Adventures" und "Serious Reflections."* Stuttgart: Deutsches Volksblatt, 1920.

1335A. Mackiewicz, Wolfgang. *Providenz und Adaptation in Defoes "Robinson Crusoe": Ein Beitrag zum Problem des pragmatischen Puritanismus*. Frankfurt: Lang, 1981.

1336. Mann, William E. *Robinson Crusoé en France: Etude sur l'influence de cette oeuvre dans la littérature française.* Paris: A. Davy, 1916.

1337. Marion, Denis. *Daniel Defoe.* Paris: Fayard, 1948.

1338. ————. "'Te Deum Laudamus' ou la vie pleine de surprises de Daniel Foe, dit Daniel Defoe." Brussels: Libris, 1943.

1339. Mathesius, V. "Daniel Defoe." *Naše dobe,* 39 (1932), 220-25.

1340. Mauriac, François. "En relisant *Moll Flanders.* Quand le romancier s'anéantit dans un personnage." *Figaro Littéraire,* 20 (1957), 1, 4.

1341. Mildebrath, Berthold W. *Die deutschen "Aventuriers" des achtzehnten Jahrhunderts.* Gräfenhainichen: Schulze, 1907.

   Discusses the relationship between the adventure-romance and the Robinsonade.

   Review: Walther Brecht, *Anzeiger für deutsches Altertum und deutsche Literatur,* 34 (1910), 175.

1342. Mirimsky, I.V. *Stati o klassikach.* Moscow, 1966.

   Treats Defoe's realism.

1343. Miyazaki, Yoshizo. "Hizokunaru Defoe." *Eigo Seinen* [*The Rising Generation*], 122 (1976), 210-12, 281-83, 326-28.

1344. Mohr, Hans-Ulrich. "Texte als funktionale Aquivalente: Mandevilles *Fable of the Bees* und Defoes *Col. Jack.*" *Of Private Vices and Publick Benefits: Beiträge zur englischen Literatur des frühen 18. Jahrhunderts.* AAF 11. Frankfort: Lang, 1979. Pp. 63-106.

1345. Mülhaupt, Frederick. *Das kaufmännische und puritanische Element in den Abenteuerromanen Daniel Defoes.* Freiburg, 1939.

1346. Mummendy, Richard. *Defoe: Robinson Crusoe. Der Ur-Robinson.* Köln, 1947.

1347. Muret, Maurice. "Pedro Serrano, le vrai Robinson Crusoe." *Journal des Débats,* 15 (1908), 595-96.

1348. Navarro-Gonzales, Alberto. *Robinson y Don Quixote*. Madrid: Ateneo, 1962.

1349. Neumeister, Sebastian. "Saint-John Perse et le mythe de Robinson." *Cahiers Saint-John Perse*, 2 (1979), 61-76.

1350. Niehaus, Agnes. *Defoes Einfluss auf Swifts Gulliver. Jahrbuch der philosophischen und naturwissenschaftlichen Fakultät*. Münster, 1920.

1351. Nolting-Hauff, Ilse. "Die betrugerliche Heirat: Realismus und Pikareske in Defoes *Moll Flanders*." *Poetica*, 3 (1970), 409-20.

1352. Nordon, Pierre. "*Robinson Crusoe*: unité et contradictions." *Archives des Lettres Modernes*, 3 (1967), 1-40.

1353. Nourrisson, Paul. *Jean-Jacques Rousseau et Robinson Crusoe*. Paris, 1931.

1354. Oda, Minoru. "Moll's Complacency: Defoe's Use of Comic Structure in *Moll Flanders*." *Studies in English Literature* (Japan), 48 (1971), 31-41.

   Although the article is printed in Japanese, an English abstract appears on pp. 187-89.

1355. Otsuka, Hisao. "Human Type in 'Robinson Crusoe.'" *Jidai* (Japan), No. 8, n.d.

1356. Otten, Kurt. *Der englische Roman von 16. zum 19. Jahrhundert*. Berlin: Erich Schmidt, 1971.

   Devotes a short section to Defoe, focusing on *Robinson Crusoe*.

1357. Papetti, Viola. "Amor sacro e amor profano in alcuni romanzi settecenteschi." *English Miscellany*, 24 (1973-74), 105-27.

1358. Parker, Alexander A. *Los pícaros en la Literatura: La Novela Picaresca en España y Europa (1599-1753)*. Translated by Rodolfo Arévalo Mackry. Madrid: Editorial Gredos, S.A., 1971.

   Published originally in English under the title *Literature and the Delinquent: The Picaresque Novel in Spain and Europe, 1599-1753* (item 791).

1359.   Partamyan, R. "Robinzon v Armyanskoi Literature."
        Literaturnaya Armeniya, 2 (1968), 92-94.

1360.   Petersen, Ulrich Horst. "Om Robinson Crusoe." *Frihed
        og Tabu: Essays*. Copenhagen: Gyldendal, 1971. Pp.
        11-15.

1361.   Pilgrim, Konrad. "Zu Defoes Weltverständnis im 3. Teil
        von *Robinson Crusoe*." *Die neueren Sprachen*, 66
        (1967), 524-34.

1362.   Pilon, Edmond. "Daniel de Foe." *Nouvelle Revue Fran-
        çaise*, 7 (1912), 141-217.

1363.   ————. "Daniel De Foe." *Portraits de Sentiments*.
        Paris, 1913.

1364.   Pire, G. "Jean-Jacques Rousseau et *Robinson Crusoe*."
        Revue de Littérature Comparée, 30 (1956), 479-96.

1365.   Polak, Léon. "Vordefoesche Robinsonaden in den Neider-
        landen." *Germanisch-romanische Monatsschrift*, 6
        (1914), 304-07.

1366.   Pollert, Hubert. *Daniel Defoes Stellung zum englischen
        Kolonialwesen*. Münster, 1928.

        Review: G.C. Moore Smith, *Review of English Studies*, 5
        (1929), 358-59.

1367.   Pompen, Fr. A. "Defoe en zijn bronnen." *Neophilologus*,
        12 (1926), 31-34.

1368.   Praviel, A. "Le père de 'Robinson': Daniel De Foe."
        Correspondant, 25 April 1931, pp. 263-78.

1369.   Praz, Mario. *Studi e svaghi inglesi*. Firenze: Sansoni,
        1937.

        Reprints "Defoe and Cellini" (item 301).

1370.   Prica, Zora. *Daniel Defoes Robinson Crusoe und Robert
        Poltocks Peter Wilkins*. Budapest: Serbische Buch-
        druckerei, 1909.

        Review: *Literaturblatt für germanische und romanische
        Philologie*, 33 (1921), n.p.

1371. Puglisi, Michele. "Herman Melville e Daniel Defoe: Un'accoppiata 'storica' revisitata." *Ponte*, 33 (1977), 931-39.

1372. Raabe, Dieter, ed. *Leben und Abenteuer des echten Robinson Crusoe*. Stuttgart: Schuler-Verl, 1949.

1373. Razi, G.M. *Madagascar dans l'oeuvre de Daniel Defoe*. L'Academie Malgache, 1978.

1374. Item deleted.

1375. Reinhold, Heinz. *Der englische Roman im 18. Jahrhundert: soziologische, geistes- und gattungsgeschichtliche Aspekte*. Stuttgart: Verlag W. Kohlhammer, 1978.
Treats Defoe's fiction as highly biographical.
Review: Heinz J. Vienken, *The Scriblerian*, 13 (1981), 82.

1376. Richard, Elie. "Robinson Crusoe et Daniel de Foe." *Les Nouvelles Littéraires*, 16 March 1940, p. 1.

1377. Ritterbusch, P. *Parlamentssouveränität und Volkssouveränität in du Staats- und Verfassungsrechtslehre Englands, Vornehmlich in der Staatslehre Defoes*. Leipzig, 1929.

1378. Rohmann, Gerd. "Neuere Arbeiten über Daniel Defoe." *Die neueren Sprachen*, 21 (1972), 226-36.

1379. Röhnsch, Martha. *Defoes Stellung zu den religiösen Strömungen seiner Zeit*. Breslau, 1933.
Reviews: Paul Dottin, *Englische Studien*, 69 (1934), 264-66; E.G. Jacob, *Anglia Beiblatt*, 45 (1934), 326-28; Rudolph Stamm, *Literaturblatt für germanische und romanische Philologie*, 57 (1936), 318-21.

1380. Rosenkranz, A. "Kreuznach--die Heimatstadt von Robinson Crusoes Vater?" *Anglia Beiblatt*, 51 (1940), 165-68.

1381. Rosin, Albert. *Lebensversicherung und ihre geistesgeschichtelichen Grundlagen*. Leipzig, 1932.

1382. Rothstein, E. "Daniel Defoe i Severnaya voina." *Voprosy istorii*, 6 (1967), 91-106.

1383. Rovetto, Matteo. "Influence ou coïncidence entre
       Robinson Crusoe de Defoe et l'*île des esclaves* de
       Marivaux." *Belfagor*, 30 (1975), 217-21.

1384. Rümann, Arthur. "Robinson und Robinsonaden in der
       Buchillustration des 18. und 19. Jahrhunderts."
       Philobiblon eine Zeitschrift für Bücherfreunde, 9
       (1936), 9-21.

1385. Sanov, V. "Taina Robinsona Kruzo." *Detskaya Litera-
       tura*, 4 (1969), 36-42.

1386. Sarnetski, D.H. "Daniel Defoe: Robinson Crusoe."
       Kölnische Zeitung (1939), Nos. 439-40.

1387. Schmidt, R. *Der Volkswille als realer Faktor des
       Verfassungsleven und Daniel Defoe.* Berichte über
       die Verhandlungen die Sachs. Akademie des Wissen-
       schaft, 76:1. Leipzig: Hirzel, 1924.

       Review: F. Liebermann, *Anglia Beiblatt*, 36 (1925),
       308-10.

1388. Schneider, Paul, ed. *Erlebte Robinsonaden: abenteuer-
       liche Fahrten und Schicksale aus den Zeiten der
       Entdeckungsreisen, nach Originalberichten.* Berlin:
       Ullstein, 1925.

1389. Schoffler, Herbert. *Protestantismus und Literatur.*
       Leipzig, 1922.

1390. Scholte, J.H. "Robinsonades." *Neophilologus*, 35
       (1951), 129-38.

1391. Schou, Søren. "Robinsons to verdener: Om Defoes
       Robinson Crusoe." *Romanteori og romananalyse.*
       Eds. Merete Gerlach-Nielsen, Hans Hertel, and Morten
       Nøjgaard. Odense: Odense Universitetsforlag, 1977.
       Pp. 186-208.

1392. Schreiber, Marianne. "Daniel Defoe, sein Leben und
       seine Werke." *12. Jahres-Bericht des sechklassigen
       Mädchen-Lyzeums in Salzburg*, von Johann Krögler.
       Salzburg: R. Kiesel, 1916. Pp. 5-25.

*   Schücking, Levin L. *The Puritan Family.* (See item
       322.)

1393. Schulte, Edvige. "Defoe, Swift e l'Accademia inglese."
       Annali Istituto Universitario Orientale, Napoli,
       Sezione Germanica, 8 (1965), 201-20.

1394. Senba, Yutaka. "Defoe no yūreijitsuwa to sono model"
       [Defoe's Ghost Story and Its Model]. Essays Presented
       to Professor Kōzō Yamakawa on the Occasion of his
       Retirement from Osaka University. Tokyo: Eihōsha
       Press, 1981. Pp. 156-67.

       Compares the Apparition of Mrs. Veal with the original
       Bargrave story.

1395. Sgard, Birgitta. "Un aspect de la révolution roman-
       tique: La traduction de Robinson Crusoe par Pétrus
       Borel." Moderna Språk, 5/ (1963), 37-49.

1396. Singer, Helmut. Daniel Defoe: A Tour Through England
       and Wales. Eine kulturgeschichtliche Studie. Leip-
       zig: Robert Noske, 1938.

1397. Skydsgaard, Niels Jørgen. En Studie i Daniel Defoes
       Jeg-Roman. Studier fra Sprog og Oldtidsforskning
       256. Copenhagen: Gad, 1964.

1398. Smit, E.M. "Een collectie betreffende Robinson Crusoe
       in de biblioteek der Rijksuniversiteit te Groningen."
       Biblioteekleven, 43 (1958), 359-71.

       Discusses Dutch editions of Crusoe.

1398A. Souiller, Didier. "Utilisation et transformation par
       Defoe dans Moll Flanders du Marriage trompeur de
       Cervantes." Revue de Littérature Comparée, 217
       (1981), 30-38.

1399. Speidel, Erich. Sprachstil und menschen Bild bei
       Daniel Defoe. Tubingen, 1961.

1400. Spina, Giorgio. "Lingua e letteratura nel mondo
       londinese: Daniel Defoe." Bollettino dell'Istituto
       de Lingui Estere (Genoa), 11 (1978), 63-71.

1401. ————. La nascita del romanzo inglese moderno: Daniel
       Defoe. Genoa: Tilgher, 1972.

1402. Stamm, Rudolf G. Der aufgeklärte Puritanismus Daniel
       Defoes. Swiss Studies in English, 1. Zürich:
       M. Niehau, 1936.

Reviews: O. Boerner, *Die neueren Sprachen*, 46 (1938), 41-42; H.W. Häusermann, *Review of English Studies*, 13 (1937), 232-35; E.G. Jacob, *Geistige Arbeit*, 5 (1938), 6; W. Kalthoff, *Anglia Beiblatt*, 48 (1937), 339-40; W. Keller, *Zeitschrift für neusprachlichen Unterricht*, 36 (1937), 53-54; P. Meissner, *Englische Studien*, 72 (1937), 112-15; G. Roorda, *English Studies*, 19 (1937), 39-40; (London) *Times Literary Supplement*, 11 July 1936, p. 580.

1403. Staverman, Werner H. "Een Nederlandse Bron van de 'Robinson Crusoe.'" *Nieuwe Taalgids*, 19 (1925), 16-26.

        See Hubbard, *A Dutch Source*, item 560.

1404. ———. *Robinson Crusoe in Nederland*. Groningen, 1907.

1405. Stockum, Th. C. van. "Robinson Crusoe, Vorrobinsonaden und Robinsonaden." *Von Friedrich Nicolai bis Thomas Mann: Aufsätze zur deutschen und vergleichenden Literaturgeschichte*. Groningen: Wolters, 1962. Pp. 24-38.

1406. Stukasa, I. [Afterword to] *Robinson Crusoe*. Vil'nyus: Vaga, 1971.

1407. Terrerôs y Guevara, Pedro de. *El Robinsón español manuscrito de fines del siglo XVIII*. Madrid, 1927.

1408. Thomas, Alain. "Essai d'analyse socio-critique d'un passage de *Moll Flanders*." *Picaresque européenne: Actes*. Ed. Edmond Cros. Montpellier: Centre d'Etudes Sociocrit, Université Paul Valéry, 1978. Pp. 181-203.

1409. Toth, Erwin. "Die Funktion des Dialogs bei Daniel Defoe." *Germanisch-romanische Monatsschrift*, 22 (1972), 240-55.

1410. Trisciuzzi, Leonardo. *Cultura e mito nei Robinson Crusoe*. Florence: La Nuova Italia, 1970.

1411. Uchida, Takeshi. "Robinson Crusoe: a Reconsideration." *Studies in English Literature* (Tokyo), 41 (1964), 19-33.

1412. Ullrich, Hermann. *Defoes Robinson Crusoe: die Geschichte eines Weltbuches*. Leipzig: Reisland, 1924. *Reviews*: Paul Dottin, *Revue Anglo-Américaine*, 3 (1925), 153-54; Walthar Fischer, *Anglia Beiblatt*, 36 (1925), 133-35; Erwin G. Gudde, *Journal of English and Germanic Philology*, 25 (1926), 132-34; Gustav Hübener, *D. Literaturz*, 1 (1924), 1945-48; W. Mahrholz, *Die Literatur* (1924), 116-17; H. Schöffler, *Englische Studien*, 59 (1925), 452-57.

1413. ————. "Einfuhrung in das Studium Daniel Defoes." *Zeitschrift für franzosich(e) und englische Unterricht*, 19 (1920), 6-29.

1414. ————. *Leben und Abenteuer des Robinson Crusoe*. Berlin: Otto Hendel, 1923.

1415. ————. "Nachwort." *Robinson Crusoe* by Daniel Defoe. Translated by M. Vischer. Leipzig, 1909. Pp. 409-43.

1416. ————. "Der Robinson-Mythus." *Zeitschrift fur Bücherfreunde*, 8 (1904-05), 1-10.

1417. ————. "Robinson und Robinsonaden in der Jugendliteratur." *Enzyklopädische Handbuch der Pädagogik*. Ed. W. Rein. 2 Auf. Langensalza, Beyer und Söhne, 7 (1908), 567-76.

1418. ————. "Unbekannte Ubersetzungen von Schriften Daniel Defoes." *Zeitschrift für Bücherfreunde*, 4 (1900), 32-35.

1419. ————. "Zu den Quellen des 'Robinson.'" *Literarische Echo*, 11 (1908-09), 154.

1420. ————. "Zum Defoeproblem." *Englische Studien*, 57 (1923), 309-15.

1421. ————. "Zum Robinsonproblem." *Englische Studien*, 55 (1920), 213-36.

1422. ————. "Zur Bibliographie der Robinsonaden. Nachträge und Ergänzungen zu meiner Robinson-Bibliographie." *Zeitschrift für Bücherfreunde*, 11 (1907-08), 444-56, 489-98.

1423. ———. "Zur Robinson-Literatur." *Literaturblatt für germanische und romanische Philologie*, 33 (1912), 105-13.

1424. ———. "Zur Textgeschichte von Defoes Robinson Crusoe." *Archiv für das Studium die neueren Sprachen und Literaturen*, 3 (1903), 93-105.

1425. ———. "Der zweihundertste Geburtstag von Defoes Robinson." *Zeitschrift für Bücherfreunde*, 11 (1919), 35-41.

1426. ———. "Zwölf Jahre Defoeforschung (1916-1928)." *Germanisch-romanische Monatsschrift*, 17 (1929), 458-69.

1427. Urnov, D.M. [Afterword to] *Selected Works of Daniel Defoe*. Moscow: Pravda, 1971.

1428. ———. *Defo*. (Žizn' zamečatel'nyx ljudej 575.) Moscow: Molodaja gvardija, 1978.

1429. ———. *Robinzon i Gulliver: Sud'by dvux literaturnyx geroev*. Moscow: Nauka, 1973.

1430. Van Beeck, Paula. *Der psychologische Gehalt in die Romanen Defoes*. Quakenbrück: Kleinart, 1931.

1431. Voisine, Jacques. "Review of *La pensée réligieuse et morale de George Eliot.*" *Revue des Sciences Humaines*, 97 (1960), 132-33.

   Believes that Eliot's treatment of free will and original sin are derived from Defoe's *Political History of the Devil*.

1432. Von Hofmannsthal, H. "Defoe. Entwurf zu einem Film." *Corona*, 5 (1935), 563-69.

1433. Wackwitz, Friedrich. *Enstehungsgeschichte von D. Defoes Robinson Crusoe*. Berlin: Mayer und Müller, 1909.

   Review: *Literaturblatt für germanische und romanische Philologie*, 23 (1912), 105-13.

1434. Wagner, Hermann. *Robinson und die Robinsonaden in unser Jugendliteratur*. Wien: Im Selbstverlage des Verfassers, 1903.

1435. Weil, Alice. *Wesen und Ursprung von Defoes Vorstellun-
gen der ubersinnlichen Welt.* Freiburg, 1927.

1436. Weimann, Robert. *Daniel Defoe: Eine Einführung in das
Romanwerk.* Wege zur Literatur, Monographien 11.
Halle: VEB Verlag, 1962.
Review: Jean Béranger, *Études Anglaises,* 16 (1963),
283-84.

1436A. ———. "Erwiderung." *Zeitschrift für Anglistik und
Amerikanistik,* 27 (1979), 258-61.

1437. ———. "Erzählerstandpunkt und *point of view.* Zu
Geschichte und Aesthetik der Perspective im eng-
lischen Roman." *Zeitschrift für Anglistik und
Amerikanistik,* 10 (1962), 396-416.

1438. ———. "Robinson Crusoe: Wirklichkeit und Utopie im
neuzeitlichen Roman." *Sinn und Form,* 21 (1969),
453-84.

1439. Weisgerber, Jean. "Aspects de l'espace romanesque:
L'Histoire du Chevalier des Grieux et de Manon Lescaut."
Etudes sur le XVIIIe siècle, II. Eds. Roland Mortier
and Hervé Hasquin. Brussels: Université de Bruxelles,
1975. Pp. 89-107.

1440. ———. "Aspects de l'espace romanesque: Moll Flanders." *Revue des Langues Vivantes,* 40 (1974), 503-10.

1441. ———. "A la recherche de l'espace romanesque:
*Lazarillo de Tormes, Les Aventures de Simplicius
Simplicissimus* et *Moll Flanders.*" *Neohelicon,* 3
(1975), 209-27.

1442. Winqvist, Margareta. *Den engelske Robinson Crusoes
sällsamma öden och äventyr genom Svenska språket.*
Stockholm: Bonniers, 1973.

Surveys Swedish editions of *Robinson Crusoe;* followed
by an English summary.

Reviews: Margot Nilson, *Barn och kultur,* 20 (1974),
139-40; Sonja Svensson, *Samlaren,* 95 (1974), 267-68.

1443. Winter, Michael. *Compendium Utopiarum: Typologie und
Bibliographie literarischer Utopien. I: Von der
Antike bis zur deutschen Fruhaufklarung.* Stuttgart:
J.B. Metzler, 1978.

Includes *Robinson Crusoe*, *An Essay upon Projects*, *The Consolidator*, and *The Protestant Monastery* in this bibliography of European literary utopias.

1443A. Wojcik, Manfred. "Zur Interpretation des *Robinson Crusoe*." *Zeitschrift für Anglistik und Amerikanistik*, 27 (1979), 5-34.

1444. Wolff, Erwin. *Der englische Roman.* [No publication data.] 1968.

Listed by Abernethy, item 1, but not confirmed by this compiler.

1445. Wolken, Fritz. "Major Ramkins' *Memoirs*, Daniel Defoe und die Anfänge des realistischen Ich-Romans." *Anglia*, 75 (1957), 411-28.

1446. Würzbach, Natascha. "Wandlungen in der Struktur der englischen Prosaerzählung vor Defoe." *Die neueren Sprachen*, 17 (1968), 585-601.

1447. Yamaguchi, Katsumasa. "Overstatement to Understatement: Defoe-Swift Oboegaki." *Annual Reports of English and American Literature, Osaka Shoin Women's College,* 15 (1978), 54-67.

Compares Defoe with Swift and concludes that Defoe uses overstatement and therefore lacks Swift's subtle irony.

Review: Zenzo Suzuki, *The Scriblerian*, 13 (1981), 85.

1448. Zeller, Hildegard. *Die Ich-Erzahlung im englische Roman.* Breslau: Priebatsch, 1933.

Treats briefly Defoe's use of the I-narrator in *Robinson Crusoe* and *Moll Flanders*.

1449. Zupancic, Peter. "'My Man Friday': Zum Motiv des edlen Wilden in der Robinsonade." *Philobiblon*, 22 (1978), 34-41.

VIII

DISSERTATIONS

1450. Achurch, Robert W. "The Literary and Historical Relations of *The Tatler* to Defoe's *Review* and the *London Gazette*." *University of North Carolina Record*, No. 429 (1946), pp. 134-35 (University of North Carolina).

1451. Andersen, Hans H. "Daniel Defoe: A Study in the Conflict Between Commercialism and Morality in the Early Eighteenth Century." *Abstracts of Theses*, University of Chicago, 9 (1930-32), 431-35.

1452. Arora, Sudesh V. "The Divided Mind: A Study of Selected Novels of Defoe and Richardson." *DAI*, 35 (1974), 3668A-69A (Kent State).

1453. Babb, Moira C.F. "Declarations of Independence: The Rebel Heroine, 1684-1800." *DAI*, 34 (1974), 5088A-89A (University of Washington).

1454. Backscheider, Paula K.R. "The Special Societies in Daniel Defoe's Novels." *DAI*, 33 (1972), 2883A-84A (Purdue University).

1455. Baer, Joel H. "Piracy Examined: A Study of Daniel Defoe's *General History of the Pirates* and Its Milieu." *DAI*, 32 (1971), 319A (Princeton University).

1456. Barker, Steven John. "Wallenberg and His English Contemporaries: A Study in Affinities." *DAI*, 41 (1980), 2130A-31A (University of Washington).

1457. Bass, Jeanette Martin. "The Confrontation of Forces in Defoe's Fiction." *DAI*, 39 (1979), 7326A (University of South Carolina).

1458. Bassein, Beth A. "Crime and Punishment in the Novels
       of Defoe, Fielding, and Godwin." *DA*, 22 (1962),
       2783 (University of Missouri).

1459. Behrens, Laurence. "Plotting the Eighteenth-Century
       Novel: Narrative Constructs from Defoe to Goldsmith."
       DAI, 35 (1975), 1613A (University of California at
       Los Angeles).

1460. Bernstein, Roslyn A. "Defoe on Education: A Comprehen-
       sive Examination of Daniel Defoe's Class Views on
       Education in His Tracts, Books of Advice and Social
       Commentary and Novels." *DAI*, 35 (1974), 1039A (New
       York University).

1461. Black, Sidney J. "The Critical Reputation of Defoe's
       Novels." Boston University, 1954.

1462. Blewett, David L. "Defoe's Art of Fiction: A Study of
       Robinson Crusoe, *Moll Flanders*, *Colonel Jack*, and
       Roxana." *DAI*, 32 (1972), 6963A-64A (University of
       Toronto).

1463. Boone, William F. "Into the Labyrinth: The Daydream
       Mode in Literature." *DAI*, 32 (1972), 5219A-20A
       (State University of New York, Buffalo).

1464. Bryant, Herbert. "The Relationship Between Defoe the
       Journalist and Defoe the Novelist." *DAI*, 34 (1974),
       5159A (University of Tennessee).

1465. Budge, Mary A. "The Rhetoric of Operation: Character
       Masks in the Fiction of Daniel Defoe." *DAI*, 31
       (1971), 4707A (State University of New York, Buffalo).

1466. Burch, Charles E. "The English Reputation of Daniel
       Defoe." *Ohio State University Abstracts of Doctors'
       Dissertations*, No. 13 (1934), pp. 17-26.

1467. Burt, Della Ann. "The Widening Arc and the Closed
       Circle: A Study of Problematic Novel Endings." *DAI*,
       40 (1980), 4011A (Indiana University).

1468. Butler, Mary Elizabeth. "The Rhetoric of Self-Conscious-
       ness and of Self-Knowledge in *Moll Flanders*, *Evelina*,
       Anna St. Ives, and *Emma*." *DAI*, 40 (1979), 5061A-62A
       (Stanford University).

1469. Campbell, Mary E. "Political Propaganda in the Early
       Verse of Defoe." Yale University, 1938.

1470. Carter, Kay C. "George Berkeley's Views on Linguistic
       Meaning." *DA*, 29 (1968), 1562A (Cornell University).

1471. Cogswell, William Burchard. "A Contrast of Defoe's
       'Moll Flanders' and 'Colonel Jack,' and Thematic
       Unity of Each." *DA*, 31 (1970), 1265A (University of
       New Mexico).

1472. Cohan, Steven M. "Fiction and the Creation of Charac-
       ter." *DAI*, 35 (1974), 1616A-17A (University of
       California at Los Angeles).

1473. Cornelius, Paul Edwin. "Languages in Seventeenth- and
       Early Eighteenth-Century Imaginary Voyages." *DA*, 23
       (1963), 3351 (Columbia University).

1474. Curtis, Laura A.G. "A Defoe Anthology: Writings on
       Politics, Economics, and History with Explanatory
       Essays and Introduction." *DAI*, 35 (1974), 1094A-
       95A (Rutgers).

1475. Danby, J.E. "The Satirical Verse of Daniel Defoe."
       *Index to Theses Accepted for Higher Degrees in the
       Universities of Great Britain and Ireland*. No. 175.
       London: London University College, 1959-60.

1476. Demarest, David Porter, Jr. "Legal Language and Situa-
       tion in the Eighteenth-Century Novel: Readings in
       Defoe, Richardson, Fielding, and Austen." *DA*, 24
       (1964), 2907 (University of Wisconsin).

1477. Dewees, Charles W., Jr. "'Vested with a Reasonable
       Soul': A Study of *The Farther Adventures of Robinson
       Crusoe*." *DAI*, 34 (1974), 7744A (University of Penn-
       sylvania).

1478. Dill, Stephen Horton. "An Analysis of Some Aspects
       of Daniel Defoe's Prose Style." *DA*, 26 (1966), 3922
       (University of Arkansas).

1479. Downie, J.A. "Daniel Defoe's 'Review' and Other
       Political Writings in the Reign of Queen Anne."
       Master's Thesis. University of Newcastle upon
       Tyne, 1973.

1480.   ————. "Robert Harley and the Press." Thesis. New-
        castle upon Tyne, 1976.

1481.   Ebner, Ivan D. "Seventeenth Century British Autobiog-
        raphy. The Impact of Religious Commitment." Stan-
        ford University, 1965.

1482.   Ewing, Mary Dessagene Crawford. "Daniel Defoe's Conduct
        Books and Their Relationship to His Novels." *DA*, 31
        (1970), 1756A (University of Texas, Austin).

1483.   Fleming, John Paul. "The Classical Retirement Theme in
        the Fiction of Defoe, Fielding, Johnson, and Gold-
        smith." *DAI*, 38 (1977), 2804A-05A (Bowling Green
        State University).

1484.   Foster, Joan C. "Daniel Defoe and the Position of
        Women in Eighteenth Century England: A Study of *Moll
        Flanders* and *Roxana*." *DAI*, 33 (1973), 5677A (Univer-
        sity of New Mexico).

1485.   Frye, Bobby J. "The Twentieth-Century Criticism of
        Robinson Crusoe and *Moll Flanders*." *DA*, 27 (1967),
        3007A-08A (University of Tennessee).

1486.   Gatling, Clover Holly. "The Strange, Surprising Ad-
        ventures of Robinson Crusoe *chez* Pixerécourt."
        DAI, 40 (1979), 1451A-52A (University of South
        Carolina).

1487.   Gay, Christopher W. "Nothing But What Was Common: The
        Language and Rhetoric of Daniel Defoe's Novels."
        DAI, 33 (1972), 2373A (Rutgers).

1488.   Geary, Robert F., Jr. "The Equivocal Virtue: Prudence
        in the Eighteenth-Century Novel." *DAI*, 32 (1972),
        4610A (University of Virginia).

1489.   Glatti, Walter. "Die Behandlung des Affekts der Furcht
        im Englischen Roman des 18. Jahrhunderts." Zurich,
        1949.

1490.   Gliserman, Martin J. "The Intersection of Biography
        and Fiction: A Psychological Study of Daniel Defoe
        and His Novels." *DAI*, 34 (1974), 5100A (Indiana
        University).

1491.   Gold, Arthur R. "The Origins of *Robinson Crusoe* in
        the Mind of Daniel Defoe." Harvard, 1965.

1492. Goldknopf, David. "Studies in the Novel's Search for Form." *DAI*, 30 (1970), 3458A-59A (Syracuse University).

1493. Goldknopf, Irma. "Crime and Prison-Experience in the Early English Novel: Defoe, Fielding, Smollett." *DA*, 29 (1968), 1207A (Syracuse University).

1494. Hackos, JoAnn T. "Defoe's *Tour* and the English Travel Narrative." *DAI*, 33 (1973), 4345A (Indiana University).

1495. Hansen, Richard Erling. "Consummate Craft: Defoe's Development of Characterization before Crusoe." *DAI*, 37 (1976), 3642A (Duke University).

1496. Hartog, Curt H. "The Prodigal Motif in Defoe and *Robinson Crusoe*." *DAI*, 32 (1972), 4611A (University of Illinois).

1497. Hawkes, Genevieve T. "Women in the Life and Fiction of Daniel Defoe." Utah State University, 1969.

1498. Healey, George H. "The Early Correspondence of Daniel Defoe (1703-1707)." *Cornell University Abstracts of Theses* (1947), 23-25.

1499. Hendley, William C., Jr. "Factional Journalism in the Age of Queen Anne: Defoe's *Review* and Its Rivals." *DAI*, 32 (1972), 3953A (University of Texas, Austin).

1500. Hewitt, Frank S. "Daniel Defoe, Dissenter." *Cornell University Abstracts of Theses* (1947), 26-29.

1501. Hill, Teresa Ellen. "The Disintegrating Rhetoric of Defoe and Marivaux: *Moll Flanders* and *La Vie de Marianne*." *DAI*, 39 (1978), 1533A-34A (State University of New York, Binghamton).

1502. Jacobson, Margaret Charlotte Kingsland. "Women in the Novels of Defoe, Richardson, and Fielding." *DAI*, 35 (1975), 7256A (University of Connecticut).

1503. James, Eustace Anthony. "Defoe's Many Voices: Aspects of the Author's Prose Style and Literary Method." *DA*, 26 (1966), 7318-19 (University of Pennsylvania).

1504. Jenkins, Marita J.A. "The Influence of the Drama on
       the Novels of Defoe and Smollett." *DAI*, 32 (1972),
       5741A (University of Texas, Austin).

1505. Kaler, Anne K. "Daniel Defoe's Version of the Picaresque
       Traditions in His Novel *Roxana*." *DAI*, 31 (1971),
       5364A (Temple University).

1506. Kaplan, Richard P. "Daniel Defoe's Views on Slavery
       and Racial Prejudice." *DAI*, 31 (1971), 6556A (New
       York University).

1507. Kazantzi, John. "Defoe and the Criminal Lives: A Study
       in the Interrelation of Biography and the Novel as
       Genres." *DA*, 25 (1964), 2962 (Boston University).

1508. Kennedy, Joyce H. "Daniel Defoe's *An Essay Upon
       Projects*: A Critical Edition." *DA*, 29 (1968), 873A
       (University of Delaware).

1509. Kiehl, James Millinger. "Epic, Mock-heroic, and Novel:
       1650-1750." *DA*, 33 (1973), 5182A-83A (Syracuse Uni-
       versity).

1510. Klopsch, Raymond Albert. "Daniel Defoe as a Historian."
       DA, 23 (1963), 4359-60 (University of Illinois).

1511. Krier, William J. "A Pattern of Limitations: the
       Heroine's Novel of the Mind." *DAI*, 34 (1973), 277A-
       78A (Indiana University).

1512. Kropf, Carl R. "Defoe as Puritan Novelist." *DA*, 29
       (1968), 1541A (Ohio State University).

1513. La Roche, Mary Heughes Gibson. "Challe, Lesage, Defoe,
       Marivaux, Prévost, and Richardson: Technical Develop-
       ments in the Early Eighteenth-Century Novel." *DAI*,
       38 (1977), 3470A (University of Michigan).

1513A. Laden, Marie-Paule. "Faces of the First Person: The
       Eighteenth-Century Novel in France and England."
       DAI, 41 (1981), 5091A.

1514. Leyasmeyer, Archibald I. "The Social Thought in Defoe's
       Colonel Jack." *DA*, 28 (1968), 3149A (Princeton Uni-
       versity).

1515. Lynch, Daniel J. "Criminals and Prisons in the Writings of Daniel Defoe." *DAI*, 34 (1973), 1921A (University of Pennsylvania).

1516. McGowan, Raymond E. "Daniel Defoe's *Moll Flanders*: Fact into Fiction." *DAI*, 35 (1974), 2232A-33A (Tulane University).

1517. McKee, John Brown. "Literary Irony and the Literary Audience: Studies in the Victimization of the Reader in Early English Fiction." *DA*, 33 (1973), 5132A-33A (Syracuse University).

1518. Major, John C. "The Role of Personal Memoirs in English Biography and Novel." University of Pennsylvania, 1934.

1519. Mason, Shirlene Rae. "Daniel Defoe's Paradoxical Stand on the Status of Women." *DAI*, 35 (1975), 7872A (University of Utah).

1520. Matchen, David Elba. "Prophet, Preacher, Mountebank: Defoe and His Methods of Persuasion in the *Review*." *DAI*, 37 (1976), 2862A (University of Tennessee).

1521. Megley, Sheila Ellen. "Daniel Defoe: Experimenter in Prose." *DAI*, 35 (1975), 5355A (University of Nebraska, Lincoln).

1522. Meier, Tom K. "Defoe and the Defense of Commerce." *DAI*, 32 (1971), 3316A (Columbia University).

1523. Merritt, Henry C. "The Life, Travels, and Adventures of John Dunton, Late of London: Author, Bookseller, and Publisher." *DAI*, 30 (1970), 5415A (Syracuse University).

1524. Miller, Nancy Kipnis. "Gender and Genre: An Analysis of Literary Femininity in the Eighteenth-Century Novel." *DAI*, 35 (1975), 6674A (Columbia University).

1525. Mills, Russell. "Settings in Fiction: A Study of Five English Novels." *DAI*, 36 (1976), 7442A-43A (Indiana University).

1526. Moore, Judith K. "Early Eighteenth-Century Literature and the Financial Revolution." *DAI*, 31 (1971), 6561A (Cornell University).

1527. Nassr, Fatma. "A Study of Two of Defoe's Long Prose
       Narratives in Relation to His Domestic Conduct Manuals."
       DAI, 42 (1982), 3165A (University of Iowa).

1528. Neman, Beth Smilay. *"The Memoirs of Major Alexander
       Ramkins* by Daniel Defoe: A Scholarly Edition." *DAI*,
       37 (1976), 2899A-900A (Miami University).

1529. Opoku, Samuel K. "The Image of Africa, 1660-1730
       (Defoe and Travel Literature)." *DA*, 29 (1968),
       235A-36A (Princeton University).

1530. Orren, Tyna Claire Thall. "True and False Accounts
       by Defoe." *DAI*, 37 (1976), 3646A (University of
       Minnesota).

1531. Paine, Robert N. "Economics and Ethics in English
       Novels, 1719-1771." George Peabody, 1955.

1532. Parker, Gillian Edith. "I. The Loss of the Millennium:
       Paradise Lost and the English Revolution. II. Pat-
       terns of Duality in Defoe's Narratives: *Robinson
       Crusoe* and *A Journal of the Plague Year*. III. Lineage
       and History in *Tess of the D'Urbervilles*." *DAI*, 38
       (1978), 6747A (Rutgers).

1533. Pettigrove, M.G. "A Study of Defoe's Concept of Charac-
       ter and His Techniques of Characterization in Rela-
       tionship to the Courtesy and Conduct Literature of
       the Seventeenth Century." University of Oxford, 1975.

1534. Item deleted.

1535. Price, David. "Defoe's *Due Preparation for the Plague*:
       An Introduction and Annotations toward an Edition."
       DAI, 31 (1971), 6564A-65A (Princeton University).

1536. Prince, Gilbert P., Jr. "Poetry and Propaganda in
       Defoe's Three Major Verse Satires During the Reign
       of William III." *DAI*, 33 (1972), 2340A (University
       of California, Santa Barbara).

1537. Pugliano, Fiore. "The Trade of Morality: The Quest
       for Moral Regeneration in *Captain Singleton*, *Robinson
       Crusoe*, *Moll Flanders*, and *Roxana*." *DAI*, 38 (1978),
       6146A-47A (University of Pittsburgh).

1538. Rasmussen, Kirk G. "The Hero: Motifs of Initiation in Eighteenth-Century British Fiction." *DAI*, 32 (1971), 1484A (University of Utah).

1539. Reuter, John E. "'A Quiet Habitation ...': The Spiritual Autobiography and the Development of the English Novel." *DA*, 29 (1968), 236A (University of Rochester).

1540. Richetti, John J. "The Uses of Fiction: 1700-1739. Popular Narrative Before Richardson." *DA*, 29 (1968), 577A (Columbia University).

1541. Ross, Ernest C. "The Development of the English Sea Novel from Defoe to Conrad." University of Virginia, n.d.

1542. Russell, Ann Z. "The Image of Women in Eighteenth-Century English Novels." *DAI*, 35 (1974), 1122A (Brandeis).

1543. Salzberg, Albert Charles. "The Problem of Irony in the Novels of Defoe." *DA*, 24 (1963), 2020-21 (New York University).

1544. Schonhorn, Manuel Robert. "Defoe's Sources and Narrative Method: *Mrs. Veal*, *Journal of the Plague Year*, *Robinson Crusoe* and *Captain Singleton*." *DA*, 25 (1964), 485-86 (University of Pennsylvania).

1545. Schrock, Thomas. "On the Basis of Defoe's Political Thought: *Robinson Crusoe*." *DA*, 25 (1964), 1129 (University of Chicago).

1546. Shifford, Kent D. "The Origins of Modern Environmental Thought: A Study of the Writings of Daniel Defoe, Denis Diderot and Karl Marx." *DAI*, 35 (1974), 3656A-57A (Northern Illinois University).

1547. Shinagel, Michael. "Daniel Defoe: The Gentleman Theme." Harvard University, 1964.

1548. Siddens, James Michael. "Defoe's Rogue Novels and the Picaresque Tradition: A Reading of *Captain Singleton*, *Moll Flanders*, *Colonel Jack*, and *Roxana*." *DAI*, 35 (1975), 5427A-28A (Ohio State University).

1549. Sill, Geoffrey M. "A Phenomenology of Theft." *DAI*, 35 (1974), 1635A (Pennsylvania State University).

1550. Singleton, Robert R. "Defoe and Criminal Biography."
       DAI, 30 (1969), 2550A (New York University).

1551. Smith, Beverlee F. "'Give Me Not Poverty, Lest I
       Steal!': Social Criticism in Selected Non-Fiction
       of Daniel Defoe, Projecting to His Three Criminal
       Novels." *DAI*, 32 (1971), 2710A (Loyola University).

1552. Snow, Malinda G. "Defoe's Puritan Context." *DAI*, 35
       (1974), 477A (Duke University).

1553. Sperry, David A. "A Study of Daniel Defoe's *Tour
       Through Great Britain*." *DA*, 11 (1950), 2226 (Uni-
       versity of Illinois).

1554. Starr, George Alexander. "Defoe and Spiritual Auto-
       biography." *DA*, 25 (1964), 3558-59 (Princeton Uni-
       versity).

1555. Starr, Nathan C. "The Sea in the English Novel from
       Defoe to Melville." Harvard, 1928.

1556. Steele, Perry Louis. "Defoe's Narrative Structure: The
       Making of the First English Novels." *DAI*, 40 (1980),
       5880A-81A (University of Texas, Austin).

1557. Swann, G.R. "Philosophical Parallelisms in Six English
       Novelists: The Conception of Good, Evil, and Human
       Nature." University of Pennsylvania, 1929.

1558. Taylor, Sheila L. "Form and Function in the Picaresque
       Novel." *DAI*, 34 (1973), 3359A (University of Cali-
       fornia, Los Angeles).

1559. Topf, Melvyn A. "An Inquiry into Some Relations Between
       the Epistemology of the Novel and Its Origins."
       DAI, 30 (1970), 5006A (Pennsylvania State Univer-
       sity).

1560. Vail, Marilyn Irene. "Transformation of Narrative
       Structure in Relation to the Role of the Female
       Protagonist in the Eighteenth-Century Novel." *DAI*,
       39 (1978), 313A (Cornell University).

1561. Van Dover, James Kenneth. "'The Only Place I Had Been
       Bless'd At': The Idea of America and the Structure of
       Defoe's Narratives." *DAI*, 42 (1982), 3614A (Bryn
       Mawr College).

1562. Vania, Rhoda Jal. "Defoe and the American Experience." *DAI*, 38 (1977), 1398A (Claremont Graduate School).

1563. Vantrease, Brenda Rickman. "The Heroic Ideal: Three Views." *DAI*, 41 (1980), 2106A (Middle Tennessee State University).

1564. Vopat, James B. "The Denial of Innocence: The Theme of Social Responsibility in the Early British Novel." *DAI*, 33 (1973), 4437A (University of Washington).

1565. Weeks, Robert L. "Defoe, Swift, and the Peace of Utrecht." *DA*, 16 (1956), 2171 (Indiana University).

1566. White, Ruth B. "The Activities of Defoe Relating to the Act of the Union, 1706-1707." *DA*, 27 (1967), 3854A-55A (Columbia University).

1567. Williams, Otho Clinton. "A Study of Daniel Defoe's Complete Englishman." *University of California Abstracts of Theses*, 17 (1950), 196.

1568. Wortman, Walter R., Jr. "Defoe as a Satirist." *DAI*, 34 (1973), 744A-45A (University of Texas, Austin).

1569. Yokley, Mary Louise Winn. "The Mask of the Poet: Irony and Ethos in Selected Poems of Daniel Defoe." *DAI*, 42 (1981), 719A (University of Houston).

AUTHOR INDEX

Included in this index are the names of authors of articles and books on Defoe, editors of collections of essays, and authors and editors of general works which include material on Defoe. The numbers following each name refer the reader to item numbers in the bibliography.

353

TITLE INDEX

All titles in the bibliography are alphabetically listed below. Like English items,
foreign-language items are indexed according
to the first substantive (non-article) word in
the title--e.g., "Der Robinson-mythus" is listed
under the R's and not the D's. Numbers follow
ing the titles refer the reader to item numbers,
not page numbers.

"A la recherche de l'espace romanesque: *Lazarillo de Tormès,
Les Aventures de Simplicius Simplicissimus*, et *Moll
Flanders*" 1441
An Account of the Conduct and Proceedings of the Pirate Gow
61
"The Activities of Defoe Relating to the Act of the Union,
1706-1707" 1566
"Addenda and Corrigenda: Moore's *Checklist* of Defoe" 23
"Additions and Refinements to Moore's *A Checklist of the
Writings of Daniel Defoe*" 16
The Advance of the English Novel 439
The Adventurer 696
*The Adversary Literature: The English Novel in the Eighteenth
Century. A Study in Genre* 415
"Afterword" (to *The Fortunes and Misfortunes of the Famous
Moll Flanders*) 800
"Afterword" (to *Robinson Crusoe*) 672
"Afterword" (to *Roxana, The Fortunate Mistress*) 887
The Age of Pope 407
"The Agentless Sentence as Rhetorical Device" 141
"Aggression, Femininity, and Irony in *Moll Flanders*" 746
Aktuelle Probleme aus der Geschichte der Medizin 1313
"Alexander Selkirk" 608
"Alexander Selkirk's 'Desert Island'" 503
"Allegory and History: A Study of Daniel Defoe's *Roxana*" 879
"The Allegory of *Robinson Crusoe*" 633
American Literature: Essays and Opinions 792
"An American Robinson Crusoe" 597

367

SUBJECT INDEX

Addison, Joseph 897
Africa 238, 510, 703, 706, 1529
Aggression 746
Aleman 718
Allegory 420, 478, 482, 524, 539, 565, 570, 581, 633, 650,
    659, 744, 806, 807, 875, 879
Alienation 871
America see under Colonies
Ancestors see under Family
Angels 109, 110. Also see Religion
Anne, Queen see under Queen Anne
Army 323, 976, 1016, 1193, 1219
Artistry 158, 209, 211, 217, 218, 242, 286, 328, 339, 343,
    349, 395, 421, 424, 444, 469, 470, 478, 544, 554, 645,
    724, 728, 763, 786, 787, 808, 809, 846, 847, 852, 855,
    861, 863, 874, 875, 926, 949, 1078
Atkins, John 620
Attributions, methods of determining 2, 80, 261, 267, 1159,
    1160, 1164, 1179, 1188
Audience 458, 554, 650, 652, 712, 795, 816, 891, 922, 923,
    939, 1031, 1094, 1284, 1284A, 1301, 1302, 1517
Autobiography see under Biography
Avery, Captain John 701, 702

Baker, Henry 295, 299, 354, 1131. Also see Family
Baker, Rev. Defoe 106
Behn, Aphra 657, 1226
Belhaven, Lord 1147, 1148
Bible see under Religion
Biography, Defoe's see under Life; methods used in fiction
    347, 349, 356, 398, 438, 455, 462, 710, 719, 735, 757, 798,
    812, 814, 832, 838, 879, 1237, 1375, 1490, 1507, 1518,
    1550; spiritual 418, 453, 496, 665, 688, 719, 1481,
    1539, 1554
Blackmore, Richard 1145
Blake, William 480
Boghurst, William 856